I0039469

ABSTRACTS
OF
Marriages AND Deaths
IN
HARFORD COUNTY, MARYLAND
NEWSPAPERS

1837–1871

Henry C. Peden, Jr.

HERITAGE BOOKS
2019

HERITAGE BOOKS

AN IMPRINT OF HERITAGE BOOKS, INC.

Books, CDs, and more—Worldwide

For our listing of thousands of titles see our website
at
www.HeritageBooks.com

Published 2019 by
HERITAGE BOOKS, INC.
Publishing Division
5810 Ruatan Street
Berwyn Heights, Md. 20740

Copyright © 2005 Henry C. Peden, Jr.

All rights reserved. No part of this book may be reproduced or
transmitted in any form or by any means, electronic or mechanical,
including photocopying, recording or by any information storage
and retrieval system without written permission from the author,
except for the inclusion of brief quotations in a review.

International Standard Book Number
Paperbound: 978-1-68034-944-3

FOREWORD

Newspapers are important primary sources for marriages and deaths, especially during times when vital records did not exist. The extant newspapers for Harford and Cecil Counties, Maryland from 1822 to 1830 were published by F. Edward Wright in 1984. From the following available newspapers for Harford County I have abstracted marriage and death information for the 35 year period from 1837 through 1871:

AI -   *The Aegis and Intelligencer*, 1864-1871

HD - *The Harford Democrat*, 1856-1871

HM - *The Madisonian (Harford & Baltimore Advertiser)*, 1837-1857

HR - *The Havre de Grace Republican*, 1868-1871

SA - *The Southern Aegis*, 1857-1864 (some times known as *The Southern Aegis and Harford County Intelligencer*)

These newspapers are available on microfilm at the Historical Society of Harford County. Marriage and death information was gleaned from various parts of them, mostly on page 2 of each issue, and not only from the "Married" and "Died" sections, but also from "Local Affairs" and "The News" items, as well as from administrator and executor notices, and removals from the voter registration lists that were occasionally published.

It should be noted that many of the newspapers have missing issues and most citizens did not place marriage and death notices in the paper. Be that as it may, I trust that genealogists and family historians will find the available information useful in their research.

Henry C. Peden, Jr.
Bel Air, Maryland
April 15, 2005

ABSTRACTS OF MARRIAGES AND DEATHS
IN HARFORD COUNTY, MARYLAND
NEWSPAPERS, 1837-1871

AARONSON, ALFORD and Miss Emma Austin m. 20 Feb 1867 by
Rev. Francis E. Church (AI 1 Mar 1867)
AARONSON, AMBROSE and Miss Annie J. Pennington, both of
Harford Co., m. 25 May 1870 by Rev. J. G. Moore (AI 3 Jun 1870)
AARONSON, GEORGE, see "Layton Aaronson," q.v.
AARONSON, LAYTON, died ---- (date not given) and the
administrator's notice stated that creditors must exhibit their legal
vouchers by 30 Jul 1869 to Mary Ann Aaronson, Alfred E.
Aaronson, and George D. Aaronson, admins. (AI 31 Jul 1868)
AARONSON, MARY ANN, see "Layton Aaronson," q.v.
AARONSON, WILLIAM F. and Miss Mattie Numbers, both of Harford
Co., m. 27 Oct 1870, in Aberdeen M. E. Church, by Rev. J. G.
Moore (AI 4 Nov 1870)
ABELL, MARY, consort of A. S. Abell, died Wed. 16 Feb 1859 in
Baltimore, after a short but severe illness, in her 42nd year; obituary
contains a brief memorial (SA 26 Feb 1859)
ADAMS, MARTHA G. (Miss) and Clayton Finley, both of Harford Co.,
m. ---- (date not given) at the Slate Ridge Manse (HD 17 Feb 1871)
ADY, EDWARD H., see "Henrietta M. Ady," q.v.
ADY, HENRIETTA M., wife of Edward H. Ady, of Towsontown,
Baltimore Co., died 29 Jul 1865, in her 39th year (AI 4 Aug 1865)
ADY, LEMUEL, see "Mrs. Gordon," q.v.
ADY, LEONARD and Mrs. Martha Treadway, both of Harford Co., m.
10 Oct 1871 by Rev. J. Roberts (SA 13 Oct 1871)
ADY, MAGGIE (Miss) and William T. Clark, both of Harford Co., m.
21 Dec 1865 by Rev. J. K. Nichols (AI 5 Jan 1866)
ADY, MARY (Miss) of Harford Co., and Lewis Roberts, of
Philadelphia, m. 18 Mar 1865, at Towsontown, by Rev. P. O.
McConnell (AI 7 Apr 1865)
ADY, SAMUEL M. and Miss Cassandra Kean, both of Harford Co., m.
Tues. 3 Jun 1862 at St. Ignatius Church by Rev. James McDevitt
(SA 7 Jun 1862)
ADY, WILLIAM M., of Harford Co., and Laura G. Eichelberger, dau. of
the late William Eichelberger, of Baltimore, m. Tues. 19 Oct 1858
at the Cathedral in Baltimore by the Most Rev. Archbishop Kenrick
(SA 6 Nov 1858)
AGNEW, GEN., see "Susanna Boyer," q.v.
AIREY, GEORGE G., of Baltimore, and Miss Fannie B. Patterson, dau.
of the late William A. Patterson, m. 21 Jun 1870 at Spesutia
Church, Perrymansville, Harford Co., by Rev. Crampton [marriage
notice indicated "No cards"] (AI 1 Jul 1870)

ALDERSON, C. DAVIS and Miss Annie Hopkins, both of Harford Co., m. Tues., 29 Sep 1863 by Rev. J. K. Kramer at the Grove Church, Harford Co. (SA 9 Oct 1863)

ALDERSON, HANNAH, consort of John Alderson, died last Sat. (HM 18 Apr 1845)

ALDERSON, JOHN, see "Hannah Alderson," q.v.

ALEXANDER, HUGH, died ---- (date not given) and the administrator's notice stated that creditors must exhibit their legal vouchers by 1 Jul 1857 to John McFadden, admin. (HD 8 Aug 1856)

ALEXANDER, JOHN J. and Miss Laura Harryman, both of Harford Co., m. 19 Oct 1871 at the Presbyterian Church in Bel Air by Rev. Finney (HD 20 Oct 1871)

ALEXANDER, JOSEPH B., formerly of Wilmington, DE, died Sun. 13 Aug 1843, in Bel Air, at the home of Joseph Hutchinson (HM 18 Aug 1843)

ALLEN, A. V. and Miss Mary E. Gordon, both of Piqua, Ohio, m. 4 Nov 1869 at the First Presbyterian Church, Piqua, by Rev. T. C. Hopkins (AI 3 Dec 1869)

ALLEN, EDWARD M., see "James Prigg," q.v.

ALLEN, ISRAEL, died ---- (date not given) and was removed from the voter registration list in the 6th District in 1870 (HR 4 Oct 1870)

ALLEN, ISRAEL JR., died ---- (date not given) and was removed from voter registration list in 1869 (HD 22 Oct 1869 and AI 1 Oct 1869)

ALLEN, RICHARD N., son of the late Dr. R. N. Allen, of Harford Co., died 24 May 1870 at Hamilton, Ohio, in his 40th year (AI 8 Jul 1870)

ALLEN, SAMUEL C., of Harford Co., died 12 Sep 1871 in Baltimore, in his 28th year (HD 22 Sep 1871)

ALLEN, SARAH, youngest dau. of Alfred D. and Sarah Allen, died 17 May 1871 in Baltimore of scarlet fever, aged 2 years, 5 months and 10 days (HR 19 May 1871)

ALLEN, THOMAS H., died ---- (date not given) and was removed from the voter registration list in the 6th District in 1870 (HR 4 Oct 1870)

ALLENDER, MARTHA, died Wed. 23 Mar 1870, in her 67th year (AI 1 Apr 1870)

ALLIBONE, ELIZABETH EYRE, dau. of Thomas Allibone, Esq., of Harford Co., and John P. Scholfield, of California, m. 19 Nov 1868 at *Brookdale Farm*, Maryland, by Rev. William A. Newbold (AI 4 Dec 1868)

ALMONY, ABRA, died ---- (date not given) and was removed from the voter registration list in the 4th District in 1870 (HR 1 Nov 1870)

AMOS, ANNIE AMELIA, dau. of Robert and Elizabeth Ann Amos, died Wed. 17 Mar 1869, aged 8 years and 9 months; obituary contains a brief memorial and a poem (AI 26 Mar 1869)

AMOS, B. SCOTT, see "Sarah Amos," q.v.

AMOS, BENJAMIN SCOTT, died 10 Mar 1865, at his residence in Harford Co., in his 79th year; he served the county as Commissioner and Collector of Tax for a number of years (AI 24 Mar 1865)

AMOS, ELIZABETH, see "Annie Amelia Amos," q.v.

AMOS, GEORGE K., see "Oliver H. Amoss," q.v.

AMOS, HENRY R., late of Ohio, but formerly of Harford Co., died 12 Oct 1859, in his 77th year, son of Mordecai Amos, dec'd., and son-in-law of the late Col. John Street, of Harford Co.; he was one of the Defenders of Baltimore in 1812 and died as he lived, a true patriot and a faithful Christian; he leaves a numerous family (SA 29 Oct 1859)

AMOS, JAMES (of A.), died ---- (date not given) and was removed from the voter registration list in the 4th District in 1868 (AI 9 Oct 1868)

AMOS, JAMES (of William), died Sat. 25 Jan 1868 in his 46th year, leaving a large number of relatives; the executor's notice stated that creditors must exhibit their legal vouchers by 28 Jan 1869 to Abraham Rutledge, admin. [sic] (AI 31 Jan 1868)

AMOS, JOHN T., died Thurs. 19 Jun 1862 at his residence, in his 84th year; the subsequent executor's notice spelled the name as "Amoss" and stated that creditors must exhibit their legal vouchers by 25 Jun 1863 to Archer H. Jarrett, exec. (SA 28 Jun 1862 and 5 Jul 1862)

AMOS, MARTHA (Miss) and Washington M. Slade, Esq., both of Harford Co., m. 29 Jan 1867 by Rev. T. S. C. Smith (AI 8 Feb 1867)

AMOS, MORDECAI, see "Henry R. Amos," q.v.

AMOS, ROBERT, see "Annie Amelia Amos," q.v.

AMOS, ROBERT C., died ---- (date not given) and the administrator's notice stated that creditors must exhibit their legal vouchers by 20 Jan 1867 to William A. Wilson, admin.; Robert Amos was removed from the voter registration list in the 4th District in 1868 (AI 26 Jan 1866 and AI 9 Oct 1868)

AMOS, SARAH, consort of the late B. Scott Amos, of Harford Co., died 7 Oct 1869, after a long and painful illness, in her 77th year (AI 29 Oct 1869)

AMOS, SARAH, died 19 Dec 1865, aged 75, at the residence of Joseph E. Maynadier in Harford Co. (AI 22 Dec 1865)

AMOS, WILLIAM, see "James Amos," q.v.

AMOS, WILLIAM (of Thomas), died 6 Apr 1859 in his 86th year (SA 16 Apr 1859)

AMOS, WILLIAM LEE, died last week at this residence near Bel Air, at an advanced age; the subsequent executor's notice spelled his surname "Amoss" and stated that creditors must exhibit their legal vouchers by 14 Nov 1871 to Garrett Amoss, exec. (AI 14 Oct 1870 and 4 Nov 1870)

AMOSS, ELIZABETH A., see "Oliver H. Amoss," q.v.

AMOSS, GARRETT, see "William Lee Amos," q.v.

AMOSS, ISAAC and Mrs. Mary Amoss, both of Harford Co., m. Tues. 17 Apr 1838 by Rev. John Galey (HM 26 Apr 1838)

AMOSS, JAMES, see "Harriet C. Estes," q.v.

AMOSS, JOHN M., died ---- (date not given) and the administrator's notice stated that creditors must exhibit their legal vouchers by 15 Jun 1860 to Thomas Glenn, admin. (SA 25 Jun 1859)

AMOSS, JOSHUA M., died ---- (date not given) and the executor's notice stated that creditors must exhibit their legal vouchers by 27 Apr 1861 to Joseph M. Streett, exec. (SA 19 May 1860)

AMOSS, LEE, see "William Young," q.v.

AMOSS, MARY (Mrs.) and Isaac Amoss, both of Harford Co., m. Tues. 17 Apr 1838 by Rev. John Galey (HM 26 Apr 1838)

AMOSS, OLIVER H., died Sat. 9 Apr 1864 at his residence, in his 64th year; the subsequent executor's notice stated that creditors must exhibit their legal vouchers by 9 May 1865 to Elizabeth A. Amoss, George K. Amoss, and Stevenson Archer, execs. (AI 15 Apr 1864 and 13 May 1864)

AMOSS, SARAH, see "Harriet C. Estes," q.v.

AMOSS, SARAH (Miss), died 19 Dec 1865, aged 75, at *Appleby* in Harford Co. (AI 5 Jan 1866)

ANDERSON, ANN, died ---- (date not given) and the executrix's notice stated that creditors must exhibit their legal vouchers by 28 May 1857 to Cassandra Renshaw, extx. (HD 6 Jun 1856)

ANDERSON, ELIZABETH, see "William Anderson" and "Zarvona Anderson," q.v.

ANDERSON, F. D., see "Maria L. Anderson," q.v.

ANDERSON, IRA, see "Joshua V. Anderson," q.v.

ANDERSON, JOSHUA V., son of Ira G. and Mary Anderson, died --- (date not given) in his 27th year, at his father's residence near Monkton (SA 20 Mar 1863)

ANDERSON, MARGARET, see "Zarvona Anderson," q.v.

ANDERSON, MARIA L. (Miss), dau. of F. D. Anderson, Esq., and James W. Hopkins, all of Harford Co., m. 26 Aug 1858 by Rev. Dashiells (SA 4 Sep 1858)

ANDERSON, MARY, see "Joshua V. Anderson," q.v.

ANDERSON, NANCY, died at her residence in Harford Co. on Thurs. 15 May 1856 at an advanced age (HD 16 May 1856)

ANDERSON, WILLIAM, see "Zarvona Anderson," q.v.

ANDERSON, WILLIAM, died ---- (date not given) and the administratrix's notice stated that creditors must exhibit their legal vouchers by 7 Jun 1871 to Elizabeth A. Anderson, admx. (AI 10 Jun 1870); W. Anderson was removed from the voter registration list in the 4th District in 1870 (AI 4 Nov 1870)

ANDERSON, WILLIAM F. and Maggie N. DeSwan, eldest dau. of C. DeSwan, all of Harford Co., m. Thurs. 16 Jun 1864 at the residence of the Bishop, the Right Rev. R. M. Coskery, in Baltimore (AI 1 Jul 1864)

ANDERSON, ZARVONA, died 13 Jul 1865, in her 3rd year, and
Margaret Anderson d. 13 Aug 1865, in her 5th year, children of
William and Elizabeth Anderson and grandchildren of George and
Margaret Lemmon; obituary contains a short poem (AI 18 Aug
1865)

ANDREW, MARY E. (Mrs.) and William Morris, both of Harford Co.,
m. 5 Apr 1870 by Rev. J. G. Moore (AI 6 May 1870)

ANDREWS, ISAAC, see "Philip Quinlan," q.v.

ANDREWS, J. R. and Miss Mary A. Robinson, both of Harford Co., m.
17 Feb 1869, in Deer Creek Chapel, by Rev. D. A. Shermer (AI 26
Feb 1869)

ARCHER, BLANCHE, see "Mary Archer," q.v.

ARCHER, DAVID F. and Catharine Susanna Stephens, both of Harford
Co., m. 9 Jan 1866, at the house of Joseph Stephens, by Rev. J. K.
Nichols (AI 26 Jan 1866)

ARCHER, FANNY VAN WICK, wife of W. H. Archer and third dau. of
the late M. Tilghman Goldsborough, of Talbot Co., died Thurs.
night 10 Nov 1870, in her 18th year (AI 18 Nov 1870)

ARCHER, HANNAH, wife of John Archer, residing on Winter's Run
near the Red School House, Harford Co., while partaking of a meal
one day last week, accidentally lodged a small rabbit bone in her
wind pipe, below the gullet, causing great pain; Dr. E. Hall
Richardson was summoned and upon his advice the Archers at once
set out for Baltimore to seek surgical aid from Prof. Nathan R.
Smith; the surgeon desired to open the windpipe and extract the
bone, but Mrs. Archer objected, so he tried to force the obstruction
out; this operation apparently lacerated the lungs, for bleeding
ensued, and Mrs. Archer expired within three hours; her body was
returned to Harford Co. and buried last Sun. (AI 9 Dec 1870)

ARCHER, HENRY W., see "Mary Scott" and "Amos Jones," q.v.

ARCHER, J. GLASGOW (Reverend), son of Thomas Archer, of Harford
Co., was in a recent railroad accident on the Panhandle Railroad and
was found dead under the sleeping car; he was a young man in his
27th year, a graduate of Dickinson College in PA and also of the
Theological Seminary in Princeton, NJ, and pastor of a Presbyterian
Church in Clearfield in western PA; he had started to St. Louis to
bring his wife and child home who were there visiting relatives; his
body was brought to Harford Co. by Dr. Hill, a member Rev.
Archer's congregation, and was buried in Churchville last Sun. [a
second article in *The Aegis & Intelligencer* gives more details about
this accident] (HR 21 Jan 1869 and AI 22 Jan 1869)

ARCHER, JAMES J., see "Oliver H. Thomas," q.v.

ARCHER, JOHN, see "Hannah Archer" and "Nannie H. Archer" and
"Oliver H. Thomas," q.v.

ARCHER, JOHN R., of Harford Co., and Miss Arabella Sutton, of
Baltimore Co., m. 5 Nov 1866 at the Parsonage in Bel Air by Rev.
J. K. Nichols (AI 9 Nov 1866)

ARCHER, JUDGE, see "Pamelia B. Archer," q.v.

ARCHER, MARY, only child of Stevenson and Blanche Archer, died 5 Aug 1856 at *Woodside*, Harford Co., aged 7 months and 5 days (HD 8 Aug 1856)

ARCHER, MARY T. (Miss), of Harford Co., and Charles S. Shepard, of Baltimore, m. 13 Sep 1870 by Rev. J. E. Reed (AI 30 Sep 1870)

ARCHER, NANNIE H. (Miss), dau. of the late Dr. John Archer, of Rock Run, Harford Co., and Oliver H. Thomas, of Bel Air, m. Tues. 1 Dec 1868 at the residence of Mrs. Constable, sister of the bride, in Cecil Co., by Rev. Squire (AI 4 Dec 1868)

ARCHER, PAMELIA B., relict of the late Judge Archer, died Thurs. 2 Apr 1863 at the residence of her son, S. Archer, in her 80th year; a second obituary states she died suddenly on 1 Apr 1863, in her 81st year, and it also contains a long memorial (SA 10 Apr 1863 and 17 Apr 1863)

ARCHER, ROBERT H. (Doctor), died ---- (date not given) at an advanced age, within the last few days; a prominent citizen who was at one time a member of the Governor's Council, he was once spoke of as the Whig candidate for Governor; for some years he has been in feeble health (HD 22 May 1857)

ARCHER, S., see "Amos Jones" and "Pamelia B. Archer," q.v.

ARCHER, STEVENSON, see "Archer H. Jarrett" and "John Holland" and "Oliver H. Amoss" and "Mary Archer," q.v.

ARCHER, THOMAS, Esq., died suddenly and unexpectedly yesterday morning [17 Feb 1870] at his residence near Churchville, aged about 60; he was a well known and widely respected citizen of Harford Co.; he was subsequently removed from the voter registration list in the 3rd District in 1870 (AI 18 Feb 1870 and 28 Oct 1870)

ARCHER, THOMAS, see "J. Glasgow Archer," q.v.

ARCHER, W. H., see Fanny Van Wick Archer," q.v.

ARMIGER, JAMES MIDDLETON, son of James R. and Marion Armiger, died 30 Nov 1870 in Baltimore, of scarlet fever, aged 7 years, 9 months and 8 days (AI 2 Dec 1870)

ARMIGER, ROBERT B., of Baltimore, and Harriet E. Chesney, of Harford Co., m. Tues. morning 21 Jun 1863, at the Parsonage, by Rev. Alex. E. Gibson (AI 15 Jul 1864)

ARMSTRONG, JAMES H. (Negro man), was shot dead last Mon. night in a rum mill in Baltimore by George Potee, a son of the proprietor; a quarrel originated over a counterfeit five cent piece which Armstrong had tendered in payment for some beer, when Potee shot him through the heart with a revolver; Potee was subsequently arrested (SA 8 Jan 1859)

ARMSTRONG, JOHN and Miss Mary Cronin, both of Harford Co., m. Tues. 17 Jan 1865 by Rev. DeWolf (AI 20 Jan 1865)

ARNOLD, ANDREW, aged about 50, was murdered last Mon. near Hagerstown, MD (struck in the head; assailant not named); only surviving family member mentioned was a dau. [name not given] (HR 29 Oct 1868)

ARTHER, REV. and Miss Cornelia E. Gillett, dau. of Dr. Jacob Gillett, formerly of Harford Co., m. 12 Dec 1837, in Guernsey Co., Ohio, by Rev. Polk (HM 28 Dec 1837)

ARTHUR, ELIZA E. and Franklin Pennington, both of Harford Co., m. 5 Sep 1867 by Rev. Thomas M. Cathcart (AI 4 Oct 1867)

ARTHUR, GEORGE, see "Joseph Arthur," q.v.

ARTHUR, JOHN THOMAS, of Baltimore Co., and Miss Rebecca Price, of Harford Co., m. 1 Jun 1869 at the Episcopal Methodist Church, Jarrettsville, by Rev. J. C. Hagey (AI 18 Jun 1869 and HD 18 Jun 1869)

ARTHUR, JOSEPH, eldest son of George and Susan Arthur, died 30 Jul 1870 at his father's residence, near Sarah Furnace, in his 31st year; he was subsequently removed from the voter registration list in the 4th District in 1870 (HD 5 Aug 1870; AI 5 Aug 1870 and 4 Nov 1870)

ARTHUR, MARY ELIZABETH, wife of John Thomas Arthur and eldest dau. of Thomas and Elizabeth Miskimmon, of Baltimore, died 1 Jul 1867 in Harford Co., in her 23rd year (AI 12 Jul 1867)

ARTHUR, SUSAN, see "Joseph Arthur," q.v.

ARTHUR, SUSANNA (Miss) and Sylvester Phelps, both of Harford Co., m. 7 Sep 1869, at the residence of the bride's father, by Rev. T. M. Cathcart (AI 17 Sep 1869)

ASHTON, BELL (Miss) and Thomas Nelson m. last Thurs. at Rock Spring Church by Rev. Snowden; Jennie Ashton was the bride's maid and Charles Streett was the groom's man; the bridal party was entertained later at the residence of Mr. N. Nelson (HD 25 Feb 1870)

ASHTON, EDWARD, died ---- (date not given) and the executor's notice stated that creditors must exhibit their legal vouchers by 1 Jun 1858 to John Ashton and Thomas Hanway, execs. (SA 5 Dec 1857)

ASHTON, ISABEL (Miss) and Thomas H. Nelson m. 17 Feb 1870 at Christ Church (Rock Spring) by Rev. W. E. Snowden (AI 18 Mar 1870)

ASHTON, JENNIE, see "Bell Ashton," q.v.

ASHTON, JOHN, see "Edward Ashton" and "Richard Ashton," q.v.

ASHTON, JOSEPH E. and Mary E. Baldwin, both of Harford Co., m. Tues. 16 Feb 1869 at Christ Church, Rock Spring, by Rev. W. F. Snowden (HD 19 Mar 1869 and AI 19 Mar 1869)

ASHTON, MAGGIE and Isaac Mechem, both of Harford Co., m. 11 Jun 1867 in Baltimore by Rev. C. W. Rankin (AI 21 Jun 1867)

ASHTON, R. DALLAS and Miss Elizabeth C. Bryant, both of Harford Co., m. Tues., 17 May 1870 at St. Andrew's Church, Baltimore, by Rev. William W. Snowden (AI 27 May 1870)

ASHTON, REBECCA, see "Margaret Ann Mechem," q.v.

ASHTON, RICHARD, died ---- (date not given) and the trustee's sale of his real estate, except what he devised his son John Ashton, will be held on 9 Feb 1856 (HD 18 Jan 1856)

ASHTON, SARAH L. and William M. Glen, of Harford Co., m. 28 Jan 1858 by Rev. Keech (SA 6 Mar 1858)

ASHTON, SUSAN (Miss) and Silas Baldwin, both of Harford Co., m. Tues. 18 Dec 1866 at Rock Spring Church by Rev. J. H. D. Wingfield (AI 21 Dec 1866)

ASHTON, WILLIAM, see "Margaret Ann Mechem," q.v.

ATKINSON, ISAAC, died ---- (date not given) and the administrator's notice stated that creditors must exhibit their legal vouchers by 17 Apr 1839 to Mahlon Atkinson, admin. (HM 18 Oct 1838)

ATKINSON, JOHN A., of Port Deposit, drowned in December 1865 while attempting to cross the Susquehanna River from Lapidum to Port Deposit on the ice; his body was found last Sat. on Watson's Island, a short distance from Havre de Grace (AI 27 Apr 1866)

ATKINSON, MAHLON, see "Isaac Atkinson," q.v.

AUNT JUDY (colored woman), familiarly known by that name to the citizens of Bel Air, died Sun. at the County Almshouse; she is believed to have reached the advanced age of 101 years (AI 16 Oct 1868)

AUSTIN, EMMA (Miss) and Alford Aaronson m. 20 Feb 1867 by Rev. Francis E. Church (AI 1 Mar 1867)

AXER, JOHN and Lizzie Heck, both of Harford Co., m. 27 Jan 1866 by Rev. W. F. Brand, rector of St. Mary's Church (AI 2 Feb 1866)

AYERS, CHARLES, SR., died 23 Jul 1870, aged 72; he was subsequently removed from the voter registration list in the 4th District in 1870 (AI 29 Jul 1870 and 4 Nov 1870)

AYERS, SUSAN J. (Miss) and John C. Hazlett, both of Harford Co., m. Wed. 28 Jul 1869 by Rev. D. A. Shermer (AI 13 Aug 1869)

AYERS, SUSANNAH (Miss), of Harford Co., and Joseph W. Sadler, of Baltimore, m. 26 Sep 1858 in Baltimore by Rev. Alexander Bosserman (SA 2 Oct 1858)

AYRES, GEORGE, see "Dr. Oliver," q.v.

AYRES, JOHN T. and Miss Sarah F. Colder, both of Harford Co., m. Thurs. evening 12 Feb 1863 at Mt. Zion M. E. Church by Rev. R. C. Haslup (SA 20 Feb 1863)

AYRES, MARY S., youngest dau. of Thomas J. and Elizabeth Ayres, died at her father's residence near Shawsville on 21 Jun 1859, in her 21st year; obituary contains a short poem (SA 2 Jul 1859)

AYRES, R. S., see "Dr. Oliver," q.v.

AYRES, THOMAS AND ELIZABETH, see "Mary Ayres," q.v.

BACHARACH (BACHRACH), SIMON, a merchant of Philadelphia who had a branch clothing and variety store at the corner of Green and St. John Streets in Havre de Grace, was spending a few weeks here doing business; he went to bed last Fri. night and was found dead the next morning; he had been affected with heart disease; an inquest revealed he died in a fit, having been subject to fits for some time (HR 11 Nov 1869 and HD 12 Nov 1869)

BACON, REBECCA G., wife of Thomas M. Bacon, died 16 Mar 1850 in Havre de Grace, aged 33, a long time member of the M. E. Church (HM 21 Mar 1850)

BACON, THOMAS M., see "Miss Cynthia Morrison," q.v.

BAER, MARY (Miss) and Jacob Emrey, both of Harford Co., m. 15 Sep 1859 by Rev. Zulauf (SA 1 Oct 1859)

BAGELEY, HANNAH WATERS, wife of John Orick Bageley and dau. of Samuel E. and Rachael Husband, neé Snowden, of Anne Arundel Co., and niece of the late Joseph Husband, died Tues. 10 Nov 1868 of typhoid fever, in her 54th year; she was m. about age 18 and became the mother of 10 children, 8 of whom are now living, the youngest being in her 11th year; some years after her marriage she joined the Presbyterian Church in Churchville, but after removing to live near Jerusalem Mills she joined Union Chapel Methodist Protestant Church and was a member for 18 years before her death; she was a frequent contributor of poetry to the *Methodist Protestant*, of Baltimore, over the signature "H.W.B." and for many years was a teacher in both private and public schools; obituary contains a memorial which includes some of the aforementioned information (AI 20 Nov 1868)

BAGELY, SAMUEL H. and Miss Martha Matilda Ewing, both of Harford Co., m. Tues. 1 Jul 1862 by Rev. Dr. Swentzel (SA 5 Jul 1862)

BAGLEY, CLARA A., dau. of J. Orrick Bagley, of Harford Co., and John B. Watkins, of Long Green, Baltimore Co., m. Thurs. 25 Mar 1869, at Monument Street M. E. Church, by Rev. Richard Norris (AI 2 Apr 1869 and 9 Apr 1869)

BAGLEY, J. ORRICK, see "Clara A. Bagley," q.v.

BAILEY, ELIZABETH (Miss), aged about 45, died last Sun. morning about 7:30; she was found in a cistern at the residence of her cousin William Bailey in Havre de Grace; from a note found under a stone in the yard it appeared she committed suicide (HD 28 Oct 1870); another obituary states Miss Elizabeth Bailey, of Havre de Grace, committed suicide last Sat. night by drowning herself in a tank of water in the yard of William Bailey, her brother-in-law; the cause of the distressing event was religious melancholy; while in this morbid state of mind she saw no escape from imaginary evils except through her own death; she left a brief note indicating her consciousness of her true condition, laying all the blame of her rash act upon herself; she was buried last Mon.; a correction was published at the request of B. F. Heath, J.P., Acting Coroner, who stated that Miss Bailey was a respectable lady who was subject to mental depression; she had retired Sat. night as usual and was found dead Sun. morning in a cistern filled with water in the yard, having drowned herself while laboring under temporary insanity; the note referred to stated that she could not bear to see others suffer from her weakness and that no blame was attached to anyone but herself for the act [*Baltimore Sun* please copy] (HR 28 Oct 1870 and 4 Nov 1870); another obituary states Lizzie Bailey, a white woman aged about 40, employed as a nurse in a family in Havre de Grace, drowned herself last Sat. night by getting into a hogshead of rain water and seating herself therein until the water rose above her head; an inquest by Judge Heath revealed she had left a note stating she was going to destroy herself and no one should bother themselves about her, as she was better off (AI 28 Oct 1870)

BAILEY, EVAN, see "Henry C. Coen," q.v.

BAILEY, MARY E. (Miss) and William H. McVey, both of Harford Co., m. 28 Apr 1870 by Rev. J. G. Moore (AI 6 May 1870)

BAILEY, OLIVER T. and Miss Cornelia Williams, both of Havre de Grace, m. Tues. morning 27 Oct 1868, at Havre de Grace, by Rev. C. F. Thomas (HD 6 Nov 1868; AI 13 Nov 1868 gave the date as 7 Oct 1868)

BAILEY, WILLIAM, see "Elizabeth Bailey," q.v.

BAILY, DANIEL L. and Miss Mary E. Scarboro, both of Harford Co., m. Thurs. 7 May 1863 by Rev. William Colburn (SA 8 May 1863)

BAKER, FREDERICK W. and Miss Sally B. Lee m. Thurs. 28 Dec 1865 in Bel Air by Rev. J. H. D. Wingfield (AI 5 Jan 1866)

BAKER, GRAFTON, died last Wed. in Havre de Grace, aged about 70 (HM 18 Sep 1851)

BAKER, HENRY, "see "Mary A. M. Hays," q.v.

BAKER, J. G., see "Mary R. Fales," q.v.

BAKER, JOHN H. (Reverend) and Miss Cornelia Stockham, dau. of Thomas Stockham, Esq., all of Harford Co., m. 21 Oct 1868, at the residence of the bride's father, by Rev. J. G. Moore (AI 6 Nov 1868) Another marriage notice stated John H. Baker and Cornelia E. Stockham, dau. of James Stockham, Esq., of Harford Co., m. Wed. 21 Oct 1868, at the bride's fathers, by Rev. Moore (HD 30 Oct 1868)

BAKER, MARY J. (Miss), dau. of Nicholas Baker, Esq., and Frank F. Bruce, both of Harford County, m. Tues. 20 Jun 1871 by Rev. Charles A. Reid (HD 30 Jun 1871)

BAKER, MARY OLIVIA, wife of William B. Baker, of near Aberdeen, died 26 Jun 1869 in her 26th year (HR 15 Jul 1869); another death notice stated Olivia Baker, wife of William B. Baker and dau. of the late Rev. Benjamin Wells, of Harford Co., died 26 Jun 1869 near Aberdeen (HD 9 Jul 1869)

BAKER, OLIVIA, see "Mary Olivia Baker," q.v.

BAKER, WILLIAM B., see "Mary Olivia Baker," q.v.

BALDWIN, CHARLOTTE (Mrs.), died 10 Mar 1868 in Harford Co., aged 76 (AI 3 Apr 1868)

BALDWIN, FRANCES, see "Samuel T. Baldwin," q.v.

BALDWIN, FRANCIS, see "Laura C. Baldwin," q.v.

BALDWIN, JAMES, died ---- (date not given) and the administrator's notice stated that creditors must exhibit their legal vouchers by 21 Sep 1870 to William Baldwin, admin. (AI 24 Sep 1869)

BALDWIN, LAURA C., wife of Francis Baldwin and dau. of J. G. and Hannah C. Robinson, of Harford Co., died 9 Jul 1868 in Abingdon, in her 20th year; obituary contains a memorial written by "J.G.M." (AI 7 Aug 1868)

BALDWIN, MARY E. and Joseph E. Ashton, both of Harford Co., m. Tues. 16 Feb 1869 at Christ Church, Rock Spring, by Rev. W. F. Snowden (HD 19 Mar 1869 and AI 19 Mar 1869)

BALDWIN, SAMUEL T., son of Samuel T. and Frances Baldwin, died 15 Dec 1862 of diphtheria, at the residence of his father near Hopewell, Harford Co., aged 15 years, 4 months and 19 days (SA 27 Dec 1862)

BALDWIN, SILAS and Miss Susan Ashton, both of Harford Co., m. Tues. 18 Dec 1866 at Rock Spring Church by Rev. J. H. D. Wingfield (AI 21 Dec 1866)

BALDWIN, WILLIAM, see "James Baldwin," q.v.

BALL, MARY E., and William F. Ely, both of Harford Co., m. Tues. 3 Jul 1866 at the Methodist Episcopal Parsonage in Bel Air by Rev. Neminger (AI 13 Jul 1866)

BANISTER, ANDREW A. W. and Miss Eliza J. Ward, both of Harford Co., m. 31 Jan 1856 by Rev. Cushing (HD 1 Feb 1856)

BANKS, CHARLES W. and Miss Emily C. Maulsby, both of Harford Co., m. Thurs. 15 Feb 1866 at Rock Spring Church by Rev. J. H. D. Wingfield (AI 23 Feb 1866)

BANKS, JANE MAULSBY, oldest child of Charles W. and Emily C. Banks, died suddenly Sun. 6 Aug 1871 at 12:20 a.m., aged 4 years, 6 months and 15 days, after suffering with diphtheria for 3 days, at Piney Point, St. Mary's Co., MD (18 Aug 1871)

BARNABY, PRISCILLA (Miss) and William Sills, both of Havre de Grace, m. 3 Nov 1868 by Rev. C. F. Thomas (HR 5 Nov 1868)

BARNARD, JAMES, died ---- (date not given) and the administrator's notice stated that creditors must exhibit their legal vouchers by 9 May 1865 to John H. Barnard, admin. (AI 10 Jun 1864)

BARNARD, JOHN H., see "James Barnard," q.v.

BARNARD, THOMAS, died in an accident on the P. W. & B. Railroad last Tues.; the gentlemanly conductor was on the accommodation train running between Havre de Grace and Baltimore and, nearing a bridge, he attempted to look out when his head came into contact with the bridge, killing him almost instantly; he had many acquaintances in Harford Co. (HD 6 Mar 1857)

BARNES, ELEANOR, see "Elisha Barnes," q.v.

BARNES, ELISHA, died suddenly 31 Jul 1856 in Scottsville in this county; he had gone for an early morning walk when he was attacked with a fit of apoplexy and died in a few minutes; the subsequent administrator's notice stated that creditors must exhibit their legal vouchers by 11 Aug 1857 to Eleanor Barnes, admx. (HD 1 Aug 1856 and 6 Feb 1857)

BARNES, GEORGE WASHINGTON and Mrs. Sarah Jane Hevern, both of Havre de Grace, m. Thurs. evening 7 Sep 1848 by Rev. Parkinson (HM 7 Sep 1848)

BARNES, JOHN, died ---- (date not given) and the executor's notice stated that creditors must exhibit their legal vouchers by 4 Apr 1844 to John H. Mitchell, exec. (HM 17 Nov 1843)

BARNES, JOHN B., see "Mary E. Barnes," q.v.

BARNES, JOHN H. and Mary E. Morgan, both of Havre de Grace, m. Tues. 26 Jun 1866 at the Presbyterian Church in Havre de Grace by Rev. Cramer (AI 6 Jul 1866)

BARNES, MARY ANN (Miss) and Mr. Christian Case, both of Havre de Grace, m. Wed. 6 Nov 1867 in Baltimore by Rev. Richard Norris (AI 27 Dec 1867)

BARNES, MARY C. (Miss) and A. A. Fletcher, both of Havre de Grace, m. 18 Jun 1871 (HR 7 Jul 1871)

BARNES, MARY E., wife of John B. Barnes and dau. of William B. Morgan, died 5 Mar 1867, in Havre de Grace, in her 24th year; obituary contains a memorial written by "J.K.C." (AI 22 Mar 1867)

BARNES, MARY K., mother of Mr. Wash. Barnes, died 20 Apr 1868, in her 81st year (AI 1 May 1868)

BARNES, THOMAS B., died suddenly 5 Nov 1870, in his 34th year (AI 11 Nov 1870)

BARNES, WASH., see "Mary K. Barnes," q.v.

BARNES, WILLIAM HENRY, a young man of Havre de Grace who had been in ill health for two or three years, died at the residence of James Hopper, Esq., on Wed. last; he was a member of the Masonic Order and also belonged to the I. O. of Odd Fellows; his funeral takes place today (HR 17 Mar 1871)

BARNES, WINSTON, see "Thomas C. Fletcher," q.v.

BARRINGTON, MINA A., of Baltimore Co., and William S. Chew, of Havre de Grace, m. Tues. 29 Sep 1868 at St. John's Church, Huntington, Baltimore Co., by Rev. William T. Johnson (HD 9 Oct 1868)

BARTON, SOPHRONIA (Miss) and William T. Hughes, both of Harford Co., m. 12 Jan 1870, at the residence of the bride's father in Harford Co., by Rev. Joseph D. Smith (AI 21 Jan 1870)

BARTON, WESLEY and Cenia Hurst, both of Harford Co., m. 26 Oct 1865 by Rev. E. Kinsey (AI 10 Nov 1865)

BARTON, WILLIAM W., of Cooptown, died Thurs. morning last week of exposure; he was found in the road near Rutledge's School House in Marshall's District and taken to the residence of John W. Rutledge where an inquest was held on his body; supposedly a stranger, he was buried at Ebenezer M. E. Church; a few minutes the burial his identity was ascertained and his wife and relatives were sent for; they had his remains taken up and re-buried on Sun. (HR 10 Mar 1871)

BASTICK, PENELOPE K., wife of John Bastick and dau. of the late Joshua Rutledge, of Harford Co., died 15 Aug 1868 in New Orleans (AI 18 Sep 1868)

BATCHELOR, SARAH E., of Baltimore, and Charles D. France, of Harford Co., m. 12 Dec 1865, at the residence of the bride's father, by Rev. B. G. W----d [illegible] (AI 22 Dec 1865)

BATEMAN, A. W., see "Redman Kean," q.v.

BATEMAN, ALFRED W., see "Winfred Kelly," q.v.

BATEMAN, ANNA P., eldest dau. of Joseph E. Bateman, Esq., and Ignatius Macatee, all of Harford Co., m. Thurs. 17 Oct 1865 by Rev. O'Connor (AI 20 Oct 1865)

BATEMAN, SAMUEL H., see "George B. Neville," q.v.

BAUSEMAN, FREDERICK, aged about 55, committed suicide last Thurs. at the residence of his sister Miss Catherine Bausemen in Lancaster, PA (SA 6 Feb 1858)

BAUSMITH, WILLIAM T., of Baltimore, and Miss Naomi A. Gilbert, of Harford Co., m. 18 Mar 1869 by Rev. George H. Zimmerman (AI 20 Mar 1868)

BAVARD, G. SR., died ---- (date not given) and was removed from the voter registration list in the 5th District in 1870 (HR 1 Nov 1870)

BAY, ASENNATH ANN, wife of Hon. Thomas Bay, died 26 Jun 1868 in Harford Co., in her 67th year (AI 10 Jul 1868)

BAY, CHARLES H., died ---- (date not given) and the administrator's notice stated that creditors must exhibit their legal vouchers by 9 Dec 1861 to Thomas Bay , admin. (SA 1 Dec 1860)

BAY, CHARLES HENRY and Miss Rebecca Jane Cairnes, both of Harford Co., m. 28 Jan 1858 by Rev. T. S. C. Smith (SA 6 Feb 1858)

BAY, HUGH, died Fri. 27 Mar 1863, in his 18th year, at the residence of his father Thomas Bay, Esq.; obituary contains a brief memorial and short verse (SA 3 Apr 1863)

BAY, JAMES M., died 25 Jul 1870, in his 64th year; the subsequent executor's notice stated that creditors must exhibit their legal vouchers by 9 Aug 1871 to Thomas Bay, exec. (AI 29 Jul 1870 and 12 Aug 1870)

BAY, JOHN W., of Baltimore, and Emma W. Galup, dau. of the late Oliver Galup, of Harford Co., m. 16 Jan 1868 at the Second Presbyterian Church, Baltimore, by Rev. George P. Hays (AI 24 Jan 1868)

BAY, KENNEDY, see "Sarah J. Bay," q.v.

BAY, SARAH J., died ---- (date not given) and the administrator's notice stated that creditors must exhibit their legal vouchers by 8 Sep 1865 to Kennedy Bay, admin. (AI 9 Sep 1864)

BAY, THOMAS, see "Asennath Ann Bay" and "Charles H. Bay" and "Hugh Bay," q.v.

BAYARD, RACHEL (Mrs.), a native of Havre de Grace, died 31 Dec 1847, leaving a large circle of friends and acquaintances (HM 13 Jan 1848)

BAYLESS, ELIZABETH S. (Miss) and Julius H. Matthews, both of Harford Co., m. Tues. 18 Dec 1866 by Rev. William A. McKee (AI 28 Dec 1866)

BAYNE, JOHN CARVILLE, aged about 19, son of John Bayne, Esq., living on Joppa Road about 3 miles from Towsontown, was shot and killed last Thurs. morning; he had gone out gunning with George Brown, and others, and about 9 o'clock they were on the place of John C. Pierce [also spelled Pearce in the article] at the Gunpowder Falls near Cromwell's Bridge; Pierce was working in his field and heard shooting, so he picked up his gun and went over the hill and found Bayne and Brown; he ordered them off his land and an altercation ensued, ending in Pierce's shooting Bayne in the upper part of the abdomen; Pierce carried the wounded man to his own house and summoned Dr. J. H. Jarrett, but Bayne died about 12 o'clock; Pierce sent the dead man home in his own wagon; later that evening he was arrested by Sheriff Burke and is now in jail [article in the *Towsontown Herald*] (AI 2 Dec 1870)

BAYNE, JOHN H. (Doctor), the eminent horticulturist of Prince George's Co., MD, died 18 Aug 1870 (AI 2 Sep 1870)

BEACHBOARD, ELIZABETH (Miss), died Tues. morning at the residence of William L. Fendall, Esq., Harford Co., in her 77th year [*Worcester Shield* please copy] (AI 25 Mar 1870)

BEAL, JAMES P. and Miss Sue J. Wilgus, both of Harford Co., m. 15 Jan 1867 at Mt. Zion M. P. Church, near Bel Air, by Rev. J. K. Nichols (AI 8 Feb 1867)

BEAL, MARY (Mrs.), died 11 Oct 1862 in the afternoon, in Baltimore, in her 95th year; she had been a member of the Methodist Episcopal Church for the last 40 years (SA 18 Oct 1962)

BEALL, WILLIAM B., see "Martha Scott," q.v.

BEALL, WILLIAM H. and Miss Rachel E. Jeffery m. 7 Oct 1869 at the residence of the Mr. Keith, in Bel Air, by Rev. George M. Berry [double wedding with William G. Jeffery and Mary E. Keith] (AI 8 Oct 1869)

BEAM, AGNES (Miss), dau. of the late Joseph Beam, died Fri. 4 Aug 1865, in her 25th year, at the residence of her mother (AI 11 Aug 1865)

BEAMAN, JAMES J., died 18 Jun 1866, aged 43, at the residence of his father in Harford Co. (AI 29 Jun 1866)

BEAUMONT, HOLLIN and Miss Mary J. Engle, both of Harford Co., m. 4 Sep 1866 at the M. E. Parsonage in Bel Air by Rev. W. M. Meminger (AI 14 Sep 1866)

BEAUMONT, LEWIS and Mary M. Groscup, both of Harford Co., m. 15 Nov 1865 by Rev. E. Kinsey (AI 24 Nov 1865)

BEAUMONT, MOLLIE J. (Miss), of Harford Co., and Dr. George W. Davis, of Baltimore, m. 26 Jan 1870 by Rev. J. S. Remsay (AI 4 Feb 1870)

BEAUMONT, THOMAS L., see "Aaron Johnson," q.v.

BEEMAN, m. E. (Mrs.), died Wed. 22 Nov 1865, aged 90, at the residence of her son Joseph Beeman in Harford Co.; funeral on Sat. 25 Nov 1865 at 10 a.m. [name of cemetery not given] (AI 24 Nov 1865)

BEEMAN, MARY, wife of J. J. Beeman, died Sun. morning 16 Dec 1867, in her 65th year (AI 20 Dec 1867)

BELT, SALLIE P. (Miss), of Montgomery Co., and Rev. Levin D. Hebron, of the East Baltimore Conference, m. on Tues. 11 Jan 1859 at Clarksburg M. E. Church by Rev. Dr. Thomas B. Sargent (SA 22 Jan 1859)

BENNETT, ---- (Negro man), was shot and killed by another Negro by the name of Norris some time after 12 o'clock last Sat. night; Norris, who keeps a boarding house for the Negro workmen at Oakington in the lower part of Harford Co., gave a party and became disappointed with the music played by another Negro (name not known) he had hired for the occasion; some others interfered and confined Norris to a small room, but he escaped through a window and obtained a double-barreled gun; as he passed around the corner of the house he discovered Bennett and a companion about to enter the house; mistaking Bennett for the musician with whom he had he difficulty, he fired the entire load into the side of Bennett's neck, killing him instantly; Norris was arrested by Officer Young on Sun. and confined in the county jail (AI 30 Nov 1866)

BENNETT, JOHN E. and Lizzie Zimmerman, only dau. of Isaac Zimmerman, Esq., of Harford Co., m. 19 Feb 1863 by Rev. Shoaff (SA 27 Feb 1863)

BENNETT, JOHN EDWARD, of Baltimore, and Amanda R. Dorney, of Harford Co., m. 12 Apr 1865 by Rev. J. S. Stuchell (AI 12 May 1865)

BENNINGTON, MILTON and Miss Lizzie Daughton, both of Harford Co., m. 19 Apr 1870, by Rev. Smith, of Slate Ridge (AI 6 May 1870)

BERNARD, JOHN, see "---- Nicholl (Nichols)," q.v.

BERRY, ESTHER R. (Mrs.), dau. [sic] of the late Jeremiah Berry, of Howard Co., died 15 Oct 1868 in Harford Co., in her 78th year (AI 6 Nov 1868)

BEVARD, GEORGE SR., died Sun. morning 14 Feb 1869, at his residence near Darlington, in his 75th year (AI 19 Feb 1869)

BILLINGSLEA, C. W., see "Richard Green," q.v.

BILLINGSLEA, CHARLTON W. JR. and Virginia McGonigall, both of Harford Co., m. 14 Jul 1869 by Rev. Brooks (AI 23 Jul 1869 and HD 30 Jul 1869; the previous HD edition on 23 Jul 1869 had mistakenly given the marriage date as 24 Jul 1869 and the AI edition listed his name without the Jr.); see "John K. Sappington," q.v.

BILLINGSLEA, ELIZABETH F. (Mrs.), died ---- (date not given) at her residence in Abingdon, Harford Co., after a few hours' illness, in her 65th year (SA 25 Dec 1858)

BILLINGSLEA, JAMES, died Wed. 19 Jan 1865 (age not given) at his residence in Harford Co., after a protracted illness (AI 20 Jan 1865)

BILLINGSLEA, JOHN W. and Elizabeth A. Crevensten, both of Harford Co., m. 1 Feb 1866 by Rev. E. Kinsey (AI 16 Feb 1866 spelled her name "Creveston"); see "Martha Crevensten," q.v.

BILLINGSLEA, MARY C. and Wesley Phillips, both of Harford Co., m. 21 Dec 1865 by Rev. E. Kinsey (AI 5 Jan 1866)

BILLINGSLEA, WILLIAM, see "Hesther Waltham," q.v.

BIRCKHEAD, C. C. AND ELIZA Y., see "Mary C. Birckhead," q.v.

BIRCKHEAD, MARY C., eldest dau. of C. C. and Eliza Y. Birckhead, died 11 Dec 1869 (AI 17 Dec 1869)

BIRCKHEAD, S. H., see "S. Lizzie Birckhead," q.v.

BIRCKHEAD, S. LIZZIE, dau. of Dr. S. H. Birckhead, of Harford Co., and H. T. Martin, of Baltimore, m. 4 Jun 1868 at Spesutia Church, Perrymansville, by Rev. S. W. Crampton (AI 12 Jun 1868)

BIRCKHEAD, SAMUEL H., see "Francis Delmas" and "George Hartman," q.v.

BIRD, GEORGE K., of Philadelphia, and Miss Sallie J. Vandiver, of Harford Co., m. 14 Feb 1871 at Havre de Grace by Rev. William H. Cooke (HD 17 Feb 1871)

BISHOP, ELIJAH, died Mon. 21 Nov 1870, at Emmorton, aged 53 (AI 25 Nov 1870); he was subsequently removed from the voter registration list in the 1st District in 1871 (HR 29 Sep 1871)

BISSELL, LIZZIE R. (Miss) and William A. Richardson m. Mon. 8 Feb 1864 by Rev. H. Singleton at the Presbyterian Church in Bel Air; a subsequent marriage notice gave his name as Dr. William S. Richardson and stated she was the dau. of the late Capt. William R. Bissell (SA 12 Feb 1864 and 19 Feb 1864)

BISSELL, R. VIRGINIA, dau. of the late Capt. William R. Bissell, and John Holland, all of Harford Co., m. 18 Oct 1865 in Bel Air by Rev. T. S. C. Smith (AI 27 Oct 1865)

BISSELL, WILLIAM R., Captain, 8th VA Regiment, C.S.A., died 17 Jul 1863 in the Hospital Camp near Gettysburg, in his 53rd year (SA 24 Jul 1863)

BLAKE, JOHN L., of Baltimore, and Miss Susie Johns, of Harford Co., m. 10 Feb 1870 at Abingdon M. E. Church, by Rev. J. G. Moore [marriage notice indicated "No cards"] (AI 18 Feb 1870)

BLANEY, WILLIAM, died ---- (date not given) and was removed from the voter registration list in the 4th District in 1871 (HR 3 Nov 1871)

BLANY, JOHN, died ---- (date not given) and was removed from the voter registration list in the 6th District in 1870 (HR 21 Oct 1870)

BOARMAN, BENJAMIN W. (Colonel), died last Tues. night at his residence near Sandy Hook; he had been in delicate health during the entire summer, but was not confined to his bed; he retired as usual that evening and died soon thereafter (AI 24 Sep 1869)

BOARMAN, FRANK, son of Franklin and Fanny Boarman, died Sat. 30 Apr 1870, aged 3 years, 1 month and 7 days; obituary contains a poem; another notice in the same newspaper stated he was a little boy of 3 or 4 years, only son of Franklin Boarman, Esq., residing in the upper part of Harford Co., had a painful accident and died on Fri. last week; he was playing in the kitchen with his favorite dog and no other family members or servants were present; he somehow upset a tea kettle of boiling water, which falling upon him, scalded him so severely as to cause his death in a short time (AI 6 May 1870)

BOARMAN, FRANKLIN and Miss Frances E. Holland, dau. of Robert W. Holland, Esq., all of Harford Co., m. Thurs. 1 Jun 1865 by Rev. T. S. C. Smith (AI 9 Jun 1865)

BOARMAN, JOSEPH, died Fri. 13 May 1864, of diphtheria, in his 20th year, at the residence of his father in Harford Co., but for the last 3 years a resident of Baltimore Co.; obituary contains a brief memorial (AI 27 May 1864)

BODDER, IRVIN W., died ---- (date not given) and the administrator's notice stated that creditors must exhibit their legal vouchers by 9 Jul 1845 to Levi D. Bodder, admin. (HM 18 Oct 1844)

BOLT, BENJAMIN, see "Alexander Russum" and "Benjamin Thompson" and "George Roberts," q.v.

BOLTON, ROBERT AND MARGARET, see "Hannah Bond Murphy,," q.v.

BONAPARTE, JEROME NAPOLEON, died in Baltimore last Fri., aged 63; his father was Jerome Bonaparte, a brother of the great first Emperor of France, and who m. Miss Elizabeth Patterson, of Baltimore, in 1803; the Emperor refused to recognize the marriage and would not allow him to bring his bride to France; he subsequently m. a second time (AI 24 Jun 1870)

BOND, ADDIE (Miss), of Cheltenham, formerly of Kentucky, and Dr. William Stump Forwood, of Harford Co., m. 6 May 1863 at St. Paul's Church at Cheltenham, near Philadelphia, by Rev. Parvin (SA 15 May 1863)

BOND, ARTHUR W. and Josephine Cecil, dau. of Owen Cecil, Esq., of Millersville, Anne Arundel Co., MD, m. 14 Dec 1870, at the residence of the bride's father, by Rev. David Hall (AI 16 Dec 1870)

BOND, GEORGE M., of Harford Co., and Annie E. Cord, dau. of William F. Cord, Esq., of Accomac Co., VA, m. 2 Jan 1868 by Rev. Edward S. Grant (AI 10 Jan 1868)

BOND, JOSHUA B., died ---- (date not given) at his residence in Louisiana, in his 60th year; a native of Harford Co., he removed to

Louisiana some years ago and became an extensive and wealthy sugar planter; during the war his home and all his buildings were set on fire by Butler's troops and all were consumed; he was confined to his bed at the time, due to a severe illness, and was carried from the house when it was fired; he leaves a large circle of relations and friends in Harford Co. (AI 24 Aug 1866)

BOND, MARY ANN, relict of the late Zachias O. Bond, died Wed. morning 3 Aug 1870 at the residence of John A. Munnikhuysen, in her 89th year (HD 3 Aug 1870)

BOND, SALLIE A. (Miss), of Baltimore, and J. Thomas Wright, of Jerusalem Mills, Harford Co., m. Thurs. 2 Feb 1865 by Rev. Andrew B. Cross (AI 10 Feb 1865)

BOND, T. E., see "Mary McCay," q.v.

BOND, THOMAS E. (Doctor), died ---- (date not given), a native of Maryland and a resident of Baltimore, as reported in the *New York Commercial*; it also indicated he joined the Methodist Episcopal Church in Baltimore in 1805, they believe, and for many years he had been chief editor of the *New York Christian Advocate and Journal* (HD 21 Mar 1856)

BOND, ZACHIAS O., see "Mary Ann Bond," q.v.

BOOTH, JAMES, see "Mary H. Booth," q.v.

BOOTH, JOHN WILKES, see "Abraham Lincoln," q.v.

BOOTH, MARY H, wife of James Booth, died 25 Jun 1864 at Perrymansville (AI 1 Jul 1864)

BOTTS, ASAEL, see "John Botts," q.v.

BOTTS, GEORGE F. and Mrs. Henrietta Forsythe, both of Harford Co., m. 17 Nov 1870 at the M. E. Parsonage, Dublin, by Rev. George M. Berry (AI 25 Nov 1870)

BOTTS, JOHN and Miss Lizzie Norris, both of Harford Co., m. 10 Nov 1864 in Bel Air (AI 25 Nov 1864)

BOTTS, JOHN, died ---- (date not given) and the administrator's notice stated that creditors must exhibit their legal vouchers by 1 Jan 1853 to Asael Botts, admin. (HM 22 Jul 1852)

BOULDIN, HARRY GOUGH, son of R. E. and Martha C. Bouldin, died Thurs. morning 20 Feb 1868, aged 5 months and 25 days (AI 28 Feb 1868)

BOULDIN, I. V. (Miss) and James R. Cadden, of Harford Co., m. Tues. 4 Apr 1865 at the Presbyterian Church, in Bel Air, by Rev. J. McKendrie Reilly (AI 7 Apr 1865)

BOULDIN, MARTHA, see "Harry Gough Bouldin," q.v.

BOULDIN, MOLLIE A. (Miss), dau. of William Bouldin, Esq., of Bel Air, and A. Preston Gilbert m. Thurs. 6 Oct 1870 at Emmanuel Church, Bel Air, by Rev. William E. Snowden (AI 14 Oct 1870 and HD 7 Oct 1870)

BOULDIN, R. E., see "Harry Gough Bouldin," q.v.

BOULDIN, RICHARD E., Captain, 7th MD Volunteers, and Martha C. Gough, dau. of Harry D. Gough, Esq., of Baltimore, m. Thurs. 4

Feb 1864 by Rev. L. F. Morgan at Charles Street M. E. Church in Baltimore (SA 12 Feb 1864); see "Harry D. Gough," q.v.

BOULDIN, WILLIAM, see "Mollie Bouldin," q.v.

BOUNCE, RACHEL (Miss) and Daniel D. Spencer, both of Harford Co., m. Thurs. 28 Aug 1862 by Rev. Shoaff (SA 6 Sep 1862)

BOUND, ROBERT, see "William S. Rushmore," q.v.

BOWMAN, ALONZO and Miss Belle S. Sweeting, both of Harford Co., m. 10 Feb 1870 by Rev. J. A. Price (AI 18 Feb 1870)

BOWYER, ANNA J., wife of the late Henry D. Bowyer, formerly of Harford Co., died 22 Jul 1868 at Bethsada, Ohio (AI 21 Aug 1868)

BOWYER, MARY L. (Miss), of Baltimore, and John Q. Stockham m. 15 Jun 1864 by Rev. J. McKendry Reiley in Baltimore (AI 24 Jun 1864 misspelled his name as "Stokham")

BOYD, HENRIETTA M., see "John J. Boyd," q.v.

BOYD, JOHN J., died ---- (date not given) and the administratrix's notice stated that creditors must exhibit their legal vouchers by 8 Aug 1844 to Henrietta M. Boyd, admx. (HM 17 Nov 1843)

BOYER, SUSANNA (or "Old Sookey" as she was familiarly called), died at the almshouse at Germantown [PA] a few days ago, aged nearly 100; she was the dau. of a Revolutionary War soldier, about whom is related a historic incident which occurred at the Battle of Germantown; Pvt. Boyer was hidden behind a stone wall at the Mennonite Meeting House when Gen. Agnew, of the British Army, together with his staff, were riding by at the time; the general remarked "I see no d----d Yankees in sight!" and Pvt. Boyer stepped from behind the wall and shot Agnew, who fell head long from his horse, killed instantly; Pvt. Boyer lived in Germantown many years afterward [article from *Lancaster Intelligencer*] (AI 25 Feb 1870)

BOYLE, GEN., see "William P. Marr," q.v.

BOYLEN, PATRICK F. and Miss Susan F. Doxen, both of Harford Co., m. 30 Aug 1866 by Rev. T. S. C. Smith (AI 7 Sep 1866)

BRADENBAUGH, WILLIAM THOMAS, died Wed. 20 Oct 1869 in Harford Co., aged 24 years and 10 months (AI 29 Oct 1869)

BRADFORD, A. W., see "Ann Calwell" and "Mark Pringle" and "Harry D. Gough," q.v.

BRADFORD, H. HARRISON and Miss Annie W. Shekell, both of Harford Co., m. 23 Jun 1865 by Rev. Nichols (AI 30 Jun 1865)

BRADY, EDWARD, died ---- (date not given) and was removed from the voter registration list in the 6th District in 1870 (HR 21 Oct 1870)

BRAMBLE, OLIVER C. and Miss Annie S. Weems, both of Harford Co., m. 4 Apr 1869 at the M. E. Parsonage, Abingdon, by Rev. J. G. Moore (AI 9 Apr 1869)

BRAND, WILLIAM F., see "William Sylvester," q.v.

BRANNAN, LAURA (Miss) and R. Stump Smith, both of Harford Co., m. 16 Dec 1862 in Baltimore by Rev. H. C. Cushing (SA 27 Dec 1862)

BRANNON, THOMAS C., died ---- (date not given) and was removed from the voter registration list in the 5th District in 1870 (HR 1 Nov 1870)

BRIGGS, GEORGE, died ---- (date not given) and the trustee's sale notice stated that his farm will be offered for sale on 19 Apr 1856 at Henry Stabler's Store in Stablersville, Baltimore Co., by Archer H. Jarrett, trustee (HD 28 Mar 1856)

BROOKE, JAMES W., died ---- (date not given) and was removed from the voter registration list in the 6th District in 1870 (HR 21 Oct 1870)

BROOKHEART, CASSANDRA, died ---- (date not given) and the executrix's notice stated that creditors must exhibit their legal vouchers by 29 Jun 1860 to Eliza Slee, extx. (SA 20 Aug 1859)

BROOKS, JAMES W., Esq., died ---- (date not given), a resident of Havre de Grace and native of this place; sorrow falls on a large family (HR 11 Feb 1870)

BROOMFIELD, WILLIAM, son of Joseph Broomfield, of Port Deposit [Cecil Co.], died ---- (date not given) at the farm of John Evans about 3 miles from Port Deposit; the lad was riding a mule, which became frightened, and he attempted to jump off, but his feet became entangled in the harness; he was dragged about a mile and when found was dead (AI 25 Aug 1865)

BROWN, ANNIE W., infant dau. of James and Susan S. Brown, died Sat. 24 Oct 1868 [age not given] (AI 13 Nov 1868)

BROWN, AQUILLA, see "Elizabeth Brown," q.v.

BROWN, B. PEYTON (Reverend), of the Baltimore Annual Conference, and Mrs. Harriet A. Dickson, dau. of Dr. J. Wilson, of Harford Co., m. 20 Apr 1869 at the Dumbarton M. E. Church in Georgetown, D.C., by Rev. Dr. McCauley (HD 23 Apr 1869)

BROWN, BENJAMIN F., died ---- (date not given) and was removed from the voter registration list in the 5th District in 1870 (AI 4 Nov 1870)

BROWN, CHARLES (Captain), died suddenly Mon. morning 4 Feb 1867, at Havre de Grace, aged 84 (AI 15 Feb 1867)

BROWN, CHARLES, died ---- (date not given) and was removed from voter registration list in 1869 [district not clarified, but either 4th, 5th or 6th] (AI 1 Oct 1869 and HD 22 Oct 1869)

BROWN, ELIZABETH, died 29 Nov 1868, aged 80, at the residence of her nephew, James Letzinger, at Lego's Point, Harford Co. (AI 22 Jan 1869)

BROWN, ELIZABETH, wife of the late Aquilla Brown, died Sat. morning 30 Dec 1871 at Churchville, in her 84th year (AI 5 Jan 1872)

BROWN, ELIZABETH A., wife of John S. Brown, of Harford Co., died 12 Sep 1870 in Baltimore [age not given] (AI 23 Sep 1870)

BROWN, GEORGE, see "John Carville Bayne," q.v.

BROWN, GEORGE W., died ---- (date not given) and was removed
from voter registration list in 1869 [district not clarified, but either
4th, 5th or 6th] (AI 1 Oct 1869 and HD 22 Oct 1869)
BROWN, JAMES, see "Annie W. Brown," q.v.
BROWN, JOHN S., see "Elizabeth A. Brown," q.v.
BROWN, JOSEPH, died 4 Dec 1837 of a pulmonary disease, aged 30
years and 9 months, a well respected citizen of Bel Air (HM 14?
Dec 1837)
BROWN, MARY, see "Samuel Barton," q.v.
BROWN, MARY (Miss), died Thurs. 26 Mar 1863, in her 73rd year, at
the residence of her nephew Mortimer F. Brown (SA 3 Apr 1863)
BROWN, MORTIMER F., see "Mary Brown," q.v.
BROWN, SUSAN, see "Annie W. Brown," q.v.
BROWN, WILLIAM, see "Samuel Burton," q.v.
BROWN, WILLIAM and Miss Charlotte A. Cullum m. Tues. 11 Oct
1864, near Harford Furnace, by Rev. R. Scott Norris (AI 25 Nov
1864)
BRUCE, FRANK F. and Miss Mary J. Baker, dau. of Nicholas Baker,
Esq., both of Harford County, m. Tues. 20 Jun 1871 by Rev.
Charles A. Reid (HD 30 Jun 1871)
BRUNDIGE, HANNAH GOVER, relict of the late James Brundige, died
31 May 1870, aged 71 (HD 3 Jun 1870)
BRYANT, ELIZABETH C. (Miss) and R. Dallas Ashton, both of
Harford Co., m. Tues., 17 May 1870 at St. Andrew's Church,
Baltimore, by Rev. William W. Snowden (AI 27 May 1870)
BRYANT, GEORGE W., of Harford Co., and Miss Mary M. Pile, of
Philadelphia, m. Tues. 31 Oct 1871 at First Presbyterian Church in
Philadelphia by Rev. Dr. H. Johnson (HR 3 Nov 1871)
BRYARLY, E. L. G. (Miss) and Charles W. Lee m. 4 Jun 1857 at the
residence of Philip Gover, Esq., in Baltimore, by Rev. Isaac P.
Cook (HD 5 Jun 1857)
BRYARLY, MARY ANN, died Wed. 13 Sep 1865 at 2 a.m., in Bel Air,
in her 67th year (AI 15 Sep 1865)
BRYARLY, ROBERT, died Sat. 15 Jan 1870 at his residence in
Baltimore, aged 59 (AI 21 Jan 1870)
BRYARLY, WAKEMAN "WAKE" (Doctor), died in his 49th year last
Sat. at the residence of his father-in-law, Dr. Gittings, at Roslin,
Baltimore Co.; he was a son of Dr. Wakeman Bryarly, an eminent
Harford Co. physician who died while his son was young; he was
educated here and lived in Bel Air until he graduated in medicine,
since which time he has lived in almost every portion of the world;
he served as surgeon in the American Army during the Mexican
War, and in the Crimean War held a commission in the Russian
service where he attained considerable distinction as well as the
Russian modification of his name into Bryarliski; afterwards he
returned to Maryland and later spent most of his time first in San
Francisco, California and then in Virginia City, Nevada; he returned

to Maryland a short time ago to end his days where they began [one obituary stated he was on a visit to his relations in Harford and Baltimore Counties when he died after a brief illness] (HD 19 Mar 1869 and AI 12 Mar 1869)

BUCHANAN, JAMES, ex-President of the United States, died 1 Jun 1868 at his residence near Lancaster, PA, in his 78th year; he was born in Franklin Co., PA on 22 Apr 1791, graduated Dickinson College in 1809, was admitted to the bar in 1812, and served as a private in the War of 1812 in the defense of Baltimore; he entered Congress in 1820 and remained in public life until the close of his Presidential term on 4 Mar 1861, after which he lived as a quite, unostentatious, private citizen on his farm until his death (AI 5 Jun 1868)

BUCKINGHAM, WILLIAM, died ---- (date not given) and the administrator's notice stated that creditors must exhibit their legal vouchers by 25 May 1862 to Charles Treusch, admin. (SA 17 Aug 1861)

BULL, ANN ELIZABETH, of Harford Co., and Uriah Johnson, of Lycoming Co., PA, m. Tues. 7 Nov 1865 by Rev. E. Kinsey (AI 10 Nov 1865)

BULL, ELIZA A., wife of William L. Bull, died Mon. 24 May 1869, in her 53rd year (AI 18 Jun 1869)

BULL, JACOB E., of Harford Co., and Miss Mary T. Sunderland, of Philadelphia, m. 5 Feb 1863 by Rev. J. H. Kean in Philadelphia (SA 13 Feb 1863)

BULL, PRISCILLA (Miss) and Rufus Jones, both of Harford Co., m. 18 Aug 1870 at the M. E. Parsonage, Dublin, by Rev. George M. Berry (AI 25 Nov 1870)

BULL, WILLIAM, died ---- (date not given) and was removed from the voter registration list in the 4th District in 1871 (HR 3 Nov 1871)

BULL, WILLIAM L., see "Eliza A. Bull," q.v.

BUNCE, MARY J. and Henry J. Lackey, both of Harford Co., m. 4 Jan 1866, at the house of William Johnson, by Rev. J. K. Nichols (AI 26 Jan 1866)

BURCH, DAVID F., died 28 Apr 1870, aged 67 (AI 6 May 1870)

BURGESS, C. W., a grocery merchant of Baltimore who was well known by the people of Harford Co., died very suddenly on Sat. morning from a spasm of the heart; he was head of the firm of C. W. Burgess & Son; for several years he represented the 5th and 6th Wards in the Second Branch of the City Council of Baltimore and was also Treasurer of the Old Town Savings Institution (HR 27 May 1870)

BURK, JOHN, formerly of Harford Co., but for some years a resident of California, died ---- (date not given) while interposing to save the life of a companion upon whom an attack had been made by an armed desperado; Burk was unarmed at the time, but threw himself between the assailant and his intended victim, and received the fatal shot which was aimed at another; he lingered for some weeks, but the wound finally proved fatal; Burk was known to the writer of these lines (name not given), having been his companion in a voyage around Cape Horn in 1849 and afterwards in many trying scenes in California; he was a young man of noble impulses who could be relied upon in any emergency; to his afflicted parents his loss is irreparable (HD 8 May 1857)

BURK, MARY (Miss), of Baltimore, and William Cross m. 5 Jul 1862 at Havre de Grace by Rev. Father Stinehiser (SA 19 Jul 1862)

BURKE, LIZZIE E. (Miss), eldest dau. of William G. Burke, Esq., and John Sawyer, both of Harford Co., m. 6 Jun 1871 by Rev. Dr. Martin (HR 23 Jun 1871)

BURKE, SHERIFF, see "John Carville Bayne," q.v.

BURKE, WILLIAM G., see "Lizzie E. Burke," q.v.

BURKE, WILLIAM H., died suddenly 2 Feb 1864 of apoplexy, in his 74th year (SA 12 Feb 1864)

BURKINS, JACOB, died 7 Mar 1869 at his residence in Dublin District, Harford Co., aged 67; the executor's notice stated that creditors must exhibit their legal vouchers by 22 Mar 1870 to John Daugherty, exec. (AI 26 Mar 1869)

BURKINS, JOSEPH E. and Miss Rosanna Gibney, both of Harford Co., m. 22 Feb 1870 by Rev. T. M. Crawford, assisted by Rev. R. Gamble (AI 4 Mar 1870)

BURKINS, JOSEPH R. and Sarah E. Jones, both of Harford Co., m. 22 May 1866 at the M. E. Parsonage in Bel Air by Rev. W. M. Meminger (AI 1 Jun 1866)

BURKINS, MARTHA (Miss) and John F. Gaither, both of Harford Co., m. 3 Mar 1870 by Rev. T. M. Crawford (AI 11 Mar 1870)

BURNETT, JOHN, see "Edwin Drum," q.v.

BURNHAM, THOMAS H., was murdered on 15 Jul 1858 by William G. Ford, a constable in Baltimore's 15th Ward; Ford, aged about 30, had spent time in the penitentiary for burglary some 10 years ago and has since then not led a very reputable life; he was convicted of the murder of Burnham in the first degree last Mon.; the penalty will be death on the scaffold (SA 9 Oct 1858)

BURTON, DR., see "Michael Doyle," q.v.

BURTON, ROBERT, see "Sarah Jane Burton," q.v.

BURTON, SAMUEL, a bachelor, aged about 60, was murdered last Fri. night at his residence in the 11th District, Baltimore Co., about 1 mile from the copper works and 11 miles from Bel Air; he was found Sat. morning, his head nearly severed from the body, with an axe, and a deep cut in his breast; William Brown, his wife Mary, who is a niece of the deceased, and her aunt Keziah Chenowith, were visiting with him at the time; the two women were arrested and committed to Towsontown jail, charged with being implicated in the killing of Mr. Burton; their story is that William Brown was beating Mr. Burton and they got frightened and left the house because he threatened to kill them as well, and they remained in the woods all night; the next morning they returned and found Mr. Burton dead; William Brown was there at the time, but left soon afterwards, telling his wife to bring his supper to him at a particular place in the woods that night and then to meet him at her mother's at the Clipper Factory two weeks hence; Brown was formerly a soldier in the army and came from Terre Haute, Indiana; it is said that Mr. Burton had promised to give Brown his place at his death if he m. his niece and it is surmised that the murder was committed in order to get hold of the property sooner (AI 1 Oct 1869)

BURTON, SARAH JANE, wife of Robert Burton, died on the morning of 3 Oct 1870, of consumption, in her 41st year (AI 7 Oct 1870)

BUSSEY, HELEN M. (Miss), of Baltimore, and Thomas Hayward, of Harford Co., m. 4 Aug 1864 by the Very Rev. Dr. Coskery, at the Archbishop's residence (AI 12 Aug 1864)

BUTLER, DAVID S., died ---- (date not given) and the administrator's notice stated that creditors must exhibit their legal vouchers by 25 Feb 1868 to Thomas Butler, admin. (AI 1 Mar 1867)

BUTLER, JOSEPH B., died ---- (date not given) and was removed from the voter registration list in the 5th District in 1871 (HR 27 Oct 1871)

BUTLER, MARY F., only dau. of Clement Butler, Esq., and William G. Roberts, all of Harford Co., m. 6 Jan 1859 by Rev. Keech (SA 15 Jan 1859)

BUTLER, ROSE and William Streett, both of Harford Co., m. Thurs. 12 Aug 1869 at the pastoral residence of St. Ignatius' Church, Harford Co., by Rev. P. F. O'Connor (AI 20 Aug 1869)

BUTLER, THOMAS, see "David S. Butler," q.v.

BUTTS, WILLIAM H. and Mary E. Gonce, eldest dau. of John T. and Catherine A. Gonce, m. 26 Oct 1869, at the Immaculate Conception, by Rev. Father Abbott (AI 19 Nov 1869)

CADDEN, JAMES R. and Miss I. V. Bouldin, of Harford Co., m. Tues. 4 Apr 1865 at the Presbyterian Church, in Bel Air, by Rev. J. McKendrie Reilly (AI 7 Apr 1865)

CAFFRIE, MR., see "Harry O'Brien Gough," q.v.

CAGE, JAMES, see "Harry Lee," q.v.

CAGE, JAMES S. and Mary Jane Turner, both of Harford Co., m. 14 Jun 1858 in Baltimore by Rev. E. J. Drinkhouse (SA 19 Jun 1858)

CAIN, JAMES, see "Matthew Cain," q.v.

CAIN, MATTHEW, died 11 Mar 1859 at his residence in Harford Co., aged 77 years and 4 months; subsequently, the executor's notice stated that creditors must exhibit their legal vouchers by 28 Mar 1860 to Sarah Cain and James M. Cain, execs. (SA 26 Mar 1859 and 20 Aug 1859)

CAIN, SARAH, see "Matthew Cain," q.v.

CAIRNES, ANNA, consort of Isaac Cairnes, died Mon. 27 Apr 1863, in her 60th year (SA 29 May 1863)

CAIRNES, GEORGE, died ---- (date not given) and the executor's notice stated that creditors must exhibit their legal vouchers by 16 Jul 1859 to William Cairnes, exec.; the administratrix's notice dated 7 Sep 1861 stated vouchers were due by 7 Sep 1862 to Mary A. Cairnes, admx. (SA 15 Jan 1859 and 5 Oct 1861)

CAIRNES, GEORGE R., see "Nicholas McComas," q.v.

CAIRNES, GEORGE RICHARD, and Miss Belle Nelson, both of Harford Co., m. 11 Feb 1869 in Baltimore by Rev. Dr. Smith (HD 19 Feb 1869 and AI 26 Feb 1869)

CAIRNES, ISAAC H. and Elizabeth Wright, both of Harford Co., m. Tues. 30 Jun 1868 by Rev. Thomas M. Cathcart (AI 10 Jul 1868); see "Sarah Hart," q.v.

CAIRNES, ISABEL R. (Miss) and George C. Kirkwood, both of Harford Co., m. Thurs. 3 Mar 1859 by Rev. T. S. C. Smith (SA 12 Mar 1859)

CAIRNES, MARTHA J., see "Nicholas McComas," q.v.

CAIRNES, MARY A., see "George Cairnes," q.v.

CAIRNES, REBECCA JANE (Miss) and Charles Henry Bay, both of Harford Co., m. 28 Jan 1858 by Rev. T. S. C. Smith (SA 6 Feb 1858)

CAIRNES, WILLIAM, see "George Cairnes," q.v.

CALDER, ANN, see "Frances Ann Calder," q.v.

CALDER, ELIZABETH, dau. of Franklin Calder, died 2 Feb 1865, in her 22nd year, at the residence of her father in Harford Co. (AI 24 Feb 1865)

CALDER, FRANCES ANN, eldest dau. of M. and Ann Calder, died 25 Jul 1868 at her father's residence in Harford Co., in her 22nd year (AI 7 Aug 1868)

CALDER, FRANKLIN P., youngest son of Martin and Nancy Calder, died 23 Jul 1870, aged 17; a subsequent obituary stated Franklin Pierce Calder, youngest son of M. and N. Calder, died Fri. 22 Jul 1870, aged 14 years, 5 months and 12 days; one obituary contains a short poem (AI 29 Jul 1870 and 12 Aug 1870; HD 19 Aug 1870)

CALDER, MARTIN AND NANCY, see "Franklin P. Calder," q.v.

CALDER, NAOMIA (Miss) and John Jeffery m. 21 Mar 1871 at the residence of the bride's father in Harford Co. by Rev. A. H. Greenfield (HD 24 Mar 1871)

CALWELL, ANN, died ---- (date not given) and the administrator's notice stated that creditors must exhibit their legal vouchers by 25 May 1845 to A. W. Bradford, admin. (HM 18 Oct 1844 and 3 Jan 1845)

CAMPBELL, ----, a man from Massachusetts who was working on the railroad bridge at Havre de Grace, fell from the structure into the river one day last week and drowned before his fellow workmen could save him; his body was returned to Massachusetts by his friends (AI 13 Jul 1866)

CAMPBELL, JOHN, died ---- (date not given) and the administrator's notice stated that creditors must exhibit their legal vouchers by 29 Apr 1870 to Henry Tenly, Admin. C.T.A. (AI 30 Apr 1869)

CAMPBELL, JOHN W., died ---- (date not given) and was removed from the voter registration list in the 4th District in 1868 (AI 9 Oct 1868)

CANNON, MARY A. and William H. Wallis, both of Harford Co., m. 13 Aug 1862 by Rev. R. H. B. Mitchell (SA 30 Aug 1862)

CANNON, SEMELIA O., died ---- (date not given) and the administratrix's notice stated that creditors must exhibit their legal vouchers by 15 May 1866 to Martha M. Gallop, admx. (AI 19 May 1865 misspelled the name as "Canon")

CANNON, WILLIAM LAWS, Captain, 1st Delaware Cavalry Regt., died Tues. 18 Jul 1863 about half past 5 o'clock, in Bel Air, in his 25th year (SA 21 Aug 1863)

CARLILE, WASHINGTON (colored man), died ---- (date not given) and the administrator's notice stated that creditors must exhibit their legal vouchers by 7 Dec 1860 to Daniel Scott, admin. (SA 17 Dec 1859)

CARLISLE, GEORGE AUSTIN, of Baltimore Co., and Miss Sallie A. Jones, dau. of Daniel Jones, Esq., of Harford Co., m. 2 Aug 1868 in Baltimore by Rev. Daniel Bowers [Richmond, VA papers please copy] (AI 7 Aug 1868)

CARLISLE, J. HOWARD (Captain and Brevet-Major), formerly of the U. S. Artillery, died Sun. 16 Dec 1866 at the residence of Mrs. Griffith near Aberdeen, Harford Co., in his 45th year (AI 21 Dec 1866)

CARR, CORONER, see "Jeremiah Tobin" and "John Lamb," q.v.

CARR, MARY (Miss) and William Simms, both of Harford Co., m. 28 Nov 1867 by Rev. Lemmon (AI 13 Dec 1867)

CARR, WILLIAM, died ---- (date not given) and was removed from the voter registration list in the 1st District in 1870 (HR 11 Nov1870)

CARROLL, BENJAMIN F., see "Clara R. Carroll," q.v.

CARROLL, CLARA R., wife of Benjamin F. Carroll, died Sat. 13 Aug 1864, aged 42, at her residence in Harford Co.; she leaves a husband and six children; obituary contains a brief memorial and short verse written by "A Friend" (AI 19 Aug 1864)

CARROLL, JOHN, see "Michael Doyle," q.v.

CARROLL, THOMAS, died ---- (date not given) and the administrator's notice stated that creditors must exhibit their legal vouchers by 17 Apr 1869 to James K. Keech, admin. (AI 24 Apr 1868)

CARSINS, JOHN, Esq., late Sheriff of Harford Co., died last Sat. morning; as an officer he was strict and humane, often exercising lenity towards those with whom the duties of his office necessarily placed within his power; as a citizen he was industrious and enterprising, and just in his dealings (HM 25 Oct 1838)

CARSINS, JOHN, see "William D. Phillips," q.v.

CARTER, ELIZA S. H., dau. of the late Durden B. Carter, Esq., of Philadelphia, and J. Henderson Springer, of Harford Co., m. Thurs. 3 Jun 1858 at the Church of the Ascension in Philadelphia (SA 12 Jun 1858)

CARTER, JOHN, died Wed. 12 Oct 1864 at his residence in Harford Co., aged about 40 (AI 14 Oct 1864)

CARVER, AARON, see "Mary M. Carver," q.v.

CARVER, ANNA E. (Miss), of Havre de Grace, and David C. Daniels, of New Castle, Lawrence Co., PA, m. 5 Jun 1866 at the M. E. Church in Havre de Grace by Rev. George W. Heyde [marriage notice states "No cards"] (AI 8 Jun 1866)

CARVER, GEORGE W. JR. and Miss Mary M. Thorpe, both of Bel Air, m. 6 May 1867 by Rev. T. S. C. Smith (AI 10 May 1867)

CARVER, MARY EMMA (Miss) and C. A. McFadden, both of Havre de Grace, m. 27 Apr 1871 at the M. E. Church by Rev. M. L. Smyser (HR 5 May 1871)

CARVER, MARY M., wife of Aaron Carver, died 24 Jul 1865 in Havre de Grace, in her 78th year (AI 4 Aug 1865)

CARVER, MR., see "John Price," q.v.

CASE, CHRISTIAN and Miss Mary Ann Barnes, both of Havre de Grace, m. Wed. 6 Nov 1867 in Baltimore by Rev. Richard Norris (AI 27 Dec 1867)

CASE, MRS., consort of Christian Case, died Sun. 3 Feb 1867, at Havre de Grace, after a painful illness (AI 15 Feb 1867)

CATHCART CHILDREN (names not given), died Thurs. morning of last week; the wife of John P. Cathcart, residing at While Hall in Baltimore Co., about 7 miles from Jarrettsville, went to visit a neighbor, leaving her two youngest children alone, a child aged about 5 months, who was in a cradle, and a dau. about 4 years old; by some means yet unknown the clothes of the little girl caught fire and when Mrs. Cathcart returned about 20 minutes later she found the little girl on the floor burned to death and the baby's clothes on fire; the baby died Sat. (HD 19 Mar 1869 and AI 19 Mar 1869)

CATHCART, JEMIMA (Miss) and Thomas Johnson, both of Marshall's District, m. Thurs. evening 19 Dec 1861 by Rev. E. Welty (SA 4 Jan 1862)

CATHCART, JOHN P., see "Cathcart Children," q.v.

CATOR, DUKIE, son of Joseph Cator, died suddenly 7 Oct 1864, age 13, after 12 years of affliction; obituary contains a short poem (AI 28 Oct 1864)

CECIL, JOSEPHINE, dau. of Owen Cecil, Esq., of Millersville, Anne Arundel Co., MD, and Arthur W. Bond m. 14 Dec 1870, at the residence of the bride's father, by Rev. David Hall (AI 16 Dec 1870)

CHAMBERLAIN, ELIZABETH (Miss), of Lapidum, Harford Co., and John L. Hunt, of New York, m. 17 Nov 1859 at the residence of B. F. Heath, Esq., at Lapidum, by Rev. H. F. Hearn (SA 26 Nov 1859)

CHAMBERLAIN, REBECCA J. and Samuel Wesley Forwood, both of Harford Co., m. 26 Jun 1860 by Rev. T. D. Valiant (SA 14 Jul 1860)

CHAMBERS, EZEKIEL F., died suddenly Wed. 30 Jan 1867 at Chestertown, MD, almost 80 years old; he was born there on 28 Feb 1788 and graduated Washington College in 1806; he was admitted to practice as an attorney in Chestertown in 1808; he was a member of the Maryland Senate in 1826 when appointed to fill a vacancy in the U. S. Senate; he was subsequently elected to that office and served until 1835; he was appointed Chief Judge of the Second Judicial Court in 1834 and was a member of the Constitutional Conventions of 1851 and 1854; he was a member of the Protestant Episcopal Church and President of the Board of Visitors for Washington College for more than 40 years; he was a captain in the War of 1812 when the British forces were in the Chesapeake Bay and his militia under Col. Reed repulsed them at a place called Bel Air; he subsequently attained the rank of Brigadier General; as a lawyer he had few equals and was an able debater, cogent reasoner and prominent actor in the great cause of Prigg against the State of PA, in which the right to recover fugitive slaves, under the U. S. Constitution, was involved (AI 8 Feb 1867)

CHANDLER, JAMES S., died last Tues., aged about 55 (HM 28 May 1847)

CHANLEY, ELIZABETH (Miss) and Jesse Ergood m. Sun. 17 Dec 1837, at Havre de Grace, by Rev. Goldsborough (HM 28 Dec 1837)

CHAPMAN, MARY E. (Miss) and Joseph W. Cunningham, both of Harford Co., m. Tues. 22 Oct 1867 by Rev. W. M. Meminger (AI 8 Nov 1867)

CHAPPELL, ROBERT, died ---- (date not given) and the trustee's sale of his real estate will be held on 9 Feb 1856 (HD 18 Jan 1856)

CHARSHEE, MISSOURI and Franklin P. Cord, both of Harford Co., m. 18 Dec 1869 at the M. E. Parsonage, in Philadelphia, by Rev. M. D. Kurtz (AI 16 Sep 1870); another marriage notice gave her name as "Missourie W. Charshee" [Bel Air papers please copy] (HR 9 Sep 1870)

CHAUNCEY, JOHN H., died ---- (date not given) and the administrator's notice stated that creditors must exhibit their legal vouchers by 28 Nov 1838 to George Henderson, admin. (HM 28 Dec 1837)

CHAUNCEY, S. REBECCA, relict of the late Benjamin Chauncey, died 28 Mar 1863 in her 55th year; obituary contains a memorial and short poem (SA 3 Apr 1863)

CHENOWITH, KEZIAH, see "Samuel Burton," q.v.

CHESNEY, HARRIET E., of Harford Co., and Robert B. Armiger, of Baltimore, m. Tues. morning 21 Jun 1863, at the Parsonage, by Rev. Alex. E. Gibson (AI 15 Jul 1864)

CHESNEY, JAMES, died 22 Dec 1868 at his residence, *Boothby Hill*, in Hall's Crossroads District, in his 85th year; a member of the Methodist Church, he m. in 1812 and his wife, in her 82nd year, is still living; they had 9 children, 7 still living; obituary contains a brief memorial (AI 26 Feb 1869); another obituary stated he was aged 83 years and 4 months (HR 7 Jan 1869); he was subsequently removed from the voter registration list of the 2nd District in 1870 (AI 4 Nov 1870)

CHESNEY, JAMES R., see "John L. Webster," q.v.

CHEW, EDWARD M., see "Margaret M. Chew," q.v.

CHEW, MARGARET M., wife of Edward M. Chew, of Deer Creek, died 17 Jan 1857, aged 45 (HD 6 Feb 1857)

CHEW, WILLIAM S., of Havre de Grace, and Mina A. Barrington, of Baltimore Co., m. Tues. 29 Sep 1868 at St. John's Church, Huntington, Baltimore Co., by Rev. William T. Johnson (HD 9 Oct 1868)

CHEYNEY, EDITH, died Wed. evening 19 Jul 1871, aged about 70, at the residence of Darlington Hoopes near Hickory (HD 28 Jul 1871)

CHIVREL, HELEN EDITH, only dau. of Mr. A. B. Chivrel, of Baltimore, and Dr. Charles Hudson, of New York, m. 21 Jan 1866 at *Oak Hill* in Harford Co. by Rev. S. Bartol [double wedding with R. Jarrett Marston and May Ella Galloway] New York and Baltimore papers please copy (AI 26 Jan 1866)

CHRISTIE, JOHN S. (Captain), of Rowlandsville, died Wed. after a short illness; he had raised a company in 1862 and was commissioned captain of Co. G, 6th MD Volunteers, but resigned before close of the war, and owned one of the largest flour mills in Cecil Co. (HR 21 Jan 1869)

CHRISTY, ANDREW, for some years past living on the farm of Ramsey McHenry, Esq., of Harford Co., was discovered last Sat. near the public road leading from Bel Air to Abingdon, about a half a mile from the last named place, in a frozen condition; he was conveyed to Abingdon and lingered in a partially insensible condition until the next day when he died; he was past middle age and supposed to have been intoxicated at the time of his exposure (AI 1 Jan 1869)

CHURCHILL, A. H., of Louisville, KY, and Almira Sutton, of Harford Co., m. 6 Jan 1857 by Rev. Sharpley (HM 15 Jan 1857)

CLARK, BARNET J., see "Barnet McComas," q.v.

CLARK, JOHN M., engineer of Camel Engine No. 43, attached to a coal train of the B. & O. Railroad, died Mon. afternoon when the engine was thrown from the track about 3 p.m. while in a curve at Union Dam, two miles east of Ellicott's Mills; it fell on Clark who was dreadfully bruised and scalded; he was taken to his mother's house in Ellicott's Mills and a telegraph was dispatched to his wife in Baltimore, but he died about 2 hours later; burial was in Ellicott's Mills yesterday; he leaves a wife and one child who reside at No. 70 Carey Street in Baltimore (HD 15 May 1857)

CLARK, WILLIAM C., died ---- (date not given) and was removed from the voter registration list in the 6th District in 1871 (HR 29 Sep 1871)

CLARK, WILLIAM T. and Miss Maggie Ady, both of Harford Co., m. 21 Dec 1865 by Rev. J. K. Nichols (AI 5 Jan 1866)

CLAUTICE, m. JOSEPH, of Baltimore, and Miss Annie Greenfield, of Harford Co., m. ---- (date not given) at the Caroline Street M. E. Parsonage, Baltimore, by Rev. John W. Hedges (AI 19 May 1865)

CLAY, JOSEPH M., died ---- (date not given) and was removed from the voter registration list in the 1st District in 1871 (HR 29 Sep 1871)

CLAY, THEODORE, eldest son of Henry Clay, died recently in the lunatic asylum in Lexington, Kentucky, where he had been confined as hopelessly insane for 38 years (AI 3 Jun 1870)

CLAYTON, JULIA A. (Miss), of Baltimore Co., and William H. Treadwell, of Harford Co., m. 25 Jan 1866, at the Parsonage in Bel Air, by Rev. J. K. Nichols (AI 2 Feb 1866)

CLOUGH, CAPT., engineer on an express train which left Baltimore last Sun., was killed when the train struck a horse about 13 miles from that city and the cars jumped the track; Charles H. Whiteford, of Baltimore, was terribly mangled (SA 2 Jul 1859)

COALE, ELIZA, eldest dau. of Isaac W. and Martha Coale, died 1 Sep 1866 of typhoid dysentery, aged 12 (AI 14 Sep 1866)

COALE, GERARD (colored), died ---- (date not given) and the administrator's notice stated that creditors must exhibit their legal vouchers by 7 Feb 1871 to Skipwith H. Coale, Admin. C.T.A. (AI 11 Feb 1870)

COALE, ISAAC, see "Eliza Coale" and "William F. Coale," q.v.

COALE, JAMES, died ---- (date not given) and the executor's notice stated that creditors must exhibit their legal vouchers by 22 Aug 1869 to John Corse and John W. Coale, execs. (AI 28 Aug 1868)

COALE, JOHN W., see "James Coale," q.v.

COALE, JOSEPH HENRY, son of Joseph A. and Mary E. Coale, died Fri. 22 Jul 1870, aged 6 months and 2 weeks; obituary contains a short poem (AI 29 Jul 1870)

COALE, JOSEPH R., died ---- (date not given) and the administrator's notice stated that creditors must exhibit their legal vouchers by 27 Apr 1865 to Sarah Ann Coale and William S. Coale, admins. (AI 17 Jun 1864)

COALE, MARTHA, see "Eliza Coale," q.v.

COALE, MARY E., see "Joseph Henry Coale" and "Skipwith Holland Coale," q.v.

COALE, S. H., see "Skipwith Holland Coale," q.v.

COALE, SARAH, see "Joseph R. Coale," q.v.

COALE, SKIPWITH H., see "Gerard Coale," q.v.

COALE, SKIPWITH HOLLAND, only child of S. H. and Mary E. Coale, died Mon. morning 19 Sep 1870 at Towsontown, Baltimore

Co., aged 15 months and 6 days (AI 23 Sep 1870 and HD 23 Sep 1870)

COALE, WILLIAM, see "Joseph R. Coale," q.v.

COALE, WILLIAM F., second son of Isaac W. Coale, died Thurs. 20 Feb 1868 at *Alton*, Harford Co., in his 19th year (AI 6 Mar 1868)

COBURN, MARY J. (Miss), of Harford Co., and Joseph St. Clair, of Cecil Co., m. 15 Sep 1869, at Abingdon, by Rev. J. G. Moore (AI 24 Sep 1869)

COCHRAN, ANNIE Z. (Miss), of Mount Vernon, Baltimore Co., and David S. Hynes, of Baltimore, m. 4 Jul 1870 by Rev. P. B. Reese (AI 12 Aug 1870)

COCHRAN, DENNIS, a workman at Tolley's lime quarries situated near the Baltimore and Harford County line, met with a painful accident last Thurs. which will probably be his death; a bank of earth caved in him, breaking his back and one of his thighs; medical aid was summoned and his condition is critical (AI 25 Jun 1869)

COCHRAN, JAMES, see "Harry Lee," q.v.

COCKRELL, IRENE L. (Miss), of Prince William Co., VA, and Robert B. Taylor, of Harford Co., m. 25 Nov 1869 at the M. E. Church South in Alexandria, VA, by Rev. Dr. Hough [*Baltimore Sun* please copy] (AI 28 Jan 1870)

COEN, HENRY C., died ---- (date not given) and the administrator's notice stated that creditors must exhibit their legal vouchers by 13 Jul 1871 to Evan Bailey, admin. (AI 15 Jul 1870); he was subsequently removed from the voter registration list of the 2nd District in 1870 (AI 4 Nov 1870)

COEN, NANCY E., died ---- (date not given) at her residence in Havre de Grace, after a lingering and painful illness, in her 67th year (AI 15 Jun 1866)

COLBURN, NATHANIEL KNIGHT, second son of Dr. H. and Elizabeth Colburn, and brother of Rev. F. A. Colburn, of Harford Co., died 24 Apr 1865 in Baltimore, after a few hours illness, in his 33rd year (AI 28 Apr 1865)

COLDER, SARAH F. (Miss) and John T. Ayres, both of Harford Co., m. Thurs. evening 12 Feb 1863, at Mt. Zion M. E. Church, by Rev. R. C. Haslup (SA 20 Feb 1863)

COLE, ABRAHAM, see "Louisa G. Nelson," q.v.

COLE, EVELINE L., youngest dau. of Joseph O. and Eveline L. Cole, died 18 Nov 1862 at Thomas Run, Harford Co., aged 5 years and 11 months; obituary contains a short poem written by "M.R.R." (SA 6 Dec 1862)

COLE, JOSEPH, died Wed. 27 Jan 1864 at his residence near Churchville, in his 55th year (SA 5 Feb 1864)

COLE, MARY A. (Miss) of Harford Co., and James A. Scott, of Adams Co., PA, m. Wed. 5 Apr 1865, in Baltimore, by Rev. John R. Nichols (AI 14 Apr 1865)

COLE, JOSEPH, see "William B. Cole" and "Eveline L. Cole," q.v.

COLE, WALTER B., see "William B. Cole," q.v.
COLE, WILLIAM B., youngest son of Joseph O. and Eveline L. Cole,
died 13 Nov 1862 at Thomas Run, Harford Co., aged 2 years and 3
months; obituary contains a short poem; a subsequent obituary
states Walter B. Cole, youngest son of Joseph O. and Eveline L.
Cole, died 13 Nov 1862 at Thomas Run, Harford Co., aged 2 years
and 3 months (SA 6 Dec 1862 and 13 Dec 1862)
COLE, WILLIAM L., son of the late J. C. Cole, died 13 Nov 1863 near
Aberdeen, of a strangulated hernia; he was skillfully operated upon
by Dr. J. Evans and Dr. Hays, but mortification afterwards set in
(SA 4 Dec 1863)
COLISON, MALINDA J., of Baltimore, and William H. Wilson, Esq., of
Harford Co., m. 6 Jan 1857 by Rev. W. Stevenson (HM 15 Jan
1857)
COLLISON, MRS. ALICE, wife of William Collison, died 24 Aug 1870
in her 29th year [Baltimore Sun and Cambridge papers please copy]
(HR 26 Aug 1870)
COLLISON, WILLIAM, see "Alice Collison," q.v.
COLORED WOMAN (unnamed wife of Peter ----), living on Swan
Creek, became intoxicated and fell in the fire last Sat., the house
burning over her head; her husband came home and saw the
desolation, became frenzied, ran off, and has not been heard of
since; they were both servants in the family of the late John L.
Griffith near Aberdeen (AI 11 Nov 1870)
CONKLING, JOHN A. and Clara A. Nelson, dau. of Jarrett Nelson,
Esq., all of Baltimore Co., m. Thurs. 1 Nov 1868, at the residence of
the bride's father, by Rev. William A. McKee (AI 20 Nov 1868)
CONLEY, PATRICK, died 17 Jul 1865, in his 53rd year, at his residence
near Shawsville (AI 18 Aug 1865)
CONNER, CHARLES A., see "Nelia R. Conner," q.v.
CONNER, NELIA R., wife of Capt. Charles A. Conner, died 20 Mar
1871, in her 30th year, of consumption, near Towsontown in
Baltimore Co. (HR 7 Apr 1871)
CONRAD, R. Y., see "Lillie Powell," q.v.
CONSTABLE, ALBERT, see "Hannah Archer Constable" and "Oliver
H. Thomas," q.v.
CONSTABLE, HANNAH ARCHER, widow of Judge Albert Constable,
died Mon. morning 24 Jul 1871 at her residence in Cecil Co. (HD
28 Jul 1871)
CONSTABLE, MRS., see "Nannie H. Archer," q.v.
COOK, C. (Reverend) and Miss Mary M. Hitchcock, dau. of Charles B.
Hitchcock, Esq., of Havre de Grace, m. Tues. 30 Jun 1868 at the
Presbyterian Church in Havre de Grace by Rev. Galey (AI 10 Jul
1868)
COOK, JAMES, of Oakington, had his leg crushed by a car of lumber
running over it on Fri. last; Dr. John M. Evans, of Havre de Grace,
assisted by Dr. McCullough, of Oakington, amputated the leg above

the knee, but the shock to his system was such that he died about eight hours after the operation (HR 30 Sep 1870)

COOK, MR., see "James McNamee," q.v.

COOLEY, AMBROSE, Esq., and Miss Carrie A. Hughes, dau. of Amos Hughes, Esq., all of Harford Co., m. 25 May 1871 at Darlington in the Parsonage of the M. E. Church South by Rev. R. Smith (HD 2 Jun 1871, HR 9 Jun 1871)

COOLEY, CHARLES, died ---- (date not given) and the administratrix's notice stated that creditors must exhibit their legal vouchers by 28 Jul 1865 to Cornelia Cooley, admx. (AI 5 Aug 1864)

COOLEY, CORNELIA, see "Charles Cooley" and "William Elliott Cooley," q.v.

COOLEY, DANIEL M., died Sun. 10 Feb 1867 at his residence in Harford Co., in his 77th year (AI 15 Feb 1867)

COOLEY, JOHN, see "William Elliott Cooley," q.v.

COOLEY, JOHN H. (Doctor) and Miss Nellie B. Elliott, dau. of William M. Elliott, Esq., both of Harford Co., m. Tues. 2 Jan 1866, at the residence of the bride's father, by Rev. S. A. Hoblitzell (AI 19 Jan 1866)

COOLEY, LIZZIE (Miss) and S. Lewis Spink, Esq., m. 10 Mar 1857 in Burlington, Iowa by Rev. S. Reynolds (HD 27 Mar 1857)

COOLEY, SARAH, died ---- (date not given)

COOLEY, WILLIAM ELLIOTT, son of Dr. John H. and Cornelia B. Cooley, died Wed. 7 Jul 1869, aged 20 months (HD 16 Jul 1869 and AI 23 Jul 1869)

CORD, AMOS, died ---- (date not given) and the administrator's notice stated that creditors must exhibit their legal vouchers by 11 Sep 1839 to Thomas Cord and John H. Cord, admins. (HM 25 Oct 1838)

CORD, ANNIE E., dau. of William F. Cord, Esq., of Accomac Co., VA, and George M. Bond, of Harford Co., m. 2 Jan 1868 by Rev. Edward S. Grant (AI 10 Jan 1868)

CORD, FRANKLIN P. and Missouri Charshee, both of Harford Co., m. 18 Dec 1869 at the M. E. Parsonage, in Philadelphia, by Rev. M. D. Kurtz (AI 16 Sep 1870); another marriage notice gave her name as "Missourie W. Charshee" [Bel Air papers please copy] (HR 9 Sep 1870)

CORD, JOHN, see "Amos Cord," q.v.

CORD, THOMAS, see "Thomas Smith" and "Amos Cord," q.v.

CORD, WILLIAM F., see "Annie E. Cord," q.v.

CORDREY, JAMES (Colored), died ---- (date not given) and the executor's notice stated that creditors must exhibit their legal vouchers by 20 Dec 1867 to John H. Kirkwood, exec. (AI 28 Dec 1866)

CORRIE, PETER, see "Officer Rigdon," q.v.

CORRIGAN, BARTHOLOMEW, died Sun. 25 Feb 1866, at his residence in Harford Co., aged 74 (AI 2 Mar 1866 spelled his name

"Corregan"); the subsequent executor's notice stated that creditors must exhibit their legal vouchers by 25 Jun 1867 to Hugh Corrigan and Frances Corrigan, execs. (AI 29 Jun 1866)

CORRIGAN, FRANCES, see "Bartholomew Corrigan," q.v.

CORRIGAN, HUGH, of Harford Co., and Sallie F. Lilly, dau. of John Lilly, Esq., of Adams Co., PA, m. 7 Oct 1862 at the Church of the Sacred Heart in Conawago, Adams Co., by Rev. Father Lilly (SA 18 Oct 1862); see "Bartholomew Corrigan," q.v.

CORSE, JOHN, see "James Coale," q.v.

COSTRUM, CHARLES (Negro), murdered his wife about 5 a.m. last Thurs. at their residence at No. 49 Holliday St. in Baltimore; their 15 year old son heard a scuffle, rushed into their room, and saw his father cut his mother's throat (AI 5 Aug 1870)

COURTNEY, BENJAMIN S., see "Sallie M. Courtney," q.v.

COURTNEY, ELLEN E. (Miss) and George W. Donn, Jr., of Washington City, m. 7 Jan 1869 at Havre de Grace by Rev. John F. Thomas (AI 15 Jan 1869)

COURTNEY, LYDIA A., youngest dau. of Benjamin S. Courtney, of Harford Co., and Thomas P. Mitchell m. 8 Dec 1868 by Rev. Dr. Dickson (AI 11 Dec 1868)

COURTNEY, MARY (Miss) and B. F. McGaw, both of Harford Co., m. 28 Nov 1837 by Rev. Finney (HM 7 Dec 1837)

COURTNEY, MARY E. (Miss) and James L. Richardson, both of Harford Co., m. Tues. 18 Jan 1859 at the Abingdon Parsonage by Rev. R. Spencer Vinton (SA 22 Jan 1859)

COURTNEY, SALLIE M., second dau. of Benjamin S. Courtney, of Harford Co., and George V. Mitchell m. 6 Dec 1866 in Baltimore by Rev. John McCron (AI 14 Dec 1866)

COURTNEY, THOMAS, see "Elizabeth Zollinger," q.v.

COWAN, JOHN, died last Sun. morning at his residence in Perrymansville (age not given), a respected and influential citizen of Harford Co. (HM 15 Jan 1857)

COWEN, HENRY, died 30 Dec 1869, aged 40 (HD 7 Jan 1870)

COWEN, SALLIE E., of Harford Co., and James Trott, of Baltimore, m. 22 Apr 1862 by Rev. Neville Rolfe (SA 3 May 1862)

COX, JACK (colored man), died last Mon. at *My Lady's Manor* in Baltimore Co., aged 110; he was familiarly called "Jack" and was the well known servant of the late Richard McGaw, Esq., and had passed the average duration of life on the birth of that gentleman in 1792; he was aged 25 when Washington resigned his commission in 1783 and attended John McGaw, the father of his "young master" as he always called him, in Annapolis on that occasion; Mr. McGaw died in 1845 and in consideration of the services of his faithful old servant bequeathed him his freedom, gave him a little farm, and settled to him an annuity of $90 per annum, which was punctually paid to old Jack to the day of his death [his obituary also appeared in the *Baltimore Sun*] (AI 4 Dec 1868)

COX, JOHN, see "Letitia Cox," q.v.

COX, LETITIA (Mrs.), died Wed. 14 Dec 1859, aged 66, at the residence of her son John Cox in Bel Air (SA 17 Dec 1859)

CRAMPTON, JOHNSON, infant son of Rev. S. W. Crampton, died Thurs. 15 Sep 1870 near Perrymansville, Harford Co. [age not given] (AI 23 Sep 1870)

CRAWFORD, MARIA A. (Miss), of New Orleans, LA, and Alexander Norris, Jr., m. Tues. 7 Jan 1868 at *Mt. Pleasant*, Harford Co., by Rev. William F. Brand (AI 24 Jan 1868)

CRAWFORD, STEPHEN B. and Miss Sue M. Love, both of Harford Co., m. ---- (date not given) at the residence of George A. Love (HD 17 Feb 1871)

CRESSWELL, MARGARET, see "William Criswell," q.v.

CRESSWELL, P. M. G., see "Oliver H. Thomas," q.v.

CREVENSTEN, ELIZABETH A. and John W. Billingslea, both of Harford Co., m. 1 Feb 1866 by Rev. E. Kinsey (AI 16 Feb 1866 spelled her name "Creveston")

CREVENSTEN, MARTHA, relict of the late Capt. George Crevensten, of Harford Co., died 7 Aug 1870, aged 77, at the residence of her son-in-law John W. Billingslea, in Harford Co.; she was a loving mother and a consistent member of the M. E. Church for 30 years; obituary contains a memorial and a short poem (AI 9 Dec 1870)

CRISWELL, WILLIAM, of Harford Co., died 21 Apr 1869, aged 53; the subsequent executrix's notice stated that creditors of "William Cresswell" must exhibit their legal vouchers by 7 May 1870 to Margaret Cresswell, extx. (AI 30 Apr 1869 and 14 May 1869)

CRONIN, MARY (Miss) and John Armstrong, both of Harford Co., m. Tues. 17 Jan 1865 by Rev. DeWolf (AI 20 Jan 1865)

CROPPER, SARAH W. (Miss), dau. of Capt. E. Cropper, and James E. Sadler, both of Havre de Grace, m. 15 Sep 1863 in Havre de Grace by Rev. Richard Norris (SA 25 Sep 1863)

CROPPS, MARION, see "Officer Rigdon," q.v.

CROSS, WILLIAM and Miss Mary Burk, of Baltimore, m. 5 Jul 1862 at Havre de Grace by Rev. Father Stinehiser (SA 19 Jul 1862)

CROW, JIM, see "Miss Smith," q.v.

CRUIKSHANK, GEORGE W., Esq., editor of the *Cecil Democrat*, Elkton, MD, and Miss Sallie Cruikshank, dau. of Thomas C. Cruikshank, Esq., of Sassafras Neck, Cecil Co., MD, m. Thurs. 25 Nov 1869 by Rev. Billipp; the editor offered congratulations to his brother editor (AI 10 Dec 1869)

CULLUM, ANNE F., fifth dau. of the late George W. Cullum, Esq., and William Greenland, all of Harford Co., m. Tues. 21 Jun 1864, at the Parsonage, by Rev. William Finney (AI 15 Jul 1864)

CULLUM, CHARLOTTE A. (Miss) and William Brown m. Tues. 11 Oct 1864, near Harford Furnace, by Rev. R. Scott Norris (AI 25 Nov 1864)

CULLUM, GEORGE, died ---- (date not given) and was removed from the voter registration list in the 1st District in 1871 (HR 29 Sep 1871)

CULLY, ROBERT J., of Harford Co., and Miss Mary F. Norris, formerly of Virginia, m. 26 Apr 1864 by Rev. Kramer, in Havre de Grace (AI 20 May 1864)

CUNNINGHAM, CHARLES, see "Clara C. Cunningham" and "Daniel M. Cunningham," q.v.

CUNNINGHAM, CHARLES S., formerly of Harford Co., died 13 Aug 1869 [place not stated], in his 35th year (AI 20 Aug 1869)

CUNNINGHAM, CLARA C., youngest child of Charles S. and Lucy V. Cunningham, died 13 Apr 1869, aged 8 months and 13 days (HD 16 Apr 1869)

CUNNINGHAM, DANIEL M., died ---- (date not given) and the administrator's notice stated that creditors must exhibit their legal vouchers by 9 Aug 1866 to George A. Cunningham and Charles S. Cunningham, admins. (AI 21 Jul 1865)

CUNNINGHAM, GEORGE, see "Daniel M. Cunningham," q.v.

CUNNINGHAM. JAMES, see "Benjamin Davis," q.v.

CUNNINGHAM, JOSEPH W. and Miss Mary E. Chapman, both of Harford Co., m. Tues. 22 Oct 1867 by Rev. W. M. Meminger (AI 8 Nov 1867)

CUNNINGHAM. LUCY, see "Charles B. Dameron" and "Clara C. Cunningham," q.v.

CUNNINGHAM, MARTHA, wife of Mortimore Cunningham, died Tues. evening 16 Feb 1869, in her 60th year (AI 26 Feb 1869)

CUNNINGHAM, MERRIKEN B., died 20 Apr 1869 in the evening, in his 58th year (HD 23 Apr 1869 and AI 23 Apr 1869)

CUNNINGHAM, MORTIMORE, see "Martha Cunningham," q.v.

CUNNINGHAM, SARAH J. (Miss), dau. of Walter Cunningham, Esq., of Harford Co., and Edwin Pairo, of Richmond, VA, m. 17 Feb 1870, at the residence of the bride's father, by Rev. George M. Berry (HD 4 Mar 1870 and AI 4 Mar 1870)

CUNNINGHAM, SUSAN, consort of Capt. Daniel M. Cunningham, died Mon. 28 Jul 1862 in Harford Co. (SA 2 Aug 1862)

CUNNINGHAM, THOMAS, see "Albert E. Tate," q.v.

CUNNINGHAM, WALTER, died Sun. 15 Nov 1868 of typhoid fever, at the residence of his father, near Dublin, Harford Co., in his 21st year (AI 20 Nov 1868); see "Sarah J. Cunningham," q.v.

CURRY, LEVI H., died suddenly 16 Apr 1869 in his 64th year (HD 23 Apr 1869)

CURRY, MATTHEW, died ---- (date not given) and was removed from voter registration list in 1869 [district not clarified, but either 4th, 5th or 6th] (HD 22 Oct 1869 and AI 1 Oct 1869)

CURRY, SOPHIA (Mrs.), died Wed. 26 May 1869 in her 72nd year [*Baltimore Sun* and Harrisburg, PA papers please copy] (HD 11 Jun 1869)

CURRY, WILLIAM T., died ---- (date not given) and the administratrix's notice stated that creditors must exhibit their legal vouchers by 7 Oct 1859 to Hannah C. Curry, admx. (SA 23 Oct 1858)

DABAUGH, MARGARET (Miss), aged 19, residing at Harrisburg, PA, was bitten on the finger by a small dog and she died in a few days from hydrophobia (AI 10 Jun 1870)

DALLAM, CHARLES W., see "Mary Louisa Davis," q.v.

DALLAM, H. CLAY, see "Mary C. Hardesty," q.v.

DALLAM, JOHN, son of John S. and Amanda Dallam, died Tues. 31 Aug 1869 at 2 p.m., after a lingering illness, at his father's residence in Bel Air, in his 13th year (AI 3 Sep 1869 and HD 3 Sep 1869)

DALLAM, JOHN PACA, of Harford Co., and Mary Goldsborough Thomas, of Talbot Co., MD, m. Thurs. 9 Oct 1862 by Rev. L. F. Morgan (SA 18 Oct 1862)

DALLAM, JOHN S., see "Sallie Dallam" and "John Dallam," q.v.

DALLAM, MARY E. (Miss) and Benjamin F. Wann, both of Harford Co., m. 29 Dec 1869 by Rev. A. D. Shermer (HD 7 Jan 1870); another marriage notice spelled his name as "Waun" and stated they m. on 28 Dec 1869 (AI 7 Jan 1870)

DALLAM, RICHARD, died Thurs. night last week at the residence of his son, Major William H. Dallam, near Bel Air, in his 82nd year; he was one of the few remaining in our midst of those who were engaged in the War of 1812, having served in Capt. Paca Smith's Co., belonging to Col. John Streett's Regt.; he was interred at Darlington, in the Friends' Meeting House grounds, and was attended to his final resting place by members of Mt. Ararat Lodge, A.F.& A.M., of which he was one of the oldest members; he was subsequently removed from the voter registration list in the 3rd District in 1870 (AI 21 Jan 1870 and HR 28 Oct 1870)

DALLAM, SALLIE, eldest dau. of John S. Dallam, Esq., and G. E. N. Lewis, all of Bel Air, m. Tues. 19 Jan 1869 at the Presbyterian Church, Bel Air, by Rev. T. S. C. Smith (AI 22 Jan 1869)

DALLAM, WILLIAM H., see "Richard Dallam," q.v.

DAMERON, CHARLES B., died ---- (date not given) and the executrix's notice stated that creditors must exhibit their legal vouchers by 10 Nov 1869 to Lucy Virginia Cunningham, extx. (AI 13 Nov 1868)

DANCE, JAMES G. and Miss Caroline Richardson, of Harford Co., m. Wed. 19 Oct 1859 at St. Ignatius Church in Hickory by Rev. McDevitt (SA 22 Oct 1859)

DANCE, PHEBE (Miss) and Edward Ensor, both of Dulaney's Valley, Baltimore Co., m. Thurs. 22 Dec 1864 by Rev. William Grafton (AI 30 Dec 1864)

DANIELS, DAVID C., of New Castle, Lawrence Co., PA, and Miss Anna E. Carver, of Havre de Grace, m. 5 Jun 1866 at the M. E.

Church in Havre de Grace by Rev. George W. Heyde [marriage notice states "No cards"] (AI 8 Jun 1866)

DAUGHERTY, JOHN, see "Jacob Burkins" and "John Yates," q.v.

DAUGHTON, LIZZIE (Miss) and Milton Bennington, both of Harford Co., m. 19 Apr 1870, by Rev. Smith, of Slate Ridge (AI 6 May 1870)

DAVENPORT, PERSIS R. (Miss) of Worcester, Massachusetts, and Thomas Marsh, of Hudson, New Hampshire m. 25 Dec 1859 in Harford Co. (SA 31 Dec 1859)

DAVIDGE, REBECCA T. (Miss), of Harford Co., and John L. Dunkel, Esq., of Baltimore, m. 4 Nov 1847 by Rev. Crampton (HM 2 Dec 1847)

DAVIDSON, DAVID and Miss Rebecca Rosezette, both of Harford Co., m. 7 Apr 1869 in Rock Spring Church by Rev. W. E. Snowden (AI 14 May 1869)

DAVIS, ALBERT, see "Lloyd Stephenson," q.v.

DAVIS, AQUILA H., died ---- (date not given) and the administrator's notice stated that creditors must exhibit their legal vouchers by 19 Dec 1867 to Larkin Davis and John T. Davis, admins. (AI 21 Dec 1866)

DAVIS, AQUILLA H. and Miss Eliza A. Jones, both of Harford Co., m. Thurs. 23 Feb 1865 by Rev. T. S. C. Smith (AI 3 Mar 1865)

DAVIS, BENJAMIN, was stabbed and killed, and James Cunningham was dangerously wounded, last Sun. evening at Port Deposit [Cecil County] by a man named Gillespie, an employee of the Port Deposit Sash Factory, who was either insane or under the influence of liquor at the time; Davis and Gillespie were both young and unmarried; Gillespie was finally disarmed and arrested at Mrs. Reynolds' Hotel (SA 21 Nov 1857)

DAVIS, FRANCES H., died 12 Oct 1868, of consumption, at the residence of her uncle, N. A. McComas, aged 20 years and 4 months; obituary contains a poem written "By Her Friend, J. Y." (AI 23 Oct 1868)

DAVIS, GEORGE C., Chief Judge of the Orphans' Court of Harford Co., died Thurs. morning [another obituary stated he died in the evening] at his residence near Churchville; he was quite advanced in years, and commanded the respect and esteem of his fellow citizens to a very large extent; the administratrix's notice stated that creditors must exhibit their legal vouchers by 29 Dec 1870 to Susan [Susanna] Davis, admx. (AI 26 Nov 1869, 31 Dec 1869 and 28 Jan 1870; HR 2 Dec 1869); he was subsequently removed from the voter registration list in the 3rd District in 1870 (HR 28 Oct 1870)

DAVIS, GEORGE W. (Doctor), of Baltimore, and Miss Mollie J. Beaumont, of Harford Co., m. 26 Jan 1870 by Rev. J. S. Remsay (AI 4 Feb 1870)

DAVIS, HENRY WINTER, see "Henry May," q.v.

DAVIS, INDIA M., of Baltimore, and Albert E. Spicer, of Harford Co., m. 21 Feb 1871 by Rev. Dr. Fuller (HD 31 Mar 1871)

DAVIS, JOHN T. and Miss Sarah E. Jones, both of Harford Co., m. Thurs. 9 May 1867, in the Friendship M. E. Church, by Rev. W. M. Meminger (AI 17 May 1867); see "Aquila H. Davis," q.v.

DAVIS, JOSHUA (colored), died ---- (date not given) and was removed from the voter registration list in the 1st District in 1871 (HR 27 Oct 1871)

DAVIS, LARKIN, see "Aquila H. Davis," q.v.

DAVIS, LUTHER M., of Harford Co., died 30 Apr 1857, in his 62nd year, at the residence of his brother (HD 8 May 1857)

DAVIS, MARY LOUISA, wife of R. S. Davis and dau. of Charles W. Dallam, formerly of Harford Co., died 28 Jun 1870 at her home near Bardolph, Illinois; obituary contains a memorial written by "M." (AI 5 Aug 1870)

DAVIS, R. S., see "Mary Louisa Davis," q.v.

DAVIS, RUTH, died ---- (date not given) and the administrator's notice stated that creditors must exhibit their legal vouchers by 2 Nov 1864 to J. H. Neville and E. O. Johnson, admins. with will (SA 20 Nov 1863)

DAVIS, SEPTIMUS (Doctor), died last Thurs. at his residence near Hall's Crossroads, aged about 55 (HM 15 Jan 1857)

DAVIS, SUSAN (SUSANNA), see "George C. Davis," q.v.

DAVIS, THOMAS R., of Baltimore, and Miss Sallie E. Murphy, of Harford Co., m. 7 Jul 1863 by Rev. Bishop (SA 31 Jul 1863)

DAVIS. HENRY G. (Mrs.), see "John C. Forwood," q.v.

DAWSON, JACOB S., died ---- (date not given) and was removed from the voter registration list in the 6th District in 1870 (HR 21 Oct 1870)

DAY, AMOS J., see "Hannah Day" and "Hannah F. Day," q.v.

DAY, ANNIE E., wife of Ishmael Day, died 6 Dec 1868, after a short illness, in her 64th year (AI 11 Dec 1868)

DAY, CHARLOTTE MARY ORSO, wife of William Y. Day, died 19 Nov 1870 at *Taylor's Mount*, Baltimore Co. (AI 2 Dec 1870)

DAY, HANNAH, widow of William G. Day, died 4 May 1869 at her residence in Harford Co., of pneumonia, in her 79th year; obituary contains a short poem; the subsequent administrator's notice stated that creditors must exhibit their legal vouchers by 16 Jun 1870 to Amos J. Day, admin. (AI 28 May 1869 and 18 Jun 1869)

DAY, HANNAH F., died 13 May 1869, of pneumonia, on the evening of the seventh day of her illness, in her 54th year; she leaves a lone sister, two brothers and a large circle of friends; the subsequent administrator's notice stated that creditors must exhibit their legal vouchers by 16 Jun 1870 to Amos J. Day, admin. (AI 28 May 1869 and 18 Jun 1869)

DAY, ISHMAEL, see "Annie E. Day," q.v.

DAY, LUTHER, of Baltimore Co., and Mrs. Sallie Everett, of Harford
Co., m. 25 Dec 1870 at the residence of the officiating minister, in
Fallston, by Elder F. Marion Hawkins, M.D., assisted by Rev.
William Shroff, of the M. E. Church (AI 30 Dec 1870)
DAY, WILLIAM G., see "Hannah Day," q.v.
DAY, WILLIAM Y., see "Charlotte Mary Orso Day," q.v.
DEAN, HARRIET and John Enlows, both of Harford Co., m. 10 Dec
1870 by Rev. W, F. Speake (AI 16 Dec 1870)
DEAVER, FORD, died 14 Jun 1869 at Back River, Baltimore Co., aged
72 (HD 18 Jun 1869)
DEAVER, GEORGE, died 22 May 1863 at his residence, *Shanty Hall*, in
his 79th year (SA 12 Jun 1863)
DEAVER, JAMES, died Sat. 16 Dec 1865 at his residence in Harford
Co., at an advanced age (AI 22 Dec 1865)
DEAVER, MARY R. (Miss), died 5 Aug 1869 near Perrymanville,
Harford Co., obituary contains a memorial and short poem written
by "G.W.S., Baltimore, MD" (AI 20 Aug 1869)
DECKER, JOHN, see "Richmond Decker," q.v.
DECKER, MARY, see "Richmond Decker," q.v.
DECKER, RICHMOND, oldest son of John and Mary J. Decker, died 26
Jul 1856 after a protracted illness, aged 21 years, 5 months and 8
days (HD 8 Aug 1856)
DECKER, SARAH V., wife of Andrew J. Decker, died 17 Oct 1865 in
Kewaunee, Wisconsin, aged 25 years, 8 months and 21 days (AI 3
Nov 1865)
DEETS, FREDERICK, died 28 Nov 1869 at his residence, near
Jarrettsville, in his 76th year (AI 10 Dec 1869)
DEEVER, DAVID, of Lancaster, PA, and Margaret C. Tucker, of
Harford Co., m. Tues. 1 May 1866 at the residence of the bride's
father, by Rev. John W. Smith (AI 4 May 1866)
DEHAVEN, MARGARET N., dau. of Jesse and Frances Dehaven, died
Fri. 5 Jan 1866, aged 14 years (AI 19 Jan 1866)
DELCAMP, died H., died ---- (date not given) and was removed from
the voter registration list in the 4th District in 1870 (HR 1 Nov 1870)
DELCAMP, JOHN, died ---- (date not given) and the administrator's
notice stated that creditors must exhibit their legal vouchers by 15
Aug 1867 to Joshua H. Scarff, admin. (AI 17 Aug 1866); he was
subsequently removed from the voter registration list in the 4th
District in 1868 (AI 9 Oct 1868)
DELCAMP, MARY A. (Miss), of Harford Co., and Charles D. Haile, of
Baltimore Co., m. Tues. 21 Apr 1863 by Rev. G. P. Hays (SA 1
May 1863)
DELMAS, FRANCIS, died ---- (date not given) and the executor's
notice stated that creditors must exhibit their legal vouchers by 18
Mar 1845 to Edward Laroque, of Baltimore, exec., or to Dr. Samuel
H. Birckhead, his agent in Harford Co. (HM 11 Apr 1845)

DEMOSS, GEORGEANNA (Miss), died 25 Apr 1863, after a short and painful illness, in her 16th year; obituary contains a long memorial and poem written by "J.T.H. Jr." (SA 22 May 1863)

DEMOSS, JAMES E. and Miss Louisa Howard, both of Jerusalem Mills, m. Sun. 15 Oct 1871 at 6 p.m., at the residence of John Hollingsworth, by Dr. F. Marion Hawkins (SA 13 Oct 1871)

DENBOW, ANNIE E. (Miss), of Harford Co., and Joseph H. Tuder, of Baltimore, m. 29 Aug 1870 by Rev. J. E. Moss (AI 2 Sep 1870)

DENNISON, MATILDA (colored woman), jumped from the P. W. & B. Railroad platform at Perryman last Sat. evening about 8:40 with an infant in her arms and she fell between the platforms; Mr. Quinn, the agent and telegraph operator, quickly seized them and held them under the platform until the train was stopped; however, a wheel had gone over her right leg and everything was done to save her life, but an amputation had to be performed; she died Sun. at 4 a.m.; the infant was placed in the care of relatives who lived in the neighborhood [*Baltimore Sun*] (HD 18 Aug 1871)

DeSWAN, ARTHUR C., of Harford Co., and Miss Kate A. Harp, of Philadelphia, m. 24 Nov 1870 at the residence of the bride's parents, No. 1026 Brown St., Philadelphia, by Rev. John Pleasonton DuHammell (AI 16 Dec 1870)

DeSWAN, C., see "Mary E. DeSwan" and "Maggie N. DeSwan," q.v.

DeSWAN, MAGGIE N., eldest dau. of C. DeSwan, and William F. Anderson, all of Harford Co.,. m. Thurs. 16 Jun 1864 at the residence of the Bishop, the Right Rev. R. M. Coskery, in Baltimore (AI 1 Jul 1864)

DeSWAN, MARY E. "MOLLIE" (Miss), second dau. of Capt. C. DeSwan, and William T. Lilly, all of Harford Co., m. 26 Apr 1866 in Baltimore by Rev. Dr. Bullock (AI 25 May 1866 and 1 Jun 1866)

DEVER, BETSY (Miss), died Thurs. 16 Mar 1866 at Darlington, Harford Co., at an advanced age [error in newspaper: Thurs. was 15 Mar and Fri. was 16 Mar] (AI 23 Mar 1866)

DEVOE, ANNIE E. (Miss), dau. of Thomas Devoe., Esq., and Benjamin L. Mason, Jr., all of Harford Co., m. 22 Dec 1868 at Bethel Church by Rev. B. F. Myers (HD 1 Jan 1869 and AI 1 Jan 1869)

DEVOE, J. FRANK and Miss Eliza G. Wright, both of Harford Co., m. Thurs. 13 Feb 1868 at the residence of the bride's father (AI 27 Mar 1868)

DEVOE, THOMAS, see "Annie E. Devoe," q.v.

DICK, JOSHUA, died ---- (date not given) and was removed from the voter registration list in the 5th District in 1870 (AI 4 Nov 1870)

DICKEY, R. (Doctor), of West Chester, PA, and Laura J. Watters, dau. of Alexander Y. Watters, Esq., m. 23 Dec 1863 in the afternoon, at the residence of the bride at *Oakland*, Harford Co., by Rev. William G. Ferguson (SA 3 Jan 1863)

DICKSON, HARRIET A. (Mrs.), dau. of Dr. J. Wilson, of Harford Co., and Rev. B. Peyton Brown, of the Baltimore Annual Conference, m.

20 Apr 1869 at the Dumbarton M. E. Church in Georgetown, D.C., by Rev. Dr. McCauley (HD 23 Apr 1869)

DICKSON, SAMUEL MIDDLETON (Reverend), of the Baltimore Annual Conference, died 13 Nov 1866 in Washington City, aged 29 years, 10 months and 10 days; he joined the Methodist Episcopal Church in his 16th year, graduated from Dickinson College at age 20, united with the Baltimore Conference in the spring of 1857, and m. Miss H. A. Wilson, of Harford Co.; he subsequently traveled to Europe, contracted bronchial difficulties that became chronic, and also suffered from consumption; mentioned his father in Georgetown; obituary contains a lengthy memorial written by "J.R.E." (AI 28 Dec 1866)

DIFFENDERFFER, ANN, died ---- (date not given) and the administrator's notice stated that creditors must exhibit their legal vouchers by 23 Aug 1866 to George W. Herring, admin. (AI 25 Aug 1865)

DIFFENDERFFER, William George, see "Harry Lee," q.v.

DIVERS, A., died ---- (date not given) and was removed from the voter registration list in the 4th District in 1871 (HR 3 Nov 1871)

DIXON, DAVID M. and Ann J. Kerr, both of Harford Co., m. Tues. 6 Jun 1865 by Rev. O'Connor (AI 9 Jun 1865)

DONAHOO, WILLIAM THOMAS, son of Joseph F. and Mary E. Donahoo, died 31 Jul 1858 in Hampstead, Baltimore Co., after an illness of 5 days of bilious fever, aged 1 year, 3 months and 24 days (SA 14 Aug 1858)

DONN, GEORGE W., JR., of Washington City, and Miss Ellen E. Courtney m. 7 Jan 1869 at Havre de Grace by Rev. John F. Thomas (AI 15 Jan 1869)

DORNEY, AMANDA R., of Harford Co., and John Edward Bennett, of Baltimore, m. 12 Apr 1865 by Rev. J. S. Stuchell (AI 12 May 1865)

DORNEY, JACKSON, see "Marmaduke P. Dove," q.v.

DORNEY, WASHINGTON, see "Harry Lee" and "James Paul," q.v.

DORSEY, A. S., see "Mary Alice Dorsey," q.v.

DORSEY, MARTHA E. (Miss), of Baltimore, and Samuel Moulton, of Cecil Co., m. 12 Sep 1869 by Rev. R. Norris (HD 24 Sep 1869; AI 24 Sep 1869 spelled his name "Moltin")

DORSEY, MARY ALICE, wife of A. S. Dorsey and dau. of Capt. John A. Webster, of the U. S. Revenue Service, died Sun. 23 Jul 1865 in Baltimore (AI 28 Jul 1865)

DOVE, MARMADUKE P., died 2 Sep 1866 at *Joppa Farm*, the residence of Jackson Dorney, in his 44th year; he leaves a large circle of friends (AI 5 Oct 1866)

DOVE, MARTHA G. (Mrs.), died Wed. morning 24 Feb 1864 in Gunpowder Neck, Harford Co., in her 68th year (SA 11 Mar 1864)

DOWLING, JAMES and Miss Georgianna Starr, both of Harford Co., m. 24 Jun 1856 at the Parsonage in Bel Air by Rev. H. C. Cushing (HD 27 Jun 1856)

DOWNS, DANIEL J. and Miss Hannah Long, both of Harford Co., m. 17 Jan 1867, at the residence of Henry Long, by Rev. B. F. Myers (AI 15 Feb 1867)

DOXEN, CHARLOTTE and Henry Jones, both of Harford Co., m. 22 Aug 1867 by Rev. T. S. C. Smith (AI 6 Sep 1867)

DOXEN, SUSAN F. (Miss) and Patrick F. Boylen, both of Harford Co., m. 30 Aug 1866 by Rev. T. S. C. Smith (AI 7 Sep 1866)

DOYLE, MICHAEL, was shot and killed by John Carroll about 6 p.m. last Sat. on the Baltimore and Harford Turnpike near Wright's Hotel; it appears that some days ago a difficulty had taken place between these men, who were neighbors, on account of a pig belonging to Doyle getting into the garden of Carroll who drove the pig away, whereupon Doyle threw stones at the house of Carroll, it is alleged, frightening his wife and causing her to faint; the matter finally terminated in a law suit, and on the day in question, as both parties were returning from the magistrate's office, the quarrel was renewed; Carroll became exasperated at something Doyle said and drew his pistol and fired two shots; the first one missed, but the second one hit him in the stomach, causing death almost instantly; a post mortem examination by Drs. Burton and E. Franklin was conducted and the above facts elicited at the coroner's inquest; Carroll was arrested by the Sheriff of Baltimore Co. and put in jail at Towsontown; his trial was held in October and the jury, after 15 minutes deliberation, returned a verdict of not guilty and he was released (AI 28 Aug 1868 and 30 Oct 1868)

DRUM, EDWIN, an Irishman, aged about 25, in the employ of John Burnett at Newark, NJ, was stabbed to death by Margaret Garraty, a servant at the North Ward Hotel, on 4 Aug 1851; Drum [whose name was also spelled "Prum" in the article] had been engaged to Garraty and another woman at the same time, and m. the latter on the previous Sunday; Garraty told her fellow servants that she was going to kill him and then either drown herself or go to New York; a case of murder and probable suicide [article from the *Newark Mercury*, 5 Aug 1851] (HM 14 Aug 1851)

DRUMMOND, JOHN BURWELL, a respectable citizen of Brunswick Co., VA, was murdered on Christmas Eve by a man named Lewis, a pardoned convict (AI 7 Jan 1870)

DULIN, ANDREW, died 22 Jul 1870 in Annapolis, in his 53rd year, at the residence of his sister Mrs. Eliza J. Mitchell (HR 29 Jul 1870)

DUNBAR, JOHN W. R. (Doctor), died Mon. 3 Jul 1871, in his 66th year [VA papers please copy] (HD 7 Jul 1871)

DUNCAN, JOSEPH M., died Sun. 10 Aug 1862 at this residence in Harford Co., aged 54 (SA 16 Aug 1862)

DUNKEL, JOHN L., Esq., of Baltimore, and Miss Rebecca T. Davidge, of Harford Co., m. 4 Nov 1847 by Rev. Crampton (HM 2 Dec 1847)

DURHAM, ABRAHAM and Miss Martha Louisa Whiteford, both of Harford Co., m. 22 Dec 1870, at the residence of the bride's mother, by Rev. James Smith (AI 23 Dec 1870)

DURHAM, DAVID, see "Dorcas Durham" and "Josephine A. B. Durham," q.v.

DURHAM, DORCAS, wife of David Durham and dau. of the late James Wood, died 22 May 1862, in her 39th year; a subsequent obituary states she was aged 39 and leaves a husband and six children; second obituary contains a short poem (SA 7 Jun 1862 and 21 Jun 1862); see "Josephine A. B. Durham," q.v.

DURHAM, JOSEPHINE AMELIA BUSLINGTON, dau. of David and Dorcas Durham, died 28 Jan 1862, aged 6 years, 8 months and 16 days; obituary contains a short poem (SA 21 Jun 1862)

DURHAM, WILLIAM A. and Miss Matilda E. Lowe, both of Harford Co., m. 2 Apr 1868, at the residence of the bride's father, by Elder William Grafton (AI 8 May 1868)

DUTTON, MARIA (old colored woman), who lived at *Walnut Grove* near Oakington, was found dead at the door of her house Sun. morning 8 Nov 1868; at first it was thought she had been murdered as she was known to have had 12 silver dollars and $25 in currency about her; 4 silver dollars were found in an old chest in her house, but the balance she had spent, as she drank very hard; coroner's jury returned a verdict that she had died by the visitation of God and not otherwise (AI 4 Dec 1868)

DUVALL, FANNIE FENDALL, dau. of William B. Duvall, of Harford Co., and George H. Kyle, of Baltimore, m. 1 Jan 1867 at *La Vista* by Rev. J. H. D. Wingfield (AI 11 Jan 1867)

DUVALL, R. BURNS and Miss Bettie B. M. Hamilton, both of Harford Co., m. Tues. 26 Nov 1867, at Rock Spring Church, by Rev. Dr. Morrison; a subsequent article in 1869 stated he was formerly of Bel Air, MD and now living in Omaha, Nebraska Territory (AI 29 Nov 1867 and 31 Dec 1869); see "Henry Giles," q.v.

DUVALL, R. E., see "John Thompson," q.v.

DUVALL, WILLIAM B., see "Fannie Fendall Duvall" and "Jer. Y. Maynadier," q.v.

DWYER, MRS., see "Kate Marsh," q.v.

ECKARD, MRS., of Carroll Co., MD, burned to death last week by the accidental explosion of a coal oil lamp (AI 31 Dec 1869)

ECKART, H. J., Esq., ex-member of the Maryland Legislature, died a few days ago in Carroll Co., MD (AI 2 Sep 1870)

ECOFF, SAMUEL JR., died Fri. 21 Oct 1864 "near the Hickory in this county," in his 18th year (AI 28 Oct 1864)

ECOFF, SAMUEL SR., died Sat. 22 Oct 1864 at his residence in Harford Co., in his 65th year (AI 28 Oct 1864)

ECTON, JOHN, see "Bill Rumsey," q.v.

EDWARD, JOHN, see "Z. Taylor McDowell," q.v.

EICHELBERGER, LAURA G., dau. of the late William Eichelberger, of Baltimore, and William M. Ady, of Harford Co., m. Tues. 19 Oct 1858 at the Cathedral in Baltimore by the Most Rev. Archbishop Kenrick (SA 6 Nov 1858)

ELECLIP, R., died ---- (date not given) and was removed from the voter registration list in the 4th District in 1870 (HR 1 Nov 1870)

ELLICOTT, ----, see "Ralph S. Lee," q.v.

ELLICOTT, MARY M., dau. of William M. Ellicott, and John B. Roberts m. 20 Jun 1871 at Friends Meeting House on Eutaw St. in Baltimore (HD 30 Jun 1871)

ELLIOTT, CASSANDRA (Miss) and William T. Hilditch m. 15 Feb 1870 at the residence of the bride's father, near Fountain Green, by Rev. George M. Berry (AI 18 Feb 1870)

ELLIOTT, LAURA H., dau. of William M. Elliott, and George F. Walker, m. Thurs. evening 27 Nov 1862, at the residence of the bride's father, by Rev. Dr. F. Swentzell (SA 13 Dec 1862)

ELLIOTT, NELLIE B. (Miss), dau. of William M. Elliott, Esq., and Dr. John H. Cooley, both of Harford Co., m. Tues. 2 Jan 1866, at the residence of the bride's father, by Rev. S. A. Hoblitzell (AI 19 Jan 1866)

ELLIOTT, WILLIAM M., see "Laura H. Elliott" and "Nellie B. Elliott," q.v.

ELLIOTT, WILLIAM M. JR., died 12 Apr 1870, aged 24, afflicted many years; obituary contains a brief memorial and a short poem; subsequent issues of two newspapers contain a longer memorial (AI 15 Apr and 29 Apr 1870; HD 29 Apr 1870)); a third memorial states, in part, our beloved Willie, an obedient and dutiful son, a loving brother, a sincere friend, and a pleasant companion (also contains a lengthy lamentation about his passing); for several years his health gradually failed and on Fri. before his death his physician informed him that his end grew nigh (HR 13 May 1870)

ELTONHEAD, WILLIAM Z., of Baltimore, and Miss Aggie L. Johns, dau. of Edward F. Johns, of Harford Co., m. 23 Jan 1867 by Rev. William A. McKee (AI 1 Feb 1867)

ELY, J. R., see "Mary Rogers," q.v.

ELY, WILLIAM F. and Mary E. Ball, both of Harford Co., m. Tues. 3 Jul 1866 at the Methodist Episcopal Parsonage in Bel Air by Rev. Neminger (AI 13 Jul 1866)

ELY, WILLIAM S. and Lavinia Strickland, both of Harford Co., m. at the M. E. Parsonage in Bel Air by Rev. W. M. Meminger (AI 1 Jun 1866)

EMORY, T. LANE and Selda Holmes, dau. of Victor Holmes, Esq., m. Thurs. 3 Nov 1864 at *Belmour*, the residence of the bride's father, in Baltimore Co. (AI 11 Nov 1864)

EMREY, JACOB and Miss Mary Baer, both of Harford Co., m. 15 Sep 1859 by Rev. Zulauf (SA 1 Oct 1859)

ENFIELD, NANCY J. (Miss) and Alfred Thomas, both of Dublin District, Harford Co., m. 21 Apr 1870 by Rev. T. M. Crawford (AI 29 Apr 1870)

ENGER, MARY, formerly of Georgetown, but late of Harford Co., and N. S. Stinchcomb m. 26 May 1857 at St. Vincent's Parsonage in Baltimore by Rev. Obermeyer (HD 5 Jun 1857)

ENGLAND, ANN, wife of Elisha England, died 8 Mar 1867 in her 68th year; obituary contains a memorial written by "A Friend" (AI 5 Apr 1867)

ENGLAND, ELISHA and Miss Frances A. Scarborough, both of Harford Co., m. 8 Dec 1870, at the residence of the bride, by Rev. George M. Berry (AI 16 Dec 1870)

ENGLAND, ELISHA, see "Abraham Rutledge" and "Ann England," q.v.

ENGLAND, JAMES and Miss Henrietta Holland, both of Harford Co., m. 27 Jan 1863 by Rev. E. Welty (SA 13 Feb 1863)

ENGLAND, MRS., see "Samuel Ulysses Holland," q.v.

ENGLE, MARY J. (Miss) and Hollin Beaumont, both of Harford Co., m. 4 Sep 1866 at the M. E. Parsonage in Bel Air by Rev. W. M. Meminger (AI 14 Sep 1866)

ENLOWS, JANE, wife of John Enlows, died suddenly on Fri. 4 Mar 1870, in Harford Co., in her 73rd year (AI 18 Mar 1870); another obituary stated Jane Enloes, wife of John Enloes, died Fri. 4 Mar 1870 in her 72nd year (HD 18 Mar 1870)

ENLOWS, JOHN and Harriet Dean, both of Harford Co., m. 10 Dec 1870 by Rev. W. F. Speake (AI 16 Dec 1870)

ENSOR, EDWARD and Miss Phebe Dance, both of Dulaney's Valley, Baltimore Co., m. Thurs. 22 Dec 1864 by Rev. William Grafton (AI 30 Dec 1864)

ERGOOD, JESSE and Miss Elizabeth Chanley m. Sun. 17 Dec 1837, at Havre de Grace, by Rev. Goldsborough (HM 28 Dec 1837)

ESHELMAN, SARAH E. (Miss) and William J. McKinney, both of Harford Co., m. 13 Jan 1870 by Rev. George M. Berry at the residence of the bride's father (HD 11 Feb 1870); another marriage notice gave their names as Miss Sarah R. Eshelman and William J. McKenney (AI 11 Feb 1870)

ESTES, HARRIET C., wife of Charles Estes and dau. of the late James W. and Sarah Amoss, of Baltimore Co., died Wed. 9 Mar 1864 at Chestertown, Kent Co., MD, in her 28th year (AI 18 Mar 1864)

EVANS, DR. J., see "William L. Cole," q.v.

EVANS, ELEANOR, see "William M. Evans" and "Ella J. Evans," q.v.

EVANS, ELLA J., second dau. of William F. and Eleanor E. Evans, died Thurs, 21 Jun 1866 in Havre de Grace, after suffering two years with consumption, in her 19th year; obituary contains a long memorial and poem (AI 17 Aug 1866)

EVANS, ISABEL C., dau. of Dr. John and Rebecca N. Evans, died 5
Dec 1863 in Havre de Grace, aged 5 years, 10 months and 1 week
(SA 18 Dec 1863)
EVANS, JOHN, see "William Broomfield" and "Isabel C. Evans," q.v.
EVANS, JOHN M., see "James Cook," q.v.
EVANS, REBECCA, see "Isabel C. Evans," q.v.
EVANS, ROBERT, died suddenly last Fri. at his residence in Cecil Co.;
for many years he was a resident of Harford Co. and a high toned
gentleman who was punctual and prompt in all his business
relations (AI 11 Jan 1867)
EVANS, WILLIAM, see "Ella J. Evans," q.v.
EVANS, WILLIAM M., son of William F. and Eleanor E. Evans, died
Fri., 8 Sep 1865 at 9:45 p.m. in Havre de Grace, of consumption,
aged 23 years, 2 months and 3 days; obituary contains a memorial
and poem written by "A.F." (AI 15 Dec 1865)
EVERETT, HARRIET (Miss) and Stephen T. Magness, both of Harford
Co., m. 7 Oct 1868 by Rev. D. A. Shermer (AI 16 Oct 1868)
EVERETT, JOHN D. and Miss Caroline E. Klinesmith, both of Harford
Co., m. 19 Jan 1865 at the Methodist Protestant Parsonage in Bel
Air by Rev. R. Scott Norris (AI 27 Jan 1865)
EVERETT, LENA, relict of the late Richard Everett, died 17 Jan 1868,
after a lingering illness, in her 82nd year; obituary contains a brief
memorial (AI 22 May 1868)
EVERETT, SALLIE (Mrs.), of Harford Co., and Luther Day, of
Baltimore Co., m. 25 Dec 1870 at the residence of the officiating
minister, in Fallston, by Elder F. Marion Hawkins, M.D., assisted
by Rev. William Shroff, of the M. E. Church (AI 30 Dec 1870)
EVERIST, JOSEPH, see "Ruth Everist," q.v.
EVERIST, RUTH, wife of Joseph Everist, died 2 Apr 1869, after a short
illness, in her 79th year (AI 9 Apr 1869)
EVERITT, CHARLOTTE, died Thurs. 20 Aug 1868, aged 62 (AI 18 Sep
1868)
EWELL, GEN., see "Oliver H. Thomas," q.v.
EWING, ANN M. (Miss) and Wilson D. West, both of Harford Co., m. 8
Aug 1867 in the M. E. Church, Dublin, by Rev. W. M. Meminger
(AI 16 Aug 1867)
EWING, G. E. N. and Sallie Dallam, eldest dau. of John S. Dallam, Esq.,
all of Bel Air, m. Tues. 19 Jan 1869 at the Presbyterian Church, Bel
Air, by Rev. T. S. C. Smith (AI 22 Jan 1869)
EWING, GEORGE W., of Dublin District, Harford Co., died Sat. 8 Nov
1862, at his residence, after an illness of 48 hours, aged 61 years, 1
month and 24 days; at age 18 he joined the Methodist Episcopal
Church, but shortly thereafter joined the Presbyterian Church of
which his father was a member; in 1829 he again became a member
of the Methodist Episcopal Church and for many years was a trustee
of "our" church in Dublin; obituary contains a memorial written by
"R.C.H." (SA 10 Jan 1863 and SA 22 Nov 1862)

EWING, MARTHA MATILDA (Miss) and Samuel H. Bagely, both of Harford Co., m. Tues. 1 Jul 1862 by Rev. Dr. Swentzel (SA 5 Jul 1862)

EWING, WILLIAM, died Mon. 18 Sep 1871 at his residence near Hopewell Crossroads, in his 76th year (HD 22 Sep 1871)

EWING, WILLIAM JR., died 17 Dec 1866, at 20 minutes before 9 o'clock in the morning, aged 27 years and 19 days, of a lingering illness of consumption of 2 years and 1 month; the disease also took two brothers and a sister; obituary contains a memorial and poem written by "A Friend" (indicating he was a dutiful son, kind father, devoted husband and confiding friend); the executrix's notice stated that creditors of William Ewing must exhibit their legal vouchers by 29 Jan 1868 to Cornelia A. Ewing, extx. (AI 8 Feb 1867 and 15 Feb 1867)

EWING, WILLIAM SR. and Miss Eliza Mitchell m. Tues. 6 Apr 1869 at Hopewell by Rev. Cochell (HD 16 Apr 1869)

FALES, MARY R., wife of E. C. Fales and dau. of J. G. Baker, Esq., of Baltimore, died Tues. 15 Oct 1867 at Hagerstown, MD, in her 23rd year (AI 25 Oct 1867)

FALLS, HENRIETTA JANE, wife of Stephen W. Falls and dau. of the late Col. Edward A. Howard, of Baltimore Co., died Thurs. 10 Mar 1870, in her 71st year (AI 1 Apr 1870)

FARLEY, OWEN, died Mon. 19 Mar 1866 at his residence in Harford Co., aged about 35; the subsequent administratrix's notice stated that creditors must exhibit their legal vouchers by 25 Apr 1867 to Jane Farley, admx. (AI 23 Mar 1866 and 11 May 1866)

FARMER, RICHARD, died ---- (date not given) and the executrix's notice stated that creditors must exhibit their legal vouchers by 19 Aug 1840 to Margaret Farmer, extx. (HM 14 Feb 1840)

FARMER. MARGARET, see "Richard Farmer," q.v.

FARNANDIS, HENRY D., see "Harry D. Gough" and "Charles Baker Hitchcock" and "Otho Scott," q.v.

FARNANDIS, WALTER, eldest son of Walter and Mary E. Farnandis, died 23 Jan 1865, in his 14th year, at the residence of his grandmother in Harford Co. (AI 27 Jan 1865)

FARR, JOHN C.,. see "Patrick Murney," q.v.

FARR, WILLIAM A., died ---- (date not given) and was removed from the voter registration list of the 6th District in 1870 (HD 7 Oct 1870 and AI 4 Nov 1870)

FARRINGER, CATHARINE, relict of the late Jacob Farringer, died 17 Jan 1863 of consumption, in her 55th year (SA 23 Jan 1863)

FENDALL, ALICE LEE and Jer. Y. Maynadier m. Tues. evening 18 Mar 1865, at the residence of William B. Duvall, Esq., by Rev. J. H. D. Wingfield (AI 21 Apr 1865)

FENDALL, CHARLES E., see "William Oldfield," q.v.

FENDALL, WILLIAM L., see "Elizabeth Beachboard," q.v.

FERRY, DANIEL, died ---- (date not given) and was removed from the voter registration list in the 4th District in 1870 (AI 4 Nov 1870)

FERRY, JOHN, died suddenly Sun. 23 Mar 1862 at his residence in Bel Air, in his 36th year; he was a native of County Tyrone, Ireland and had resided here only 3 or 4 years (SA 29 Mar 1862)

FIFE, ELIZABETH (Mrs.), died Mon. 8 May 1865 at her residence in Harford Co., aged 89 (AI 12 May 1865)

FIFE, JAMES, died ---- (date not given) and was removed from the voter registration list in the 4th District in 1868 (AI 9 Oct 1868)

FINLEY, CASSANDRA (Miss), of Lancaster Co., PA, and Charles H. A. Whiteford m. Tues. 4 Dec 1866 at the residence of Philip H. Love, near Bel Air, by Rev. T. M. Crawford of York Co., PA (AI 7 Dec 1866)

FINLEY, CLAYTON and Miss Martha G. Adams, both of Harford Co., m. ---- (date not given) at the Slate Ridge Manse (HD 17 Feb 1871)

FINLEY, REBECCA (Miss) and Ralph H. Thomas, both of Harford Co., m. 5 Jan 1858 at the Parsonage in Bel Air by Rev. H. C. Cushing (SA 16 Jan 1858)

FINNEY, GEORGE J., of Harford Co., and Lou. L. Webster, dau. of the officiating clergyman, m. 26 Apr 1865 in Baltimore by Rev. Dr. Webster (AI 5 May 1865)

FINNEY, MARGARET, wife of Rev. William Finney, died Sat. morning 22 Jul 1865 in her 76th year (AI 28 Jul 1865)

FINNEY, WILLIAM JR., son of William and Margaret Finney, died 11 Dec 1862 in Amador Co., California; he was far from home, but cared for by many Christian friends (SA 16 Jan 1863)

FINNEY, WILLIAM, see "John R. Paxton" and "Margaret Finney," q.v.

FISH, MARION, died 4 Aug 1869; her obituary is essentially a long poem written "By Her Attending Physician" (AI 24 Sep 1869)

FISHER, CAROLINE (Mrs.), died suddenly on 2 Apr 1871 at her residence near Burlingham, Meigs Co., Ohio, in her 65th year (HD 14 Apr 1871)

FISHER, EDWARD, died ---- (date not given) and the administrator's notice stated that creditors must exhibit their legal vouchers by 22 Jan 1864 to Joseph M. Streett, admin. (SA 3 Apr 1863)

FITZNER, PETER, of Havre de Grace, was brought to Bel Air jail last Wed. and charged with an assault with the intent to kill Louis Oberman and George Koonin of that place; wounds of a very serious nature were inflicted Tues. night with a large beef butcher's sticking knife, 12 inches long; it is supposed one of the wounded parties will die (SA 14 May 1859)

FLAHARTY (FLAHERTY), SARAH E. (Mrs.) and Samuel Whann, both of Harford Co., m. 25 Nov 1869 by Rev. George M. Berry (AI 17 Dec 1869 and HD 17 Dec 1869)

FLETCHER, A. A. and Miss Mary C. Barnes, both of Havre de Grace, m. 18 Jun 1871 (HR 7 Jul 1871)

FLETCHER, ELIZABETH S., see "William S. Fletcher," q.v.

FLETCHER, HENRY C., was murdered last Sat. [15 Nov 1857] near Nelson's Mill by Andrew Thompson; looked upon by the neighborhood as a desperate character, Thompson lived unhappily with his wife and at the time of this occurrence was beating her; Fletcher was passing by and, hearing the noise, stopped and went into the house and remonstrated with Thompson as to the impropriety of his conduct; he was immediately struck on the head with a heavy briar hook, fracturing his skull and killing him instantly; a young man named Trout was passing in the road with a gun when Thompson made after him with a knife; he attempted to shoot, but his gun snapped, so he retreated and made his escape; Thompson was subsequently caught and arrested in Baltimore in May 1858; his trial took place in November 1858 and he was found guilty of murder in the second degree (SA 21 Nov 1857 and 20 Nov 1858)

FLETCHER, JOHN, died ---- (date not given) and the executor's notice stated that creditors must exhibit their legal vouchers by 27 Oct 1847 to William Michael, exec. (HM 2 Apr 1847)

FLETCHER, JOHN, see "Septimus Fletcher," q.v.

FLETCHER, ROBERTA C., wife of Spencer D. Fletcher and dau. of Mrs. Hannah Lee, of Bel Air, died Sat. 29 Sep 1866 at Lowood in Accomac Co., VA (AI 5 Oct 1866)

FLETCHER, SEPTIMUS, died ---- (date not given) and the administrator's notice stated that creditors must exhibit their legal vouchers by 19 Oct 1872 to John Fletcher, admin. (HR 27 Oct 1871)

FLETCHER, THOMAS C., died ---- (date not given) and the administrator's notice stated that creditors must exhibit their legal vouchers by 1 Oct 1847 to Winston Barnes, admin. (HM 19 Mar 1847)

FLETCHER, WILLIAM S. and Miss Elizabeth S. Fletcher, both of Accomac Co.,. VA, m. 28 Nov 1867 in Emmanuel Church, Accomac Co., by Rev. Mr. Haughton (AI 13 Dec 1867)

FLOWERS, CHARLOTTE M. (Mrs.), died 29 Apr 1869 in her 40th year, Harford Co., not living more than a week or ten days after her attack; she leaves a husband and several small children; obituaries contain a memorial and a poem (HD 7 May 1869 and AI 14 May 1869)

FLOWERS, HANNAH A. and James Wilgus, both of Harford Co., m. 2 Jan 1866 by Rev. E. Kinsey at the M. E. Parsonage in Bel Air [Baltimore papers please copy] (AI 5 Jan 1866)

FOARD, A. J. (Doctor) and Miss Ella R. Todd, both of Baltimore, m. 2 Nov 1871 in the evening, at the Universalist Church in Baltimore, by Rev. Alexander Kent (SA 10 Nov 1871)

FOARD, JOHN B., died Thurs. 1 May 1862 at his residence in Harford Co., in his 65th year (SA 10 May 1862)

FOLEY, JAMES, see "---- Washington," q.v.

FORBES, MARTHA ELIZABETH, consort of Rev. M. L. Forbes, died 2 Jul 1871, in her 54th year (HD 7 Jul 1871)

FORD, WILLIAM G., see "Thomas H. Burnham," q.v.

FORSYTHE, ALEXANDER, died ---- (date not given) and was removed from the voter registration list in the 5th District in 1870 (AI 4 Nov 1870); see "George Forsythe," q.v.

FORSYTHE, GEORGE, died ---- (date not given) and the executor's notice stated that creditors must exhibit their legal vouchers by 14 Nov 1864 to Alexander Forsythe, exec. (SA 20 Nov 1863)

FORSYTHE, HENRIETTA (Mrs.) and George F. Botts, both of Harford Co., m. 17 Nov 1870 at the M. E. Parsonage, Dublin, by Rev. George M. Berry (AI 25 Nov 1870); see "William Forsythe," q.v.

FORSYTHE, WILLIAM, died ---- (date not given) and the executrix's notice stated that creditors must exhibit their legal vouchers by 7 Mar 1865 to Henrietta Forsythe, extx. (AI 18 Mar 1864)

FORSYTHE, WILLIAM SR., died ---- (date not given) and the administrator's notice stated that creditors must exhibit their legal vouchers by 20 Aug 1856 to William Forsythe, admin. (HM 11 Oct 1855)

FORWOOD, GEORGE D., of Harford Co., and Miss Laura P. Smithson, of Cecil Co., m. 23 Nov 1867 at Port Deposit by Rev. Henry Branch (AI 29 Nov 1867)

FORWOOD, H. J. and Frank Hanway, both of Harford Co., m. Thurs. 26 Mar 1862 at Rock Spring Church by Rev. R. J. Keeling (SA 3 Apr 1863)

FORWOOD, JAMES J., see "Sarah S. Forwood," q.v.

FORWOOD, JAMES O. and Miss R. Susan Hanna, both of Harford Co., m. Tues. 26 Mar 1867, in Baltimore, by Rev. Dr. Hays (AI 5 Apr 1867)

FORWOOD, JOHN C., formerly of Harford Co., died 28 Dec 1857 at the residence of Mrs. Henry G. Davis in Clark Co., Alabama (SA 23 Jan 1858)

FORWOOD, MARY (Miss) and Ira George, both of Harford Co., m. 7 Oct 1871 by Rev. A. H. Greenfield at the minister's residence in Bel Air (SA 13 Oct 1871)

FORWOOD, MARY H., see "Parker Forwood," q.v.

FORWOOD, PARKER (Doctor), died ---- (date not given) at his residence in Harford Co., aged 69 (AI 2 Feb 1866); the subsequent executrix's notice stated that creditors must exhibit their legal vouchers by 8 Mar 1867 to Mary H. Forwood, extx. (AI 20 Apr 1866)

FORWOOD, SAMUEL W., died ---- (date not given) and was removed from the voter registration list in the 4th District in 1870 (AI 4 Nov 1870)

FORWOOD, SAMUEL WESLEY and Rebecca J. Chamberlain, both of Harford Co., m. 26 Jun 1860 by Rev. T. D. Valiant (SA 14 Jul 1860)

FORWOOD, SARAH S., wife of James J. Forwood and dau. of Thomas M. James, died 17 May 1859 in Harford Co., of consumption, in her 27th year (SA 28 May 1859)

FORWOOD, W. S. (Doctor) and Miss Pamela Wilson, both of Harford Co., m. 16 Jun 1857 at the 2nd Presbyterian Church in Baltimore by Rev. Smith (HD 19 Jun 1857)

FORWOOD, WILLIAM STUMP (Doctor), of Harford Co., and Miss Addie Bond, of Cheltenham, formerly of Kentucky, m. 6 May 1863 at St. Paul's Church at Cheltenham, near Philadelphia, by Rev. Parvin (SA 15 May 1863)

FOSTER, ELIZABETH A. (Miss) and Edward Curry Wright m. 1 Jul 1856 at the Exeter Street Parsonage in Baltimore by Rev. J. S. Martin (HD 4 Jul 1856)

FOSTER, GRACE, see "John Kelly Foster," q.v.

FOSTER, HENRY, see "Rebecca Foster," q.v.

FOSTER, JANETTE and Thomas R. Mister, of Anne Arundel Co., MD, m. 4 Jan 1863 in Baltimore by Rev. Williams of the Baptist Church (SA 10 Jan 1863)

FOSTER, JOHN KELLY, son of William and Grace Foster, died 2 Aug 1851 in Baltimore, in the morning, aged 1 year, 2 months and 3 days (HM 14 Aug 1851)

FOSTER, LYDIA, see "Rebecca Foster," q.v.

FOSTER, REBECCA, youngest dau. of Henry and Lydia R. Foster, died Fri. morning 4 Feb 1870 in her 18th year (HR 11 Feb 1870)

FOSTER, WILLIAM, see "John Kelly Foster," q.v.

FOY, ISAAC W., died 13 Oct 1867 near Perrymansville, Harford Co., in his 39th year (AI 18 Oct 1867)

FOY, JOHN B., see "Samuel Lawder," q.v.

FRANCE, CHARLES D., of Harford Co., and Sarah E. Batchelor, of Baltimore, m. 12 Dec 1865, at the residence of the bride's father, by Rev. B. G. W----d [illegible] (AI 22 Dec 1865)

FRANCE, RICHARD, died ---- (date not given) and was removed from the voter registration list in the 1st District in 1870 (HR 1 Nov 1870)

FRANCIES, J. ALBERT and Miss Emma V. Henry, both of Baltimore Co., m. 14 May 1871 in Towsontown, at the residence of the bride's mother, by Dr. F. M. Hawkins of the Christian Church (HR 23 Jun 1871)

FRANKLIN, DR. E., see "Michael Doyle," q.v.

FREANER, WILLIAM, a soldier of the War of 1812, died last week in Hagerstown, MD, aged 80 (AI 15 Apr 1870)

FREDERICK, HENRY, while engaged in walling up a well for John Joshua Streett on Deer Creek last Wed., had his skull fractured by the falling of a bucket of stone; Drs. Hayward and Richardson were summoned, but there was little prospect of recovery; he died Thurs., aged about 50, and leaves a wife and several children; the subsequent administratrix's notice stated that creditors must exhibit their legal vouchers by 29 Jun 1869 to Margaretta Frederick, admx.

[the latter notice spelled the name "Fredrick"] (AI 19 Jun 1868 and 26 Jun 1868 and 3 Jul 1868)

FREEBORN, SAMUEL, was found dead last Fri. in a lady's traveling trunk on the steamer *Fortress Monroe* which had arrived in Baltimore; the owner of the trunk gave a statement to police last Sat. night [long account in the *Baltimore Sun*]; she said her name was Mary Louisa Linder, a native of Germany, aged about 37, who had resided in Norfolk, VA prior to the war, and acknowledged herself to be a woman of lewd habits; she had lived with the deceased about 3 months and shortly after their meeting he enlisted as a private in the 20th New York Cavalry stationed at Norfolk; he soon after went on leave, but overstaying his time, he was afraid to go back and became a deserter; he remained concealed in her house and later decided to make his escape by hiding in her traveling trunk, stating he actually tried it before the trip and came out without injury; the plan was that once in Baltimore, he would make his escape and she could return to Norfolk; however, upon arriving, she had the trunk taken to a boarding house on Watson Street and later opened it to find him dead; Marshal Carmichael subsequently handed her over to Col. Woolly (AI 6 Jan 1865)

FREEMAN, WILLIAM, of Baltimore Co., and Miss Elizabeth Walker, of Harford Co., m. 11 Nov 1847 by Rev. McJilton (HM 2 Dec 1847)

FRENCH, ELLA L., formerly of Baltimore, and William K. Hunter, of Baltimore, m. 12 Dec 1867 by Rev. John McCron (AI 10 Jan 1868)

FRIEZE, J. THOMPSON, see "Eliza A. Pennington," q.v.

FUCHS, ABRAHAM, a native of Prussia, died 1 Dec 1837, aged 43 (HM 14? Dec 1837)

FULFORD, ALEXANDER, of Baltimore, and Miss Frances S. Hays, dau. of Thomas A. Hays, Esq., of Harford Co., m. 16 Mar 1847 by Rev. Dr. Wyatt (HM 19 Mar 1847)

FULLER, SARAH L. (Mrs.), of Baltimore, and J. T. Hunter, of Harford Co., m. 17 Mar 1863 in Baltimore by Rev. E. D. Owens (SA 1 May 1863)

FULTON, EMMA, dau. of William H. Fulton, Esq., of Philadelphia, and S. H. Mearns, of Cecil Co., m. 4 Oct 1865, at the residence of the bride's father, by Rev. Dr. Henry (AI 13 Oct 1865)

FULTON, JAMES A., see "James Kean," q.v.

FULTON, W. JACKSON, of Philadelphia, and Miss M. Effie Michael, dau. of the late Capt. Henry Michael, of Michaelsville, MD, m. 19 Dec 1866 at the residence of George W. Michael, Esq., by Rev. McKee [*Baltimore Sun* please copy] [marriage notice indicated "No cards"] (AI 28 Dec 1866)

FULTON, WILLIAM H., see "Emma Fulton," q.v.

GAILEY, ROBERT, died ---- (date not given) and was removed from the voter registration list in the 4th District in 1868 (AI 9 Oct 1868); see "Augustus Kurtz," q.v.

GAILEY, SARAH, widow of Robert Gailey, died 14 May 1869, of pneumonia, at the residence of her son in Harford Co., in her 67th year; she leaves a son and many friends (AI 28 May 1869)

GAITHER, JOHN F. and Miss Martha Burkins, both of Harford Co., m. 3 Mar 1870 by Rev. T. M. Crawford (AI 11 Mar 1870)

GALLAGHER, FRANCIS, Esq., died 10 Dec 1866 in Baltimore, of consumption, in his 53rd year; he was unm. and had but one near relation living in this country, a brother who resides in Connecticut and who was with him during his illness; he had represented Baltimore in the House of Delegates and was one of the earliest advocates for the abolition of imprisonment for debt in this State; he was a lieutenant in the Federal Army during the war and had been in declining health for some time; he had a considerable reputation as a stump speaker and on November first had made a speech from the court house steps (AI 14 Dec 1866)

GALLAGHER, SUSAN (Miss), a young lady residing at Perrysville, PA, was struck and killed by lightning last Wed. while sitting on her porch (SA 9 Jul 1859)

GALLEY, LIZZIE (Miss), only dau. of Robert Galley, Esq., of *Locust Grove*, Harford Co., and T. Streett Gemmill, of Freeport, Illinois, m. 10 May 1860 by Rev. A. Hartman (SA 19 May 1860)

GALLION, ELIZABETH C., see "Joshua F. Gallion," q.v.

GALLION, JACOB H., died Wed. 13 Oct 1869 at his residence in Aberdeen, Harford Co. [age not given] (AI 29 Oct 1869); he was subsequently removed from the voter registration list of the 2nd District in 1870 (AI 4 Nov 1870)

GALLION, JAMES and Miss Rachel Marsh, both of Harford Co., m. 7 Feb 1867 at the residence of Joseph Starr (AI 15 Feb 1867)

GALLION, JINNIE M., second dau. of Martha J. and John W. Gallion, died 18 Jan 1867 in Harford Co., in her 14th year; obituary contains a poem written by "M.J.C." (AI 15 Feb 1867)

GALLION, JOHN, see "Jinnie M. Gallion," q.v.

GALLION, JOSHUA F., died ---- (date not given) and the administrator's notice stated that creditors must exhibit their legal vouchers by 10 Oct 1871 to Elizabeth C. Gallion and James L. Richardson, admins. (AI 14 Oct 1870); he was subsequently removed from the voter registration list of the 2nd District in 1870 (AI 4 Nov 1870)

GALLION, MARTHA, see "Jinnie M. Gallion," q.v.

GALLOP, MARTHA M., see "Semelia O. Cannon," q.v.

GALLOP, OLIVER, died ---- (date not given) and the executrix's notice stated that creditors must exhibit their legal vouchers by 24 Mar 1863 to Catherine Gallop, extx.(SA 5 Apr 1862); see "Emma W. Galup," q.v.

GALLOWAY, ABSALOM, of Marshall Co., Illinois, and Mrs. Avarilla B. Whitaker, of Harford Co., m. 20 Sep 1866 by Rev. J. K. Nichols (AI 5 Oct 1866)

GALLOWAY, ELIZABETH (Mrs.), consort of Capt. Peter Galloway, died 23 Feb 1871 at her residence of a protracted illness (HR 3 Mar 1871)

GALLOWAY, MAGGIE J. and Lewis Griffith, both of Aberdeen, Harford Co., m. 28 Aug 1865 by Rev. James M. Maxwell (AI 1 Sep 1865)

GALLOWAY, MARY A. and William H. Smithson, both of Harford Co., m. 4 Oct 1868 in the evening at the Parsonage of Exeter Street M. E. Church [in Baltimore] by Rev. J. A. Price (HD 9 Oct 1868)

GALLOWAY, MAY ELLA, youngest dau. of the late Capt. William Galloway, of Baltimore, and Hon. R. Jarrett Marston, of New York, m. 21 Jan 1866 at *Oak Hill* in Harford Co. by Rev. S. Bartol [double wedding with Charles Hudson and Helen Edith Chivrel]; surname was spelled "Gallaway" in the paper [New York and Baltimore papers please copy] (AI 26 Jan 1866)

GALLOWAY, PETER, and Miss Louisa Jennes, both of Havre de Grace, m. 11 Jan 1865, at Jefferson Street M.E. Church in Baltimore, by Rev. Richard Norris (AI 20 Jan 1865)

GALLOWAY, PETER, see "Elizabeth Galloway," q.v.

GALLOWAY, SAMUEL, Esq., well known citizen of Harford Co. and a brother of Mr. Galloway, Assessor of Internal Revenue in the 2nd District, died Wed. morning from a stroke of apoplexy which prostrated him on Tues. evening while on a visit to the residence of his brother-in-law Charles H. Giles, Esq., a short distance from Bel Air; this was the second attack he had suffered in the past two years; he was one of the oldest residents of Bel Air, having commenced the merchandising business here many years ago in partnership with the late N. W. S. Hays and Thomas A. Hays (AI 10 Jun 1870 and HR 10 Jun 1870)

GALLOWAY, SARAH, wife of Samuel Galloway, died Mon. 7 Mar 1864 at her residence in Bel Air, aged 61 (SA 11 Mar 1864)

GALLUP, CLARA (Miss) and H. C. Osmond, both of Havre de Grace, m. 5 Jan 1871 by Rev. William Cooke (HR 3 Feb 1871)

GALLUP, THOMAS F., committed suicide last Sun. night by throwing himself into the river from Simmons' Wharf in Havre de Grace; he was about 35 years of age and lived in the lower part of Harford Co.; he had exhibited symptoms of derangement of the mind, supposedly caused by the death of his wife about a year or two ago; his body was recovered Mon. morning, by dragging the river, and taken in charge by his friends; an inquest in the same newspaper indicated he had mentioned to someone that he was going to die that night; his clothes were later found neatly arranged on Simmons' Wharf as if to go in swimming; the verdict was voluntary drowning caused by mental aberration (AI 5 Jun 1868)

GALUP, EMMA W., dau. of the late Oliver Galup, of Harford Co., and John W. Bay, of Baltimore, m. 16 Jan 1868 at the Second

Presbyterian Church, Baltimore, by Rev. George P. Hays (AI 24 Jan 1868)

GARRATY, MARGARET, see "Edwin Drum," q.v.

GARRETT, ANNIE, see "Winter Garrett," q.v.

GARRETT, JAMES, see "Winter Garrett," q.v.

GARRETT, SAMUEL, see "Sarah A. Garrett," q.v.

GARRETT, SARAH ANN, wife of Samuel Garrett, died Mon. 20 Sep 1869 near Shawsville, in her 57th year (AI 24 Sep 1869, which mistakenly gave the date of death as 20 Sep 1868); Sarah A. Garrett, wife of Samuel Garrett, of Harford Co., died 20 Sep 1869, aged 56 (AI 17 Dec 1869 and HD 17 Dec 1869)

GARRETT, WINTER, only child of James H. and Annie R. Garrett, died 17 Dec 1871, aged 3 years and 12 days (AI 19 Jan 1872)

GARRETTSON, E. C., of Baltimore Co., and Miss Lydia M. Groscup, of Harford Co., m. 19 Mar 1863 by Rev. E. Welty (SA 3 Apr 1863); see "Laura E. Garrettson," q.v.

GARRETTSON, GEORGE H. and Miss Sarah R. Whitson, both of Harford Co., m. Thurs. 6 Jan 1870, at Friendship Meeting House, by Rev. Daniel Reese (AI 14 Jan 1870)

GARRETTSON, LAURA ELIZABETH, dau. of E. C. and Lydia A. Garrettson, died Sat. 24 Jun 1871, in her 4th year; obituary contains a poem (HD 30 Jun 1871)

GARRETTSON, LYDIA, see "Laura E. Garrettson," q.v.

GARRISON, ANN, relict of Samuel J. Garrison, died 16 Nov 1870, in Baltimore, in his 71st year (AI 25 Nov 1870)

GARRISON, JOHN and Rebecca Spedden, both of Harford Co., m. Mon. 2 May 1864 by Rev. E. Kinsey (AI 6 May 1864)

GARRISON, SAMUEL J., see "Ann Garrison," q.v.

GAVIT, SUSAN, dau. of Capt. J. Gavit, of East Baltimore St. near Ann St., aged 17, was severely burned at her father's residence when an ethereal lamp exploded around 8:30 p.m. last Sat.; a passing gentleman rushed in to help and Drs. Inloes, Cockrill and Monkur were called in, but despite their efforts she died about 9:30 p.m. Sun. (HD 26 Jun 1857)

GEMMILL, JAMES, of York Co., PA, and Miss Ann Norris, of Harford Co., m. Thurs. 21 Dec 1837 by Rev. Samuel Parke (HM 28 Dec 1837)

GEMMILL, T. STREETT, of Freeport, Illinois, and Miss Lizzie Galley, only dau. of Robert Galley, Esq., of *Locust Grove*, Harford Co., m. 10 May 1860 by Rev. A. Hartman (SA 19 May 1860)

GEORGE, IRA and Miss Mary Forwood, both of Harford Co., m. 7 Oct 1871 by Rev. A. H. Greenfield at the minister's residence in Bel Air (SA 13 Oct 1871)

GIBNEY, ROSANNA (Miss) and Joseph E. Burkins, both of Harford Co., m. 22 Feb 1870 by Rev. T. M. Crawford, assisted by Rev. R. Gamble (AI 4 Mar 1870)

GILBERT, A. PRESTON and Miss Mollie A. Bouldin, dau. of William Bouldin, Esq., all of Bel Air, m. Thurs. 6 Oct 1870 at Emmanuel Church, Bel Air, by Rev. William E. Snowden (AI 14 Oct 1870 and HD 7 Oct 1870); see "Bennett Gilbert," q.v.

GILBERT, ABRAHAM A., died 31 Jan 1864 at *Blue Rock*, Harford Co., aged 39 years, 7 months and 2 days, leaving a large circle of friends; obituary contains a short poem; the subsequent administrator's notice stated that creditors must exhibit their legal vouchers by 19 Mar 1865 to Mary Jane Gilbert, admx. (SA 5 Feb 1864; AI 25 Mar 1864)

GILBERT, ALICE E. (Miss) and Charles S. Waterman, both of Harford Co., m. Tues. 19 Feb 1867 by Rev. T. S. C. Smith (AI 22 Feb 1867)

GILBERT, AMERICA A. (Miss), dau. of Amos Gilbert, Esq., of Harford Co., and Elias G. Selby, of Carroll Co., m. 2 May 1867 by Rev. T. S. C. Smith (AI 10 May 1867)

GILBERT, AMOS, see "America A. Gilbert," q.v.

GILBERT, BENNETT, died ---- (date not given) and the administrator's notice stated that creditors must exhibit their legal vouchers by 1 Jan 1864 to Martha S. Gilbert and A. Preston Gilbert, admins. (SA 10 Jan 1863); see "Elizabeth Ann Pritner" and "Hannah S. Gilbert" and "Preston McComas," q.v.

GILBERT, CHARLES (colored), see "Harry Lee," q.v.

GILBERT, ELIZA JANE, eldest dau. of Parker Gilbert, died 28 Feb 1869, aged 27; she was a member of the Methodist Episcopal Church; obituary contains a memorial written by "K.C." (AI 2 Apr 1869)

GILBERT, ELLEN B. wife of George Gilbert and dau. of the later Preston McComas, died Sun. morning 11 Jul 1869, in her 54th year, after a long and painful illness (HD 16 Jul 1869)

GILBERT, FRANKLIN, see "John Gilbert," q.v.

GILBERT, GEORGE, see "Ellen B. Gilbert," q.v.

GILBERT, HANNAH S. (Miss), dau. of the late Bennett Gilbert, Esq., of Harford Co., and J. Rich Grier, of Philadelphia, m. Tues. 4 Oct 1864 by Rev. William Finney (AI 21 Oct 1864)

GILBERT, JOHN, died ---- (date not given) and the administrator's notice stated that creditors must exhibit their legal vouchers by 6 Jun 1868 to Franklin Gilbert, admin. (AI 7 Jun 1867)

GILBERT, JOHN N., see "Sarah A. Gilbert," q.v.

GILBERT, MARTHA, see "Bennett Gilbert," q.v.

GILBERT, MARY JANE, see "Abraham A. Gilbert," q.v.

GILBERT, NAOMI A. (Miss), of Harford Co., and William T. Bausmith, of Baltimore, m. 18 Mar 1869 by Rev. George H. Zimmerman (AI 20 Mar 1868)

GILBERT, PARKER, see "Eliza Jane Gilbert," q.v.

GILBERT, SARAH A., dau. of John N. and Sarah Gilbert, died Sat. 6 Sep 1851, aged 7 years, 4 months and 18 days (HM 18 Sep 1851)

GILES, CHARLES H., see "Samuel Galloway," q.v.

GILES, HENRY (colored), died ---- (date not given) and the administrator's notice stated that creditors must exhibit their legal vouchers by 25 Apr 1866 to R. Burns Duvall, admin. (AI 5 May 1865)

GILLAND, SARAH FRANCES and William H. Grupy, both of Harford Co., m. 25 May 1857 by Rev. McKeith (HD 29 May 1857)

GILLESPIE, ----, see "Benjamin Davis," q.v.

GILLETT, CORNELIA E. (Miss), dau. of Dr. Jacob Gillett, formerly of Harford Co., and Rev. Mr. Arther m. 12 Dec 1837, in Guernsey Co., Ohio, by Rev. Polk (HM 28 Dec 1837)

GILMORE, COLUMBUS K., of Port Deposit, Cecil Co., MD, and Emma L. W. Weaver, of Pottsville, Schuylkill Co., PA, m. 20 Jul 1869 by Rev. H. Branch (AI 30 Jul 1869)

GITTINGS, DR., see "Wakeman Bryarly," q.v.

GLACKEN, MARTHA A. (Miss), of Lancaster Co., PA, and Sylvester Wheeler, of Harford Co., m. 4 Feb 1869 at St. Ignatius Church by Rev. Father O'Connor [*Lancaster Intelligencer* please copy] (HD 19 Feb 1869 and AI 12 Feb 1869)

GLADDEN, JACOB, died ---- (date not given) and was removed from the voter registration list in the 4th District in 1868 (AI 9 Oct 1868)

GLEASON, CORNELIUS, of Havre de Grace, a brakeman on the P. W. & B. Railroad, was run over by a passenger train near Chester last Mon. might and was instantly killed; he leaves aged parents (HR 6 Jan 1871)

GLEN, WILLIAM M. and Sarah L. Ashton, of Harford Co., m. 28 Jan 1858 by Rev. Keech (SA 6 Mar 1858)

GLENN, CLEMENT, died ---- (date not given) and the administrator's notice stated that creditors must exhibit their legal vouchers by 4 Oct 1866 to Thomas Glenn, admin. (AI 10 Nov 1865); see "Nathaniel Glenn," q.v.

GLENN, ELIZABETH, consort of Nathaniel Glenn, died Mon. 21 Apr 1862, in her 70th year (SA 26 Apr 1862)

GLENN, F. B., see "Richard Glenn" and "John L. Glenn," q.v.

GLENN, JOHN L. and Miss Lizzie Whiteford, both of Harford Co., m. Tues. 6 Sep 1870 at the residence of F. B. Glenn, Bel Air, by Rev. W. B. Brown (AI 9 Sep 1870)

GLENN, MR., see "Charles E. Markland," q.v.

GLENN, NATHANIEL, died Sun. 20 Apr 1862, in his 71st year; a subsequent executor's notice stated that creditors of Nathan Glenn must exhibit their legal vouchers by 29 Apr 1863 to Clement Glenn, exec. (SA 26 Apr 1862 and 3 May 1862)

GLENN, RICHARD ALFRED, son of Frank B. and Priscilla Glenn, died Fri. night 5 Aug 1870, aged 6 months and 3 days (HD 12 Aug 1870 and AI 12 Aug 1870)

GLENN, SARAH F. (Miss) and Dr. Martin L. Jarrett, both of Harford Co., m. 31 Jan 1867, at Bethel, by Rev. B. F. Myers [double wedding; see "Thomas B. Jarrett," q.v.] (AI 15 Feb 1867)

GLENN, THOMAS, died ---- (date not given) and was removed from the voter registration list in the 4th District in 1870 (HR 1 Nov 1870); see "Clement Glenn," q.v.

GOLDSBOROUGH, m. TILGHMAN, see "Fanny Van Wick Archer," q.v.

GONCE, MARY E., eldest dau. of John T. and Catherine A. Gonce, and William H. Butts m. 26 Oct 1869, at the Immaculate Conception, by Rev. Father Abbott (AI 19 Nov 1869)

GORDON, FRANKLIN, died Sat. 17 Mar 1866 at Union Mills, Harford Co., in his 25th year (AI 23 Mar 1866)

GORDON, MARY E. (Miss) and A. V. Allen, both of Piqua, Ohio, m. 4 Nov 1869 at the First Presbyterian Church, Piqua, by Rev. T. C. Hopkins (AI 3 Dec 1869)

GORDON, MRS., died Sat. 10 Mar 1866, in her 96th year, at the residence of her son-in-law Lemuel Ady, in Harford Co. (AI 16 Mar 1866)

GORDON, SUSAN M. (Miss) and Philip C. Greenfield, both of Baltimore Co., m. 1 Jun 1865 by Rev. Philip Clark (AI 9 Jun 1865)

GORRELL, HANNAH AMELIA, dau. of Joseph and S. J. Gorrell, died 14 Mar 1868, aged 1 year and 24 days (AI 20 Mar 1868)

GORRELL, JAMES T. and Miss Elizabeth Hendon, both of Harford Co., m. 2 Aug 1871 at the Washington House in Bel Air by Rev. T. M. Cathcart (HD 4 Aug 1871)

GORRELL, JOSEPH, see "Hannah Amelia Gorrell," q.v.

GOUGH, CHARLES H., see "Harry O'Brien Gough," q.v.

GOUGH, HARRY D., died Mon. 2 Dec 1867 about 10 p.m., aged about 76 (another obituary stated he died in his 77th year), at the residence of his son-in-law, Capt. Richard E. Bouldin, near Bel Air; in early life he adopted the sea as a business or profession, but soon abandoned it and turned to other pursuits; during the War of 1812 he was a soldier at Baltimore; he was elected to the Maryland House of Delegates and served for a number of years as a County Commissioner for Harford Co.; in 1845 her was appointed Clerk of the Harford County Court by Gov. Thomas G. Pratt and served until 1851 when he was superseded by a change in the Constitution of the State; in 1862 he was appointed Weigher of Livestock in Baltimore by Gov. A. W. Bradford; he was also one time Deputy Sheriff of Harford Co., and was several times Clerk to the Board of County Commissioners, School Commissioner for Harford Co., Committee Clerk during several sessions of the Maryland Legislature, etc. *[sic]*; in politics he was originally a Whig and when it was dissolved he became a leader of the Know Nothing or American Party; during the late war between the two sections of our country he became a Union man and afterwards a member of the Republican Party; his lengthy obituary also contains a memorial written by H. D. Farnandis which was read before the Court yesterday, the day of his funeral [information from two obituaries in the same newspaper]; a third obituary contains a memorial and short poem written by "A.E.G., Baltimore, December 12, 1867" (AI 6 Dec 1867 and 3 Jan 1868); see "Mrs. Gough," q.v.

GOUGH, HARRY O'BRIEN, son of the late Harry D. Gough, Esq., of Harford Co., had been suffering from an attack of illness which had left him in a critical invalid condition, died suddenly 28 May 1870, from congestion of the brain, in California [age not given]; he left Harford Co. for California in 1850 shortly after the close of the Mexican War; his obituary contains a brief memorial from an unidentified San Francisco newspaper; a subsequent newspaper article stated Charles H. Gough, after an absence of 20 years (stating he left Bel Air to go to San Francisco in 1849), returned to Harford Co. from California with the remains of his two brothers, Harry O. Gough and William Thomas Gough, Esq., both of whom recently died in that state; he was accompanied by Mr. Caffrie, a close friend, who assisted him last Wed. in their interment in the old family graveyard at Southampton, near Bel Air (AI 17 Jun 1870 and 23 Sep 1870)

GOUGH, MARTHA C., dau. of Harry D. Gough, Esq., of Baltimore, and Capt. Richard E. Bouldin, of the 7th MD Volunteers, m. Thurs. 4 Feb 1864 by Rev. L. F. Morgan at Charles Street M. E. Church in Baltimore (SA 12 Feb 1864)

GOUGH, MRS., consort of H. D. Gough, Esq., died last Mon. evening at her residence near Bel Air, after a protracted illness (HM 17 May 1844)

GOUGH, S. J., see "Hannah Amelia Gorrell," q.v.

GOUGH, WILLIAM THOMAS, died Sun. afternoon 26 May 1867, of erysipelas of the head, in Aurora, Nevada; in consequence of the very precarious state of his father's health at the time, his brothers in California kept back the news of the death of their brother until one or the other could arrive here from the Pacific coast, which they had designed to do in the summer or early fall; however, matters over which they had no control prevented their arrival in Baltimore until late in December; the death of his son at the time it occurred would have been to him a terrible shock, one which his frail condition could not have withstood; this young man grew to manhood among us and gave great promise of eminence in his profession; we parted with him for the last time on 6 Jul 1854 in New York City, on his way to California, from whence he removed to Aurora [information taken in part from the *Esmeralda Union* in Nevada] (AI 3 Jan 1868); see "Harry O'Brien Gough," q.v.

GOVENS, JEHU, died ---- (date not given) and was removed from the voter registration list in the 4th District in 1870 (HR 3 Nov 1871)

GOVER, CASSIE A. (Miss), dau. of the late James A. Gover, Esq., and Dr. W. W. Hopkins, all of Harford Co., m. Tues. 26 Nov 1867 at St. John's Church, Havre de Grace, by the rector, Rev. Henry B. Martin, M.D. (AI 29 Nov 1867 and 6 Dec 1867)

GOVER, ELIZABETH (Miss), died Thurs. 21 Feb 1867 at the residence of her brother-in-law, Samuel M. Lee, in her 57th year (AI 1 Mar 1867)

GOVER, GEORGE OLIVER, son of George P. and Juliet A. Gover, died 25 Dec 1857, aged 21 years, 2 months and 10 days (SA 26 Dec 1857)

GOVER, GERARD, see "James A. Gover," q.v.

GOVER, JAMES A., died Fri. 24 May 1867 at his residence near Havre de Grace, in his 63rd year (AI 31 May 1867); the administrator's notice stated that creditors must exhibit their legal vouchers by 28 Jun 1868 to Gerard Gover, admin. (AI 5 Jul 1867); he was subsequently removed from voter registration list of the 6th District in 1869 (HD 22 Oct 1869); see "Cassie A. Gover" and "Sarah M. Gover," q.v.

GOVER, SARAH M. (Miss), dau. of the late James A. Gover, Esq., and William F. Knight, of Clarke Co., VA, m. Tues. 10 Dec 1867 at St. John's Church, Havre de Grace, by Rev. Henry B. Martin, M.D.. (AI 27 Dec 1867)

GRACE, LUTHER and Miss Gracey H. Pritchett, both of Easton, MD, m. Tues. 23 Nov 1869 at Christ Church, Easton, Talbot Co., by Rev. Orlando Hutton (AI 3 Dec 1869)

GRACY, JAMES, died Wed. 5 Jun 1867 near Bel Air, aged about 54; he leaves a wife (AI 28 Jun 1867)

GRAFTON, BASIL, of Forest Hill, died last Fri. morning from the inflammation of a stab wound to the breast and lung received some 3 weeks ago [Thurs. 6 May 1869] at Forest Hill, about 4 miles from Bel Air, at the hands of his friend Joseph Parks [spelled Parkes in one article]; Grafton was treated by Dr. E. Hall Richardson and the dangerous wound was thought not to be necessarily fatal, but a critical one; Parks is now in Bel Air jail and deeply distressed at the result of his reckless drunken act; they are both men of families; Grafton leaves a widow and children (AI 14 May and 4 Jun 1869 and HR 3 Jun 1869); another account indicated Parks was a painter at Grafton's Shop from which place he and Grafton had left together in a wagon; at Forest Hill they had an altercation which led to the stabbing; the subsequent administrator's notice stated that creditors must exhibit their legal vouchers by 31 May 1870 to Corbin Grafton, admin. (AI 21 May 1869 and 4 Jun 1869); additional accounts of the incident and murder trials were subsequently published; Parks was found guilty of manslaughter in February 1870 (AI 26 Nov 1869 and 3 Dec 1869 and 4 Mar 1870)

GRAFTON, BASIL and Miss Margaret C. Grafton, both of Harford Co., m. 21 Jun 1866 by Rev. J. K. Nichols (AI 29 Jun 1866 spelled his name "Bazil")

GRAFTON, JAMES A. and Miss Julia A. McComas, both of Harford Co., m. Mon. 6 May 1867 at the M. E. Parsonage, in Bel Air, by Rev. A. H. Greenfield (AI 10 May 1867)

GRAFTON, MARGARET (Miss) and Henry Pohlar, both of Harford Co., m. 18 Jul 1867 by Rev. T. S. C. Smith (AI 26 Jul 1867)

GRAFTON, MARGARET C. (Miss) and Basil Grafton, both of Harford Co., m. 21 Jun 1866 by Rev. J. K. Nichols (AI 29 Jun 1866 spelled his name "Bazil")

GRAFTON, MARTHA A. (Miss) and James M. Rogers, both of Harford Co., m. 27 Sep 1866 at the Parsonage in Bel Air by Rev. J. N. Nichols (AI 5 Oct 1866)

GRAFTON, SARAH and James K. Martin, both of Harford Co., m. 8 Feb 1866, at the M. E. Parsonage, by Rev. E. Kinsey (AI 16 Feb 1866)

GRASON, MR., ex-Governor of Maryland (elected 1838) and former member of both branches of the State Legislature, died Thurs. 3 Jul 1868 at his residence in Queen Anne's Co., in his 83rd year (AI 10 Jul 1868)

GREEN, ----, see "Charles McCormick," q.v.

GREEN, RICHARD, died ---- (date not given) and the executor's notice stated that creditors must exhibit their legal vouchers by 8 Jun 1862 to C. W. Billingslea, exec. (SA 24 Aug 1861)

GREENFIELD, A. H., see "Louisa Shultz," q.v.

GREENFIELD, ANNIE (Miss), of Harford Co., and M. Joseph Clautice, of Baltimore, m. ---- (date not given) at the Caroline Street M. E. Parsonage, Baltimore, by Rev. John W. Hedges (AI 19 May 1865)

GREENFIELD, MARY E. (Miss) and Robert G. Taylor, both of Harford Co., m. 31 May 1867 by Rev. T. S. C. Smith (AI 7 Jun 1867)

GREENFIELD, PHILIP C. and Miss Susan M. Gordon, both of Baltimore Co., m. 1 Jun 1865 by Rev. Philip Clark (AI 9 Jun 1865)

GREENFIELD, SAMUEL J. and Miss Mary E. Sanders, both of Harford Co., m. 25 Nov 1856 by Rev. H. C. Cushing (HD 28 Nov 1856)

GREENFIELD, SAMUEL J. K., died ---- (date not given) and the administrator's notice stated that creditors must exhibit their legal vouchers by 16 Feb 1861 *(sic)* to William Sanders, admin. (SA 13 Apr 1861) [the notice was dated 16 Feb 1860, but was not published in the paper until 13 Apr 1861]

GREENLAND, ELLA E., see "Harry Hays Greenland," q.v.

GREENLAND, HARRY HAYS, died 4 Sep 1868, aged 11 years, 6 months and 16 days, of dysentery, and Ella E. Greenland, died 18 Sep 1868, aged 13 years and 1 month, of the same disease, children of John Amos and Ruth Cornelia Greenland (AI 23 Oct 1868)

GREENLAND, HOLLAND, residing near Churchville, some weeks ago met with a severe accident by falling from an ox cart, which he was driving, and striking his head on a stone; paralysis has supervened and he now lies in a critical condition; he has been under the constant care of Dr. T. H. Roberts, but there seems to be a strong probability of an ultimate fatal result (AI 30 Jul 1869)

GREENLAND, JOHN, see "Harry Hays Greenland," q.v.

GREENLAND, RUTH, see "Harry Hays Greenland," q.v.

GREENLAND, WILLIAM and Anne F. Cullum, fifth dau. of the late George W. Cullum, Esq., all of Harford Co., m. Tues. 21 Jun 1864, at the Parsonage, by Rev. William Finney (AI 15 Jul 1864)

GREENLEAF, WILLIAM, of Vermont, and Miss Kate Seneca, dau. of Dorus Seneca, of Havre de Grace, m. on the morning of 17 Jan 1867 at Havre de Grace by Rev. Hyde (AI 25 Jan 1867)

GREGORY, JOHN, was murdered in Baltimore last Sat. evening; an argument had taken place earlier between he and Owen Shields, but it was broken up by Gregory's brother-in-law; the disagreement apparently did not end there because Gregory's badly hacked up body was found Sun. morning by a watchman of the Middle District at the corner of Hillen and East Sts.; Gregory, a young man about age 28, had been m. about 7 weeks and lived on Hillen St.; Shields also lived on Hillen St. and officers proceeded there and arrested him while in his bed; they found his shirt and pantaloons covered with blood [article from the *Baltimore Clipper* contains more details] (HM 19 Aug 1852)

GRICE, JEREMIAH and Miss Catherine Reynolds, both of Harford Co., m. 14 Feb 1871 at the residence of the bride's father, David Reynolds, Esq., by Rev. George M. Berry (HD 31 Mar 1871)

GRIER, BENNETT GILBERT, only child of J. Rich and Hannah S. Grier, died 30 Jun 1867 at Philadelphia, aged 1 year, 7 months and 13 days (AI 12 Jul 1867)

GRIER, HANNAH, see "J. Rich Grier" and "Bennett Gilbert Grier," q.v.

GRIER, J. RICH, of Philadelphia, and Miss Hannah S. Gilbert, dau. of the late Bennett Gilbert, Esq., of Harford Co., m. Tues. 4 Oct 1864 by Rev. William Finney (AI 21 Oct 1864); see "Bennett Gilbert Grier," q.v.

GRIER, SAMUEL, see "Mrs. Welsh," q.v.

GRIFFIN, AMELIA (Mrs.), died Wed. 16 Mar 1870, in her 74th year (AI 8 Apr 1870)

GRIFFITH, A. G., see "Martha Rebecca Griffith," q.v.

GRIFFITH, EDWARD, died 4 Jul 1867 in Harford Co., in his 86th year; the subsequent executor's notice stated that creditors must exhibit their legal vouchers by 17 Jul 1868 to Robert Mickle and William G. Wetherall, execs. (AI 12 Jul 1867 and 19 Jul 1867)

GRIFFITH, ELLA, see "Martha R. Griffith," q.v.

GRIFFITH, G. S. JR. and Ella Michael, youngest dau. of Ethan Michael, of Harford Co., m. Tues. 14 Jun 1864 at Spesutia Church by Rev. Crampton (AI 1 Jul 1864)

GRIFFITH, GOLDSBOROUGH, see "Martha R. Griffith," q.v.

GRIFFITH, JOHN, died intestate and without issue about 1855 [there was an equity case involving his heirs in Harford and Baltimore Counties] (HD 20 Feb 1857)

GRIFFITH, JOHN L., died ---- (date not given) and the administratrix's notice stated that creditors must exhibit their legal vouchers by 26

Jun 1866 to Priscilla Griffith, admx. (AI 30 Jun 1865); see "Colored Woman" and "Sallie B. Griffith," q.v.

GRIFFITH, LEWIS and Miss Maggie J. Galloway, both of Aberdeen, Harford Co., m. 28 Aug 1865 by Rev. James M. Maxwell (AI 1 Sep 1865)

GRIFFITH, MARTHA REBECCA, only dau. of Ella and Goldsborough S. Griffith, Jr., died Tues. evening 28 Jun 1870, aged 3 years, 3 months and 9 days, of whooping cough, at the farm of A. G. Griffith in Harford Co. (AI 1 Jul 1870)

GRIFFITH, MRS., see "J. Howard Carlisle," q.v.

GRIFFITH, PRISCILLA, see "John L. Griffith," q.v.

GRIFFITH, SALLIE B. (Miss), dau. of the late John L. Griffith, Esq., and Otho S. Lee, all of Harford Co., m. Thurs. 14 Mar 1867 by Rev. S. W. Compton (AI 22 Mar 1867)

GRIFFITH, WILLIAM, died ---- (date not given) and was removed from the voter registration list in the 6th District in 1870 (HR 4 Oct 1870)

GRIFFITH, WILLIAM E. and Fannie R. Wilson, eldest dau. of Isaac Wilson, both of Baltimore, m. 8 May 1862 by Rev. William N. Elliott of Elkton, MD (SA 17 May 1862)

GROOME, GEORGE F., of Baltimore, and Miss Margaret Silver, of Harford Co., m. 19 Aug 1851 by Rev. Finney (HM 28 Aug 1851)

GROOME, JOHN C. (Colonel), died last Fri. evening at his residence in Elkton, Cecil Co., in his 67th year; he was a member of the bar and as a politician he was mild though firm in his views; he was of the old Whig school until that party ceased to exist and then attached himself to the Democratic Party, becoming their candidate for Governor in 1858; he was also a director in the Philadelphia, Baltimore & Wilmington Railroad Company for a number of years; buried in Elkton last Tues. at 11 o'clock (AI 7 Dec 1866)

GROSCUP, FREDERICK, see "Sarah E. Groscup," q.v.

GROSCUP, LYDIA M. (Miss), of Harford Co., and E. C. Garrettson, of Baltimore Co., m. 19 Mar 1863 by Rev. E. Welty (SA 3 Apr 1863)

GROSCUP, MARY M. and Lewis Beaumont, both of Harford Co., m. 15 Nov 1865 by Rev. E. Kinsey (AI 24 Nov 1865)

GROSCUP, SARAH E. (Miss), dau. of Rev. Frederick Groscup, all of Harford Co., and Harman H. Scarborough m. 19 Nov 1868 at Friendship M. E. Church by Rev. William A. McKee [*Baltimore Sun* please copy] (AI 11 Dec 1868)

GROSS, J. THOMAS and Miss Jennie Wetherill, both of Harford Co., m. 21 Dec 1871 by Rev. J. C. Hagey (AI 12 Jan 1872)

GRUPY, WILLIAM H. and Sarah Frances Gilland, both of Harford Co., m. 25 May 1857 by Rev. McKeith (HD 29 May 1857)

GUYTON, CHARLES T., eldest son of John and Mary Ann Guyton, died Tues. 22 Mar 1870, aged 37 (AI 25 Mar 1870)

GUYTON, JAMES (of Benjamin), died ---- (date not given) and the executor's notice stated that creditors must exhibit their legal vouchers by 26 Aug 1869 to Samuel W. James, exec. (AI 28 Aug 1868)

GUYTON, JOHN, see "Charles T. Guyton," q.v.

GUYTON, JOSIAH, see "Sarah Guyton," q.v.

GUYTON, MARY, see "Charles T. Guyton," q.v.

GUYTON, SALLIE (Miss), of Harford Co., and Alpheus Murphy, of the borough of Washington, PA, m. Thurs. 17 Jan 1867, in said borough, by Rev. R. V. Dodge (AI 8 Feb 1867)

GUYTON, SARAH, died ---- (date not given), aged 75, at the residence of her brother Josiah Guyton, near Shawsville (SA 20 Mar 1863)

GWINN, GEORGIE (Miss) and Dr. Charles A. Shure m. 24 Jun 1869 at Port Deposit, Cecil Co., by the bride's brother Rev. W. R. Gwinn, assisted by Rev. H. Branch and Rev. W. E. England (AI 2 Jul 1869)

HAILE, CHARLES D., of Baltimore Co., and Miss Mary A. Delcamp, of Harford Co., m. Tues. 21 Apr 1863 by Rev. G. P. Hays (SA 1 May 1863)

HAINES, DeWILTON, died ---- (date not given) and was removed from the voter registration list of the 6th District in 1870 (HD 7 Oct 1870 and AI 4 Nov 1870)

HAIR, JACOB D., see "Warren Roebock," q.v.

HALL, ALVERDA, see "Aquila Hall," q.v.

HALL, ANDREW, see "J. Sidney Hall," q.v.

HALL, AQUILA, Esq., died 9 Sep 1870 at his residence near Abingdon, in his 80th year; he was one of the Association of Baltimore Defenders and was one of the oldest citizens of this county [newspaper contains two death notices]; the subsequent executor's notice stated that creditors must exhibit their legal vouchers by 14 Nov 1871 to Thomas W. Hall and Alverda Hall, execs. (AI 16 Sep 1870 and 25 Nov 1870); "Aquilla Hall" was subsequently removed from the voter registration list of the 6th District in 1870 (HD 7 Oct 1870 and 4 Nov 1870)

HALL. CAROLINE, see "Nannie Day Hall" and "Carrie A. Hall," q.v.

HALL, CARRIE A., youngest dau. of Thomas W. and Caroline A. Hall, died Thurs. 4 Aug 1864, at *Lauretum* in Harford Co., in her 7th year (AI 12 Aug 1864)

HALL, CHARLOTTE JANE, died ---- (date not given) and the executrix's notice stated that creditors must exhibit their legal vouchers by 15 Jun 1869 to Charlotte Ramsay Hall, extx. (AI 19 Jun 1868)

HALL, EDWARD C., see "Eliza Hall," q.v.

HALL, EDWARD H. and Miss Lydia B. Hayes, both of Harford Co., m. Thurs. 10 Feb 1870, in Emmanuel Church, by Rev. William E. Snowden [marriage notice indicated "No cards"] (AI 18 Feb 1870)

HALL, ELIZA, consort of the late Edward C. Hall, died 10 Apr 1869 in her 69th year (HD 16 Apr 1869)

HALL, GEORGE WILLIAM, died Thurs. 26 Jul 1866 at his residence; he was a prominent citizen of Harford Co. (AI 27 Jul 1866)

HALL, HENRY (Major), died 7 Dec 1854 in Harford Co., in his 71st year (HM 14 Dec 1854)

HALL, JOHN SIDNEY, died Sat. morning 2 Jul 1864 at his residence near Perrymansville, in his 61st year (AI 8 Jul 1864); the subsequent executor's notice stated that creditors must exhibit their legal vouchers by 26 Jul 1865 to Andrew Hall, exec. (AI 5 Aug 1864)

HALL, JOHN W., of Baltimore Co., and Miss Susan Slade, youngest dau. of Dixon Slade, of Harford Co., m. Thurs. 21 Dec 1837 by Rev. Andrew B. Cross (HM 28 Dec 1837)

HALL, NANNIE DAY, dau. of Thomas W. and Caroline A. Hall, died 22 Jul 1864, at *Lauretum* in Harford Co., after a short and painful illness, in her 12th year (AI 29 Jul 1864)

HALL, PATTIE W. (Miss), dau. of Thomas W. Hall, Esq., of Harford Co., and Major John U. Mayo m. Wed. 16 Jun 1869 in St. Mary's Church, Harford Co., by Rev. William F. Brand (AI 18 Jun 1869; HD 18 Jun 1869 spelled her name "Patty")

HALL, THOMAS, see "Nannie Day Hall" and "Carrie A. Hall" and "Aquila Hall" and "Pattie W. Hall," q.v.

HAMILTON, BETTIE B. M. (Miss) and R. Burns Duvall, both of Harford Co., m. Tues. 26 Nov 1867 at Rock Spring Church by Rev. Dr. Morrison (AI 29 Nov 1867)

HAMILTON, E. A. (Miss) and Charles W. Lee, both of Harford Co., m. 27 Jul 1870, in Baltimore, by Rev. P. C. Brooks (AI 2 Dec 1870 and HD 2 Dec 1870)

HAMILTON, H. E. (Mrs.), see "Thomas G. Howard," q.v.

HAMMOND, DOMINICK, see "Nellie Hammond," q.v.

HAMMOND, NELLIE E. (Miss), dau. of Dominick Hammond, of Baltimore Co., and James H. Wann, of Harford Co., m. 3 Dec 1868 at the Green Street M. P. Church by Rev. T. D. Valiant (HD 1 Jan 1869 and AI 1 Jan 1869)

HANCOCK, A. M., see "David E. Thomas, Jr.," q.v.

HANKS, HANNAH E., see "Hannah E. Hauks (Hawks)," q.v.

HANNA, ALEXANDER, brother of Robert N. Hanna, died almost instantly last Wed. 7 Jun 1865 while superintending the cutting of some timber from their farm about 1 mile from Churchville; in felling a tree in the woods, it caught against another, a limb of which was broken off, falling on Mr. Hanna and causing his death, in his 65th year [information contained in two notices in this newspaper] (AI 9 Jun 1865)

HANNA, ANNA MARIA, dau. of William Hanna, Jr., of Churchville, and J. Wesley Hanna m. Thurs. 26 Nov 1857 in Baltimore at the Second Presbyterian Church by Rev. Dr. Happer, of Canton, China (SA 5 Dec 1857)

HANNA, H. ELLEN (Miss) and Amentis T. Patterson, both of Harford Co., m. 12 Mar 1857 by Rev. William Finney (HD 20 Mar 1857)

HANNA, J. WESLEY and Anna Maria Hanna, dau. of William Hanna, Jr., of Churchville, m. Thurs. 26 Nov 1857 in Baltimore at the

Second Presbyterian Church by Rev. Dr. Happer, of Canton, China (SA 5 Dec 1857)

HANNA, JAMES A., see "Jane Hanna," q.v.

HANNA, JANE, eldest dau. of James A. Hanna, died Fri. 25 Sep 1863, aged 8 years (SA 9 Oct 1863)

HANNA, JANE, wife of William Hanna, Sr., died Mon. 11 Jan 1868 *[sic]* near Bel Air, in her 76th year (AI 15 Jan 1869)

HANNA, JANE, see "Eliza Ann Smith," q.v.

HANNA, JOHN CALVIN and Miss Lucretia G. Mechem, both of Harford Co., m. 22 Dec 1859 by Rev. W. F. P. Noble (SA 31 Dec 1859); see "Lucretia G. Hanna," q.v.

HANNA, LUCRETIA G., wife of John C. Hanna and dau. of William Mechem, died Mon. 24 Oct 1870, in her 34th year; one obituary contains a brief memorial (AI 28 Oct 1870 and HD 28 Oct 1870)

HANNA, R. SUSAN (Miss) and James O. Forwood, both of Harford Co., m. Tues. 26 Mar 1867, in Baltimore, by Rev. Dr. Hays (AI 5 Apr 1867)

HANNA, ROBERT, died Wed. 15 Apr 1868 at his residence near Fountain Green, in his 81st year (AI 17 Apr 1868); the administrator's notice stated that creditors must exhibit their legal vouchers by 5 Sep 1869 to Stephen B. Hanna, admin. (AI 11 Sep 1868)

HANNA, ROBERT E. and Florence Slee, both of Harford Co., m. 12 Sep 1867 (AI 20 Sep 1867)

HANNA, ROBERT N., see "Alexander Hanna," q.v.

HANNA, STEPHEN B., see "Robert Hanna," q.v.

HANNA, WILLIAM, see "Eliza Ann Smith" and "Anna Maria Hanna" and "Jane Hanna," q.v.

HANSON, A. B. and Miss Annie E. Middleton, both of Harford Co., m. 1 Dec 1864 by Rev. Hays (AI 9 Dec 1864)

HANSON, ANNA E. (Mrs.), wife of Foard B. Hanson, died Wed. 16 Mar 1864 at Churchville (AI 18 Mar 1864)

HANSON, F. B. and M. C. Wakeland, both of Harford Co., m. 10 Jan 1867 by Rev. J. S. Stuchell (AI 18 Jan 1867)

HANWAY, FRANK and H. J. Forwood, both of Harford Co., m. Thurs. 26 Mar 1862 at Rock Spring Church by Rev. R. J. Keeling (SA 3 Apr 1863)

HANWAY, HATTIE E. (Miss) and John G. Rouse, both of Harford Co., m. Wed. 25 Apr 1866 by Rev. J. K. Nichols (AI 4 May 1866)

HANWAY, THOMAS, died Sun. 27 Jul 1862 at his residence near Harford Furnace (SA 2 Aug 1862); see "Edward Ashton," q.v.

HANWAY, WASHINGTON, died ---- (date not given) and was removed from the voter registration list in the 4th District in 1871 (HR 3 Nov 1871)

HARDESTY, MARY C., died ---- (date not given) and the administrator's notice stated that creditors must exhibit their legal vouchers by 7 Jan 1871 to Richard C. Hardesty and H. Clay Dallam, admins. (AI 14 Jan 1870)

HARKINS, CLARENCE K., youngest son of John H. Harkins, died 15 Oct 1865 at the residence of William Harkins, in Darlington, aged 7 months and 14 days (AI 27 Oct 1865)

HARKINS, ELIZZIE R., wife of John H. Harkins, died 23 Mar 1865 at Churchville, in her 31st year; obituary contains a poem written "By A Sincere Friend" (AI 31 Mar 1865)

HARKINS, HESTER J. (Miss) and John T. Ward, both of Harford Co., m. 20 May 1868 by Rev. D. A. Shermer at the Methodist Protestant Church in Bel Air (AI 22 May 1868)

HARKINS, HETTIE (Miss) and Martin J. Purselle, Esq., both of Harford Co., m. Thurs. 7 Sep 1865 at 4 p.m., at the residence of John Rogers, Esq., by Rev. A. H. Greenfield (AI 15 Sep 1865)

HARKINS, HOWARD, son of John H. and Sallie E. Harkins, died 7 Sep 1870, aged 7 months and 22 days; one obituary contains a short poem (AI 30 Sep 1870; HD 23 Sep 1870 states he died 5 Sep 1870)

HARKINS, JOHN, see "Howard Harkins," q.v.

HARKINS, JOHN A. and Miss Lizzie K. Toy, dau. of John Toy, Esq.., of Baltimore Co., m. 3 Mar 1859 by Rev. Hart (SA 12 Mar 1859)

HARKINS, JOHN H. and Miss Sallie E. Toy, both of Harford Co., m. 11 Nov 1868 by Rev. R. A. Norris (AI 18 Dec 1868); see "Clarence K. Harkins" and "Elizzie R. Harkins," q.v.

HARKINS, JOSEPH AUGUSTUS (Captain) and Miss Lurenna Slade Robinson, both of Harford Co., m. 21 Dec 1865 by Rev. J. K. Nichols (AI 5 Jan 1866)

HARKINS, LAVINIA ANN, third dau. of William and Martha A. Harkins, died 15 Feb 1859 at 6 p.m., after a lingering illness, aged 19 years and 6 months; obituary contains a short poem (SA 26 Feb 1859)

HARKINS, MARTHA, youngest dau. of William and Martha A. Harkins, died Sun. 9 Feb 1863 at 1½ o'clock in the morning, aged 16 years and 4 months; obituary contains a memorial written by "J.W.H." (SA 13 Feb 1863)

HARKINS, SALLIE, see "Howard Harkins," q.v.

HARKINS, WILLIAM, see "Lavinia Ann Harkins" and "Clarence K. Harkins" and "Martha Harkins," q.v.

HARLAN, DAVID, see "Oleita Herbert Harlan" and "Philip Lawson Lee," q.v.

HARLAN, MARGARET, see "Oleita Herbert Harlan," q.v.

HARLAN, OLEITA HERBERT, only dau. of Surgeon David Harlan, U.S.N., and Margaret R. Harlan, died 23 Aug 1866 in Harford Co., of typhoid fever, aged 18 (AI 31 Aug 1866)

HARLEY, JOHN, see "John Murphy," q.v.

HARMAN, AGNES E. and John Hitchcock m. 7 Apr 1868 by Rev. Thomas M. Cathcart (AI 17 Apr 1868)

HARP, KATE A (Miss), of Philadelphia, and Arthur C. DeSwan, of Harford Co., m. 24 Nov 1870 at the residence of the bride's parents, No. 1026 Brown St., Philadelphia, by Rev. John Pleasonton DuHammell (AI 16 Dec 1870)

HARRIS, ANDREW W., of Cecil Co., and Letitia J. Scarborough, of Harford Co., m. Fri. 27 Jul 1866 in Elkton by Rev. M. D. Kurtz (AI 10 Aug 1866)

HARRIS, GEORGE, see "Alexander Russum" and "Benjamin Shears" and "George Roberts," q.v.

HARROD, WILLIAM, died Mon. 21 Apr 1862, in his 74th year; for many years prior to his death he had been the Crier of the Circuit Court for Harford Co. (SA 26 Apr 1862)

HARRY, JOHN, died ---- (date not given) and the administrator's notice stated that creditors must exhibit their legal vouchers by 1 Aug 1848 to Joel Harry, admin. (HM 13 Jan 1848)

HARRYMAN, HEZEKIAH, died ---- (date not given) and the administrator's notice stated that creditors must exhibit their legal vouchers by 16 Jul 1864 to William W. Harryman, admin. (SA 17 Jul 1863)

HARRYMAN, LAURA (Miss) and John J. Alexander, both of Harford Co., m. 19 Oct 1871 at the Presbyterian Church in Bel Air by Rev. Finney (HD 20 Oct 1871)

HARRYMAN, MR., see "Adam Treusch," q.v.

HARRYMAN, WILLIAM W., died Fri. morning last week [age not given]; he had been an invalid for 2 years and confined to his bed by his disease, which was of the nature of neuralgia or an acute nervous affection *[sic]* from which his sufferings were of the most intense character (AI 29 Oct 1869); he was subsequently removed from the voter registration list in the 3rd District in 1870 (HR 28 Oct 1870)

HART, ASA, died 20 Aug 1865 at the residence of John V. St. Clair in Harford Co., in his 76th year (AI 10 Nov 1865)

HART, SARAH, died ---- (date not given) and the administrator's notice stated that creditors must exhibit their legal vouchers by 12 Jun 1869 to Isaac H. Cairnes, admin. (AI 19 Jun 1868)

HARTMAN, ALBERT D., was killed last Thurs. about 7:30 p.m. in Loganville, 7 miles south of York, PA; the wagon of George Hartman, Jr. had collided with a wagon driven by Michael Hartman whose son Albert D. Hartman was walking nearby when the collision occurred; an argument sprang up and George struck Albert in the head with a club or other weapon; Albert recently kept a store at the corner of George and King Sts.; both assailants were about age 23 and were distant relatives; all resided in Springfield Twp.; Albert died of his injury at 11 p.m.; George was arrested by Constable Wallick and put in jail by Squire Treger to await the action of the law (HR 11 Feb 1869)

HARTMAN, GEORGE, see "Albert D. Hartman," q.v.

HARTMAN, GEORGE, died ---- (date not given) and the administrator's notice stated that creditors must exhibit their legal vouchers by 24 Sep 1862 to Samuel H. Birckhead, admin. (SA 28 Sep 1861)

HARTMAN, GEORGE, died ---- (date not given) and was removed from the voter registration list in the 4th District in 1870 (AI 4 Nov 1870)

HARTMAN, MICHAEL, see "Albert D. Hartman," q.v.

HARVEY, SUSIE (Miss), of Harford Co., and John H. Lowe, of Baltimore, m. 9 Jul 1868 at the Christian Church in Baltimore by Rev. Alfred N. Gilbert (AI 17 Jul 1868)

HARWARD, ANNA "ANNIE" E., wife of Walter Harward, died Sun. 7 Aug 1870, at Abingdon, in her 37th year (AI 19 Aug 1870 and HD 19 Aug 1870); see "Clara Edna Harward" and "Lillian Helen Harward," q.v.

HARWARD, CLARA EDNA, youngest dau. of Walter and Annie E. Harward, died Tues. 15 Feb 1870, aged 2 years and 1 month (HD 25 Feb 1870 and AI 25 Feb 1870)

HARWARD, JAMES H., son of William H. and Kate F. Harward, died 5 Apr 1869 in the afternoon, near Churchville, aged 18; one obituary contains a brief memorial and poem written by "S.W." (AI 9 Apr 1869); another obituary contains a lengthy memorial written by "A Friend" (HD 16 Apr 1869)

HARWARD, KATE, see "James H. Harward" and "Walter Edwin Harward," q.v.

HARWARD, LILLIAN HELEN, dau. of Walter and Annie E. Harward, died Sun. 27 Feb 1870, after a brief illness, aged 6 years and 3 months (AI 11 Mar 1870)

HARWARD, WALTER, see "Clara Edna Harward" and "Lillian Helen Harward" and Anna E. Harward," q.v.

HARWARD, WALTER EDWIN, son of William H. and Kate F. Harward, died 5 Apr 1870, aged 4 years and 6 months; one obituary contains a short poem (AI 8 Apr 1870 and HD 15 Apr 1870)

HARWARD, WILLIAM, see "James H. Harward" and "Walter Edwin Harward," q.v.

HARWARD, WILLIAM C., of Philadelphia, formerly of Harford Co., and Miss E. Dora Zimmerman, youngest dau. of John and Elizabeth Zimmerman, m. 9 Apr 1870 at the residence of the bride's father in Baltimore Co. (HD 15 Apr 1870)

HAUKS (HAWKS), HANNAH E., of Harford Co., and William S. Rushmore, of Queen's Co., NY, m. 3 Oct 1867, at Robert Bound's, by Rev. W. M. Meminger [two marriage notices, one of which mistakenly gave his name as "Rushwood" and another which mistakenly gave her name as "Hanks"] (AI 11 Oct 1867 and 18 Oct 1867)

HAWKINS, JOHN W., see "John H. Russell," q.v.

HAYES, LYDIA B. (Miss) and Edward H. Hall, both of Harford Co., m. Thurs. 10 Feb 1870, in Emmanuel Church, by Rev. William E. Snowden [marriage notice indicated "No cards"] (AI 18 Feb 1870)

HAYGHE. H. C., died ---- (date not given) and was removed from the voter registration list in the 4th District in 1870 (HR 1 Nov 1870)

HAYS, ARCHER (Doctor), formerly of Harford Co., son of the late N. W. S. Hays, died 26 Sep 1870 near Rodney, Mississippi, of typhoid fever; he graduated from the Maryland Univ. School of Medicine, went South some years before the war, and served as a surgeon in the Confederate Navy; he leaves a widow and several children (AI 14 Oct 1870)

HAYS, Dr., see "William L. Cole," q.v.

HAYS, ELLEN M. (Miss), of Harford Co., David C. Robinson, of California, m. Wed. 24 Aug 1870, at Dublin Southern Methodist Church, Harford Co., by Rev. Crawford [Easton, MD papers please copy] (AI 26 Aug 1870)

HAYS, FRANCES S. (Miss), dau. of Thomas A. Hays, Esq., of Harford Co., and Alexander Fulford, of Baltimore, m. 16 Mar 1847 by Rev. Dr. Wyatt (HM 19 Mar 1847)

HAYS, G. T. (Mrs.), see "Noah Phillips," q.v.

HAYS, GEORGE T., see "Mary A. M. Hays," q.v.

HAYS, MARY A. M. (Miss), oldest dau. of the late Rev. Dr. Hays, of Virginia, and granddau. of the late Dr. Henry Baker, of Frederick Co., died ---- (date not given) at the residence of her brother-in-law Dr. George T. Hays (HD 20 Jun 1856)

HAYS, MRS. THOMAS A., relict of the late Thomas A. Hays, died Wed. evening 6 Apr 1870 [age not given]; funeral will take place from her late residence to Rock Spring Church on Sat. 9 Apr 1870 at 10 a.m. (AI 8 Apr 1870)

HAYS, N. W. S., died Mon. 20 Apr 1863 at his residence in Harford Co., in his 77th year (SA 24 Apr 1863); see "Archer Hays" and "Samuel Galloway," q.v.

HAYS, NANCY (Mrs.), an aged lady of Richmond, VA, was found in her home dead, one day last week, having died from starvation, it was ascertained, some three weeks before the fact became known; her husband was living with her, but was demented to such a degree as not to be able to appreciate the sad state of affairs, and was almost dead himself from starvation, when found (AI 15 Apr 1870)

HAYS, THOMAS A., died Sun. morning 26 Jul 1868 at half past 1 o'clock, leaving a wife and 7 children (AI 7 Aug 1868); see "Mrs. Thomas A. Hays" and "Frances S. Hays" and "Samuel Galloway," q.v.

HAYWARD, DR., see "Henry Frederick," q.v.

HAYWARD, THOMAS, of Harford Co., and Miss Helen M. Bussey, of Baltimore, m. 4 Aug 1864 by the Very Rev. Dr. Coskery, at the Archbishop's residence (AI 12 Aug 1864)

HAZLETT, JOHN C. and Miss Susan J. Ayers, both of Harford Co., m. Wed. 28 Jul 1869 by Rev. D. A. Shermer (AI 13 Aug 1869)

HEAPS, SARAH J. (Miss) and Samuel M. Whiteford, both of Harford Co., m. 14 Dec 1865 by Rev. Smith (AI 22 Dec 1865)

HEATH, B. F., see "Elizabeth Bailey" and "John L. Hunt," q.v.

HEATH, JUDGE, see "Lizzie Bailey," q.v.

HEATON, JOHN, died ---- (date not given) and the executor's notice stated that creditors must exhibit their legal vouchers by 16 Sep 1868 to Nelson Merryman and John Heaton, execs. (AI 20 Sep 1867)

HEBRON, LEVIN D. (Reverend), of the East Baltimore Conference, and Miss Sallie P. Belt, of Montgomery Co., m. on Tues. 11 Jan 1859 at Clarksburg M. E. Church by Rev. Dr. Thomas B. Sargent (SA 22 Jan 1859)

HECK, LIZZIE and John Axer, both of Harford Co., m. 27 Jan 1866 by Rev. W. F. Brand, rector of St. Mary's Church (AI 2 Feb 1866)

HEMP, ELIZABETH, wife of Thomas Hemp, died 14 Apr 1845 (HM 18 Apr 1845)

HENDERSON, GEORGE, see "John H. Chauncey," q.v.

HENDON, ELIZABETH (Miss) and James T. Gorrell, both of Harford Co., m. 2 Aug 1871 at the Washington House in Bel Air by Rev. T. M. Cathcart (HD 4 Aug 1871)

HENLEY, MARTIN, died ---- (date not given) and the administratrix's notice stated that creditors must exhibit their legal vouchers by 30 Jan 1868 to Mary Henley, admx. (AI 8 Feb 1867)

HENRY, DANIEL, died 25 Oct 1862 at his residence, 9½ miles on the Philadelphia Turnpike in Baltimore Co., of heart disease and typhoid fever (SA 8 Nov 1862)

HENRY, EMMA V. (Miss) and J. Albert Francies, both of Baltimore Co., m. 14 May 1871 in Towsontown at the residence of the bride's mother by Dr. F. M. Hawkins of the Christian Church (HR 23 Jun 1871)

HENRY, ROBERT, see "Lewis Horton," q.v.

HENZE, AUGUSTUS, see "Charles Saalfield," q.v.

HERBERT, GEORGE, see "Jane Herbert," q.v.

HERBERT, JANE, widow of George Herbert, died Wed. 22 Jul 1863, aged 93 (SA 31 Jul 1863)

HERBERT, R. C., of Perrymansville, and Lottie Whistler, of Harford Co., m. 11 Jan 1866, at the house of Mr. Whistler, by Rev. J. K. Nichols (AI 26 Jan 1866)

HERMAN, WILLIAM, infant son of Margaret A. and William Herman, died 5 Sep 1862 in Bel Air (SA 13 Sep 1862)

HERMAN, WILLIAM, see "Mary Jane Peterson," q.v.

HERRICK, SETHANNA ELIZABETH, only child of Major S. W. and Hattie S. Herrick, died 21 May 1867 in Beverly, NJ, of typhoid fever, aged 2 years and 11 months (AI 31 May 1867)

HERRING, GEORGE W., see "Ann Diffenderffer," q.v.

HERRMAN, JOSIAH M. and Miss Mary Jane Wann, both of Harford Co., m. 12 May 1868 by Rev. D. A. Shermer at the Methodist Protestant Church in Bel Air (AI 22 May 1868)

HERRMAN, MOLLIE L., only child of Joseph and Mary Jane Herrman, died 27 Jul 1870, aged 1 year and 4 days; one obituary contains a poem written by "S." and another obituary contains a short poem, author not named (AI 5 Aug 1870 and HD 5 Aug 1870)

HERRON, JAMES (Reverend), died Sun. 14 Jan 1866 at *Castle Blaney*, Harford Co., in his 98th year; he was a native of County Down, Ireland and a resident in the U. S. for the last 70 years (AI 19 Jan 1866)

HERRON, JAMES and Mrs. Elizabeth Reynolds, both of Harford Co., m. Thurs. 4 Jun 1863 by Rev. R. J. Keeling (SA 12 Jun 1863)

HERRON, LEVIN WATERS, son of Rev. L. D. and S. P. Herron, died 28 May 1871 in Darlington, aged 7 months (HD 30 Jun 1871)

HEVERN, SARAH JANE (Mrs.) and George Washington Barnes, both of Havre de Grace, m. Thurs. evening 7 Sep 1848 by Rev. Parkinson (HM 7 Sep 1848)

HEWITT, ELIZZIE (Miss), of Baltimore, and R. J. Rogers, of Harford Co., m. 27 Aug 1863 in Baltimore by Rev. T. D. Valiant (SA 4 Sep 1863)

HICKMAN, JOHN, of Chandlersville, Illinois, had recently murdered his fourth wife, having killed two of the first ones in PA (AI 31 Dec 1869)

HICKS, THOMAS HOLLIDAY, former Governor of Maryland, died Mon. 13 Feb 1865 in Washington, D.C., of paralysis, aged 65; he was born in Dorchester Co., MD and was a U. S. Senator at the time of his death; "though not a man of great intellect, he was nevertheless a man of much business talent" (AI 17 Feb 1865)

HILD, JOHN W., died ---- (date not given) and the administratrix's notice stated that creditors must exhibit their legal vouchers by 17 Oct 1869 to Sarah Hild, admx. (AI 23 Oct 1868)

HILDITCH, WILLIAM T. and Miss Cassandra Elliott m. 15 Feb 1870 at the residence of the bride's father, near Fountain Green, by Rev. George M. Berry (AI 18 Feb 1870)

HILL, DR., see "J. Glasgow Archer," q.v.

HILL, FRANCIS, died ---- (date not given) and the administrator's notice stated that creditors must exhibit their legal vouchers by 1 Apr 1859 to Herman Stump, Jr., admin. (SA 23 Oct 1858)

HILLES, JESSE JR. and Miss Mary C. Sadler, dau. of Thomas Sadler, all of Harford Co., m. Thurs. 19 Jan 1865 in Havre de Grace by Rev. W. C. Langdon (AI 10 Feb 1865)

HINDES, SAMUEL, Esq., died last Tues. evening at his residence in Baltimore, aged 62, well known head of the firm of Samuel Hindes & Son, hat manufacturers; he formerly filled the office of sheriff of the city and was connected with the Exeter Street Methodist Episcopal Church for many years; he had recently been chosen

Chief Manager of the Great National Camp Meeting to be held in Havre de Grace next month (HR 10 Jun 1870)

HINDS, ELIZABETH, relict of the late William Hinds, died 8 Aug 1863 near Shawsville, in her 92nd year (SA 4 Sep 1863)

HITCHCOCK, AMELIA, died ---- (date not given) and the administrator's notice stated that creditors must exhibit their legal vouchers by 6 Aug 1863 to Elijah Rockhold, admin. (SA 9 Aug 1862)

HITCHCOCK, CHARLES BAKER, died ---- (date not given) and the trustee's sale notice stated that his real estate will be offered for public sale on 10 Jun 1856 by Henry D. Farnandis, trustee (HD 16 May 1856); see "Elisha Lewis," q.v.

HITCHCOCK, JOHN and Agnes E. Harman m. 7 Apr 1868 by Rev. Thomas M. Cathcart (AI 17 Apr 1868)

HITCHCOCK, MARY M. (Miss), dau. of Charles B. Hitchcock, Esq., of Havre de Grace, and Rev. C. Cook m. Tues. 30 Jun 1868 at the Presbyterian Church in Havre de Grace by Rev. Galey (AI 10 Jul 1868)

HITCHELL, EDWARD, of Denton, Caroline Co., MD was murdered last Sat. by a Negro who was subsequently arrested and jailed, as reported in the *Centreville Observer* (AI 10 Dec 1869)

HOBBS, SARAH (Miss) and Wesley W. Levy, both of Harford Co., m. Wed. 29 Nov 1837 in Baltimore by Rev. E. L. Everett (HM 7 Dec 1837)

HOGG, ALEXANDER and Virginia M. Welbourne, both of Baltimore, m. 5 Jan 1865 in that city by Rev. John W. Williams (AI 13 Jan 1865)

HOLLAHAN, MRS., wife of Patrick Hollahan, buried last Sun. (HR 25 Dec 1868)

HOLLAND, ANN, dau. of Oliver S. and Susan J. Holland, died 15 Sep 1867 at the residence of her grandfather, in Harford Co., aged 3 months and 11 days; obituary contains a poem written by "Her Mother" (AI 4 Oct 1867)

HOLLAND, CASSANDRA (Mrs.), died 10 Aug 1871 at the residence of Ephraim Holland near Perrymansville, aged 116 years and without doubt the oldest person in the Co.; it is said she was quite active and in full possession of her faculties up to the time of her death (HR 25 Aug 1871)

HOLLAND, E. B. and Miss Joanna Rutledge, both of Harford Co., m. Thurs. 3 Aug 1865 at Rock Spring Church by Rev. J. H. D. Wingfield (AI 11 Aug 1865)

HOLLAND, ELIJAH B., see "Robert W. Holland," q.v.

HOLLAND, EPHRAIM, see "Cassandra Holland," q.v.

HOLLAND, FRANCES E. (Miss), dau. of Robert W. Holland, Esq., and Franklin Boarman, all of Harford Co., m. Thurs. 1 Jun 1865 by Rev. T. S. C. Smith (AI 9 Jun 1865)

HOLLAND, HENRIETTA (Miss) and James England, both of Harford Co., m. 27 Jan 1863 by Rev. E. Welty (SA 13 Feb 1863)

HOLLAND, JOHN and R. Virginia Bissell, dau. of the late Capt. William R. Bissell, all of Harford Co., m. 18 Oct 1865 in Bel Air by Rev. T. S. C. Smith (AI 27 Oct 1865); see "Oleita Holland," q.v.

HOLLAND, JOHN, died Sun. 11 Aug 1867 at his residence in Bel Air, in his 30th year; the administrator's notice of sale stated that his personal property would be sold, and a two-acre lot in Bel Air, with a new dwelling and substantial fencing, would be available for leasing on 31 Aug 1867 by R. Virginia Holland and Stevenson Archer, admins. (AI 23 Aug 1867)

HOLLAND, OLEITA, only child of John and R. Virginia Holland, died Thurs. 23 May 1867, aged 6 months; obituary contains a poem (AI 31 May 1867)

HOLLAND, OLIVER, see "Ann Holland" and "Samuel Ulysses Holland," q.v.

HOLLAND, R. VIRGINIA, see "John Holland," q.v.

HOLLAND, ROBERT W., died Sun. 3 Jun 1866 at his residence in Harford Co., in his 74th year; he served in the War of 1812 and was among the defenders of Baltimore; he later held successively the positions of County Commissioner, Judge of the Orphans' Court, and member of the State Legislature; he had been in declining health for several years and his death was therefore not unlooked for [newspaper contains two death notices]; the subsequent executor's notice stated that creditors must exhibit their legal vouchers by 25 Jun 1867 to Robert W. Holland and Elijah B. Holland, execs. (AI 8 Jun 1866 and 29 Jun 1866)

HOLLAND, ROBERT W., see "Frances E. Holland," q.v.

HOLLAND, SAMUEL ULYSSES, only child of Oliver S. and Susan J. Holland, and grandson of Mrs. England, died 17 Mar 1867 of congestion of the lungs, at the residence of his grandmother, aged 14 months and 15 days; obituary contains a short poem (AI 5 Apr 1867)

HOLLAND, SUSAN, see "Ann Holland" and "Samuel Ulysses Holland," q.v.

HOLLINGSWORTH, died P., see "Daniel Pope," q.v.

HOLLINGSWORTH, JOHN, see "James E. Demoss," q.v.

HOLLINGSWORTH, JOHN H., of Harford Co., and Miss Ellen Oden, of Baltimore, m. 5 Nov 1868 by Rev. D. A. Shermer (AI 13 Nov 1868)

HOLLIS, JACOB C., see "Lewis D. Michael," q.v.

HOLLOWAY, HATTIE W., dau. of William and Sallie A. Holloway, died Mon. 25 Aug 1867 at the residence of her father in Harford Co., aged 10 months and 14 days (AI 8 Nov 1867)

HOLLOWAY, HUGH S., died ---- (date not given) and the administrator's notice stated that creditors must exhibit their legal vouchers by 5 Sep 1869 to Henry C. Stump, admin. (AI 11 Sep 1868)

HOLLOWAY, KATE V. (Miss) and George J. Johnson, both of Harford Co., m. 24 Nov 1870 at *Rumney*, the residence of the bride's father, by Rev. Moore (HD 2 Dec 1870 and AI 2 Dec 1870)

HOLLOWAY, SALLIE, see "Hattie W. Holloway," q.v.

HOLLOWAY, WILLIAM, see "Hattie W. Holloway," q.v.

HOLLOWAY, WILLIAM and Sarah A. Hopkins, both of Harford Co., m. 11 Jan 1865 in Bel Air by Rev. H. L. Singleton (SA 15 Jan 1864)

HOLMES, CHARLES H., of Baltimore Co., and Miss Mary Virginia Lefevre, of Harford Co., m. Thurs. 5 May 1864 by Rev. N. H. Schenck, rector of Emanuel Church in Baltimore (AI 20 May 1864)

HOLMES, SELDA, dau. of Victor Holmes, Esq., and T. Lane Emory m. Thurs. 3 Nov 1864 at *Belmour*, the residence of the bride's father, in Baltimore Co. (AI 11 Nov 1864)

HOOKER, EDWARD G., of Harford Co., and Lizzie Horney, of Baltimore, m. 8 Mar 1859 in Baltimore by Rev. I. P. Cook (SA 19 Mar 1859)

HOOPES, CHARLES, died ---- (date not given) and the executor's notice stated that creditors must exhibit their legal vouchers by 13 Dec 1871 to William H. Hoopes, exec. (AI 16 Dec 1870)

HOOPES, DARLINGTON, see "Edith Cheyney" and "Joseph Trimble" and "Ann Trimble," q.v.

HOOPES, WILLIAM H., see "Charles Hoopes," q.v.

HOOPMAN, ISAAC, see "Lucinda A. Hoopman," q.v.

HOOPMAN, JACOB, died ---- (date not given) and the administrator's notice stated that creditors must exhibit their legal vouchers by 1 Jul 1857 to John W. Hoopman and Jacob W. Hoopman, admin. (HM 11 Dec 1856)

HOOPMAN, LUCINDA A., wife of Isaac Hoopman and dau. of the late Rowland and Catherine Rogers, died 24 Oct 1871 in Guernsey Co., Ohio, aged 64 (SA 10 Nov 1871)

HOPKINS, AMANDA, see "James Lee Hopkins" and "Charles Lee Hopkins," q.v.

HOPKINS, ANNIE, see "Mary E. Hopkins" and "Martha Hopkins" and "Elizabeth Hopkins," q.v.

HOPKINS, ANNIE (Miss) and C. Davis Alderson, both of Harford Co., m. Tues., 29 Sep 1863 by Rev. J. K. Kramer at the Grove Church, Harford Co. (SA 9 Oct 1863)

HOPKINS, CHARLES LEE, son of Amanda and the late Lee Hopkins, died 21 Jan 1869 in Harford Co., in his 22nd year; obituary contains a memorial written by "C." (AI 12 Feb 1869)

HOPKINS, ELIZABETH, youngest child of H. H. and Annie C. Hopkins, died Wed. afternoon 2 Mar 1870, aged 3 months (AI 25 Mar 1870)

HOPKINS, EPHRAIM, Esq., died 20 Jun 1869, in his 85th year, at his
residence near Darlington; a native of Harford Co., he lived upon
the estate inherited by him from his father and devoted his life to
agricultural pursuits; a gentleman of the old school, he has been
endeared to and connected with this community for a longer space
than is ordinarily allotted to mortals (AI 25 Jun 1869)

HOPKINS, GEORGE, see "Sarah A. Hopkins," q.v.

HOPKINS, GEORGE S. and Miss Annie M. McCummings, both of
Harford Co., m. 17 May 1870 in Dublin, MD by Rev. George M.
Berry (HD 3 Jun 1870)

HOPKINS, H. H., see "Mary E. Hopkins" and "Martha Hopkins" and
"Elizabeth Hopkins," q.v.

HOPKINS, JACOB II, died ---- (date not given) and was removed from
the voter registration list of the 2nd District in 1870 (AI 4 Nov 1870)

HOPKINS, JAMES LEE, died ---- (date not given) and the
administrator's notice stated that creditors must exhibit their legal
vouchers by 6 Nov 1864 to Amanda Hopkins, admx. (SA 27 Nov
1863)

HOPKINS, JAMES W. and Miss Maria L. Anderson, dau. of F. D.
Anderson, Esq., all of Harford Co., m. 26 Aug 1858 by Rev.
Dashiells (SA 4 Sep 1858)

HOPKINS, LEE, see "Charles Lee Hopkins," q.v.

HOPKINS, MARTHA, youngest child of H. H. and Annie C. Hopkins,
died Mon. morning 19 Jun 1871 at 1:30 (HD 30 Jun 1871)

HOPKINS, MARY ELIZABETH, youngest dau. of H. H. and Annie C.
Hopkins, died Wed. afternoon 2 Mar 1870, aged 3 months (HR 4
Mar 1870)

HOPKINS, MELISSA R. (Miss), eldest dau. of Richard Hopkins, of
Sunny Dell, Harford Co., and T. J. McCausland, of *Locust Valley
Farm*, Harford Co., m. 17 Dec 1867 at the Grove Church by Rev.
K. J. Kramer (AI 24 Jan 1868)

HOPKINS, PRISCILLA W., wife of Dr. Thomas C. Hopkins, died in
Havre de Grace on Thurs. 21 Sep 1871, in her 61st year (HD 29 Sep
1871)

HOPKINS, RACHEL, wife of the late Samuel Hopkins, of Harford Co.,
died last Sun., aged 72, shedding gloom over a large number of
relatives and friends (HM 1 Oct 1847)

HOPKINS, RICHARD, died ---- (date not given) and the executor's
notice stated that creditors must exhibit their legal vouchers by 18
Aug 1855 to John H. Mitchell, exec. (HM 14 Dec 1854); see
"Melissa R. Hopkins," q.v.

HOPKINS, ROBERT, see "Z. Taylor McDowell," q.v.

HOPKINS, SAMUEL, see "Rachel Hopkins," q.v.

HOPKINS, SARAH A. (Miss), dau. of George Hopkins, Esq., all of
Harford Co., and George W. Walker m. 26 Nov 1868 at Rock Run
M. E. Church by Rev. J. G. Moore, assisted by Rev. Groschell (AI 4
Dec 1868)

HOPKINS, SARAH A. and William Holloway, both of Harford Co., m. 11 Jan 1865 in Bel Air by Rev. H. L. Singleton (SA 15 Jan 1864)

HOPKINS, THOMAS C., see "Priscilla W. Hopkins," q.v.

HOPKINS, W. W. (Doctor) and Miss Cassie A. Gover, dau. of the late James A. Gover, Esq., all of Harford Co., m. Tues. 26 Nov 1867 at St. John's Church, Havre de Grace, by the rector, Rev. Henry B. Martin, M.D.. (AI 29 Nov 1867 and 6 Dec 1867)

HOPKINS, WAKEMAN B., see "William McNutt," q.v.

HOPPER, JAMES, see "William M. Hopper" and "William Henry Barnes," q.v.

HOPPER, JOHN A., see "Henry Steinrider," q.v.

HOPPER, MR., see "Unknown Colored Man," q.v.

HOPPER, SALLIE, see "William M. Hopper," q.v.

HOPPER, WILLIAM M., son of James and Sallie E. Hopper, died 9 Apr 1871 in his 3rd year (HR 14 Apr 1871)

HORNER, MARIA LANSDALE, wife of John W. Horner, of Philadelphia, and dau. of the late William M. Lansdale, of *Bloomsbury*, Harford Co., died Tues. morning 24 Aug 1858 (SA 4 Sep 1858)

HORNEY, LIZZIE, of Baltimore and Edward G. Hooker, of Harford Co., m. 8 Mar 1859 in Baltimore by Rev. I. P. Cook (SA 19 Mar 1859)

HORTON, LEWIS, died ---- (date not given) and the executor's notice stated that creditors must exhibit their legal vouchers by 25 Feb 1865 to Robert Henry, exec. (AI 25 Mar 1864)

HOSKINS, ANGELINE, see "Sarah Martha Hoskins," q.v.

HOSKINS, HARRIET A. (Miss) and David Preston m. 25 Dec 1867 at the residence of the bride's father, Jesse Hoskins (AI 3 Jan 1868)

HOSKINS, JESSE, see "Sarah Martha Hoskins" and "Sarah Johnson," q.v.

HOSKINS, MR., died last Sun. morning at his residence near Bel Air, at an advanced age, an exemplary and respectable citizen (HM 14 Feb 1840)

HOSKINS, SARAH MARTHA, eldest dau. of Jesse and Angeline Hoskins, died 14 Feb 1868, aged 25 (AI 21 Feb 1868)

HOSMER, ELBRIDGE WARREN, of Massachusetts, and Miss Indiana Clark Woodhouse, of Havre de Grace, m. Sun. evening 27 Jan 1867 at the Episcopal Church in Havre de Grace by Rev. Dr. Henry B. Martin (AI 1 Feb 1867)

HOWARD, EDWARD A., see "Henrietta Jane Falls," q.v.

HOWARD, GEORGE N., youngest son of Leonard J. and Sarah A. Howard, died Mon. 28 Aug 1871, aged 2 years, 10 months and 12 days (HR 8 Sep 1871)

HOWARD, LEONARD, see "George N. Howard," q.v.

HOWARD, LOUISA (Miss) and James E. Demoss, both of Jerusalem Mills, m. Sun. 15 Oct 1871 at 6 p.m., at the residence of John Hollingsworth, by Dr. F. Marion Hawkins (SA 13 Oct 1871)

HOWARD, MARY FRANCES, only dau. of Sarah and Leonard
Howard, died 11 Mar 1864, aged 5 years; obituary contains a brief
memorial and verse (AI 1 Apr 1864)

HOWARD, SARAH, see "George N. Howard," q.v.

HOWARD, THOMAS, died Thurs. 7 Jun 1864 at his residence (age not
given) in Harford Co. (AI 15 Jul 1864)

HOWARD, THOMAS G. (Captain), died 20 Nov 1867 at the residence
of Mrs. H. E. Hamilton in Bel Air, in his 70th year; he was one of
the oldest members of the Odd Fellow's fraternity; in his habits he
was essentially domestic, always preferring the peace and quiet of
home to the uncertain shiftings and turmoils of public life; he leaves
a large circle of relations and friends [Frederick papers please copy]
(AI 29 Nov 1867 and 6 Dec 1867), he was subsequently removed
from the voter registration list in the 4th District in 1868 (AI 9 Oct
1868)

HOWLETT, ANDREW J., died ---- (date not given) and the executrix's
notice stated that creditors must exhibit their legal vouchers by 12
Nov 1868 to Mary E. Howlett, extx. (AI 15 Nov 1867)

HOWLETT, ELIZA L. (Miss) and Archibald Wallace, both of Harford
Co., m. 9 Jan 1868 by Rev. T. M. Crawford [of York Co., PA] (AI
17 Jan 1868)

HOWLETT, JAMES G., son of the late Andrew B. Howlett, died 31
May 1870 at the residence of his mother, in Harford Co., aged 11
(AI 24 Jun 1870)

HUDSON, CHARLES (Doctor), of New York, and Helen Edith Chivrel,
only dau. of Mr. A. B. Chivrel, of Baltimore, m. 21 Jan 1866 at *Oak
Hill* in Harford Co. by Rev. S. Bartol [double wedding with R.
Jarrett Marston and May Ella Galloway] New York and Baltimore
papers please copy (AI 26 Jan 1866)

HUFF, ABRAHAM, died ---- (date not given) and the administratrix's
notice stated that creditors must exhibit their legal vouchers by 18
Jul 1866 to Guluelma P. Huff, admx. (AI 21 Jul 1865)

HUFF, SARAH R. (Miss), and William J. Thompson, both of Harford
Co., m. 11 Jan 1870 by Rev. George M. Berry at the residence of
the bride (HD 11 Feb 1870 and AI 21 Jan 1870)

HUGHES, AMOS, see "Carrie A. Hughes" and "Mary C. Hughes," q.v.

HUGHES, C. KATE (Miss) and George B. Silver, both of Harford Co.,
m. Tues. 28 Nov 1865, at the residence of the lady's father, by Rev.
Samuel Bayless (AI 8 Dec 1865)

HUGHES, CARRIE A. (Miss), dau. of Amos Hughes, Esq., and
Ambrose Cooley, Esq., all of Harford Co., m. 25 May 1871 at
Darlington in the Parsonage of the M. E. Church South by Rev. R.
Smith [*Baltimore Sun* please copy] (HD 2 Jun 1871, HR 9 Jun
1871)

HUGHES, EMILY J. (Miss), of Baltimore Co., and James T. Meads, of
Harford Co., m. 8 Jan 1863, at the residence of the bride's father, by
Rev. T. S. Smith (SA 16 Jan 1863)

HUGHES, GEORGE W., of Baltimore, died 14 Mar 1862 near St. Petersburg, Russia, in his 44th year; for many years he was in charge of the Patterson, NJ Railroad and during the past 12 years was General Superintendent of Machinery in the employ of Messrs. Winans, Harrison & Williams, of St. Petersburg (SA 10 May 1862)

HUGHES, JOHN, see "Virginia E. Hughes," q.v.

HUGHES, MARY C. (Miss), second dau. of Amos Hughes, and Robert P. Mitchell m. 15 Jan 1867 by Rev. J. K. Cramer (AI 1 Feb 1867)

HUGHES, PARKER M., died ---- (date not given) and was removed from the voter registration list in the 6th District in 1870 (HR 21 Oct 1870)

HUGHES, THOMAS S., of Baltimore, and Miss Sallie A. Silver, dau. of the late Samuel B. Silver, of Harford Co., m. 8 Jun 1865 at the bride's residence in Harford Co., by Rev. John K. Cramer (AI 16 Jun 1865)

HUGHES, VIRGINIA E., dau. of John Hughes, Esq., of Baltimore Co., and E. Madison Mitchell, of Prince George's Co., formerly of Harford Co., m. 22 Dec 1870, at the residence of the bride's parents, by Rev. J. A. Price, assisted by Rev. Samuel Register, D.D. (AI 30 Dec 1870)

HUGHES, WILLIAM T. and Miss Sophronia Barton, both of Harford Co., m. 12 Jan 1870, at the residence of the bride's father in Harford Co., by Rev. Joseph D. Smith (AI 21 Jan 1870)

HUGHES, ZENAS, died Sun. 30 Jan 1870 at his residence in Harford Co., in his 88th year; the subsequent executor's notice stated that creditors must exhibit their legal vouchers by 22 Feb 1871 to John H. Kirkwood, exec. (AI 18 Feb and 25 Feb 1870)

HUNT, JOHN L., of New York, and Miss Elizabeth Chamberlain, of Lapidum, Harford Co., m. 17 Nov 1859 at the residence of B. F. Heath, Esq., at Lapidum, by Rev. H. F. Hearn (SA 26 Nov 1859)

HUNTER, EDWARD, aged 50, convicted in New York of killing his wife, was sentenced to serve the remainder of his natural life in the State prison (AI 17 Jun 1864)

HUNTER, EMILY, of Baltimore, formerly of Harford Co., third dau. of George W. and Mary E. Hunter, and Zeley W. Porter, of Vermont, m. 11 Aug 1870 by Rev. S. B. Blake (AI 30 Sep 1870)

HUNTER, J. T., of Harford Co., and Mrs. Sarah L. Fuller, of Baltimore, m. 17 Mar 1863 in Baltimore by Rev. E. D. Owens (SA 1 May 1863)

HUNTER, MAGGIE (Miss), of Baltimore Co., and Robert A. Nelson, of Harford Co., m. 15 Oct 1868 by Rev. T. M. Cathcart (AI 23 Oct 1868)

HUNTER, WILLIAM K., of Baltimore, and Ella K. French, formerly of Baltimore, m. 12 Dec 1867 by Rev. John McCron (AI 10 Jan 1868)

HURST, CENIA and Wesley Barton, both of Harford Co., m. 26 Oct 1865 by Rev. E. Kinsey (AI 10 Nov 1865)

HUSBAND, JOSEPH, see "Hannah Waters Bageley," q.v.

HUSBAND, RACHAEL, see "Hannah Waters Bageley," q.v.

HUSBAND, SAMUEL, see "Hannah Waters Bageley," q.v.

HUSBANDS, SARAH G., relict of the late Joseph Husbands, died Fri. 18 Jul 1851, in her 71st year (HM 18 Sep 1851)

HUTCHINS, N. J. (Doctor), died Mon. 30 May 1864 at his residence, *Church Hill,* Baltimore Co., in his 50th year (AI 10 Jun 1864)

HUTCHINSON, ANNIE M. (Mrs.), of Harford Co., and Elijah B. Phipin, of Wicomico Co., MD, m. 28 Apr 1869 at the M. E. Parsonage. Bel Air, by Rev. George M. Berry (HD 7 May 1869 and AI 14 May 1869)

HUTCHINSON, JOSEPH, see "Joseph B. Alexander," q.v.

HUTTON, GILPIN O. and Miss Fanny Kirk, both of Harford Co., m. 5 Dec 1867 in the Presbyterian Church, Bel Air, by Rev. T. S. C. Smith (AI 13 Dec 1867)

HYNES, DAVID S., of Baltimore, and Miss Annie Z. Cochran, of Mount Vernon, Baltimore Co., m. 4 Jul 1870 by Rev. P. B. Reese (AI 12 Aug 1870)

ILEY, JACOB and Miss Lucinda Warner, both of Harford Co., m. 6 Dec 1859 by Rev. Zulauf (SA 31 Dec 1859)

IRWIN, DEBORAH L., wife of the late Capt. Jesse Irwin, died 19 Mar 1870 in Havre de Grace at the residence of her son-in-law John Hopkins, in her 68th year (HR 22 Apr 1870)

IRWIN, JESSE, see "Deborah L. Irwin," q.v.

IVES, ALBERT, son of Thomas J. Ives, Esq., died last Sun. at 6 p.m., at his father's residence in Havre de Grace, in his 19th year (AI 23 Aug 1876)

IVY, WILLIAM NASH, died 25 Jan 1859 of consumption, at the residence of his father in Louisiana, in his 27th year; he was born near Norfolk, VA, was educated at the Academy in Bel Air, and has spent much of his time in Bel Air since (SA 12 Feb 1859)

JACKSON, RICHARD I., died ---- (date not given) and his personal property will be sold at Darlington on 20 Apr 1871 by J. P. Silver, admin. (HD 7 Apr 1871)

JACKSON, SAMUEL, see "Charles Price," q.v.

JACOBS, HETTY S., widow of Rev. Charles W. Jacobs, of the Methodist P. Church, died 11 Nov 1861 at the residence of Hon. Judge J. H. Price (SA 16 Nov 1861)

JAMES, KATE (Miss) and James Sherndan, both of Harford Co., m. 31 Dec 1868, at home, by Rev. J. G. Moore (HD 19 Feb 1869 and AI 12 Feb 1869)

JAMES, MARY E., second dau. of Thomas James, Esq., died Fri. 29 Sep 1871 at the residence of Dr. John C. Polk in Abingdon (HD 20 Oct 1871)

JAMES, SAMUEL W., see "James Guyton," q.v.

JAMES, SOPHIA J. (Miss) and William P. Loflin, both of Harford Co., m. 20 Dec 1871, at Smith's Chapel, by Rev. J. H. Baker [double wedding with Thomas C. Mahan and Louisa Loflin] (AI 19 Jan 1872)

JAMES, THOMAS M., see "Sarah S. Forwood," q.v.

JAMES, WILLIAM S., formerly of Harford Co., died 16 Jul 1869 at his residence in Baltimore Co., in his 39th year (HD 23 Jul 1869 and AI 23 Jul 1869)

JARRETT, ARCHER H., Esq., of Bel Air, died Wed. night in Cumberland, MD when he fell from a window, according to a dispatch received by Hon. Stevenson Archer; none of the particulars have yet been received; the next edition of the newspaper reported Mr. Jarrett had been to Jordan Springs, VA and left there on his way to Bedford, PA, traveling in company with John Ritchie, Esq., of Baltimore; they reached Cumberland, MD on the Baltimore & Ohio Railroad on Wed. evening 7 Jul 1869 and decided to spend the night; each retired to his room on the third floor of the Revere House; some time later Mr. Ritchie was awakened by a noise of a person having fallen to the ground below and hastened to the window; he immediately gave the alarm and went below, shocked to find the nearly extinct body of Mr. Jarrett; it is supposed he had arisen from his bed and gone to the window for fresh air, as he was in the habit of doing this at home, being sometimes troubled with a difficulty in breathing; he somehow lost his balance and fell to his death [article contains more details about the accident]; he was brought home to Bel Air and interred Sat. morning at Christ Church (Rock Spring), the order of Free Masons turning out in large numbers; he was in his 44th year, a member of the Harford Bar for 15 or 16 years, and intimately connected with the business and political affairs of his native county; he leaves a widow (HD 16 Jul 1869; AI 9 Jul and 16 Jul 1869 and 17 Sep 1869)

JARRETT, ARCHER H., see "George Briggs" and "John T. Amos" and "Luther M. Jarrett," q.v.

JARRETT, DEVROW, died ---- (date not given) and was removed from the voter registration list in the 4th District in 1868 (AI 9 Oct 1868)

JARRETT, J. H., see "John Carville Bayne," q.v.

JARRETT, JULIA A., died ---- (date not given) and the administrator's notice stated that creditors must exhibit their legal vouchers by 17 Mar 1863 to Abraham Jarrett, admin. (SA 22 Mar 1862)

JARRETT, LEFEVRE, Esq., died very suddenly in that city on Fri. of last week; he was attacked with illness in a street car and being conveyed to his home lived but a few hours; heart disease was supposed to be the cause of death; he had just been re-elected to his second term; he leaves many relations and friends in Harford Co. (AI 4 Mar 1870); he was President of the Board of Police Commissioners; long article about his accomplishments (HD 4 Mar 1870)

JARRETT, LUTHER M., died ---- (date not given) and the trustee's sale notice stated that his real estate will be offered for public sale at the store of William B. Jarrett in Jarrettsville on 21 Mar 1857 by Archer H. Jarrett, trustee (HD 13 Mar 1857)

JARRETT, MARTIN L. (Doctor) and Miss Sarah F. Glenn, both of Harford Co., m. 31 Jan 1867, at Bethel, by Rev. B. F. Myers [double wedding; see "Thomas B. Jarrett," q.v.] (AI 15 Feb 1867)

JARRETT, THOMAS B. and Miss Kate H. Miller, both of Harford Co., m. 31 Jan 1867, at Bethel, by Rev. B. F. Myers [double wedding; see "Martin L. Jarrett," q.v.] (AI 15 Feb 1867)

JARRETT, WILLIAM B., see "Luther M. Jarrett," q.v.

JAY, ALICE M., eldest dau. of John and Mary Jay, of Harford Co., died 15 Oct 1870 (AI 21 Oct 1870)

JECKEL, ---- (two unnamed children with that surname), aged 8 and 15, were mortally injured [date not given] when the walls of a city school building at Alleghany City, PA, recently burned, and fell in on the following day (AI 31 Dec 1869)

JEFFERIES, BENJAMIN and Miss Rebecca E. Litzinger, both of Harford Co., m. 28 Jul 1868 by Rev. J. G. Moore (AI 7 Aug 1868)

JEFFERY, JOHN and Miss Naomia Calder m. 21 Mar 1871 at the residence of the bride's father in Harford Co. by Rev. A. H. Greenfield (HD 24 Mar 1871)

JEFFERY, JOSEPHINE, dau. of Thomas and S. A. Jeffery, died 17 Feb 1863 at *Westwood* in Harford Co., after a long and painful illness, aged 25 years and 24 days; obituary contains a brief memorial written by "M.V.K." (SA 13 Mar 1863)

JEFFERY, RACHEL E. (Miss) and William H. Beall m. 7 Oct 1869 at the residence of the Mr. Keith, in Bel Air, by Rev. George M. Berry [double wedding with William G. Jeffery and Mary E. Keith] (AI 8 Oct 1869)

JEFFERY, THOMAS AND S. A., see "Josephine Jeffery," q.v.

JEFFERY, WILLIAM G. and Miss Mary E. Keith m. 7 Oct 1869 at the residence of the bride's father, in Bel Air, by Rev. George M. Berry [double wedding with Rachel E. Jeffery and William H. Beall] (AI 8 Oct 1869)

JENKINS, MR., a farm laborer, died ---- (date not given) in Herefordshire, aged 107, leaving a dau. aged 85; he had his wits to the end and was a great smoker, some people will be happy to hear (HD 21 Apr 1871)

JENKINS, ELIZABETH A., died ---- (date not given) and the administrator's notice stated that creditors must exhibit their legal vouchers by 25 Jul 1860 to Daniel Scott, admin. (SA 24 Sep 1859)

JENNES, LOUISA (Miss) and Peter Galloway, both of Havre de Grace, m. 11 Jan 1865, at Jefferson Street M. E. Church in Baltimore, by Rev. Richard Norris (AI 20 Jan 1865)

JENNINGS, MARTHA A., dau. of John and Mary Jennings, died 8 Oct 1863 near Norristown, Harford Co., in his 31st year; obituary contains a memorial that mentions her parents, sisters and brothers (SA 30 Oct 1863)

JESSUP, JOSHUA, Esq., died Wed. of last week at his residence in Dulaney's Valley, Baltimore co., in his 63rd year; he was esteemed as a gentleman of great worth and integrity, and for some years was a director of the Mutual Fire Insurance Company of Harford [AI 3 Sep 1869)

JEWENS, WILLIAM, of Harford Co., and Miss Margaret Lyon, of Baltimore, m. 4 Feb 1869 in Baltimore by Rev. D. Bowers (HD 19 Feb 1869)

JEWETT, JOSEPH H., see "Ann Smith" and "Robert Stewart," q.v.

JOHNS, ----, died ---- (date not given), aged about 7, eldest son of Stephen S. Johns, Esq., of Harford Co., was playing in the barn a few days ago, climbed up a cart bed which was standing by the fence and it fell on him, crushing him and causing almost instant death (HD 8 May 1857)

JOHNS, AGGIE L. (Miss), dau. of Edward F. Johns, of Harford Co., and William Z. Eltonhead, of Baltimore, m. 23 Jan 1867 by Rev. William A. McKee (AI 1 Feb 1867)

JOHNS, EDWARD F., see "Aggie L. Johns," q.v.

JOHNS, HENRY H., died ---- (date not given) and the administrator's notice stated that creditors must exhibit their legal vouchers by 29 May 1862 to Marill J. Johns and John Streett, admins. (SA 22 Jun 1861)

JOHNS, LIZZIE, youngest dau. of the late Dr. Benjamin T. Johns, of Charles Co., MD, and Dr. Edward P. Keech, of Baltimore, m. Tues. 21 Nov 1865 in Baltimore, by Rev. Meyer Lewin, assisted by Rev. S. E. Grammer (AI 24 Nov 1865)

JOHNS, MARILL J., see "Henry H. Johns," q.v.

JOHNS, STEPHEN S., see "---- Johns" and "Moses Webster," q.v.

JOHNS, SUSIE (Miss), of Harford Co., and John L. Blake, of Baltimore, m. 10 Feb 1870 at Abingdon M. E. Church, by Rev. J. G. Moore [marriage notice indicated "No cards"] (AI 18 Feb 1870)

JOHNSON, AARON, died ---- (date not given) and the administrator's notice stated that creditors must exhibit their legal vouchers by 1 Jun 1864 to Thomas L. Beaumont, admin. (SA 5 Jun 1863)

JOHNSON, BARNET, see "Thomas Johnson," q.v.

JOHNSON, CHARLES A. and Miss Charlotte F. Lamb, both of Harford Co., m. 3 Sep 1868 by Rev. D. A. Shermer (HD 2 Oct 1868; AI 18 Sep 1868 and 9 Oct 1868)

JOHNSON, E. O., "Ruth Davis," q.v.

JOHNSON, GEORGE J. and Miss Kate V. Holloway, both of Harford Co., m. 24 Nov 1870 at *Rumney*, the residence of the bride's father, by Rev. Moore (HD 2 Dec 1870 and AI 2 Dec 1870)

JOHNSON, ISAAC, died ---- (date not given) and the administrator's notice stated that creditors must exhibit their legal vouchers by 19 Oct 1860 to E. Hall Richardson, admin. (SA 5 Nov 1859)

JOHNSON, JOHN, died Mon. 20 Nov 1865 at the residence of William B. Norris in Harford Co., at an advanced age; he was a prominent merchant and head of the various firms for more than a quarter of a century who conducted the Bush Store and Mills (AI 24 Nov 1865)

JOHNSON, JOHN L., died Thurs. 28 Sep 1871, in his 78th year; obituary contains a poem written by "M. A. J." (HD 20 Oct 1871)

JOHNSON, SARAH, formerly of New York, died "on third day morning, 7th of 10th month, 1871" at the residence of her son-in-law Jesse Hoskins, in her 84th year (SA 10 Nov 1871)

JOHNSON, SIDNEY, see "William M. Magraw," q.v.

JOHNSON, THOMAS (of Barnet), died 20 Oct 1867 at his residence in Harford Co., in his 41st year (AI 25 Oct 1867)

JOHNSON, THOMAS and Miss Jemima Cathcart, both of Marshall's District, m. Thurs, evening 19 Dec 1861 by Rev. E. Welty (SA 4 Jan 1862)

JOHNSON, URIAH, of Lycoming Co., PA, and Ann Elizabeth Bull, of Harford Co., m. Tues. 7 Nov 1865 by Rev. E. Kinsey (AI 10 Nov 1865)

JOHNSON, WILLIAM F. and Miss Hannah M. Richardson, both of Harford Co., m. 25 Nov 1869 by Rev. George M. Berry (AI 28 Jan 1870)

JOHNSON, WILLIAM, see "Henry J. Lackey," q.v.

JONES, AMOS, died ---- (date not given); the Equity Court ordered on 16 Mar 1847 that creditors must file their accounts with the auditor, S. Archer, before 1 May 1847; another newspaper notice reported the sale of his property by Henry W. Archer, Trustee, some time prior to 1 Jan 1847 (HM 2 Apr 1847)

JONES, AZARIAH, see "William Jones," q.v.

JONES, ELIZA A. and Aquilla H. David, both of Harford Co., m. Thurs. 23 Feb 1865 by Rev. T. S. C. Smith (AI 3 Mar 1865)

JONES, ELLEN C. (Miss) and Henry A. Smith, both of Harford Co., m. 27 Feb 1871 at the residence of the bride's father, John P. Jones, Esq., near Dublin, MD, by Rev. George M. Berry (HD 7 Apr 1871)

JONES, GEORGE W., see "Hugh Jones," q.v.

JONES, HENRY and Charlotte Doxen, both of Harford Co., m. 22 Aug 1867 by Rev. T. S. C. Smith (AI 6 Sep 1867)

JONES, HUGH, died ---- (date not given) and the executor's notice stated that creditors must exhibit their legal vouchers by 22 Mar 1865 to George W. Jones, exec. (AI 1 Apr 1864)

JONES, JAMES T., died ---- (date not given) and was removed from the voter registration list in the 5th District in 1871 (HR 27 Oct 1871)

JONES, JOHN P., see "Ellen C. Jones," q.v.

JONES, R. EMMETT, see "Coleman Yellott," q.v.

JONES, REBECCA, consort of the late Samuel R. Jones, died Sun. 15 May 1864 at her residence in Aberdeen, in her 48th year (AI 10 Jun 1864)

JONES, ROBERT, aged about 28, committed suicide on Mon. morning 5 Dec 1870 about 8 o'clock; he resided in the neighborhood of Prospect in the 5th District, Harford Co., and had been laboring under derangement of the mind for some time; an inquest by Squire Orr showed that, in the absence of his family, he suspended himself from a rafter in the garret of the house in which he resided; the jury rendered their verdict accordingly (AI 16 Dec 1870)

JONES, ROBERT R., died ---- (date not given) and the administrator's notice stated that creditors must exhibit their legal vouchers by 10 Mar 1869 to Hugh C. Whiteford, admin. (AI 13 Mar 1868)

JONES, RUFUS and Miss Priscilla Bull, both of Harford Co., m. 18 Aug 1870 at the M. E. Parsonage, Dublin, by Rev. George M. Berry (AI 25 Nov 1870)

JONES, SALLIE A. (Miss), dau. of Daniel Jones, Esq., of Harford Co., and George Austin Carlisle, of Baltimore Co., m. 2 Aug 1868 in Baltimore by Rev. Daniel Bowers [Richmond, VA papers please copy] (AI 7 Aug 1868)

JONES, SAMUEL R., see "Rebecca Jones," q.v.

JONES, SARAH E. (Miss) and John T. Davis, both of Harford Co., m. Thurs. 9 May 1867, in the Friendship M. E. Church, by Rev. W. M. Meminger (AI 17 May 1867)

JONES, SARAH E. and Joseph R. Burkins, both of Harford Co., m. 22 May 1866 at the M. E. Parsonage in Bel Air by Rev. W. M. Meminger (AI 1 Jun 1866)

JONES, WILLIAM, died ---- (date not given) and the executor's notice stated that creditors must exhibit their legal vouchers by 23 Aug 1870 to Azariah Jones, exec. (AI 27 Aug 1869)

JUDD, ANNIE, wife of John Judd, died at her residence in Harford Co., in her 71st year (AI 6 Mar 1868)

JUDD, JOHN, of Harford Co., and Miss Laura J. Walter, formerly of Baltimore Co., m. Tues. 24 Nov 1868 at St. Ignatius Church, near the Hickory, by Rev. P. F. O'Connor (AI 18 Dec 1868)

KANE, MARY, see "William Kane," q.v.

KANE, WILLIAM AND MRS. MARY KANE, although of the same name, were not related; both died suddenly last Thurs. night in the lower end of Havre de Grace and were buried in the Catholic Cemetery last Sun. (HR 20 May 1869)

KEAN, CASSANDRA (Miss) and Samuel M. Ady, both of Harford Co., m. Tues. 3 Jun 1862 at St. Ignatius Church by Rev. James McDevitt (SA 7 Jun 1862)

KEAN, H. LIZZIE and James H. Michael, both of Harford Co., m. 12 Feb 1863 at Spesutia Church by Rev. S. W. Crampton (SA 20 Feb 1863)

KEAN, JAMES, Esq., President of the last Board of County Commissioners, ex-Sheriff of Harford Co., and one of our most useful citizens, died last Fri. evening at his residence near Hickory; funeral took place Sun. morning at St. Ignatius Church, of which he was a prominent member; another article indicated the County Commissioners passed a resolution on 27 Mar 1871 in his honor (HD 31 Mar 1871); he was honored with a "Memorial of Respect" by the Harford County Commissioners on Mon. 27 Mar 1871 and it was published in the newspaper; sympathies were extended to his family; the memorial was written by James A. Fulton, Clerk (HR 31 Mar 1871); see "George Rider" and "Priscilla Kean," q.v.

KEAN, JOHN, died ---- (date not given) and the executor's notice stated that creditors must exhibit their legal vouchers by 15 Sep 1860 to Chloe Kean and James Kean, execs. (SA 24 Sep 1859)

KEAN, JOHN, died ---- (date not given) and was removed from the voter registration list in the 3rd District in 1870 (HR 28 Oct 1870)

KEAN, PRISCILLA (Miss), youngest dau. of James Kean, Esq., of Harford Co., died Fri. 15 Feb 1867; one obituary contains a poem written by "S.J.J." (AI 22 Feb 1867 and 8 Mar 1867)

KEAN, REDMAN, died ---- (date not given) and the notice to creditors stated they must exhibit their legal vouchers by 1 Aug 1857 to A. W. Bateman, atty. (HD 20 Feb 1857)

KEANE, MARY A. (Miss) and Jacob Minnick, both of Harford Co., m. 25 Aug 1870 at 7½ o'clock, in the M. P. Parsonage, Bel Air, by Rev. D. A. Shermer [Baltimore County papers please copy] (AI 30 Sep 1870)

KEATING, THOMAS J., of Queen Anne's Co., and Sallie F. Webster, dau. of Henry Webster, Esq., of Harford Co., m. 12 Jun 1862 in Harford Co. by Rev. Dr. A. Webster (SA 21 Jun 1862)

KEATINGE, GEORGE, editor of the *Madisonian* newspaper which was published some years ago in Havre de Grace, died 22 Jan 1868, in Havre de Grace, in his 68th year; one lengthy death notice stated, in part, that he served in the War of 1812 at Baltimore and also participated in the Battle of Bladensburg; it is said he published the first penny daily paper every published in Baltimore, after which he removed to Accomac Co., on the Eastern Shore of Virginia, and for a time published a paper in that county; about 1833 or 1834 he began publishing the *Madisonian* in Bel Air for some years and also established *The Port Deposit Rock* in Port Deposit ; about 1842 he commenced publication of the *Madisonian* in Havre de Grace for some years, sold out, and started *The Register* in Towsontown, Baltimore Co.; he soon abandoned it, returned to Havre de Grace, and started *The Visitor*, which was his last newspaper; he was frequently a candidate for public office, but never elected to any, we believe, except for serving as Clerk to the County Commissioners and as Justice of the Peace; he was born in Baltimore and was generous and kind, not without his faults, and a stranger to fear; some three or four years before his death, at an advanced age, he lost his mind, except at very short intervals, and so remained up to the time of his death [two of the articles misspelled his name as "Keating"] (AI 31 Jan 1868 and 7 Feb 1868 and 14 Feb 1868)

KEECH, EDWARD P. (Doctor), of Baltimore, and Lizzie Johns, youngest dau. of the late Dr. Benjamin T. Johns, of Charles Co.,

MD, m. Tues. 21 Nov 1865 in Baltimore, by Rev. Meyer Lewin, assisted by Rev. S. E. Grammer (AI 24 Nov 1865)

KEECH, JAMES K., see "Thomas Carroll," q.v.

KEECH, SAMUEL C., Esq., died Fri. 4 Nov 1864 of typhoid fever, at Charlotte Hall, MD, in his 26th year (AI 11 Nov 1864)

KEEN, AQUILLA D., died ---- (date not given) and the executor's notice stated that creditors must exhibit their legal vouchers by 30 Apr 1862 to George B. Keen and John K. Sappington, execs. (SA 24 Aug 1861)

KEEN, AQUILLA SR., died ---- (date not given) and the administrator's notice stated that creditors must exhibit their legal vouchers by 30 Jul 1845 to William J. Keen, admin. (HM 18 Oct 1844)

KEEN, BENEDICT H., see "George Bartol Keen," q.v.

KEEN, GEORGE BARTOL, died 6 May 1865 at his residence near Perrymansville, in his 28th year; obituary contains a poem written in Baltimore by "Mary" on 14 May 1865; the executor's notice stated that creditors must exhibit their legal vouchers by 23 May 1866 to Benedict H. Keen, exec. (AI 26 May 1865); see "Aquilla D. Keen," q.v.

KEEN, JAMES, see "Sallie Gaskins Keen," q.v.

KEEN, LOTTIE D. (Miss), dau. of Nathaniel B. Keen, of *Woodley Cottage*, Harford Co., and R. W. Preece, of Baltimore, m. 14 Nov 1867 at Grove Presbyterian Church by Rev. John C. Cramer (AI 29 Nov 1867)

KEEN, MARY, see "Sallie Gaskins Keen," q.v.

KEEN, NATHANIEL B., see "Lottie D. Keen," q.v.

KEEN, SALLIE GASKINS, dau. of James T. and Mary C. Keen, died 2 Jul 1867 at Perrymansville, Harford Co., aged 16 months (AI 12 Jul 1867)

KEEN, SUSAN E. (Miss) and George T. Wareham, both of Harford Co., m. Wed. 6 Jul 1853 by Rev. T. S. C. Smith, of Havre de Grace (HM 7 Jul 1853)

KEEN, TIMOTHY, Esq., died 25 Nov 1847 at his residence *Sidney Park*, Harford Co., in his 69th year, after a protracted illness of two years (HM 2 Dec 1847)

KEEN, WILLIAM J., see "Aquilla Keen," q.v.

KEITH, MARY E. (Miss) and William G. Jeffery m. 7 Oct 1869 at the residence of the bride's father, in Bel Air, by Rev. George M. Berry [double wedding with Rachel E. Jeffery and William H. Beall] (AI 8 Oct 1869)

KELCHNER, MAGGIE R. (Miss), dau. of Peter Kelchner, stove dealer, and Mr. J. N. Spencer, all of Havre de Grace, m. 25 May 1869, at the residence of the bride, by Rev. M. L. Smiser (AI 18 Jun 1869 and 25 Jun 1869, of which the former edition spelled the name as "Kelsner")

KELLER, SOPHRONA, died 17 Feb 1869, aged 17, at the residence of her mother in Baltimore Co. (HD 5 Mar 1869)

KELLOGG, SARAH (Miss) and William R. Wallis, both of Harford Co., m. 7 Feb 1867, at the residence of the bride's father, by Rev. W. M. Meminger (AI 15 Feb 1867)

KELLY, JULIA, see "Martin Kelly," q.v.

KELLY, MARTIN, died ---- (date not given) and the administratrix's notice stated that creditors must exhibit their legal vouchers by 7 Jun 1870 to Julia Kelly, admx. (AI 11 Jun 1869)

KELLY, WINFRED, died ---- (date not given) and the administrator's notice stated that creditors must exhibit their legal vouchers by 13 Oct 1865 to Alfred W. Bateman, admin. (AI 14 Oct 1864)

KELSNER (KELCHNER), PETER, see "Maggie R. Kelchner," q.v.

KEMP, ANNE T., dau. of Thomas Kemp, and Charles Russell, son of Thomas Russell, all of Harford Co., m. 3 Mar 1869 at the residence of the bride's father and according to the order of the Society of Friends (HD 19 Mar 1869)

KEMP, EDWIN CLYDE, youngest son of Thomas E. and Binnie G. Kemp, died at Oak Grove, Baltimore Co., aged 1 year, 5 months and 15 days (AI 19 Aug 1870)

KEMP, THOMAS, see "Anne T. Kemp" and "Edwin Clyde Kemp," q.v.

KENCADE, JOHN, died ---- (date not given) and was removed from the voter registration list in the 6th District in 1870 (HR 4 Oct 1870)

KENDLY, CHARLES B., died Thurs. 2 Feb 1865 at his residence in Harford Co., in his 36th year (AI 10 Feb 1865)

KENLY, OLIVER G. and Lou. E. Stewart m. 1 Oct 1867 at St. Vincent's Church by Rev. Father Myers (AI 11 Oct 1867)

KENNARD, HARKLESS (colored), died ---- (date not given) and was removed from the voter registration list in the 1st District in 1871 (HR 29 Sep 1871)

KENNARD, J. H., see "Edward A. Moore," q.v.

KENNEDY, JOHN P. (Hon.), of Baltimore, died last week at Newport, RI, while serving as Secretary of the Navy (AI 26 Aug 1870)

KENNEDY, JOHN S. and Margaret Polk, both of Harford Co., m. 2 May 1866, at Mr. J. Wann's, by Rev. W. M. Meminger (AI 4 May 1866)

KENNEDY, WILLIAM, see "George W. Magness," q.v.

KENT, GRIER, died ---- (date not given) and was removed from the voter registration list in the 4th District in 1871 (HR 3 Nov 1871)

KERBY, JAMES H. and Mary Louisa Love m. 26 Dec 1863 by Rev. William R. Mills (SA 20 Feb 1863)

KERNAN, JULIA (Mrs.), died 8 Mar 1863 in Baltimore, in her 33rd year (SA 20 Mar 1863)

KERR, ANN J. and David M. Dixon, both of Harford Co., m. Tues. 6 Jun 1865 by Rev. O'Connor (AI 9 Jun 1865)

KERR, FRANCIS D., of Harford Co., and Miss Elizabeth E. McCauley, of Anne Arundel Co., m. Sat. 7 Nov 1868 at St. John's Church, Baltimore, by Rev. Father McManus (AI 13 Nov 1868 and 20 Nov 1868)

KERR, HERMAN D., see "Lydia S. Kerr," q.v.

KERR, LYDIA S., wife of Herman D. Kerr, died 17 Sep 1866 in Harford Co., in her 67th year [*West Chester Jeffersonian* and *York Gazette* in PA please copy] (AI 28 Sep 1866)

KERR, PATRICK A., died 26 Oct 1866 in his 24th year, after a short but painful illness; obituary contains a memorial written by "A Friend" (AI 23 Nov 1866)

KEY, PHILIP BARTON, Esq., U. S. District Attorney, while conversing with a gentleman at the corner of Pennsylvania Ave. and 16th St. in Washington, D.C., was accosted by Daniel E. Sickles, U. S. Congressman from New York City, who, after a few words of altercation, drew a revolver and laid him dead at his feet [this lengthy article contains considerable details about Sickles' life (and wife), but very little about Key] (SA 5 Mar 1859)

KILGORE, JAMES and Miss Susan E. Whiteford, both of Harford Co., m. 9 Jan 1868 by Rev. T. M. Crawford, of York Co., PA, assisted by Rev. J. D. Smith and Rev. J. Y. Cowhick (AI 17 Jan 1868)

KILROY, JOHN, died Wed. 14 Apr 1868 at his residence, in his 79th year; a native of Castle Bar, County Mayo, Ireland, he came to this country about 4 years ago and was in all things an honest and upright man (AI 15 May 1868)

KIMBLE, A. W., see "Harriet Kimble," q.v.

KIMBLE, HARRIET, wife of A. W. Kimble, died 4 Jun 1866 near Harford Furnace, aged 49 (AI 15 Jun 1866)

KIND, MR., see "Miss Poplar," q.v.

KING, JOHN R. and Miss Elizabeth B. Robinson, both of Harford Co., m. 3 Jun 1858 by Rev. Thomas Stuart C. Smith (SA 19 Jun 1858)

KINNEY, T. M., see "A. J. McCausland," q.v.

KIRK, FANNY (Miss) and Gilpin P. Hutton, both of Harford Co., m. 5 Dec 1867 in the Presbyterian Church, Bel Air, by Rev. T. S. C. Smith (AI 13 Dec 1867)

KIRK, MARGARET A. (Miss) and William H. Smith, both of Harford Co., m. Wed. 3 Jun 1863 by Rev. Welty (SA 12 Jun 1863)

KIRK, THOMAS (colored), died ---- (date not given) and was removed from the voter registration list in the 1st District in 1871 (HR 27 Oct 1871)

KIRKWOOD, GEORGE C. and Miss Isabel R. Cairnes, both of Harford Co., m. Thurs. 3 Mar 1859 by Rev. T. S. C. Smith (SA 12 Mar 1859)

KIRKWOOD, ISABELLA C., wife of George C. Kirkwood, died 29 Jan 1870 in Harford Co., in he 28th year; she leaves 6 children, the youngest not two years old; obituary contains a short poem by "R.K." (AI 18 Feb 1870)

KIRKWOOD, J. HENDERSON, see "Miss Smith," q.v.

KIRKWOOD, JOHN B., died 4 Jul 1868 at his residence in Marshall's District, Harford Co., in his 65th year; the administrator's notice stated that creditors must exhibit their legal vouchers by 31 Aug 1869 to Robert Kirkwood, admin. (AI 4 Sep 1868); he was subsequently removed from the voter registration list in the 4th District in 1868 (AI 9 Oct 1868)

KIRKWOOD, JOHN H., see "James Cordrey" and "Lee Wilson" and "Zenas Hughes," q.v.

KIRKWOOD, ROBERT, see "John B. Kirkwood," q.v.

KLINESMITH, CAROLINE E. (Miss) and John D. Everett, both of Harford Co., m. 19 Jan 1865 at the Methodist Protestant Parsonage in Bel Air by Rev. R. Scott Norris (AI 27 Jan 1865)

KNIGHT, JOHN BARNES, died 25 Oct 1865 at his residence near Magnolia, aged 56; obituary contains a poem [Baltimore, MD and Martinsburg, VA papers please copy] (AI 10 Nov 1865)

KNIGHT, MARY (Miss) and David Parlett, both of Harford Co., m. 28 Dec 1865 by Rev. J. K. Nichols (AI 5 Jan 1866)

KNIGHT, WILLIAM F., of Clarke Co., VA, and Miss Sarah M. Gover, dau. of the late James A. Gover, Esq., m. Tues. 10 Dec 1867 at St. John's Church, Havre de Grace, by Rev. Henry B. Martin, M.D.. (AI 27 Dec 1867)

KNOTT, FRANCIS A. and Miss Susan Winfield, both of Bel Air, m. 28 Nov 1837 by Rev. Kirtz (HM 14 Dec 1837)

KOONIN, GEORGE, see "Peter Fitzner," q.v.

KRAMER, SAMUEL and Miss Matilda Shane, dau. of the late Rev. Joseph Shane, all of Baltimore, m. Mon. evening 21 Feb 1870 by Rev. Dr. Ryan, assisted by Rev. G. W. Cooper (AI 25 Feb 1870)

KUNKEL, JACOB (Hon.), formerly a member of Congress from Western Maryland, died last Thurs. in Frederick City, of consumption (AI 15 Apr 1870)

KURTZ, AUGUSTUS, died ---- (date not given) and the administrator's notice stated that creditors must exhibit their legal vouchers by 21 May 1858 to Robert Gailey, admin. (SA 1 Aug 1857)

KYLE, GEORGE H., of Baltimore, and Fannie Fendall Duvall, dau. of William B. Duvall, of Harford Co., m. 1 Jan 1867 at *La Vista* by Rev. J. H. D. Wingfield (AI 11 Jan 1867)

LACKEY, HENRY J. and Mary J. Bunce, both of Harford Co., m. 4 Jan 1866, at the house of William Johnson, by Rev. J. K. Nichols (AI 26 Jan 1866)

LAFFERTY, MR., a hand on one of Vandiver & Simmons' vessels, fell over board while rowing a small boat last Thurs. evening and drowned near the Furnace Wharf; he was known to be under the influence of alcohol at the time; his body washed ashore near the Old Bay Fishery one week later (HR 13 May 1869 and 20 May 1869)

LAMB, CHARLOTTE F. (Miss) and Charles A. Johnson, both of Harford Co., m. 3 Sep 1868 by Rev. D. A. Shermer (HD 2 Oct 1868; AI 18 Sep 1868 and 9 Oct 1868)

LAMB, JOHN, of New York, aged about 32, died suddenly at Wilson's Hotel on Baltimore St., near North, in Baltimore City; he checked in Sun. afternoon and at 4 a.m. his heavy breathing attracted those in

an adjoining room; Dr. J. F. Speck was called, but Lamb died at
6:30 a.m., apparently from heart disease, according to Dr. Speck
and Coroner Carr; the deceased had no identification papers, but
had registered as John Lamb (HR 11 Feb 1869)

LAMPLUGH, MAGGIE (Miss), died last Tues. after a long and painful
sickness; she was the fourth death in the Lamplugh family in the
last 15 months (HR 26 Nov 1868)

LANSDALE, WILLIAM M., see "Maria Lansdale Horner," q.v.

LAROQUE, EDWARD, see "Francis Delmas," q.v.

LAWDER, GEORGIANNA (Miss) and W. A. Myers, both of Havre de
Grace, m. 16 Jan 1869 at the Episcopal Church by Rev. H. B.
Martin (HR 28 Jan 1869)

LAWDER, SAMUEL, died ---- (date not given) and the administrator's
notice stated that creditors must exhibit their legal vouchers by 17
Dec 1863 to John B. Foy, admin. (SA 27 Dec 1862)

LEAGUE, WILLIAM, died ---- (date not given) in Baltimore, after a
short but severe illness (HM 7 Dec 1837)

LEAKLE, WILLIAM, recently appoint Leather Inspector for Frederick
City by Gov. Bowie, died with paralysis in that place one day last
week (AI 31 Dec 1869)

LEATTOR, M. C. and H. P. Sutor m. Wed. morning 13 Aug 1843, at St.
John's Church, by Rev. Billopp (HM 18 Aug 1843)

LEE, BETTIE, youngest dau. of the late Josiah Lee, Esq., of Bel Air,
died 4 Nov 1870 in Baltimore [age not given] (AI 18 Nov 1870)

LEE, CHARLES W. and Miss E. L. G. Bryarly m. 4 Jun 1857 at the
residence of Philip Gover, Esq., in Baltimore, by Rev. Isaac P.
Cook (HD 5 Jun 1857)

LEE, CHARLES W. and Miss E. A. Hamilton, both of Harford Co., m.
27 Jul 1870, in Baltimore, by Rev. P. C. Brooks (AI 2 Dec 1870 and
HD 2 Dec 1870)

LEE, DAVID, see "William P. Stephenson," q.v.

LEE, ELIZABETH C., dau. of Josh T. and Hannah R. Lee, died 4 Feb
1869, aged 2 months and 22 days (AI 26 Feb 1869)

LEE, FRANCES A. and Dr. William G. Wilson, both of Harford Co., m.
15 Apr 1867, at the residence of the bride's mother, by Rev. W. M.
Meminger (AI 26 Apr 1867)

LEE, GEN., see "Coleman Yellott," q.v.

LEE, GEORGE, died last Sat. evening, aged about 50; his body was
found in the woods about 2 miles from Bel Air last Sun. morning;
an inquest was held that day and the jury rendered a verdict of death
from intemperance and exposure (SA 8 Dec 1860)

LEE, HANNAH, widow of the Richard D. Lee, died Sat. 28 Mar 1868 in
Bel Air, in her 64th year (AI 3 Apr 1868); see "Roberta C. Fletcher"
and "Elizabeth C. Lee," q.v.

LEE, HARRY, and J. M. Sewell and Septimus Sewell, all of Abingdon,
drowned last Fri. when their boat capsized while crabbing on Bush
River near the P. W. & B. Railroad bridge; their bodies were

recovered for burial (HR 12 Aug 1869); another newspaper account gave the names of those involved as Dr. John C. Pope, James Cochran, James Cage, Washington Dorney and his two sons (not named), William George Diffenderffer, James M. Sewell, Septimus D. Sewell, Harry Lee and Josiah Lee (nephews of the last two named), Charles Sewell (son of Septimus D. Sewell), and a colored boy employed by the Sewells, plus two others (names unknown); Harry Lee, aged about 22, single, was buried in Greenmount Cemetery, with Rev. Henry Lee officiating; James Sewell and Septimus D. Sewell, both m. with families, were buried in Abingdon (HD 13 Aug 1869); another newspaper gave the names of the thirteen people as Dr. John C. Polk, James M. Sewell, Septimus D. Sewell, Harry Lee, Josiah Lee, George Diffenderffer, James Cochran, Wash. Dorney, Albert Dorney, Edward Hall, William Hall, James Cage, and a colored man in the employ of S. D. Sewell; it also contains more details about the accident, mentioning a colored man named Charles Gilbert who went to the sunken boat and brought in the body of James M. Sewell; he leaves a widow, but no children; he and S. D. Sewell were buried in the family burying ground near Abingdon; Harry Lee, aged about 22, son of the late Josiah Lee and brother of Josiah Lee, Jr., was found floating a considerable distance away; he and his brother had just returned from a tour through Europe; he was buried in Greenmount Cemetery in Baltimore (AI 13 Aug 1869)

LEE, HENRY, see "Harry Lee," q.v.

LEE, JOHN H. and Miss Mary Rodley, both of Baltimore, m. 16 Mar 1871 by Rev. Richard Norris (HD 31 Mar 1871)

LEE, JOHN N., died ---- (date not given) and the trustee's sale of lots of real estate in Havre de Grace will be held on 15 Jul 1871 (HR 16 Jun 1871)

LEE, JOHN T., see "William E. Lee," q.v.

LEE, JOSH T., see "Elizabeth C. Lee," q.v.

LEE, JOSIAH, see "Bettie Lee" and "Harry Lee," q.v.

LEE, NANNIE, see "Richard Dallam Lee," q.v.

LEE, OTHO S. and Miss Sallie B. Griffith, dau. of the late John L. Griffith, Esq., all of Harford Co., m. Thurs. 14 Mar 1867 by Rev. S. W. Compton (AI 22 Mar 1867); see "William Oldfield," q.v.

LEE, PHILIP LAWSON, died ---- (date not given) and the administrator's notice stated that creditors must exhibit their legal vouchers by 1 Aug 1848 to David Harlan, admin. (HM 13 Apr 1848)

LEE, RALPH S., died Wed. 12 Mar 1862 at Jerusalem Mills, aged 82; obituary contains information from the *Baltimore Sun* which stated he was a quiet and unobtrusive man, a member of the Society of Friends; his father and the elder Ellicott, who established Ellicott's Mills, were friends and neighbors in PA, from which they both migrated to Maryland about a century ago, the father locating

himself at Jerusalem in Harford Co. and Ellicott locating at
Ellicott's Mills, then in Anne Arundel Co. (SA 22 Mar 1862)

LEE, REBECCA, see "William E. Lee," q.v.

LEE, REVERDY, see "Richard Dallam Lee," q.v.

LEE, RICHARD D., see "Alice Parker" and "Hannah Lee," q.v.

LEE, RICHARD DALLAM, son of Reverdy J. and Nannie Lee, died 26
Oct 1870 at Rowlandsville, Red River, Texas, aged 4 (AI 25 Nov
1870)

LEE, ROBERT E. (General), died in Lexington, VA, last Wed. morning
at 9:30, of congestion of the brain, aged 63 years, 8 months and 22
days; a resolution was passed in his honor at the Masonic Temple in
Baltimore on 15 Oct 1870 by the officers, soldiers and sailors of the
Southern Confederacy residing in Maryland who served under him
during the war (HD 14 Oct 1870; AI 14 Oct and 21 Oct 1870)

LEE, SALLY B. (Miss) and Frederick W. Baker m. Thurs. 28 Dec 1865
in Bel Air by Rev. J. H. D. Wingfield (AI 5 Jan 1866)

LEE, SAMUEL M., see "Elizabeth Gover," q.v.

LEE, WILLIAM E., son of John T. and H. Rebecca Lee, died 12 Aug
1867, aged 3 weeks; obituary contains a poem (AI 23 Aug 1867)

LEFEVRE, MARY VIRGINIA (Miss), of Harford Co., an Charles H.
Holmes, of Baltimore Co., m. Thurs. 5 May 1864 by Rev. N. H.
Schenck, rector of Emanuel Church in Baltimore (AI 20 May 1864)

LEMMON, GEORGE, see "Margaret Lemmon" and "Zarvona
Anderson," q.v.

LEMMON, MARGARET, wife of George Lemmon, Sr., died Sun. 6
Aug 1866 in her 65th year [see "Zarvona Anderson," q.v.] (AI 18
Aug 1865)

LESTER, MARTHA, died ---- (date not given) and the administrator's
notice stated that creditors must exhibit their legal vouchers by 23
Jun 1871 to Herman Stump, admin. (AI 1 Jul 1870)

LETZINGER, JAMES, see "Elizabeth Brown," q.v.

LEVY, JOHN, died ---- (date not given) and the administrator's notice
stated that creditors must exhibit their legal vouchers by 8 Nov
1854 to Ezekiel Moulton, admin. (HM 19 Jan 1854)

LEVY, WESLEY W. and Miss Sarah Hobbs, both of Harford Co., m.
Wed. 29 Nov 1837 in Baltimore by Rev. E. L. Everett (HM 7 Dec
1837)

LEWIN, JOHN, died ---- (date not given) and the executor's notice
stated that creditors must exhibit their legal vouchers by 21 Nov
1869 to David Pyle, exec. (AI 4 Dec 1868)

LEWIS, ----, see "John Burwell Drummond," q.v.

LEWIS, A. J., see "Margaret W. Robertson," q.v.

LEWIS, ELISHA, died ---- (date not given) and the executor's notice
stated that creditors must exhibit their legal vouchers by 31 Jan
1869 to Hannah S. Lewis and Charles B. Hitchcock, execs. (AI 7
Feb 1868); he was subsequently removed from voter registration list
in 1869 (HD 22 Oct 1869 and AI 1 Oct 1869)

LEWIS, HANNAH S., see "Elisha Lewis," q.v.

LEWIS, MILTON T., of Lancaster, PA, and Miss Isadore Ross, of Harford Co., m. 29 Dec 1867 by Rev. T. M. Crawford, of York Co., PA (AI 17 Jan 1868)

LIDDELL, THOMAS, of Wisconsin, and Mary Rodham, of Harford Co., m. 28 Jan 1864, at the residence of the bride's father, by Rev. H. Singleton (SA 5 Feb 1864)

LILLY, JOHN, see "Sallie F. Lilly," q.v.

LILLY, SALLIE F., dau. of John Lilly, Esq., of Adams Co., PA, and Hugh Corrigan, of Harford Co., m. 7 Oct 1862 at the Church of the Sacred Heart in Conawago, Adams Co., by Rev. Father Lilly (SA 18 Oct 1862)

LILLY, WILLIAM T. and Miss Mary E. "Mollie" DeSwan, second dau. of Capt. C. DeSwan, all of Harford Co., m. 26 Apr 1866 in Baltimore by Rev. Dr. Bullock (AI 25 May 1866 and 1 Jun 1866)

LINCOLN, ABRAHAM, President of the United States, was shot by John Wilkes Booth at Ford's Theatre in Washington, D.C. on 14 Apr 1865 and died the next day [this newspaper contains two articles about the assassination, one from the *Baltimore Gazette* and one from the *New York Daily News*] (AI 21 Apr 1865) [Booth was a native of Harford Co.; articles about him, his family, and his death appeared in *The Aegis & Intelligencer* on 28 Apr 1865 and 5 May 1865, and part of his diary was published on 24 May 1867]

LINDER, MARY LOUISA, see "Samuel Freeborn," q.v.

LINDSAY, MARY "MOLLIE" (Miss), of Alleghany Co., PA, and Rev. John R. Paxton, the successor of Rev. William Finney, in charge of the Presbyterian Church at Churchville, m. 10 Nov 1870 in Alleghany Co. [two marriage notices in same newspaper] (AI 18 Nov 1870)

LINGAN, MARY SOPHIA, only dau. of John F. and Lizzie A. Lingan, died 2 Feb 1871, aged 2 years and 9 months; obituary included a short poem (HD 17 Feb 1871)

LITZINGER, REBECCA E. (Miss) and Benjamin Jefferies, both of Harford Co., m. 28 Jul 1868 by Rev. J. G. Moore (AI 7 Aug 1868)

LIVEZY, THOMAS, of Harford Co., and Miss Sylvania Stewart, of Philadelphia, m. 19 Aug 1868 by Rev. T. S. C. Smith (AI 4 Sep 1868)

LOCK, JOHN, said to have been the last soldier of the revolution belonging to the army who enlisted in Morristown, died at Chester [PA] on 12 Jun 1846, aged 96 (HM 25 Jun 1846)

LOFLIN, LOUISA (Miss) and Thomas C. Mahan, both of Harford Co., m. 20 Dec 1871, at Smith's Chapel, by Rev. J. H. Baker [double wedding with William P. Loflin and Sophia J. James] (AI 19 Jan 1872)

LOFLIN, WILLIAM P. and Miss Sophia J. James, both of Harford Co., m. 20 Dec 1871, at Smith's Chapel, by Rev. J. H. Baker [double wedding with Thomas C. Mahan and Louisa Loflin] (AI 19 Jan 1872)

LONG, HANNAH (Miss) and Daniel J. Downs, both of Harford Co., m. 17 Jan 1867, at the residence of Henry Long, by Rev. B. F. Myers (AI 15 Feb 1867)

LONG, HENRY, see "Hannah Long" and "John H. Long," q.v.

LONG, JOHN H., only son of Henry Long, died 14 Sep 1871, aged 22 years and 3 months; obituary contains a poem written by "L.E.B." (SA 13 Oct 1871)

LONGNECKER, JOHN H., died 11 Nov 1870 at his residence in Towsontown, Baltimore Co., in his 53rd year; born in Lancaster Co., PA, he removed to Baltimore Co. many years ago and engaged in politics; he unsuccessfully ran three times for Sheriff under the Whig Party, but was subsequently elected County Clerk and served until the election which followed the adoption of the Constitution of 1867; he received an appointment in the Custom House at Baltimore during President Grant's administration, which position he held at the time of his death; he was an uncompromising politician, and at one time conducted the *Baltimore County American*, with considerable ability and success (AI 18 Nov 1870)

LOVE, EMMA J. (Miss) and George A. Reasin, both of Baltimore, m. 28 May 1867 by Rev. J. J. Stockton (AI 14 Jun 1867)

LOVE, MARY LOUISA and James H. Kerby m. 26 Dec 1863 by Rev. William R. Mills (SA 20 Feb 1863)

LOVE, PHILIP H., see "Charles H. A. Whiteford," q.v.

LOVE, SUE M. and Stephen B. Crawford, both of Harford Co., m. ---- (date not given) at the residence of George A. Love (HD 17 Feb 1871)

LOWE, GEORGE, see "Mrs. Lowe," q.v.

LOWE, JOHN H., of Baltimore, and Miss Susie Harvey, of Harford Co., m. 9 Jul 1868 at the Christian Church in Baltimore by Rev. Alfred N. Gilbert (AI 17 Jul 1868)

LOWE, MATILDA E. (Miss) and William A. Durham, both of Harford Co., m. 2 Apr 1868, at the residence of the bride's father, by Elder William Grafton (AI 8 May 1868)

LOWE, MRS., wife of George Lowe, was murdered by her husband (date not given); his trial is now progressing in the court at Frederick, MD (HM 17 Nov 1843)

LUCKEY, FANNY, dau. of Joshua G. and Mary S. Luckey, died 8 Jun 1870 of dropsy of the brain, aged 3 years, 1 month and 8 days; obituary contains a poem written by "J.G.L." (AI 17 Jun 1870)

LUCY, LIZZIE B., only dau. of Prof. Thomas Lucy, of Baltimore, and M. Crook Whiteford, of Harford Co., m. 27 Jul 1869 by Rev. Dr. Dalrymple [marriage notice indicated "No cards"] (AI 13 Aug 1869)

LYNCH, ELIZABETH, died ---- (date not given) and the administrator's notice stated that creditors must exhibit their legal vouchers by 7 Sep 1864 to William H. Lynch, admin. (SA 11 Sep 1863)

LYNCH, P. H., died ---- (date not given) and was removed from the voter registration list in the 4th District in 1868 (AI 9 Oct 1868)

LYNCH, WILLIAM H., see "Elizabeth Lynch," q.v.

LYON, MARGARET (Miss), of Baltimore, and William Jewens, of Harford Co., m. 4 Feb 1869 in Baltimore by Rev. D. Bowers (HD 19 Feb 1869)

LYONS, ELIJAH, see "Maria McDonal," q.v.

LYTLE, JAMES, died 10 Mar 1864 in his 59th year, after a brief but painful illness, at his residence near Federal Hill, Harford Co.; obituary contains a brief memorial and poem; the subsequent executor's notice stated that creditors must exhibit their legal vouchers by 4 May 1865 to Robert A. Lytle and William K. Lytle, execs. (AI 29 Apr 1864 and 6 May 1864); see "Mary Lytle," q.v.

LYTLE, JOHN H., of Magnolia, MD, and Sallie M. Taylor, youngest dau. of J. J. Taylor, of Norristown, PA, m. 16 Jun 1869, at the residence of the bride's father, by Rev. Hardin Wheat (AI 25 Jun 1869)

LYTLE, MARY, widow of James Lytle, died Wed. 9 Mar 1870 in Harford Co., in her 79th year; obituary contains a poem (AI 25 Mar 1870)

LYTLE, ROBERT A., died Thurs. 13 Oct 1864 at his residence "near the Hickory in this county," aged 57 (AI 21 Oct 1864); see "James Lytle," q.v.

LYTLE, WILLIAM K., see "James Lytle," q.v.

MACATEE, ANNIE, see "Margaret Macatee," q.v.

MACATEE, ELLEN S., died ---- (date not given) and the administrator's notice stated that creditors must exhibit their legal vouchers by 11 Apr 1864 to Ignatius G. Macatee, admin. (SA 15 May 1863)

MACATEE, IGNATIUS and Anna P. Bateman, eldest dau. of Joseph E. Bateman, Esq., all of Harford Co., m. Thurs. 17 Oct 1865 by Rev. O'Connor (AI 20 Oct 1865); see "Ellen S. Macatee" and "Margaret Macatee," q.v.

MACATEE, MARGARET, only dau. of Ignatius J. and Annie Macatee, died 18 Oct 1869, aged about 2 years (HD 22 Oct 1869)

MACATEE, SARAH JANE, eldest dau. of Thomas and Ruth E. Macatee, died 28 Jun 1862, in her 7th year (SA 12 Jul 1862)

MACLEAN, JOHN JR., of Princeton, NJ, Licentiate of the Presbytery of New Brunswick, NJ, died 27 Jul 1870 at *Brookdale Farm*, Harford Co., in his 33rd year (AI 5 Aug 1870)

MADDEN, JOHN T., died 13 Sep 1851, formerly of Harford Co., but for the last 20 years a resident of Baltimore (HM 18 Sep 1851)

MAFFIT, SAMUEL S., died Tues., 24 May 1864 at his residence in Elkton, in his 46th year; formerly Comptroller of the State Treasury (AI 10 Jun 1864)

MAGAW, JANE, wife of Samuel Magaw, Esq., died Wed. 26 Apr 1865 in Bel Air, in her 72nd year (AI 28 Apr 1865)

MAGNESS, GEORGE W., son of the late John Magness, died Thurs. afternoon 11 Aug 1870, aged 15; he was sitting in the yard of William Kennedy, for whom he worked, on the outskirts of Churchville, and was feeding grain to some fowls beneath a tree when a thunderstorm passed over; a lightning stroke descended and killed him instantly; he was in close proximity to a wire clothes line which attracted the death shaft and passed it into his body; he was a member of the village Sabbath school and was much esteemed for his good qualities [one newspaper contains two death notices] (AI 19 Aug 1870 and HD 19 Aug 1870)

MAGNESS, JOHN, died Sat. 9 Jan 1864 at his residence in Harford Co., in his 68th year; obituary contains a brief memorial; the subsequent administrator's notice stated that creditors must exhibit their legal vouchers by 27 Jan 1865 to Lee Magness, admin. (SA 5 Feb 1864); see "George W. Magness," q.v.

MAGNESS, JOHN R., who lived near Aberdeen, was found last Sat. morning frozen to death within a mile of his home; he had arrived at Aberdeen on the evening train from Baltimore and started on foot for home, about 2 miles distant; nothing was heard from him until he was found as above stated (SA 8 Jan 1864)

MAGNESS, LEE, see "John Magness," q.v.

MAGNESS, MARTHA, died Fri. 8 Mar 1867 at Sandy Hook, in her 14th (?) year; obituary contains a short poem written by "F." (AI 15 Mar 1867)

MAGNESS, STEPHEN T. and Miss Harriet Ann Everett, both of Harford Co., m. 7 Oct 1868 by Rev. D. A. Shermer (AI 16 Oct 1868)

MAGNESS, WILLIAM M., died Sun. evening 10 Mar 1867, in his 65th year; obituary contains a short verse (AI 29 Mar 1867)

MAGRAW, EMILY W., wife of the late Henry S. Magraw, died 25 Mar 1870, in her 52nd year (AI 1 Apr 1870)

MAGRAW, HENRY S., a member of the Maryland House of Delegates from Cecil Co., died last Fri. morning shortly after 8 o'clock in Washington, D.C., having been taken with apoplexy on the previous Tues., unable to speak but recognized his acquaintances; he was born at West Nottingham in Cecil Co. and was educated at the Academy at that place; he studied law in Lancaster, PA and was admitted to the bar in Pittsburgh where he practiced for a number of years; in politics he was a Democrat and served 3 years as State Treasurer in PA for 3 years; within the past few years he purchased the old homestead of his father in Cecil Co. where his family resided at the time of his death; he was interred in West Nottingham Cemetery last Tues. (AI 8 Feb 1867); see "Emily W. Magraw," q.v.

MAGRAW, JAMES C., Chief Judge of the Orphans' Court of Baltimore Co., died last Fri. at his residence near Lutherville, in his 65th year;

obituary contains some information from the *Baltimore Sun* (AI 10 Jul 1868)

MAGRAW, JAMES M. (Doctor) and Miss Kate W. Stump m. 1 Jun 1869 at *Perry Farm*, Cecil Co., by Rev. T. S. C. Smith (AI 11 Jun 1869); see "Robert M. Magraw," q.v.

MAGRAW, ROBERT M., died ---- (date not given) and the administrator's notice stated that creditors must exhibit their legal vouchers by 26 Jun 1867 to James M. Magraw, admin. (AI 29 Jun 1866)

MAGRAW, ROBERT M., a young man, died Wed. evening last week at the residence of his father Samuel M. Magraw, Esq., stricken by consumption, having been an invalid for a considerable period before his death; he leaves a large circle of attached friends; he was subsequently removed from the voter registration list in the 3rd District in 1870 (AI 8 Apr 1870 and HR 28 Oct 1870)

MAGRAW, SAMUEL M, see "Robert M. Magraw," q.v.

MAGRAW, WILLIAM M., Esq., died suddenly ---- (date not given) in Baltimore; he was born in Cecil Co., the youngest son of Rev. Dr. James Magraw; after his father's death he moved to Western Virginia and engaged as a contractor in the U. S. mail service, being the first person to carry the mail across the plains to Utah Territory; he was afterwards appointed by President Buchanan to superintend the construction of an overland mail road across the plains to connect with roads from San Francisco; the work was suspended due to difficulties with the inhabitants of Utah and the Indians in that vicinity; he volunteered under Gen. Sidney Johnson, then in command of the U. S. Army en route to enforce the laws in that region; he was subsequently engaged as a transporter of supplies to the army in Utah and New Mexico; lately he had been residing on his farm in Allegany Co., MD and was on a visit to Baltimore when he died; his remains were followed to Greenmount Cemetery last Sat. by his relatives and friends [*Baltimore Sun* 11 Apr 1864] (AI 15 Apr 1864)

MAHAN, JOSEPH L., postmaster at Elkton, MD, died 7 Aug 1869 after a few days' illness (AI 13 Aug 1869)

MAHAN, THOMAS C. and Miss Louisa Loflin, both of Harford Co., m. 20 Dec 1871, at Smith's Chapel, by Rev. J. H. Baker [double wedding with William P. Loflin and Sophia J. James] (AI 19 Jan 1872)

MAHN, M. (Reverend), rector of St. Paul's Parish, Baltimore, died Sat. after a long illness; he was a native of Nansemond Co., VA (AI 9 Sep 1870)

MANN, SAMUEL B., of Flemington, NJ, and Emma Sullivan, dau. of the late James T. Sullivan, of Havre de Grace, m. 3 Jan 1865 by Ref. James K. Cramer (AI 27 Jan 1865)

MARKLAND, CHARLES E., died very suddenly last Sat. at the hotel of Mr. Glenn in Bel Air; he had arrived in town an hour before his death for the purpose of taking his commission as a Justice of the Peace, a capacity in which he had served for 30 years; he qualified in the clerk's office and walked across the street to Mr. Glenn's where he died in 15 or 20 minutes after entering the house; he complained of great uneasiness about the heart just a few minutes before; Dr. William S. Richardson was called immediately, but he died before the doctor arrived; Markland was in his 69th year, a native of the Eastern Shore of Maryland, and he lived in Baltimore previous to his removal to Harford Co. some 40 years ago; at one time he engaged in the mercantile business at Darlington, but for many years had been involved in school teaching and performing the duties of a Justice of the Peace; he attached himself to the Methodist Episcopal Church early in life, was a man with a mild and amiable disposition, and had few or no enemies (AI 1 May 1868); see "Charles M. McCann," q.v.

MARR, WILLIAM P., and ---- Boyle, son of Gen. Boyle of Kentucky, students of the New Jersey College, were killed by the cars near Milton, PA, yesterday, while crossing the railroad track in a buggy [notice in *Baltimore Sun*]; these two young men had been residing in Bel Air, MD for some months past, pursing their studies with Rev. John McKelway, principal of the Bel Air Academy; they left this place but a few weeks since, to spend their holidays in Pennsylvania, the home of Mr. Marr; their untimely decease has fallen with a great shock on the many friends they had made here (AI 14 Jan 1870)

MARRIOTT, EUGENE E., of Baltimore Co., and Miss Mary Louisa Trott, eldest dau. of the late Dr. George L. Trott, formerly of Louisiana, m. 9 Jul 1870, in the Second Presbyterian Church, by Rev. Dr. Edwards (AI 15 Jul 1870)

MARSH, JAMES, see "Kate Marsh," q.v.

MARSH, KATE, aged about 32, murdered her four children and slashed the throat of her mother Mrs. Dwyer, aged about 53, at their residence at No. 99 Central Ave. in Baltimore yesterday afternoon; the children were James (aged 8), William (aged 6), Mary Jane (aged 4) and Georgie (aged about 2); William Marsh, the husband, was a barber and had abandoned his family about a year ago; he had gone south to seek employment and being consumptive at the time, he is supposed by many to have died [this long article contains more details about these horrible murders] (HD 29 Apr 1870)

MARSH, GEORGIE AND MARY JANE, see "Kate Marsh," q.v.

MARSH, RACHEL (Miss) and James Gallion, both of Harford Co., m. 7 Feb 1867 at the residence of Joseph Starr (AI 15 Feb 1867)

MARSH, THOMAS, of Hudson, New Hampshire, and Miss Persis R. Davenport, of Worcester, Massachusetts, m. 25 Dec 1859 in Harford Co. (SA 31 Dec 1859)

MARSH, WILLIAM, see "Kate Marsh," q.v.

MARSHALL, JAMES H. and Miss Anna Wileman, both of Harford Co.,
m. 19 Jul 1871 in Havre de Grace by Rev. William H. Cooke (HD
28 Jul 1871 and HR 28 Jul 1871)

MARSHALL, SARAH, wife of Thomas Marshall, formerly of Harford
Co., died 12 Sep 1863 at her residence, No. 118 South Paca St.
[Baltimore], in her 74th year (SA 25 Sep 1863)

MARSHALL, THOMAS, see "Sarah Marshall," q.v.

MARSTON, R. JARRETT (Hon.), of New York, and May Ella
Galloway, youngest dau. of the late Capt. William Galloway, of
Baltimore, m. 21 Jan 1866 at *Oak Hill* in Harford Co. by Rev. S.
Bartol [double wedding with Charles Hudson and Helen Edith
Chivrel]; marriage notice spelled the name as "Gallaway" [New
York and Baltimore papers please copy] (AI 26 Jan 1866)

MARTIN, BARBARY, wife of Patrick Martin, died 1 Apr 1870 in Havre
de Grace, in her 30th year (HR 22 Apr 1870)

MARTIN, DANIEL, died ---- (date not given) and the administratrix's
notice stated that creditors must exhibit their legal vouchers by 22
Jan 1869 to Priscilla Martin, admx. (AI 24 Jan 1868)

MARTIN, H. T., of Baltimore, and S. Lizzie Birckhead, dau. of Dr. S. H.
Birckhead, of Harford Co., m. 4 Jun 1868 at Spesutia Church,
Perrymansville, by Rev. S. W. Crampton (AI 12 Jun 1868)

MARTIN, HENRY STEVENS, son of Richard T. and Mary E. Martin,
died Tues.19 Jul 1870, aged 7 months and 11 days (AI 22 Jul 1870)

MARTIN, JAMES K. and Sarah Grafton, both of Harford Co., m. 8 Feb
1866, at the M. E. Parsonage, by Rev. E. Kinsey (AI 16 Feb 1866)

MARTIN, MARY, see "Henry Stevens Martin," q.v.

MARTIN, PATRICK, see "Mrs. Barbary Martin," q.v.

MARTIN, PRISCILLA, see "Daniel Martin," q.v.

MARTIN, RICHARD, see "Henry Stevens Martin," q.v.

MARTIN, ROBERT N., a Baltimore Judge, died last Wed. at Saratoga
(AI 22 Jul 1870)

MARTIN, WILLIAM, died Sun. 25 Oct 1868 near Aberdeen, in his 22nd
year (AI 13 Nov 1868)

MASON, BENJAMIN L. JR. and Miss Annie E. Devoe, dau. of Thomas
Devoe, Esq., all of Harford Co., m. 22 Dec 1868 at Bethel Church
by Rev. B. F. Myers (HD 1 Jan 1869 and AI 1 Jan 1869)

MASSEY, SALLIE B., see "Mary E. McCoy," q.v.

MATHER, THOMAS, died Fr. 1 Feb 1867 at his residence in Harford
Co., in his 72nd year (AI 8 Feb 1867)

MATHEWS, LEMUEL E. and Mrs. Ella A. Mitchell, both of Harford
Co., m. 22 Feb 1870, at the parsonage of the Caroline Street M. E.
Church, by Rev. Joseph R. Wheeler (AI 4 Mar 1870)

MATHIAS, JACOB, of Westminster, MD, aged about 75, died last Sat.
morning when he ran to catch a train on the Northern Central
Railway; he and his granddau. (not named) boarded and took their
seats at the Calvert Station and when they arrived at the Hanover
Station he left the train to get some lemonade at Mr. Geisner's

public house; suddenly the train's bell rang and he ran to catch it, but when he grabbed for the step railing of the middle car he missed and fell beneath the wheels; both legs were cut off and his skull was fractured; he was recovered and remained conscious, but died about 15 minutes later; he was once a representative from Carroll Co. to the State Legislature and at the time of his death he was President of the Farmers and Mechanics Bank of Carroll Co. in Westminster (HD 26 Jun 1857)

MATTHEWS, EPHRAIM S., died ---- (date not given) and the administrator's notice stated that creditors must exhibit their legal vouchers by 4 Jun 1869 to L. E. Matthews, admin. (AI 12 Jun 1868)

MATTHEWS, ISAAC G., of Howard Co., and Miss A. Helen Sappington, dau. of Dr. John K. Sappington, of Harford Co., m. Tues. 14 Jun 1864 by Rev. William Finney, at *Blenheim*, the residence of the bride's father (AI 24 Jun 1864)

MATTHEWS, JACOB FORWOOD, one of the old time gentlemen, died 20 Sep 1868 at his farm *Matthews' Enlargement* on Romney Neck, in his 74th year; obituary contains a brief memorial written by "G.T.H." (AI 23 Oct 1868)

MATTHEWS, JULIUS H. and Miss Elizabeth S. Bayless, both of Harford Co., m. Tues. 18 Dec 1866 by Rev. William A. McKee (AI 28 Dec 1866)

MATTHEWS, L. E., see "Ephraim S. Matthews," q.v.

MATTHEWS, LEMUEL E. and Mrs. Ella A. Mitchell, both of Harford Co., m. 23 Feb 1870 at the Parsonage of the Caroline Street M. E. Church [in Baltimore] by Rev. Joseph R. Wheeler (HD 4 Mar 1870)

MAULSBY, EMILY C. (Miss) and Charles W. Banks, both of Harford Co., m. Thurs. 15 Feb 1866 at Rock Spring Church by Rev. J. H. D. Wingfield (AI 23 Feb 1866)

MAULSBY, JANE, widow of Gen. Israel D. Maulsby, died Thurs. 14 Jan 1864 at her residence near Bel Air, aged 74 (SA 22 Jan 1864)

MAULSBY, ISRAEL, see "Jane Maulsby," q.v.

MAULSBY, MRS., wife of Col. William P. Maulsby, formerly of Harford Co., but now of Frederick, died Tues. 4 Jun 1867 at Hagerstown, where she had gone to visit her friends; she had been ill for several weeks [information from *Frederick Examiner*] (AI 14 Jun 1867); see "William Weeks," q.v.

MAULSBY, WILLIAM, see "Mrs. Maulsby," q.v.

MAXWELL, JAMES W., Esq., an attorney and son of Mr. J. L. Maxwell at Port Deposit, died last Tues. afternoon at the Howard House in Elkton, after a short illness, probably from erysipelas of which he was subject to attacks; he left a large circle of relatives and friends, and was buried in the family burying ground at West Nottingham Presbyterian Church (AI 5 May 1865)

MAY, GEORGE, a young man, native of Cheltonham, England, was instantly killed near Newark Station on Thurs. afternoon, by being run over by Engine No. 48; he was a traveler on his way from New

York to Baltimore and while walking on the tracks opposite the on-
coming locomotive he apparently deliberately stepped on the other
track; his remains were taken in charge by the station master (AI 4
Dec 1868)

MAY, HENRY, died 25 Sep 1866, in his 50th year, while on a visit to his
relatives in Baltimore; he was born in the District of Columbia and
as a lawyer and orator he had no equals; in 1854 he was nominated
by the Democratic Party to serve in the House of Representatives,
but was defeated by Henry Winter Davis; he was again chosen in
1861 and in September of that year he was arrested and imprisoned,
as were many thousands of others, without the slightest cause or the
least show of justice; his health was much impaired by his
confinement, which did not last long, and after his release from Fort
Lafayette he resumed his congressional duties [obituary contains a
quote from the *Baltimore Gazette* regarding his exemplary
character] (AI 5 Oct 1866)

MAYNADIER, GEORGE Y. and Miss Laura P. Moores, dau. of the late
A. Paca Moores, Esq., of Harford Co., m. Wed. 26 Oct 1870 at
Emmanuel Church, Bel Air, by Rev. William E. Snowden (HD 28
Oct 1870 and AI 28 Oct 1870); see "Isaac Pitt," q.v.

MAYNADIER, HENRY E., Major, 12th Inf., U. S. Army (Brevet Lieut.
Colonel), died 3 Dec 1868 at Oglethorpe Barracks, Savannah, GA
(AI 18 Dec 1868)

MAYNADIER, JER. Y. and Alice Lee Fendall m. Tues. evening 18 Apr
1865 [first marriage notice stated 18 Mar 1865] at the residence of
William B. Duvall, Esq., by Rev. J. H. D. Wingfield (AI 21 Apr
1865 and 28 Apr 1865)

MAYNADIER, JOSEPH E., see "Sarah Amos," q.v.

MAYO, JOHN U. (Major) and Miss Pattie W. Hall, dau. of Thomas W.
Hall, Esq., of Harford Co., m. Wed. 16 Jun 1869 at St. Mary's
Church, Harford Co., by Rev. William F. Brand (AI 18 Jun 1869;
HD 18 Jun 1869 spelled her name "Patty")

McABEE, ELIZABETH A., died Mon. 18 Feb 1867 at Harford Furnace,
in her 43rd year, after a long and painful illness; obituary contains a
poem (AI 15 Mar 1867)

McALISTER, CAROLINE and F. C. Stevens, both of Washington, D.C.,
m. 25 Nov 1869 in Baltimore by Rev. John Poisal (AI 24 Dec 1869)

McCAFFERTY, MICHAEL, died ---- (date not given) and on 16 Jul
1858 the Circuit Court ordered Alice McCafferty, admx., to sell his
real estate by 16 Sep 1858 (SA 31 Jul 1858)

McCANN, CHARLES, see "Elizabeth McCann," q.v.

McCANN, CHARLES MERRICK, son of Mary E. McCann, died 9 Jan
1865, aged 3 years and 4 months, at the residence of his grandfather
Charles E. Markland, Esq., in Dublin, MD [obituary contains a
poem] (AI 17 Mar 1865)

McCANN, ELIZABETH, wife of Charles McCann, died 5 Dec 1870 at
   Dublin, Harford Co., aged 69; obituary contains a brief memorial
   and a short poem by "Anna" (AI 9 Dec 1870)
McCANN, MARY E., see "Charles Merrick McCann," q.v.
McCAULEY, ELIZABETH E. (Miss), of Anne Arundel Co., and Francis
   D. Kerr, of Harford Co., m. Sat. 7 Nov 1868 at St. John's Church,
   Baltimore, by Rev. Father McManus (AI 13 Nov 1868 and 30 Nov
   1868)
McCAUSLAND, A. J., a native of Harford Co., and son of Robert
   McCausland, formerly of Dublin, Harford Co., was shot and killed
   on 25 Dec 1864 in the Territory of Montana by T. M. Kinney, his
   business partner; Kinney was subsequently tried and found not
   guilty by reason of self-defense [article contains more details from
   the *Montana Post*] (AI 20 Oct 1865)
McCAUSLAND, ANN, died ---- (date not given) and the administrator's
   notice stated that creditors must exhibit their legal vouchers by 14
   Mar 1861 to Thomas J. McCausland, admin. (SA 19 May 1860)
McCAUSLAND, ELIZABETH, relict of the late Maj. George
   McCausland, died Tues. 22 Apr 1862, in her 80th year; obituary
   contains a brief memorial written by "C." (SA 3 May 1862)
McCAUSLAND, GEORGE (Captain), of Gen. Evans' Staff, and son of
   the late Gen. Robert McCausland, of West Feliciana, LA, died 18
   Sep 1862 upon the plains of Manassas, VA; obituary contains a
   poem written by "C." (AI 29 Jun 1866)
McCAUSLAND, GEORGE (Major), see "Elizabeth McCausland," q.v.
McCAUSLAND, ROBERT, see "A. J. McCausland" and "George
   McCausland," q.v.
McCAUSLAND, T. J., of *Locust Valley Farm*, Harford Co., and Miss
   Melissa R. Hopkins, eldest dau. of Richard Hopkins, of *Sunny Dell*,
   Harford Co., m. 17 Dec 1867 at the Grove Church by Rev. K. J.
   Kramer (AI 24 Jan 1868)
McCAY, MARY A. (Miss), died 1 Nov 1871 at the residence of Dr. T.
   E. Bond near Fallston (SA 10 Nov 1871)
McCOMAS, ANN A. and Charles W. Pyle, both of Harford Co., m. 8
   Dec 1870 at the M. P. Parsonage, Bel Air, by Rev. D. A. Shermer
   (AI 23 Dec 1870)
McCOMAS, BARNET, died ----(date not given) at the residence of
   Barnet J. Clark, in Harford Co., in his 86th year (AI 16 Dec 1864)
McCOMAS, CHARLOTTE A., consort of Robert McComas, of
   Baltimore, died ---- (date not given), aged 43 (AI 24 Jan 1868)
McCOMAS, DANIEL M., died ---- (date not given) and was removed
   from the voter registration list in the 1st District in 1870 (HR 1 Nov
   1870)
McCOMAS, GILBERT, of Abingdon, died ---- (date not given) of a
   violent cold which he contracted during the late cold weather (HD
   18 Jan 1856)

McCOMAS, JAMES, died last Mon. when he was thrown from his horse and a wagon, heavily loaded with iron ore, ran over him; he died within an hour; he had resided in the upper part of Harford Co. and leaves a large circle of friends and relatives (AI 8 Jun 1866); see "Nicholas McComas," q.v.

McCOMAS, JOHN G., of Baltimore, and Miss Catherine E. Pennington, dau. of the late William O. Pennington, of Havre de Grace, m. 13 Jul 1852 by Rev. Cyrus Huntingdon (HM 22 Jul 1852)

McCOMAS, JULIA A.(Miss) and James A. Grafton, both of Harford Co., m. Mon. 6 May 1867 at the M. E. Parsonage, in Bel Air, by Rev. A. H. Greenfield (AI 10 May 1867)

McCOMAS, NICHOLAS, of Jarrettsville, a young man who had seduced and promised, but refused, to marry a young girl, Miss Martha J. Cairnes, was shot and killed by Miss Cairnes last Sat. afternoon about 6 o'clock; she had followed him to the back porch of a public house, took aim with a Colt revolver, and presumably killed him with the first shot, although she fired four or five times at him; she then mounted her horse and rode home; she turned herself in to authorities in Bel Air the next morning; she was shortly thereafter tried for murder and was found not guilty after 10 minutes deliberation by the jury (HR 15 Apr 1869 and 13 May 1869); other detailed accounts were reported in other newspapers, indicating Miss Martha Jane Cairnes was about 30 years old and Nicholas McComas (of James) was about 5 years her senior; on 1 Jan 1869 she had given birth to a child of which McComas was the reputed father; it was later reported that George R. Cairnes was charged as an accessory to the killing [considerable details about the murder, the trial, and testimony are in *The Aegis & Intelligencer* in May, 1869] (HD 16 Apr and 23 Apr 1869 and 7 May 1869; AI 16 Apr 1869 and 7 May, 14 May and 21 May 1869)

McCOMAS, PRESTON, died ---- (date not given) and the administrator's notice stated that creditors must exhibit their legal vouchers by 29 Aug 1838 to Bennett Gilbert, admin. (HM 7 Dec 1837 and 26 Apr 1838); see "Ellen B. Gilbert," q.v.

McCOMAS, ROBERT, see "Charlotte A. McComas," q.v.

McCOMBS, ----, a son of A. P. McCombs, of Havre de Grace, drowned last Fri. when he went out sailing near Furnace Wharf; it appears the small boy was knocked overboard by the boom and drowned before help could arrive (AI 31 May 1867)

McCOMBS, ALEX., died --- (date not given) and an inquest was held on his body at the P. W. & B. Railroad depot in Havre de Grace on Sun. afternoon; the verdict was that he died from exposure which brought on fits and spasms; he was from the float of Mr. Osborn and lived in Philadelphia, but no one there knew of him at the place where he said he had lived; he was buried at the expense of the town (AI 1 May 1868)

McCOMMONS, HELEN J., died Sat. 21 Apr 1866, aged 6 years, Avarilla McCommons died Sun. 22 Apr 1866, aged 2 years, Kate V. McCommons died Thurs. 26 Apr 1866, aged 8 years, and George H. McCommons died Tues. 1 May 1866, aged 6 months, all children of John and Phebe J. McCommons; they died of malignant scarlatina at their parents' residence near the Hickory; another article stated that four of the six children of John McCommons, who resides near Hickory, died from scarlet fever in the space of ten days; the two remaining children also have the disease, one of which is quite ill and the other is gradually improving; the disease has not spread to other households (AI 4 May 1866)

McCORMICK, CHARLES, a native of PA, died Sat. entirely friendless and without means; he was an unfortunate prisoner who was so badly beaten on 27 Mar 1869 at the Bel Air jail by the lunatic Green (an insane man who was also confined in the jail) that he died from his injuries (AI 2 Apr 1869 and HR 8 Apr 1869)

McCORMICK, FRED., Ensign, U. S. Navy, and Acting Navigator of the U. S. Steamer *Ossipee,* of the North Pacific Squadron, died at sea on 25 Jul 1868, of malarious fever, in his 25th year; he was the eldest child of J. M. and M. J. McCormick; a memorial written by the officers of the steamer was published later and contained some of the aforementioned information (AI 28 Aug 1868 and 11 Sep 1868)

McCORMICK, J. M., see "Fred. McCormick," q.v.

McCORMICK, JAMES ALBERT, son of James M. and M. J. McCormick, died Thurs. 16 Dec 1869, in his 19th year (AI 24 Dec 1869)

McCORMICK, JAMES M., see "Rebecca McCormick," q.v.

McCORMICK, M. J., see "James Albert McCormick" and "Fred. McCormick," q.v.

McCORMICK, REBECCA, dau. of James M. McCormick, Esq., of Harford Co., and Lieut. J. K. P. Ragsdale, U.S.N., m. 18 Nov 1869, at Poplar Grove, by Rev. W. E. Snowden; the editor noted that along with the above notice he received a slice of beautiful cake (AI 26 Nov 1869)

McCOURTNEY, NEWTON and Miss Adelia Thomas, both of Harford Co., m. 20 Jan 1870 by Rev. D. A. Shermer (AI 28 Jan 1870)

McCOURTNEY, SAMUEL, died ---- (date not given) and the administrator's notice stated that creditors must exhibit their legal vouchers by 27 Oct 1870 to J. T. McCourtney and Matilda McCourtney, admins. (AI 29 Oct 1869)

McCOY, JOHN C., died ---- (date not given) and the administrator's notice stated that creditors must exhibit their legal vouchers by 19 Sep 1866 to Joseph McCoy, admin. (AI 22 Sep 1865)

McCOY, JOSEPH, see "John C. McCoy," q.v.

McCOY, MARY E., dau. of Richard B. and Nancy McCoy, of Harford Co., died 18 Mar 1868 at Ercildoun Boarding School, Chester Co.,

PA, aged 18; a memorial was prepared at a meeting of the students on 22 Mar 1868 and submitted for publication by Georgie A. Palmer, President, and Sallie B. Massey, Secretary (AI 27 Mar 1868 and 3 Apr 1868)

McCULLOUGH, CLARENCE EUGENE, son of Dr. J. Haines and Maria A. McCullough, died 17 May 1869, of hydrocephalus, aged 19 months [*Baltimore Daily Sun* and Cecil County papers please copy] (AI 28 May 1869); another obituary states Clarence McCullough, infant son of Dr. and Eliza McCullough, died 16 May 1869 at Oakington; obituary includes a poem written by "Blanche, Aberdeen, 20 May 1869" (HD 28 May 1869)

McCULLOUGH, DR., see "James Cook" and "Clarence E. McCullough," q.v.

McCULLOUGH, ELIZA, see "Clarence E. McCullough," q.v.

McCULLOUGH, JAMES T., see "William McMullen," q.v.

McCULLOUGH, MARIA, see "Clarence E. McCullough," q.v.

McCULLOUGH, SUSAN (Miss) and William Welch, both of Baltimore Co., m. 16 Feb 1869 by Rev. Creaver (HD 5 Mar 1869)

McCUMMINGS, ANNIE M. (Miss) and George S. Hopkins, both of Harford Co., m. 17 May 1870 in Dublin, MD, by Rev. George M. Berry (HD 3 Jun 1870)

McCURDY, MATTIE (Miss), of York Co., PA, and Abraham R. Streett, of Harford Co., m. 6 Jan 1859 by Rev. Crawford (SA 15 Jan 1859)

McDONAL, MARIA, died ---- (date not given) and the administrator's notice stated that creditors must exhibit their legal vouchers by 6 Oct 1869 to Elijah Lyons (colored), admin. (AI 9 Oct 1868)

McDONALD, ALEXANDER, residing near Trenton, NJ, died last Tues. morning from hydrophobia, having been bitten by a small dog about 2 weeks previously (AI 31 Dec 1869)

McDONALD, P., who resides near Long Green Valley, Baltimore Co., was returning from the city in his market wagon last Sat. when some portion of his harness broke while descending a hill near the Great Gunpowder in Dulaney's Valley; the horse attached to the wagon began kicking furiously, inflicting such severe injuries on Mr. McDonald that he died from his wounds on the same day (AI 18 Jun 1869)

McDOWELL, Z. TAYLOR, drowned on Wed. while driving logs in the Susquehanna River above Port Deposit; 6 men were in a small boat that capsized, 3 drowned, names not known at the time; a subsequent article indicated Z. Taylor McDowell and two colored men named John Edward and Robert Hopkins drowned 24 Nov 1868 near Steel's Island while driving logs for the Susquehanna Boom Co. (HR 26 Nov 1868 and AI 4 Dec 1868); see "Z. Taylor McDowell" q.v.

McFADDEN, C. A. and Miss Mary Emma Carver, both of Havre de Grace, m. 27 Apr 1871 at the M. E. Church by Rev. M. L. Smyser (HR 5 May 1871)

McFADDEN, JOHN, died ---- (date not given) and the executor's notice stated that creditors must exhibit their legal vouchers by 11 Jan 1865 to John K. McFadden, exec. (SA 15 Jan 1864)

McFADDEN, JOHN, died last week at his residence in Churchville; *John McFadden, Esq.*, was one of the oldest citizens of this county (AI 16 Sep 1870); a subsequent issue states *John D. McFadden* died 8 Sep 1870, at Churchville, aged 68 (AI 30 Sep 1870); other newspaper editions state *John B. McFadden* was removed from the voter registration list in the 3rd District in 1870 (HR 28 Oct 1870 and AI 30 Sep 1870); see "Hugh Alexander," q.v.

McFARLAND, GEORGE and Mrs. Rosanna O'Keefe m. 5 Sep 1858 at Long Green by Rev. J. A. Walter [*Baltimore County Advocate* (MD) and *Chester County Jeffersonian* (PA) please copy] (SA 11 Sep 1858)

McGAW, ALBERT, died ---- (date not given) and was removed from the voter registration list in the 1st District in 1871 (HR 3 Nov 1871)

McGAW, B. F. and Miss Mary Courtney both of Harford Co., m. 28 Nov 1837 by Rev. Finney (HM 7 Dec 1837)

McGAW, ELIZA A. (Miss) and Frederick O. Mitchell, both of Harford Co., m. Thurs. 26 May 1864 (AI 27 May 1864)

McGAW, JOHN, died Sun. 5 Apr 1863 at his residence in Bush, in his 67th year; the subsequent executor's notice stated that creditors must exhibit their legal vouchers by 7 May 1864 to Robert McGaw and William E. McGaw, execs. (SA 3 Apr 1863 and 15 May 1863)

McGAW, JOHN, see "Jack Cox," q.v.

McGAW, RICHARD, see "Sally A. McGaw" and Jack Cox," q.v.

McGAW, ROBERT, see "John McGaw," q.v.

McGAW, SALLY A., relict of Richard McGaw, died ---- (date not given) at her residence in Harford Co., aged 61 (AI 29 Jun 1866)

McGAW, WILLIAM, see "John McGaw," q.v.

McGAW, WILLIAM E., died ---- (date not given) and the administrator's notice stated that creditors must exhibit their legal vouchers by 24 Feb 1869 to William Pannell, admin. (AI 28 Feb 1868)

McGONIGAL, DANIEL and Miss Avarilla Smith, both of Harford Co., m. Thurs. 27 Sep 1838, in Baltimore, by Rev. John Smith (HM 18 Oct 1838)

McGONIGALL, DANIEL, died ---- (date not given) and was removed from the voter registration list in the 1st District in 1870 (HR 1 Nov 1870)

McGONIGALL, VIRGINIA, and Charlton W. Billingslea, Jr., both of Harford Co., m. 14 Jul 1869 by Rev. Brooks (AI 23 Jul 1869 and HD 30 Jul 1869; the previous HD edition on 23 Jul 1869 had mistakenly given the marriage date as 24 Jul 1869 and the AI edition listed his name without the Jr.)

McGRA, MARY ANN (Miss) and Edward O'Brien, both of Harford Co., m. 29 Dec 1844 by Rev. J. Larkin (HM 3 Jan 1845)

McGUIGON, MICHAEL HENRY, son of John and Catherine McGuigon, died 13 Feb 1869 of scarlet fever, aged 6 years and 3 months (HD 19 Feb 1869)

McGUIRE, DANIEL, died ---- (date not given) and was removed from the voter registration list in "1867, 1868 & 1869" [specific year not stated and district not clarified, but either 4th, 5th or 6th] (AI 1 Oct 1869)

McGUIRK, PETER, was killed in a railroad accident yesterday morning about 4 a.m.; the baggage car on the P. W. & B. Railroad was thrown from the track near Perrymansville in Harford Co. and McGuirk was instantly killed; several other employees were slightly injured; McGuirk had worked for the railroad for 14 years [additional details about the accident are given in the article] (SA 9 Oct 1858)

McHENRY, RAMSEY, see "Andrew Christy," q.v.

McILVAIN, GEORGE W. and Rachel A. Ramsay, dau. of Dr. Samuel J. Ramsey, all of Harford Co., m. 9 Oct 1867, at the residence of the bride's father, by Rev. Edward A. Colburn (AI 1 Nov 1867)

McKELWAY, JOHN, see "William P. Marr," q.v.

McKENDLESS, JAMES W. and Miss Lizzie Walker, both of Harford Co., m. Tues. 6 Dec 1864 by Rev. Hoblitzell (AI 9 Dec 1864)

McKINNEY, WILLIAM J. and Miss Sarah E. Eshelman, both of Harford Co., m. 13 Jan 1870 by Rev. George M. Berry at the residence of the bride's father (HD 11 Feb 1870); another newspaper gave their names as William J. McKenney and Miss Sarah R. Eshelman (AI 11 Feb 1870)

McMORRIS, GEORGE and Miss Rachel A. Sills, both of Harford Co., m. 19 Sep 1871 by Rev. John Roberts (HD 22 Sep 1871)

McMULLEN, WILLIAM, died ---- (date not given) and the Circuit Court for Cecil County in Chancery ordered that the sale made by James T. McCullough, Trustee of the deceased's real estate, be ratified unless cause to the contrary can be shown by 23 Oct 1854 (HM 31 Aug 1854)

McNAMEE, JAMES, died 7 Aug 1866 at his residence on Mr. Cook's farm, near Havre de Grace, in his 66th year (AI 17 Aug 1866)

McNUTT, SAMUEL G., see "William McNutt," q.v.

McNUTT, WILLIAM, died ---- (date not given) and the administrator's notice stated that creditors must exhibit their legal vouchers by 18 Dec 1838 to Wakeman B. Hopkins and Samuel G. McNutt, admins. (HM 28 Jun 1838)

McVEY, LOUISA WAREHAM, dau. of John T. and S. Louisa McVey, died suddenly Sun. 27 Aug 1871, aged 4 years, 1 month and 14 days (HR 1 Sep 1871)

McVEY, WILLIAM H. and Miss Mary E. Bailey, both of Harford Co., m. 28 Apr 1870 by Rev. J. G. Moore (AI 6 May 1870)

MEADS, JAMES T., of Harford Co., and Miss Emily J. Hughes, of Baltimore Co., m. 8 Jan 1863, at the residence of the bride's father, by Rev. T. S. Smith (SA 16 Jan 1863)

MEADS, WILLIAM, of Baltimore, and Marian Rutledge, of Harford Co., m. 27 Feb 1867 at the Methodist Parsonage at Broadway in Baltimore by Rev. J. W. Black (AI 15 Mar 1867)

MEARNS, S. H., of Cecil Co., and Emma Fulton, dau. of William H. Fulton, Esq., of Philadelphia, m. 4 Oct 1865, at the residence of the bride's father, by Rev. Dr. Henry (AI 13 Oct 1865)

MECHEM, H. EVERETT, of Chicago, IL, and Miss Jennie E. Vansant, of Harford Co., m. 19 Oct 1870 at the Washington House, Bel Air, by Rev. D. A. Shermer (AI 21 Oct 1870)

MECHEM, ISAAC, died ---- (date not given) and the executor's notice stated that creditors must exhibit their legal vouchers by 9 Aug 1860 to Richard Mechem and William Mechem, execs. (SA 20 Aug 1859)

MECHEM, ISAAC and Maggie Ashton, both of Harford Co., m. 11 Jun 1867 in Baltimore by Rev. C. W. Rankin (AI 21 Jun 1867)

MECHEM, LUCRETIA G. (Miss) and John Calvin Hannah, both of Harford Co., m. 22 Dec 1859 by Rev. W. F. P. Noble (SA 31 Dec 1859)

MECHEM, MARGARET ANN, wife of Isaac Mechem and eldest dau. of William and Rebecca Ashton, died 16 Dec 1868, aged 21 (AI 8 Jan 1869)

MECHEM, WILLIAM, see "Lucretia G. Hanna," q.v.

MERRYMAN, ELLIE (Miss) and Dr. James Watt, both of Harford Co., m. 19 Dec 1865 by Rev. Crever (AI 22 Dec 1865)

MERRYMAN, NELSON, see "John Heaton," q.v.

MICHAEL, CALEB, see "Laura E. Michael," q.v.

MICHAEL, CALVIN and Miss Ann Martha Mitchell, both of Harford Co., m. last Tues. evening by Rev. Finney (HM 17 Apr 1856)

MICHAEL, DANIEL, died last Tues. at his residence near Hall's Crossroads, aged about 80; an honest man of industrious habits who had acquired considerable property, he was a member of the Presbyterian Church and the father of a large family (HM 28 Jul 1853)

MICHAEL, ELLA, youngest dau. of Ethan Michael, of Harford Co., and G. S. Griffith, Jr. m. Tues. 14 Jun 1864 at Spesutia Church by Rev. Crampton (AI 1 Jul 1864)

MICHAEL, ETHAN, see "Ella Michael," q.v.

MICHAEL, GEORGE W., see "M. Effie Michael" and "Mary S. Michael," q.v.

MICHAEL, HELEN ELIZABETH, wife of William B. Michael, died 9 May 1862 at Perrymansville, Harford Co., in her 29th year (SA 17 May 1862)

MICHAEL, HENRY, see "M. Effie Michael," q.v.

MICHAEL, JACOB, see "William Osborn," q.v.

MICHAEL, JAMES H. and H. Lizzie Kean, both of Harford Co., m. 12 Feb 1863 at Spesutia Church by Rev. S. W. Crampton (SA 20 Feb 1863); see "Lewis D. Michael," q.v.

MICHAEL, LAURA E. (Miss), dau. of the late Caleb Michael, of Harford Co., and Edward Rutledge Price, of Baltimore, m. 19 Jan 1865 at the residence of the bride in Harford Co. (AI 27 Jan 1865)

MICHAEL, LEWIS D., died ---- (date not given) and the administrator's notice stated that creditors must exhibit their legal vouchers by 12 Jan 1868 to James H. Michael and Jacob C. Hollis, admin. (AI 18 Jan 1867)

MICHAEL, M. EFFIE (Miss), dau. of the late Capt. Henry Michael, of Michaelsville, MD, and W. Jackson Fulton, of Philadelphia, m. 19 Dec 1866 at the residence of George W. Michael, Esq., by Rev. McKee [*Baltimore Sun* please copy] [marriage notice indicated "No cards"] (AI 28 Dec 1866)

MICHAEL, MARY SUSANNAH, wife of George W. Michael and dau. of the late William Thompson, of Otter Point, died 30 Oct 1871 at Gravelly Farm near Michaelsville (SA 10 Nov 1871)

MICHAEL, MICHAEL B., see "Helen Elizabeth Michael," q.v.

MICHAEL, OWEN, Esq., died Fri. morning about 1 o'clock, near Hickory, after a short illness of typhoid pneumonia; he was a plain farmer who adhered to the golden rule during a lifetime which did not exceed, if it reached, three score years (HD 31 Mar 1871)

MICHAEL, WILLIAM, see "John Fletcher," q.v.

MICHENER, JOHN D., died ---- (date not given) in Cecil Co. and the executor's notice stated that creditors must exhibit their legal vouchers by 2 Feb 1868 to Aaron J. Michener and Amos J. Michener, execs. (AI 15 Mar 1867)

MICKLE, ROBERT, see "Edward Griffith," q.v.

MIDDLETON, ANNIE E. (Miss) and A. B. Hanson, both of Harford Co., m. 1 Dec 1864 by Rev. Hays (AI 9 Dec 1864)

MILES, ELIHU, died 20 May 1867 in Chestertown, in his 47th year (AI 31 May 1867)

MILLER, ANDREW T. and Ann Maria Wilgus m. 6 Aug 1867 by Rev. W. M. Meminger (AI 16 Aug 1867)

MILLER, JOSEPH, see "Rachel Tracey," q.v.

MILLER, KATE H. (Miss) and Thomas B. Jarrett, both of Harford Co., m. 31 Jan 1867, at Bethel, by Rev. B. F. Myers [double wedding; see "Martin L. Jarrett," q.v.] (AI 15 Feb 1867)

MILLER, SOLOMON and Miss Susan Reynard, both of Harford Co., m. 1 Sep 1848 by Rev. Park (HM 8 Feb 1849)

MILLIGAN, ELLA (Miss), of Lancaster Co., PA, and J. Oscar Stearns, of Harford Co., m. Tues. 17 Nov 1868 at the Presbyterian Parsonage in Bart Township, near Georgetown, PA, by Rev. J. M. Rittenhouse (AI 27 Nov 1868)

MINNICK, CYRUS, see "Mary E. Warden," q.v.

MINNICK, JACOB and Miss Mary A. Keane, both of Harford Co., m. 25 Aug 1870 at 7½ o'clock, in the M. P. Parsonage, Bel Air, by Rev. D. A. Shermer [Baltimore County papers please copy] (AI 30 Sep 1870)

MISKIMMON, ELIZABETH, see "Mary Elizabeth Arthur," q.v.

MISKIMMON, ROBERT, died ---- (date not given) and the administrator's notice stated that creditors must exhibit their legal vouchers by 8 Jun 1864 to Daniel Scott, admin. (SA 12 Jun 1863)

MISKIMMON, THOMAS, see "Mary Elizabeth Arthur," q.v.

MISTER, THOMAS R., of Anne Arundel Co., MD, and Janette Foster m. 4 Jan 1863 in Baltimore by Rev. Williams of the Baptist Church (SA 10 Jan 1863)

MITCHELL, ALEXANDER, of Philadelphia, and Miss Henrietta Stump m. 27 Apr 1865, at *Perry Farm* in Cecil Co., by Rev. T. S. C. Smith (AI 5 May 1865)

MITCHELL, AMANDA S. (Miss), dau. of Bernard Mitchell, Esq., and John L. Williams m. Tues. 21 Jan 1868 at St. John's Church, Havre de Grace, by Rev. Henry B. Martin, M.D. (AI 24 Jan 1868)

MITCHELL, ANN MARTHA (Miss) and Calvin Michael, both of Harford Co., m. last Tues. evening by Rev. Finney (HM 17 Apr 1856)

MITCHELL, BERNARD, see "Eliza Mitchell," q.v.

MITCHELL, DANIEL, died Sat. 18 Nov 1865 at the residence of his sister in Harford Co., aged about 60 (AI 24 Nov 1865)

MITCHELL, E. MADISON, of Prince George's Co., formerly of Harford Co., and Virginia E. Hughes, dau. of John Hughes, Esq., of Baltimore Co., m. 22 Dec 1870, at the residence of the bride's parents, by Rev. J. A. Price, assisted by Rev. Samuel Register, D.D. (AI 30 Dec 1870)

MITCHELL, EDWARD, died Wed. evening 23 Nov 1870, in his 58th year (AI 25 Nov 1870)

MITCHELL, ELIZA, wife of Bernard Mitchell, died 23 Feb 1859 at Havre de Grace, in her 53rd year (SA 5 Mar 1859)

MITCHELL, ELIZA (Miss) and William Ewing, Sr., m. Tues. 6 Apr 1869 at Hopewell by Rev. Cochell (HD 16 Apr 1869)

MITCHELL, ELIZA J., see "Andrew Dulin," q.v.

MITCHELL, ELIZABETH, relict of the late Evan Mitchell, of Harford Co., died 8 Feb 1870, in her 86th year (AI 27 May 1870)

MITCHELL, ELLA A. (Mrs.) and Lemuel E. Mathews, both of Harford Co., m. 23 Feb 1870, at the parsonage of the Caroline Street M. E. Church, by Rev. Joseph R. Wheeler (HD 4 Mar 1870; AI 4 Mar 1870 mistakenly states 22 Feb 1870)

MITCHELL, EVAN, see "Elizabeth Mitchell," q.v.

MITCHELL, FREDERICK O. and Miss Eliza A. McGaw, both of Harford Co., m. Thurs. 26 May 1864 (AI 27 May 1864)

MITCHELL, GEORGE V. and Sallie M. Courtney, second dau. of
Benjamin S. Courtney, of Harford Co., m. 6 Dec 1866 in Baltimore
by Rev. John McCron (AI 14 Dec 1866)
MITCHELL, JANE, see "Parker Mitchell," q.v.
MITCHELL, JOHN H., see "John Barnes" and "Richard Hopkins," q.v.
MITCHELL, JOSEPH (Doctor), formerly of Harford Co., died 25 Apr
1870 at his residence in Steubenville, Ohio [age not given] (AI 27
May 1870)
MITCHELL, MARY A. (Miss) and John L. Williams, both of Harford
Co., m. Thurs. 28 Jan 1864 at St. John's Church, Havre de Grace,
by Rev. W. C. Langdon (SA 5 Feb 1864)
MITCHELL, PARKER, died ---- (date not given) and the administrator's
notice stated that creditors must exhibit their legal vouchers by 9
Oct 1839 to Jane Mitchell, admin. (HM 18 Oct 1838)
MITCHELL, ROBERT P. and Miss Mary C. Hughes, second dau. of
Amos Hughes, m. 15 Jan 1867 by Rev. J. K. Cramer (AI 1 Feb
1867)
MITCHELL, THOMAS P. and Lydia A. Courtney, youngest dau. of
Benjamin S. Courtney, of Harford Co., m. 8 Dec 1868 by Rev. Dr.
Dickson (AI 11 Dec 1868)
MONKS, EDWARD T. and Miss Ellen C. Treadway, both of Harford
Co., m. 13 Aug 1866 at the Parsonage in Bel Air by Rev. J. K.
Nichols (AI 17 Aug 1866); see "John E. Treadway," q.v.
MONKS, JOHN C. and Miss Tabitha E. Whitaker, both of Harford Co.,
m. 5 Mar 1857 in Baltimore by Rev. G. F. Adams (HD 13 Mar
1857)
MONTGOMERY, CAROLINE A., wife of Dr. James Montgomery, for
many years a resident of Harford Co., died Mon. 27 Nov 1865 in
Baltimore (AI 1 Dec 1865)
MONTGOMERY, JAMES, see "Caroline A. Montgomery," q.v.
MONTGOMERY, JOHN, see "---- Nicholl (Nichols)," q.v.
MOORE, E. J. B., see "James Moore," q.v.
MOORE, EDWARD A., died 25 Mar 1856, in his 28th year, at the
residence of J. H. Kennard in Baltimore Co.; he was member of the
Kent Co. Bar (HD 4 Apr 1856)
MOORE, JAMES, died Sat. 8 Oct 1864 at his residence in Harford Co.,
aged about 66 (AI 28 Oct 1864); the subsequent administrator's
notice stated that creditors must exhibit their legal vouchers by 23
Nov 1865 to E. J. B. Moore, exec. (AI 13 Jan 1865)
MOORE, MARY JANE, eldest dau. of Patrick and Mary Moore, died 18
Sep 1868 at *Home Farm*, the residence of S. W. Raymond, Esq.,
aged 6 years, 6 months and 4 days; one obituary contains a short
poem (AI 9 Oct 1868; HD 2 Oct 1868)
MOORE, PATRICK, see "Mary Jane Moore," q.v.
MOORE, WILLIAM W., a youth, was skating a few days ago and fell
through the ice on the Susquehanna River near Wrightsville, PA
and drowned (SA 5 Feb 1859)

MOORES, A. PACA, see "Laura P. Moores," q.v.

MOORES, HENRY C., son of the late Dr. Samuel L. and Marie N. Moores, of Baltimore Co., died suddenly 9 Jul 1870 at 2 a.m., aged 29, leaving a wife and large circle of friends; he was interred in Baltimore Cemetery on Sun. 10 Jul (AI 15 Jul 1870)

MOORES, LAURA P. (Miss), dau. of the late A. Paca Moores, Esq., of Harford Co., and George Y. Maynadier m. Wed. 26 Oct 1870 at Emmanuel Church, Bel Air, by Rev. William E. Snowden (HD 28 Oct 1870 and AI 28 Oct 1870)

MOORES, MARIE, see "Henry C. Moores," q.v.

MOORES, RACHEL ELIZABETH, dau. of the late Dr. Samuel Lee Moores, of Baltimore Co., died Fri. 29 Feb 1864 in Baltimore (SA 26 Feb 1864)

MOORES, SAMUEL, see "Henry C. Moores," q.v.

MOORES, SAMUEL LEE, See "Rachel Elizabeth Moores," q.v.

MORDEW, ISABELLA, dau. of Anthony and Margaret Mordew, of Harford Co., died 28 Jun 1864 in Baltimore Co. (AI 27 Jan 1865)

MORGAN, EDWARD, died 25 Sep 1863 in Harford Co., aged 76; for many years he was a resident of Baltimore; obituary contains a poem; the subsequent administrator's notice stated that creditors must exhibit their legal vouchers by 19 Oct 1864 to Edward D. Richardson, admin. (SA 2 Oct 1863 and 23 Oct 1863); see "Julia Morgan," q.v.

MORGAN, JULIA (Miss), dau. of Edward Morgan, Esq., and Edward D. Richardson, of Donaldsonville, Louisiana, m. 13 Nov 1847 in Harford Co., by Rev. Keech (HM 2 Dec 1847)

MORGAN, MARGARET, died ---- (date not given) and the executor's notice stated that creditors must exhibit their legal vouchers by 4 Aug 1847 to Ephraim Hopkins, exec. (HM 30 Apr 1847)

MORGAN, MARY E. and John H. Barnes, both of Havre de Grace, m. Tues. 26 Jun 1866 at the Presbyterian Church, in Havre de Grace, by Rev. Cramer (AI 6 Jul 1866)

MORGAN, PAULINA C., see "William H. Morgan," q.v.

MORGAN, R. L., see "Benjamin Silver," q.v.

MORGAN, ROBERT E., see "T. Hamilton Morgan," q.v.

MORGAN, T. HAMILTON, died ---- (date not given) and the executor's notice stated that creditors must exhibit their legal vouchers by 23 Jul 1863 to Robert E. Morgan, exec. (SA 2 Aug 1862)

MORGAN, THOMAS E., of Washington, D.C., and Miss L. Jennie Osborn, dau. of Amos Osborn, Esq., of Harford Co., m. 17 Feb 1870 at the Presbyterian Church, Havre de Grace, by Rev. William H. Cooke (AI 25 Feb 1870 and HD 25 Feb 1870; HR 19 Feb 1870 gave her name as "Miss Jennie Osborne" and his name as "T. L. Morgan, Esq.")

MORGAN, THOMAS H., died Wed. 30 Apr 1862 at his residence near Mill Green, Harford Co., in his 70th year (SA 10 May 1862)

MORGAN, WILLIAM B., see "Mary E. Barnes," q.v.

MORGAN, WILLIAM H., formerly of Baltimore, died 13 Oct 1864 at his residence in Harford Co., in his 69th year (AI 21 Oct 1864)

MORGAN, WILLIAM H., Esq., of Harford Co., was attacked with paralysis on Fri. last week and died at his residence on Mon. 6 Jun 1870 morning, in his 59th year; an energetic businessman, he was at one time Collector for the 5th District (AI 10 Jun 1870 and 24 Jun 1870); the subsequent administratrix's notice stated that creditors must exhibit their legal vouchers by 8 Aug 1871 to Paulina C. Morgan, admx. (AI 12 Aug 1870)

MORRIS, JOSHUA B., died ---- (date not given) and the administrator's notice stated that creditors must exhibit their legal vouchers by 10 Feb 1864 to Mansel E. Morrison, admin. (SA 6 Mar 1863)

MORRIS, WILLIAM and Mrs. Mary E. Andrew, both of Harford Co., m. 5 Apr 1870 by Rev. J. G. Moore (AI 6 May 1870)

MORRISON, ALICE, dau. of Susan and Mansel Morrison, died Sun. 7 Dec 1862 at the residence of her father in Harford Co., aged 13 (SA 13 Dec 1862)

MORRISON, ARAMINTA G., wife of Hugh J. Morrison, died Sun. 23 Jul 1871, in her 58th year (HD 28 Jul 1871)

MORRISON, CYNTHIA (Miss), aged 46, died 9 Jul 1869 in Havre de Grace at the residence of her brother-in-law Thomas M. Bacon, Esq.; she had joined the Methodist Episcopal Church in 1860 and remained a member all her life (HR 15 Jul 1869)

MORRISON, GEORGE C., son of M. E. and S. E. Morrison, of Harford Co., died 14 Sep 1867 near Hempstead, Austin Co., Texas, of yellow fever, in his 28th year (AI 4 Oct 1867)

MORRISON, HUGH J., see "Araminta G. Morrison," q.v.

MORRISON, M. E., see "George C. Morrison," q.v.

MORRISON, MANSEL E., see "Joshua B. Morris," q.v.

MORRISON, MARY FRANCES, infant dau. of Robert D. and Mary Frances Morrison, of Baltimore, died 8 Jul 1870 at night (AI 15 Jul 1870)

MORRISON, S. E., see "George C. Morrison," q.v.

MOULTON, EZEKIEL, see "John Levy" and "Matthew Moulton," q.v.

MOULTON, MATTHEW, died ---- (date not given) and the executor's notice stated that creditors must exhibit their legal vouchers by 21 Nov 1844 to Ezekiel Moulton, exec. (HM 17 May 1844)

MOULTON, SAMUEL, of Cecil Co., and Miss Martha E. Dorsey, of Baltimore, m. 12 Sep 1869 by Rev. R. Norris (HD 24 Sep 1869; AI 24 Sep 1869 misspelled his name as "Moltin")

MULDOON, THOMAS, aged 10, son of Mrs. Muldoon, a widow, living at the corner of Camden St. and Charles St. in Baltimore, died accidentally at the Pratt Street Depot last evening about 6 o'clock; the boy had just left the tobacco manufactory of Messrs. A. and J. Bonn where he was employed and, crossing the street, thoughtlessly posted himself against the side of the gateway leading to the depot; while occupied in eating a cake, one of the passenger cars of the

Cumberland train accidentally jammed him against the wall, crushing his head and breast in a dreadful manner; he lived but a few minutes; his mother was sent for but arrived soon after his death; her piteous cries were truly heart rending; we learn she had also been dependent on her son's earnings to support herself and her five other fatherless children (HM 17 May 1844)

MUNNIKHUYSEN, FANNY H., dau. of John A. Munnikhuysen, Esq., and James D. Watters, all of Harford Co., m. Tues. evening 20 Oct 1868 at the M. P. Church, Bel Air, by Rev. T. D. Valiant (AI 23 Oct 1868)

MUNNIKHUYSEN, JOHN A., see "Mary Ann Bond," q.v.

MUNNIKHUYSEN, WILLIAM, of Harford Co., and Louise Wyatt, of Winchester, VA, m. 10 Nov 1869 at Christ Church, Winchester, by Rev. J. B. Avirett (AI 26 Nov 1869)

MURNEY, PATRICK, died ---- (date not given) and the notice stated that creditors must exhibit their demands to John C. Farr, exec., No. 112 Chesnut St., Philadelphia; notice dated 15 Dec 1843 (HM 17 May 1844)

MURPHY, ALPHEUS, of the borough of Washington, PA, and Miss Sallie Guyton, of Harford Co., m. Thurs. 17 Jan 1867, in said borough, by Rev. R. V. Dodge (AI 8 Feb 1867)

MURPHY, ELIZABETH H., wife of William B. Murphy, formerly of Harford Co., died 19 Jan 1864 at Louisville, KY, in her 64th year (SA 12 Feb 1864)

MURPHY, HANNAH (Miss), dau. of Timothy Murphy of Havre de Grace, who had been living in Baltimore for some months, died accidentally last Fri. evening when the coal oil can she used to ignite kindling exploded, setting her clothes on fire; she died from the effects on Sat. morning; her remains were brought to Havre de Grace on Sun. and interred in the Catholic Cemetery; she was in her 18th year (HR 27 May 1870)

MURPHY, HANNAH BOND, wife of Isaac T. Murphy, Esq., of Louisville, Kentucky, and dau. of Rev. Robert Bolton and the late Margaret Bolton, of Harford Co., died 1 Nov 1867 at Louisville, in her 38th year, leaving a husband and a large family of children; burial in Cave Hill Cemetery near Louisville (AI 15 Nov 1867)

MURPHY, ISAAC T., see "Hannah Bond Murphy," q.v.

MURPHY, JOHN, was murdered (date not given) in Harford Co. and John Harley was indicted for the crime; his trial was removed to Cecil Co. in November 1858 (SA 20 Nov 1858)

MURPHY, SALLIE E. (Miss), of Harford Co., and Thomas R. Davis, of Baltimore, m. 7 Jul 1863 by Rev. Bishop (SA 31 Jul 1863)

MURPHY, TIMOTHY, died 25 Oct 1870, in his 55th year, at the residence of his son (HR 28 Oct 1870); see "Miss Hannah Murphy," q.v.

MURPHY, WILLIAM B., see "Elizabeth H. Murphy," q.v.

MURRY, SARAH (Miss) and Richard A. Sands, both of Baltimore, m. 27 Feb 1865 by Rev. Dr. Dunning (AI 7 Apr 1865)

MYERS, ALEXANDER K. (Captain), died 21 Aug 1871, in his 68th year, at Havre de Grace (HR 25 Aug 1871); Alex. K. Myers was subsequently removed from the voter registration list in the 6th District in 1871 (HR 27 Oct 1871)

MYERS, ELIZABETH (Mrs.), aged 87, died very suddenly last Sun. morning at the residence of her son Capt. J. Kendall Myers (HR 28 Apr 1871)

MYERS, GEORGE W., an old gentleman who lived alone at Swansbury Mills, was found dead in his bed last Sun. morning (HD 24 Mar 1871)

MYERS, J. KENDALL, see "Elizabeth Myers," q.v.

MYERS, W. A. and Miss Georgianna Lawder, both of Havre de Grace, m. 16 Jan 1869 at the Episcopal Church by Rev. H. B. Martin (HR 28 Jan 1869)

MYERS, WILLIAM, see "William H. Thomson," q.v.

NANKEEVIS, SAMUEL, an English preacher, was convicted at Pottsville, PA recently, of murder in the first degree, for killing his infant child (AI 24 Dec 1869)

NASH, JANE E. (Miss), of Harford Co., and William H. Tammany, of Cecil Co., m. 14 Oct 1868 (AI 16 Oct 1868)

NASH, JOHN, who left Baltimore yesterday morning for the camp meeting at Aberdeen, Harford Co., was overcome by the heat shortly after his arrival; medical attention was prompt, but he died in a short time; physicians indicate death was caused by apoplexy, super-induced by the heat; his body was returned last evening to his residence on Ann St., near Bank St., in Baltimore [article also appeared in the *Baltimore Sun*] (AI 27 Aug 1869)

NEGRO PETER ----, see "Colored Woman," q.v.

NEIL, ADDIE R. (Miss), dau. of Francis Neil, Esq., of Baltimore, and William H. Vanderford, Esq., editor of the *Democratic Advocate*, Westminster, MD, m. Thurs. 25 Nov 1869 at Loyola College, Baltimore, by Rev. Father Boone [her surname was given as both Neil and Neal]; the editor of *The Aegis & Intelligencer* offered his congratulations to his brother editor (AI 10 Dec 1869)

NELSON, AQUILLA, see "Louisa G. Nelson" and "Frances Nelson," q.v.

NELSON, B. J., died ---- (date not given) and was removed from the voter registration list in the 4th District in 1868 (AI 9 Oct 1868)

NELSON, BELLE (Miss) and George Richard Cairnes, both of Harford Co., m. 11 Feb 1869 in Baltimore by Rev. Dr. Smith (HD 19 Feb 1869 and AI 26 Feb 1869)

NELSON, BENNETT, see "George Nelson," q.v.

NELSON, CLARA A., dau. of Jarrett Nelson, Esq., and John A. Conkling, all of Baltimore Co., m. Thurs. 1 Nov 1868, at the residence of the bride's father, by Rev. William A. McKee (AI 20 Nov 1868)

NELSON, DAVID D., son of William and Sarah Nelson, died Thurs. 2 Feb 1865 at the residence of his father in Harford Co. (AI 10 Feb 1865)

NELSON, FRANCES, relict of the late Aquilla Nelson, died Sun. evening 12 Sep 1847 at her residence in Bush River Neck, Harford Co., after a short but severe illness, in her 73rd year (HM 17 Sep 1847); see "Louisa G. Nelson," q.v.

NELSON, GEORGE, died ---- (date not given) and the executor's notice stated that creditors must exhibit their legal vouchers by 26 Mar 1864 to Bennett Nelson, exec. (SA 3 Apr 1863)

NELSON, GEORGE H., see "Hannah Nelson," q.v.

NELSON, HANNAH, died ---- (date not given) and the administrator's notice stated that creditors must exhibit their legal vouchers by 24 Mar 1863 to George H. Nelson, admin. (SA 22 Mar 1862)

NELSON, HENRY, died ---- (date not given) and the administratrix's notice stated that creditors must exhibit their legal vouchers by 30 Jan 1868 to Mary A. Nelson, admx. (AI 8 Feb 1867)

NELSON, JAMES, died Mon. 8 Jan 1866, aged 45, at his residence in Harford Co. (AI 2 Feb 1866)

NELSON, JAMES B., died 30 Mar 1868, in his 33rd year (AI 17 Apr 1868)

NELSON, JARRETT, see "Clara A. Nelson," q.v.

NELSON, LOUISA G., dau. of the late Aquilla and Frances Nelson, died 21 Sep 1869 at Locust Point in Harford Co. [age not given] (AI 8 Oct 1869); the subsequent administrator's notice stated that creditors must exhibit their legal vouchers by 13 Nov 1870 to Abraham Cole, admin. (AI 19 Nov 1869 misspelled her name as "Lousia")

NELSON, N., see "Thomas Nelson," q.v.

NELSON, ROBERT A., of Harford Co., and Miss Maggie Hunter, of Baltimore Co., m. 15 Oct 1868 by Rev. T. M. Cathcart (AI 23 Oct 1868)

NELSON, SARAH, see "David D. Nelson," q.v.

NELSON, THOMAS and Miss Bell Ashton m. last Thurs. at Rock Spring Church by Rev. Snowden; Jennie Ashton was the bride's maid and Charles Streett was the groom's man (HD 25 Feb 1870)

NELSON, THOMAS H. and Miss Isabel Ashton m. 17 Feb 1870 at Christ Church (Rock Spring) by Rev. W. E. Snowden (AI 18 Mar 1870)

NELSON, WILLIAM, died Fri. 19 Mar 1869 at his residence near Swanbury, aged 57 (AI 2 Apr 1869); see "David D. Nelson," q.v.

NELSON, WILLIAM, Esq., and Mrs. Elizabeth Stansbury, both of Harford Co., m. Mon. evening 16 Apr 1838 by Rev. Andrew B. Cross (HM 26 Apr 1838)

NEVILLE, ELIZABETH, see "John Neville," q.v.

NEVILLE, GEORGE B., died ---- (date not given) and the administrator's notice stated that creditors must exhibit their legal vouchers by 19 Jul 1863 to Samuel H. Bateman, admin. (SA 2 Aug 1862); see "John Neville," q.v.

NEVILLE, J. H., see "Ruth Davis," q.v.

NEVILLE, JOHN, died 26 Sep 1861 at his residence, *Oak Grove*, Harford Co., after a long and painful illness, in his 75th year; obituary contains a brief memorial written by "T.B.B." (SA 5 Oct 1861); the subsequent executor's notice stated that creditors must exhibit their legal vouchers by 15 Oct 1862 to Elizabeth Neville and George B. Neville, execs. (SA 26 Oct 1861)

NICHOLL (NICHOLS), ----, was murdered in Harford Co. in 1858 (exact date not given) and John Montgomery and John Bernard were indicted for the crime; Montgomery was subsequently convicted of the crime and sentenced to 18 years in the state penitentiary; Bernard was acquitted (SA 27 Nov 1858 and 14 May 1859)

NICOLS, MOLLIE M., youngest dau. of Thomas C. Nicols, Esq., and J. C. O'Brien, of Baltimore, m. 17 Dec 1868 at the residence of the bride's father in Easton, MD, by Rev. Dr. Kenney (AI 15 Jan 1869)

NICOLS, THOMAS AND MARTHA, see "Mollie H. O'Brien," q.v.

NORRIS, ---- (Negro), see "---- Bennett (Negro)," q.v.

NORRIS, ALEXANDER, see "J. Charles Norris" and "Unknown Negro," q.v.

NORRIS, ALEXANDER JR. and Miss Maria A. Crawford, of New Orleans, LA, m. Tues. 7 Jan 1868 at *Mt. Pleasant*, Harford Co., by Rev. William F. Brand (AI 24 Jan 1868)

NORRIS, ANN (Miss), of Harford Co., and James Gemmill, of York Co., PA, m. Thurs. 21 Dec 1837 by Rev. Samuel Parke (HM 28 Dec 1837)

NORRIS, CASSANDRA, relict of Septimus Norris and dau. of the late John W. Stump, died 18 Jun 1865 at Lancaster, PA; the subsequent executor's notice in Harford Co. stated that creditors must exhibit their legal vouchers by 24 Oct 1866 to Octavius Norris, exec.; a later notice indicated the public sale of her personal property will be held on 26 Sep 1866 at *Woodside,* near Thomas Run P. O., by Octavius J. Norris, exec. (AI 30 Jun 1865 and 10 Nov 1865 and 21 Sep 1866)

NORRIS, CORNELIA (Miss) and Daniel Scott, Esq., both of Harford Co., m. Wed. 18 Nov 1863 (SA 20 Nov 1863)

NORRIS, G. SMITH, see "J. Charles Norris," q.v.

NORRIS, J. CHARLES, son of Alexander Norris, Esq., of Harford Co., died 8 Sep 1865 at Columbus, GA, aged 32; the subsequent administrator's notice in Harford Co. gave his full name as John Charles Norris and stated that creditors must exhibit their legal vouchers by 21 Mar 1867 to G. Smith Norris and Mary J. Norris, admins. (AI 22 Sep 1865 and 23 Mar 1866

NORRIS, LIZZIE (Miss) and John Botts, both of Harford Co., m. 10 Nov 1864 in Bel Air (AI 25 Nov 1864)

NORRIS, MARY ANN, died on the 14th day of the 8th month, 1870, at the residence of James T. Watson, Harford Co., in her 77th year (AI 19 Aug 1870)

NORRIS, MARY F. (Miss), formerly of Virginia, and Robert J. Cully, of Harford Co., m. 26 Apr 1864 by Rev. Kramer in Havre de Grace (AI 20 May 1864)

NORRIS, MARY J., see "J. Charles Norris," q.v.

NORRIS, OCTAVIUS, see Cassandra Norris," q.v.

NORRIS, SEPTIMUS, died 18 Sep 1862 at his residence in Philadelphia, in his 44th year (SA 27 Sep 1862); see "Cassandra Norris," q.v.

NORRIS, SOPHIA C., dau. of William B. Norris, Esq., and Richard E. Webster, all of Harford Co., m. 6 Jun 1867 at St. Luke's Church, Baltimore, by Rev. William F. Brand (AI 14 Jun 1867)

NORRIS, WILLIAM B., see "John Johnson" and "Sophia C. Norris," q.v.

NORRIS, WILLIAM J. and Miss Alverda Scarff, both of Harford Co., m. Thurs. 20 Oct 1870 at the M. P. Parsonage, Jarrettsville, by Rev. J. C. Hagey (HD 28 Oct 1870 and AI 28 Oct 1870)

NOUNAN, MICHAEL, died 18 Sep 1867 near Bel Air, aged 84; obituary contains a short poem (AI 27 Sep 1867)

NUMBERS, JAMES, died ---- (date not given) and the administratrix's notice stated that creditors must exhibit their legal vouchers by 29 Dec 1869 to Sarah J. Numbers, admx. (AI 1 Jan 1869)

NUMBERS, MATTIE (Miss) and William F. Aaronson, both of Harford Co., m. 27 Oct 1870, in Aberdeen M. E. Church, by Rev. J. G. Moore (AI 4 Nov 1870)

O'BRIEN, EDWARD and Miss Mary Ann McGra, both of Harford Co., m. 29 Dec 1844 by Rev. J. Larkin (HM 3 Jan 1845)

O'BRIEN, J. C., of Baltimore, and Mollie M. Nicols, youngest dau. of Thomas C. Nicols, Esq., m. 17 Dec 1868 at the residence of the bride's father in Easton, MD, by Rev. Dr. Kenney (AI 15 Jan 1869)

O'BRIEN, MOLLIE H., wife of J. C. O'Brien and youngest dau. of Thomas C. and Martha Nicols, died 2 Oct 1869 at the residence of her father in Easton, MD, aged 29 years and 10 months; obituary contains a brief memorial (AI 14 Oct 1869)

O'DONNELL, FRANCIS, was killed in a railroad accident in Jersey City, NJ while working for the Patterson Railroad about 9 p.m. last Fri.; he was thrown from the platform under the wheels and killed instantly (HM 2 Sep 1852)

O'KEEFE, ROSANNA (Mrs.) and George McFarland m. 5 Sep 1858 at Long Green by Rev. J. A. Walter [*Baltimore County Advocate* (MD) and *Chester County Jeffersonian* (PA) please copy] (SA 11 Sep 1858)

O'NEILL, JAMES, of Havre de Grace, was killed last week in Frederick Co., VA near Cedar Creek bridge on the Baltimore and Strasburg

Branch Railroad; the gang of which he was master was blowing their way through a heavy vein of limestone; three blasts had been prepared when it was discovered that one of the fuses was defective; O'Neill went forward to remedy the situation and when he pulled out the safety fuse the blast ignited, and his body was blown literally to pieces; his death has deprived a large family of its protector (HR 25 Feb 1870 and HD 4 Mar 1870)

O'NEILL, JOHN, died ---- (date not given) and the executor's notice stated that creditors must exhibit their legal vouchers by 29 Feb 1839 to William O'Neill, exec. (HM 24? May 1838)

O'NEILL, WILLIAM, see "John O'Neill," q.v.

OBERMAN, LOUIS, see "Peter Fitzner," q.v.

ODEN, ELLEN (Miss), of Baltimore, and John H. Hollingsworth, of Harford Co., m. 5 Nov 1868 by Rev. D. A. Shermer (AI 13 Nov 1868)

OLDFIELD, WILLIAM JR., late Sergeant of Co. B, 8th Cavalry Bttn., M. N. G., was buried last Wed. at Mt. Zion Church, near his residence, with military honors by his comrades; the funeral was one of the largest ever seen in this neighborhood [Bel Air], notwithstanding the bad condition of the roads; a resolution in his honor was passed at the company's meeting on 16 Feb 1870 and published by Capt. Otho S. Lee, chairman, and Charles E. Fendall, secretary (AI 18 Feb 1870)

OLDFIELD, WILLIAM, see "Benjamin Shears," q.v.

OLIVER, DR., an Englishman and agent of an immigration company, was killed on Thurs. morning last week at Charlottesville, VA, by George Ayres, a planter of Fauquier Co., VA, for seducing the dau. of the latter, while visiting his house a few months ago; a subsequent newspaper article indicated R. S. Ayers, who was tried at Charlottesville for the killing of Dr. Oliver, had been acquitted (AI 24 Dec 1869 and 23 Sep 1870)

ONION, JOSEPH B. J., died ---- (date not given) and the administrator's notice stated that creditors must exhibit their legal vouchers by 11 Oct 1865 to Lloyd D. Onion, admin. (AI 14 Oct 1864)

ORR, SQUIRE, see "Robert Jones," q.v.

OSBORN, AMOS, see "L. Jennie Osborn" and "Sarah E. Osborn," q.v.

OSBORN, BENNETT, died Mon. 23 Sep 1867 at his brother's residence, Michaelsville, Harford Co., in his 58th year (AI 4 Oct 1867)

OSBORN, L. JENNIE, dau. of Amos Osborn, Esq., of Harford Co., and Thomas E. Morgan, of Washington, D.C., m. 17 Feb 1870 at the Presbyterian Church, Havre de Grace, by Rev. William H. Cooke (AI 25 Feb 1870; HD 25 Feb 1870; HR 19 Feb 1870 gave her name as "Miss Jennie Osborne" and his name as "T. L. Morgan, Esq.")

OSBORN, LUTHER and Miss Sallie R. Wells, dau. of Joseph Wells, Esq., all of Harford Co., m. 10 Dec 1868, at home, by Rev. J. G. Moore (AI 25 Dec 1868)

OSBORN, MR., see "Alex. McCombs," q .v.

OSBORN, SARAH E. (Miss), dau. of Amos Osborn, of Harford Co., died Fri. morning 22 Apr 1859, in her 21st year; obituary contains a memorial (SA 7 May 1859)

OSBORN, WILLIAM, died ---- (date not given) and the administrator's notice stated that creditors must exhibit their legal vouchers by 24 Sep 1840 to Jacob Michael, admin. (HM 21 Nov 1839)

OSBORNE, JENNIE (Miss), see "L. Jennie Osborn," q.v.

OSMOND, H. C. and Miss Clara Gallup, both of Havre de Grace, m. 5 Jan 1871 by Rev. William Cooke (HR 3 Feb 1871)

OWENS, JAMES JR., see "Edward Reynolds," q.v.

OWENS (OWINGS), JOHN T., of Charlestown, Cecil Co., a section supervisor on the passenger train from Baltimore to Philadelphia, left the city at 7:25 p.m. and when it neared Magnolia Station ran over a cow and jumped the tracks; Owens remained under the locomotive near the fire box for two hours before being extricated; he died from his injuries the next night (HR 19 Aug 1870); another newspaper stated John T. Owings, track supervisor on the P. W. & B. Railroad who was severely injured by the accident on Philadelphia Road near Magnolia Station last Sat. night, died yesterday morning; he was a member of the Masonic fraternity; a delegation of the Knights Templar of Baltimore will attend his funeral from his residence in Perryville, Cecil Co., today [another article described the train wreck in detail] (HD 19 Aug 1870)

PACA, JAMES C., see "John P. Paca," q.v.

PACA, JOHN P. (of Edward), died ---- (date not given) and his uncle William B. Paca and cousins John P. Paca and James C. Paca were accused of murdering him, but they were found not guilty by verdict of a jury in Caroline Co., MD on 24 Mar 1866 [*Easton Journal*] (AI 30 Mar 1866)

PACA, WILLIAM (Colonel), died Thurs. of last week at *Wye Oak*, his residence in Queen Anne's Co., MD, of bilious dysentery, followed by paralysis, in his 70th year; in former years he took a great interest in politics, was spoken of for Governor of the state, and was a man of great wealth [notice was copied from the *Baltimore Sun*] (AI 9 Sep 1870)

PACA, WILLIAM B., see "John P. Paca," q.v.

PAIRO, EDWIN, of Richmond, VA, and Miss Sarah J. Cunningham m. 17 Feb 1870 at the residence of the bride's father, Walter Cunningham, Esq., by Rev. George M. Berry (HD 4 Mar 1870 and AI 4 Mar 1870)

PALMER, GEORGIE A., see "Mary E. McCoy," q.v.

PANNELL, ISABELLA W., youngest dau. of the late James Pannell, of Harford Co., and A. Henry Strausbaugh, of Howard Co., MD, m. 30 Oct 1862 at *Silverton*, in Harford Co., by Rev. William Finney (SA 8 Nov 1862)

PANNELL, JAMES, died ---- (date not given) and the executor's notice stated that creditors must exhibit their legal vouchers by 18 Dec 1855 to William F. Pannell, exec. (HM 1 Mar 1855); see "Isabella W. Pannell" and "Susan Pannell," q.v.

PANNELL, SUSAN, relict of the late James Pannell, died Wed. 30 Apr 1862 at the residence of her son-in-law, Mr. Silver, in her 72nd year (SA 10 May 1862)

PANNELL, WILLIAM, see "James Pannell" and "William E. McGaw," q.v.

PANTZ, MR., see "Thomas Woolen," q.v.

PARKER, ALICE, wife of Dr. James H. Parker and dau. of the late Richard D. Lee, Esq., of Harford Co., died Thurs. 16 Nov 1865 at Onancock in Accomac Co., VA (AI 24 Nov 1865)

PARKER, JAMES H., see "Alice Parker," q.v.

PARKER, JOSEPH, died ---- (date not given) and the executor's notice stated that creditors must exhibit their legal vouchers by 31 Feb [sic] 1841 to Joseph C. Parker, exec. (HM 10 Oct 1840); see "Margery Parker," q.v.

PARKER, MARGERY, died ---- (date not given) and the administrator's notice stated that creditors must exhibit their legal vouchers by 21 Nov 1844 to Joseph C. Parker, admin. (HM 8 Dec 1843); see "Joseph Parker," q.v.

PARKS, JOSEPH, see "Basil Grafton," q.v.

PARLETT, DAVID and Miss Mary Knight, both of Harford Co., m. 28 Dec 1865 by Rev. J. K. Nichols (AI 5 Jan 1866)

PARLETT, ELIZABETH E. (Miss) and Thomas H. Poteet, both of the Fourth District, Harford Co., m. 31 Jul 1862 by Rev. E. Welty (SA 9 Aug 1862)

PATTERSON (PATTISON), SAMUEL, see "Agnes Patterson," q.v.

PATTERSON, AGNES (Miss), dau. of the late Samuel Patterson, and A. D. R. Spencer, all of Havre de Grace, m. 10 Jun 1869 at the residence of the bride, Havre de Grace, by Rev. W. H. Cook [Philadelphia, PA and San Francisco, CA papers please copy] (AI 18 Jun 1869 and 2 Jul 1869; the former newspaper edition spelled the name as "Pattison")

PATTERSON, AMENTIS T. and Miss H. Ellen Hanna, both of Harford Co., m. 12 Mar 1857 by Rev. William Finney (HD 20 Mar 1857)

PATTERSON, CORDELIA P., died on the morning of 25 Aug 1868, in her 20th year; she was a consistent member of the Episcopal Church; obituary contains a long memorial and a short poem written by a friend "M." in Harford Co., 29 Aug 1868 (AI 4 Sep 1868)

PATTERSON, ELIZABETH, see "Jerome Napoleon Bonaparte," q.v.

PATTERSON, FANNIE B. (Miss), dau. of the late William A. Patterson, and George G. Airey, of Baltimore, m. 21 Jun 1870 at Spesutia Church, Perrymansville, Harford Co., by Rev. Crampton [marriage notice indicated "No cards"] (AI 1 Jul 1870)

PATTERSON, FREDERICK E., Esq., of Harford Co., and Lillie Powell, youngest dau. of Dr. F. W. Powell, formerly of Loudoun Co., VA, m. Wed. morning 7 Dec 1870 at the residence of the Hon. R. Y. Conrad in Winchester, VA, by Rev. W. C. Meredith [marriage notice indicated "No cards"] (AI 16 Dec 1870); see "William A. Patterson," q.v.

PATTERSON, SAMUEL, see "Agnes Patterson," q.v.

PATTERSON, WILLIAM ALFRED, died Thurs. 14 Jan 1864 at his residence near Perrymansville, in his 51st year; being a member of the Harford Bar, a resolution was adopted in his honor on 22 Feb 1864 and subsequently published (SA 22 Jan 1864 and 26 Feb 1864) the administrator's notice stated that creditors must exhibit their legal vouchers by 7 Apr 1865 to Frederick E. Patterson, admin. (AI 15 Apr 1864); see "Fannie B. Patterson," q.v.

PAUL, JAMES, died 27 Feb 1863, in his 66th year, at the residence of Washington Dorney in Harford Co.; the subsequent executor's notice stated that creditors must exhibit their legal vouchers by 12 Mar 1864 to Washington Dorney, exec. (SA 20 Mar 1863 and 3 Apr 1863)

PAXTON, JOHN R. (Reverend), the successor of Rev. William Finney, in charge of the Presbyterian Church at Churchville, and Miss Mary "Mollie" Lindsay, of Alleghany Co., PA, m. 10 Nov 1870 in Alleghany Co. [two marriage notices in same newspaper] (AI 18 Nov 1870)

PAYNE, BENJAMIN N., Esq., aged 63, died suddenly Sat. evening at Towsontown in Baltimore Co.; he had been in the city that day and returned home on the cars at 6:30 p.m., stopping to see a friend upon his return to Towsontown, where he died almost immediately of heart disease; he leaves a large family of children, all grown; he served Baltimore Co. in the House of Delegates in 1847 as an independent democrat; he later served 4 years as a Judge of the Orphans' Court for Baltimore County, retiring from office when the Union party came into power in 1862; he served 2 years as a Justice of the Peace and was also a Director of the Harford Mutual Fire Insurance Co. in Harford Co.; at the time of his death he was extensively engaged as a real estate agent (AI 4 Mar 1870 and HD 4 Mar 1870)

PAYNE, ELLEN, died ---- (date not given) and the administrator's notice stated that creditors must exhibit their legal vouchers by 21 Apr 1871 to John Payne, Admin. C.T.A. (AI 29 Apr 1870)

PAYNE, JOHN, see "Ellen Payne," q.v.

PEABODY, GEORGE, the celebrated philanthropist and banker, died Thurs. night 4 Nov 1869 in London, of congestion of the lungs, in his 71st year, after spending last summer in Virginia Springs in order to recruit his delicate health; his popularity in England, on account of his munificent charities, is not less in this country, and the Queen has herself thanked him for his interest in the poor of her kingdom [his death was mentioned in two articles in the same issue of the newspaper and a third notice appeared in the subsequent issue]; the steamer *Monarch* left England for America on 21 Dec 1869 with the body of George Peabody on board (AI 12 Nov and 19 Nov 1869 and 24 Dec 1869; HD 12 Nov 1869 contains a long article about him and the Peabody Institute, among other things)

PENNINGTON, ANNIE J. (Miss) and Ambrose Aaronson, both of Harford Co., m. 25 May 1870 by Rev. J. G. Moore (AI 3 Jun 1870)

PENNINGTON, CARROLL of Harford Co., and Miss Nannie S. Philips, of Cecil Co., m. 22 Apr 1869, at the house of T. W. Reed, by Rev. Thomas M. Cathcart (HD 30 Apr 1869; AI 30 Apr 1869 gave his name as "Carvill")

PENNINGTON, CATHERINE E. (Miss), dau. of the late William O. Pennington, of Havre de Grace, and John G. McComas, of Baltimore, m. 13 (18?) Jul 1852 by Rev. Cyrus Huntingdon (HM 22 Jul 1852)

PENNINGTON, ELIZA A., died ---- (date not given) and the executor's notice stated that creditors must exhibit their legal vouchers by 12 May 1869 to J. Thompson Frieze, exec. (AI 15 May 1868)

PENNINGTON, FRANKLIN and Eliza E. Arthur, both of Harford Co., m. 5 Sep 1867 by Rev. Thomas M. Cathcart (AI 4 Oct 1867)

PENNINGTON, WILLIAM, see "Catherine E. Pennington," q.v.

PETERS, JAMES S., died ---- (date not given) and Mary D. Peters was admx. of his estate and Charles P. Peters was the agent for the sale of his fruit trees at the Concordville Nursery (HM 11 Dec 1856)

PETERS, PHILIP, died ---- (date not given) and the administrator's notice stated that creditors must exhibit their legal vouchers by 15 May 1863 to Thomas M. Ricketts, admin. (SA 7 Jun 1862)

PETERSON, ELIAS, see "Margaret Ann Peterson," q.v.

PETERSON, JAMES, see "Mary Jane Peterson," q.v.

PETERSON, MARGARET ANN, wife of Elias Peterson, died Wed. 17 Aug 1864, aged 35 [*Cecil Democrat* and *Easton Journal* please copy] (AI 2 Sep 1864)

PETERSON, MARY JANE, dau. of James Peterson, died Sun. 30 Apr 1865 at the residence of William Herman, Esq., in Bel Air, in her 15th year (AI 5 May 1865)

PHELPS, MARY E. (Miss) and William Winstanley m. 26 Mar 1868, at the residence of the bride's father, by Rev. Thomas M. Cathcart (AI 17 Apr 1868)

PHELPS, SYLVESTER and Miss Susanna Arthur, both of Harford Co., m. 7 Sep 1869, at the residence of the bride's father, by Rev. T. M. Cathcart (AI 17 Sep 1869)

PHILIPS, JETER, the wife murderer, was hung last Fri. at Richmond, VA (AI 29 Jul 1870)

PHILIPS, NANNIE S. (Miss), of Cecil Co., and Carroll Pennington, of Harford Co., m. 22 Apr 1869, at the house of T. W. Reed, by Rev.

Thomas M. Cathcart (HD 30 Apr 1869; AI 30 Apr 1869 gave his name as "Carvill")

PHILLIPS, JOHN, see "Noah Phillips," q.v.

PHILLIPS, NOAH (Colonel), died Sun. 8 Feb 1863 at his residence in Frederick Co., MD, aged 85; formerly a prominent Whig politician, but lately acting with the Democratic party, he served in the last war with Great Britain and was the father of Capt. John Phillips and great uncle to Mrs. Dr. G. T. Hays of Harford Co. (SA 27 Feb 1863)

PHILLIPS, WESLEY and Mary C. Billingslea, both of Harford Co., m. 21 Dec 1865 by Rev. E. Kinsey (AI 5 Jan 1866)

PHILLIPS, WILLIAM D., died ---- (date not given) and the administrator's notice stated that creditors must exhibit their legal vouchers by 5 Sep 1838 to John Carsins, admin. (HM 12 Apr 1838)

PHIPIN, ELIJAH B., of Wicomico Co., MD, and Mrs. Annie M. Hutchinson, of Harford Co., m. 28 Apr 1869 at the M. E. Parsonage, Bel Air, by Rev. George M. Berry (AI 14 May 1869 and HD 7 May 1869)

PIERCE, JOHN C., see "John Carville Bayne," q.v.

PILE, MARY M. (Miss), of Philadelphia, and George W. Bryant, of Harford Co., m. Tues. 31 Oct 1871 at First Presbyterian Church in Philadelphia by Rev. Dr. H. Johnson (HR 3 Nov 1871)

PITT, ISAAC (Negro), died ---- (date not given) and the executor's notice stated that creditors must exhibit their legal vouchers by 23 Apr 1865 to George Y. Maynadier, exec. (AI 29 Apr 1864)

PLUMER, CORA LEVINS, only dau. of R. L. and Comfort Plumer, died Sat. 26 Nov 1870, aged 3 years, 1 month and 1 day (HR 2 Dec 1870)

POCOCK, MARY E. (Miss), aged 18 years and 9 months, died Mon. 19 Jun 1871 at her father's residence in Marshall's District (HR 23 Jun 1871); another obituary stated she died 19 Jun 1871 of consumption, in her 19th year, at the residence of her father, Salem Pocock, in Marshall's District; a memorial states she had been converted last fall at Mr. J. W. Rutledge's school house and shortly after joined the M. E. Church at Ebenezer, where her father was class leader (HD 30 Jun 1871)

POCOCK, SALEM, see "Mary E. Pocock," q.v.

POHLAR, HENRY and Miss Margaret Grafton, both of Harford Co., m. 18 Jul 1867 by Rev. T. S. C. Smith (AI 26 Jul 1867)

POLK, JOHN C., see "Mary E. James," q.v.

POLK, LIZZIE, dau. of Dr. John C. Polk, of Harford Co., and Eugene H. Pomeroy, of New York, m. Tues. 21 Nov 1865 at St. Mary's Church, Harford Co., by Rev. W. F. Brand (AI 1 Dec 1865)

POLK, MARGARET and John S. Kennedy, both of Harford Co., m. 2 May 1866 at Mr. J. Wann's, by Rev. W. M. Meminger (AI 4 May 1866)

POMEROY, EUGENE H., of New York, and Lizzie Polk, dau. of Dr. John C. Polk, of Harford Co., m. Tues. 21 Nov 1865 at St. Mary's Church, Harford Co., by Rev. W. F. Brand (AI 1 Dec 1865)

POOLE, HANNAH C., died 4 Jun 1863, aged 22, at the residence of her father John Poole (SA 19 Jun 1863)

POPE (POLK), JOHN C., see "Harry Lee," q.v.

POPE, DANIEL, aged about 80, died suddenly last Tues. morning in Fallston while on a trip to Baltimore with his grandson Mr. D. P. Hollingsworth; he was a member of Society of Friends; D. P. had started to Baltimore with a load of hay and was accompanied by his grandfather as far as Fallston; Pope was walking near the team and suddenly collapsed; he was carried to a nearby store where he died within a few minutes [one obituary mistakenly gave the grandson's name as M. P. Hollingsworth]; the subsequent executor's notice stated that creditors must exhibit their legal vouchers by 17 Dec 1869 to George A. Pope and Daniel P. Hollingsworth, execs. (HR 17 Dec 1868; AI 4 Dec, 11 Dec and 18 Dec 1868)

POPE, GEORGE A., see "Daniel Pope," q.v.

POPLAR, MOLLIE (Miss), one of Capt. James Poplar's children, aged about 2 years, was playing on Wed. last with several small children on the porch of Mr. Kind's house when she was pushed over the railing and fell on her head on the stone payment below; she died on Sat. evening last; a subsequent newspaper notice stated Mollie Poplar, dau. of James and Effie Poplar, died 12 Oct 1870, aged 2 years and 4 months (HR 14 Oct 1870 and 21 Oct 1870)

PORTER, ZELEY W., of Vermont, and Emily Hunter, of Baltimore, formerly of Harford Co., third dau. of George W. and Mary E. Hunter, m. 11 Aug 1870 by Rev. S. B. Blake (AI 30 Sep 1870)

POTEE, GEORGE, see "James H. Armstrong," q.v.

POTEET, THOMAS H. and Miss Elizabeth E. Parlett, both of Fourth District, Harford Co., m. 31 Jul 1862 by Rev. E. Welty (SA 9 Aug 1862)

POTEET, WILLIAM, a resident in the upper part of Harford Co., was dangerously if not fatally wounded last week while in the act of arresting a man supposed to be a deserter; he was shot in the face, tearing away much of one jaw; the perpetrator escaped (SA 4 Sep 1863)

POWELL, LILLIE, youngest dau. of Dr. F. W. Powell, formerly of Loudoun Co., VA, and Frederick E. Patterson, Esq., of Harford Co., m. Wed. morning 7 Dec 1870 at the residence of the Hon. R. Y. Conrad in Winchester, VA, by Rev. W. C. Meredith [marriage notice indicated "No cards"] (AI 16 Dec 1870)

PRATT, THOMAS G., see "Harry D. Gough," q.v.

PREECE, R. W., of Baltimore, and Miss Lottie D. Keen, dau. of Nathaniel B. Keen, of *Woodley Cottage*, Harford Co., m. 14 Nov 1867 at Grove Presbyterian Church by Rev. John C. Cramer (AI 29 Nov 1867)

PRESBURY, GEORGE, see "Martha Sykes," q.v.

PRESTON, ABRAHAM, see "Fanny Preston," q.v.

PRESTON, AVARILLA J. (Mrs.), of Harford Co., died 11 Oct 1859, in her 76th year [*Baltimore Sun* please copy] (SA 29 Oct 1859)

PRESTON, DAVID and Miss Harriet A. Hoskins m. 25 Dec 1867 at the residence of the bride's father, Jesse Hoskins (AI 3 Jan 1868)

PRESTON, ELIZA, see "Harriet Ann Preston," q.v.

PRESTON, ELIZA A., died ---- (date not given) and the executor's notice stated that creditors must exhibit their legal vouchers by 14 Sep 1866 to James B. Preston, exec. (AI 22 Sep 1865)

PRESTON, ELIZABETH, died ---- (date not given) and the executor's notice stated that creditors must exhibit their legal vouchers by 22 May 1862 to Otho Scott, exec. (SA 26 Oct 1861)

PRESTON, FANNY (colored), died ---- (date not given) and the administrator's notice stated that creditors must exhibit their legal vouchers by 19 Jun 1869 to Abraham Cooper (colored), admin. (AI 26 Jun 1868)

PRESTON, HARRIET ANN, died Sun. 7 Mar 1869, aged 4 years, and Jane Preston died Mon. 8 Mar 1869, aged 3 years, of measles, children of Henry and Eliza Preston (AI 12 Mar 1869)

PRESTON, HENRY, see "Harriet Ann Preston," q.v.

PRESTON, J. ALEXANDER, see "Jacob A. Preston," q.v.

PRESTON, JACOB A. (Doctor), died 2 Aug 1868 at his residence in Harford Co., in his 72nd year; the subsequent administrator's notice stated that creditors must exhibit their legal vouchers by 10 Aug 1869 [mistakenly typeset as 1868] to J. Alexander Preston and John F. Preston, admins. (AI 31 Jul 1868 and 14 Aug 1868); see "John W. Preston, Esq.," q.v.

PRESTON, JAMES B., see "Eliza A. Preston," q.v.

PRESTON, JANE, see "Harriet Ann Preston," q.v.

PRESTON, JOHN W. and Miss Mary Lizzie Tucker, dau. of William Tucker, Esq., all of Harford Co., m. Thurs. 4 Feb 1869 by Rev. William A. McKee (AI 12 Feb 1869)

PRESTON, JOHN W., Esq., died Fri. 6 Jul 1866 at *The Vineyard,* his residence in Harford Co., after two years of suffering; obituary contains a brief memorial written by "M."; the administrator's notice stated that creditors must exhibit their legal vouchers by 20 Aug 1867 to Jacob A. Preston, admin.; a subsequent administrator's notice stated that creditors must exhibit their legal vouchers by 10 Aug 1869 [mistakenly typeset as 1868] to John F. Preston, admin. de bonis non (AI 13 Jul 1866 and 17 Aug 1866 and 14 Aug 1868)

PRESTON, SARAH (Mrs.), died last Wed. morning, at an advanced age (HM 8 Apr 1841)

PRICE, CHARLES, died ---- (date not given) and the administrator's notice stated that creditors must exhibit their legal vouchers by 1 Jul 1848 to Samuel Jackson, admin. (HM 20 Jan 1848)

PRICE, EDWARD RUTLEDGE, of Baltimore, and Miss Laura E.
Michael, dau. of the late Caleb Michael, of Harford Co., m. 19 Jan
1865 at the residence of the bride in Harford Co. (AI 27 Jan 1865)

PRICE, J. H., see "Hetty S. Jacobs," q.v.

PRICE, JOHN (Negro), was found dead last Mon. in the woods near
Swan Creek, not far from the Philadelphia & Baltimore Turnpike,
with two bullet holes in his head; he had been fishing for Mr.
Carver and left the shore for his home in Havre de Grace on that
morning and had $70 or $80 on his person, none of which was
found when his body was discovered; prior to the incident some
persons in the neighborhood saw him walking into the woods and
two shots were heard, but no notice was taken of it at the time (AI
25 May 1866)

PRICE, MARY A., of Baltimore Co., and B. F. Sterling, of Harford Co.,
m. 27 Dec 1868 in Baltimore by Rev. Munsey (HD 1 Jan 1869)

PRICE, REBECCA (Miss), of Harford Co., and John Thomas Arthur, of
Baltimore Co., m. 1 Jun 1869 at the Episcopal Methodist Church in
Jarrettsville by Rev. J. C. Hagey of the Methodist Episcopal Church
(AI 18 Jun 1869 and HD 18 Jun 1869)

PRICE, VINIE (Miss), of Baltimore Co., and Dr. J. E. Robertson, of
Harford Co., m. 28 Mar 1865 at the residence of S. D. Price on East
Monument St. in Baltimore, by Rev. Charles Reid (AI 14 Apr 1865)

PRIGG, JAMES (colored), died ---- (date not given) and the
administrator's notice stated that creditors must exhibit their legal
vouchers by 12 Feb 1869 to Edward M. Allen, admin. (AI 14 Feb
1868)

PRIGG, WILLIAM H. and Miss Eleanora Robinson, both of Harford
Co., m. 13 Mar 1856 at St. Ignatius Church by Rev. Walter (HD 28
Mar 1856)

PRINGLE, MARK, late of Harford Co., died ---- (date not given) and the
notice stated that creditors are to call upon A. W. Bradford, admin.
de bonis non, for their share of the final assets per Order of the
Court dated 16 Feb 1847; an article called "Affairs at Hopewell"
appeared in *The Aegis and Intelligencer* over 22 years later and
gave some recollections about "Mark Pringle, Esq., long since
dead" (HM 26 Mar 1847 and AI 2 Apr 1869)

PRITCHETT, GRACEY H. (Miss) and Luther Grace, both of Easton,
MD, m. Tues. 23 Nov 1869 at Christ Church, Easton, Talbot Co.,
by Rev. Orlando Hutton (AI 3 Dec 1869)

PRITNER, ELIZABETH ANN, died ---- (date not given) and the
administrator's notice stated that creditors must exhibit their legal
vouchers by 6 Oct 1863 to Bennett Gilbert, admin. (SA 18 Aug
1862)

PROCTOR, ELIZABETH, died 25 Oct 1870 at 6:20 a.m., aged 80 years,
1 month and 28 days (AI 4 Nov 1870)

PROCTOR, JOHN C., of Baltimore Co., and Mollie E. Scotten, of Harford Co., m. Thurs. 28 Oct 1869 by Rev. Marsh (AI 19 Nov 1869)

PROCTOR, JOSHUA, of Baltimore Co., and Miss Frances Shannon, of Harford Co., m. 25 Feb 1858 by Rev. H. B. Ridgaway (SA 6 Mar 1858)

PRUM, EDWIN, see "Edward Drum," q.v.

PUE, ----, dau. of Mr. and Mrs. Michael E. Pue, Esq., died last Mon. afternoon; the family had set fire to brush from their garden and some of the children amused themselves by jumping over the fire; the little girl's clothing caught fire and she was burned so horribly that she survived but a few hours; a little boy who attempted to rescue her was also severely burned; Mrs. Pue was on a visit to Baltimore at the time (HD 27 Feb 1857)

PURSELLE, MARTIN J., Esq., and Miss Hettie Harkins, both of Harford Co., m. Thurs. 7 Sep 1865 at 4 p.m., at the residence of John Rogers, Esq., by Rev. A. H. Greenfield (AI 15 Sep 1865)

PUSEY, EDWIN M., died ---- (date not given) and the administrator's notice stated that creditors must exhibit their legal vouchers by 22 Dec 1847 to David Pyle, admin. (HM 2 Apr 1847)

PYLE, CHARLES W. and Ann A. McComas, both of Harford Co., m. 8 Dec 1870 at the M. P. Parsonage, Bel Air, by Rev. D. A. Shermer (AI 23 Dec 1870)

PYLE, DAVID, see "Edwin M. Pusey" and "John Lewin," q.v.

QUARLES, CHARLOTTE, died ---- (date not given) and the executor's notice stated that creditors must exhibit their legal vouchers by 11 Aug 1863 to Edward Quarles, exec. (SA 23 Aug 1862)

QUARLES, VIRGINIA, of Harford Co., and David E. Thomas, Jr., of Baltimore, m. 2 Sep 1865 at *Oak Hall*, the residence of Hon. A. M. Hancock, by Rev. W. F. Brand (AI 8 Sep 1865)

QUINLAN, JAMES, see "John F. Quinlan" and "Susanna Quinlan," q.v.

QUINLAN, JOHN F., of Baltimore, died suddenly Tues. 4 Jul 1865, in his 53rd year, at the residence of his brother James S. Quinlan in Harford Co. (AI 21 Jul 1865)

QUINLAN, PHILIP, died ---- (date not given) and the administrator's notice stated that creditors must exhibit their legal vouchers by 27 Oct 1847 to Isaac Andrews, admin. (HM 1 Jan 1847)

QUINLAN, SUSANNA, relict of James Quinlan, died last Sun. morning at her residence in Harford Co., aged 101; up to a short time previous to her death she was active and moved about with the activity of one a half century her junior [a second death notice in the same newspaper stated she was in her 102nd year] (AI 18 Oct 1867)

QUINLIN, PHILIP T., farmer, and Miss Elizabeth H. Taylor, both of Harford Co., m. Thurs. 26 Mar 1857 by Rev. Crawford (HD 27 Mar 1857)

QUINN, JIM, see "Miss Smith," q.v.

QUINN, MR., see "Matilda Dennison," q.v.

RAGSDALE, J. K. P. (Lieutenant, U.S.N.) and Rebecca McCormick, dau. of James M. McCormick, Esq., of Harford Co., m. 18 Nov 1869, at Poplar Grove, by Rev. W. E. Snowden; the editor noted that along with the above notice he received a slice of beautiful cake (AI 26 Nov 1869)

RAITT, CASSANDRA A., wife of the late Charles H. Raitt, died 26 Feb 1870, aged 59 (HD 4 Mar 1870 and AI 4 Mar 1869)

RAITT, CHARLES H., died 28 Aug 1867 at his residence, *Liberty Mills* in Harford Co., in his 69th year; the subsequent administrator's notice stated that creditors must exhibit their legal vouchers by 5 Sep 1868 to Franklin Whitaker, admin. (AI 6 Sep 1867 and 20 Sep 1867)

RAMPLEY, JAMES (Captain), died 13 Feb 1858 at his residence in the upper part of Harford Co.; he lived a quiet, unobtrusive life and died in full enjoyment of his mental faculties (SA 20 Feb 1858)

RAMPLEY, THOMAS, aged about 55, died last Mon. afternoon about 1 o'clock while mowing a field in the 5th District, Harford Co.; he was overcome by the heat and Dr. Hayward was sent for, but his condition grew worse and he died a short time later (AI 1 Jul 1870)

RAMSAY, NATHAN (colored), died 7 Oct 1864 at *Blenheim* farm (age not given); he was the honest and faithful servant of Dr. John K. Sappington (AI 18 Oct 1864)

RAMSAY, RACHEL A., dau. of Dr. Samuel J. Ramsey, and George W. McIlvain, all of Harford Co., m. 9 Oct 1867, at the residence of the bride's father, by Rev. Edward A. Colburn (AI 1 Nov 1867)

RAMSAY, SAMUEL, see "Rachel A. Ramsay," q.v.

RAYMOND, S. W., see "Mary Jane Moore," q.v.

REASIN, GEORGE A. and Miss Emma J. Love, both of Baltimore, m. 28 May 1867 by Rev. J. J. Stockton (AI 14 Jun 1867)

REASIN, HANNAH E., see "William H. Reasin," q.v.

REASIN, WILLIAM H., died Mon. 4 Mar 1867 at his residence in Havre de Grace, in his 51st year, having been in very feeble health for the last year; he leaves a large circle of friends and relations; in early life he adopted the profession or business of architecture and many of his monuments adorn the thoroughfares of Baltimore; he was kind and benevolent, yet stern and unswerving in the performance of his duties, with a mind many degrees above ordinary [newspaper contains two death notices]; the subsequent administratrix's notice stated that creditors must exhibit their legal vouchers by 19 Apr 1868 to Hannah E. Reasin, admx. (AI 8 Mar 1867 and 3 May 1867); William H. Reason was removed from the voter registration list in 1869 (HD 22 Oct 1869 and AI 1 Oct 1869)

REED, CHARLES ALEXANDER, son of James W. and Mary E. Reed, died 1 Jul 1859 in Bel Air, aged 6 months; obituary contains a poem (SA 16 Jul 1859)

REED, JAMES, see "Charles A. Reed," q.v.

REED, JENNIE N. (Miss), of Baltimore, and W. H. H. Zimmerman, of
Baltimore Co., m. Thurs. 4 Jun 1863 in Harford Co. by Rev. H.
Dunning (SA 12 Jun 1863)

REED, LAURA (Miss) and John H. Russell m. 27 Dec 1871 by Rev.
George M. Berry (AI 5 Jan 1872); another marriage notice stated
Miss Susan Reed and John H. Russell m. 27 Dec 1871, at the
residence of John W. Hawkins, by Rev. George M. Berry (HD 5 Jan
1872)

REED, MARY, see "Charles A. Reed," q.v.

REED, MOLLIE E. (Miss), of Baltimore, and John S. Worthington, of
Harford Co., m. 24 May 1870, in Baltimore, by Rev. Edward
Kinsey (AI 17 Jun 1870)

REED, T. W., see "Carroll Pennington," q.v.

REED, THOMAS H. C. and Drucie Worthington, dau. of Charles
Worthington, Esq., both of Harford Co., m. Thurs. 20 Dec 1866 at
St. Peter's Church, Baltimore, by Rev. Julius E. Grammer (AI 28
Dec 1866)

REED, W. H. W., of Harford Co., and Lizzie Seymour, dau. of Col. John
Seymour, of Baltimore Co., m. 7 Dec 1865 by Rev. L. A. Lefevre
(AI 22 Dec 1865)

REESE, ANNIE O. and James M. Sewell, both of Harford Co., m. 12
Oct 1865 at the Parsonage by Rev. Dr. Backus (AI 20 Oct 1865)

REIGHART, E. C. (Hon.), oldest member of the bar at Lancaster, PA,
died on Mon. last (AI 24 Dec 1869)

RENSHAW, CASSANDRA, see "Ann Anderson," q.v.

REYNARD, SUSAN (Miss) and Solomon Miller, both of Harford Co.,
m. 1 Sep 1848 by Rev. Park (HM 8 Feb 1849)

REYNOLDS, CATHERINE (Miss) and Jeremiah Grice, both of Harford
Co., m. 14 Feb 1871 at the residence of the bride's father, David
Reynolds, Esq., by Rev. George M. Berry (HD 31 Mar 1871)

REYNOLDS, DAVID, see "Catherine Reynolds," q.v.

REYNOLDS, EDWARD, died ---- (date not given) and the executor's
notice stated that creditors must exhibit their legal vouchers by 5
Jun 1863 to James Owens, Jr., exec. (SA 14 Jun 1862)

REYNOLDS, ELIZABETH (Mrs.) and James Herron, both of Harford
Co., m. Thurs. 4 Jun 1863 by Rev. R. J. Keeling (SA 12 Jun 1863)

REYNOLDS, MATTHEW, died ---- (date not given) and was removed
from the voter registration list in the 6th District in 1870 (HR 21 Oct
1870)

REYNOLDS, MRS., see "Benjamin Davis," q.v.

RICHARDSON, AMANDA, dau. of Edward Arnold Richardson, died
Thurs. 3 Sep 1863, in her 18th year; she was the third dau. to die in a
brief period; obituary contains a brief memorial (SA 11 Sep 1863)

RICHARDSON, BERTIE (Miss) and Benjamin Wells, both of Harford
Co., m. 15 Jun 1870, in Aberdeen M. E. Church, by Rev. J. G.
Moore (AI 24 Jun 1870)

RICHARDSON, CAROLINE (Miss), of Harford Co., and James G. Dance m. Wed. 19 Oct 1859 at St. Ignatius Church in Hickory by Rev. McDevitt (SA 22 Oct 1859)

RICHARDSON, DR., see "Henry Frederick," q.v.

RICHARDSON, E. HALL, see 'Hannah Archer" and "Basil Grafton" and "Isaac Johnson," q.v.

RICHARDSON, EDWARD A., see "Amanda Richardson," q.v.

RICHARDSON, EDWARD D., of Donaldsonville, Louisiana, and Miss Julia Morgan, dau. of Edward Morgan, Esq., m. 13 Nov 1847, in Harford Co., by Rev. Keech (HM 2 Dec 1847); see "Edward Morgan," q.v.

RICHARDSON, HANNAH M. (Miss) and William F. Johnson, both of Harford Co., m. 25 Nov 1869 by Rev. George M. Berry (AI 28 Jan 1870)

RICHARDSON, HARRIET, died Sat. 30 Apr 1859 at the residence of her brother Vincent Richardson, Harford Co., in her 75th year (SA 7 May 1859)

RICHARDSON, HENRY, see "Kate H. Richardson," q.v.

RICHARDSON, HENRY B., died ---- (date not given) and the administratrix's notice stated that creditors must exhibit their legal vouchers by 30 Jun 1869 to Martha A. Richardson, admx. (AI 3 Jul 1868)

RICHARDSON, JAMES, son of Vincent and Margaret Richardson, died 17 May 1856 in his 14th year, at the residence of his parents on Deer Creek (HD 23 May 1856)

RICHARDSON, JAMES L. and Miss Mary E. Courtney, both of Harford Co., m. Tues. 18 Jan 1859 at the Abingdon Parsonage by Rev. R. Spencer Vinton (SA 22 Jan 1859); see "Joshua F. Gallion," q.v.

RICHARDSON, JOHN W., died last Mon. of paralysis, at his residence, No. 10 Aisquith St., Baltimore [age not given]; he had many friends and relations in Harford Co. (AI 8 Apr 1870)

RICHARDSON, KATE H., eldest dau. of Henry Richardson, Esq., of Bel Air, and Guillermo A. Zell, of New York, m. Tues. 17 May 1870, at St. Ignatius Church, by Rev. Father O'Connor (AI 20 May 1870)

RICHARDSON, MARGARET, see "James Richardson," q.v.

RICHARDSON, MARGARET ELLEN (Miss), died Fri. 21 Jan 1864 (age not given) at the residence of her brother-in-law in Bel Air, after a lingering illness (SA 29 Jan 1864)

RICHARDSON, MARTHA A., see "Henry B. Richardson," q.v.

RICHARDSON, SAMUEL P., died 3 Oct 1863 at his residence, aged 28 (SA 16 Oct 1863)

RICHARDSON, VINCENT, see "James Richardson" and "Harriet Richardson," q.v.

RICHARDSON, WILLIAM A. and Miss Lizzie R. Bissell m. Mon. 8 Feb 1864 by Rev. H. Singleton at the Presbyterian Church in Bel Air; a subsequent marriage notice gave his name as Dr. William S.

Richardson and stated she was the dau. of the late Capt. William R. Bissell (SA 12 Feb 1864 and 19 Feb 1864)

RICHARDSON, WILLIAM S., see "Charles E. Markland," q.v.

RICKETTS, THOMAS M., formerly of Harford Co., died Sat. morning 6 May 1865 at his son's residence in Catonsville, Baltimore Co., in his 65th year (AI 12 May 1865); see "Philip Peters," q.v.

RICKEY, WAKEMAN and Miss Isabella Scarborough, both of Harford Co., m. 14 Feb 1871 at the residence of the bride's father, near Dublin, MD, by Rev. George M. Berry (HD 31 Mar 1871)

RIDER, E. A., son of the late George Rider, of Harford Co., died 4 Nov 1869 at Council Bluffs, Nebraska, aged about 47, having suffered from an affliction of the lungs for a number of years; he was engaged at an early day in the freighting business on the plains and leaves a son in Iowa City; obituary contains a brief memorial (AI 26 Nov 1869)

RIDER, GEORGE, died Fri. 17 Feb 1865 at his residence in Harford Co., in his 56th year; the subsequent executor's notice stated that creditors must exhibit their legal vouchers by 24 Feb 1866 to James Kean, exec. (AI 24 Feb 1865 and 3 Mar 1865); see "E. A. Rider," q.v.

RIFFLE, ELIZABETH, died ---- (date not given) and the executor's notice stated that creditors must exhibit their legal vouchers by 10 Jun 1856 to Thomas Riffle, exec. (of Baltimore); another notice advertised for sale her large brick house and a frame house, with lots, near the Canal Basin in Havre de Grace (HM 11 Oct 1855 and 11 Dec 1856)

RIGDON, LLOYD, died 30 Jan 1858, in his 32nd year [Baltimore papers please copy] (SA 13 Feb 1858)

RIGDON, OFFICER, was killed in 1858 (exact date not given) by Marion Cropps who was tried and convicted of murder in the first degree in Baltimore County last Tues.; his accomplice Peter Corrie, of Baltimore, was subsequently tried in February, found guilty, and sentenced to be hung on 18 Mar 1859 (SA 15 Jan 1859 and 26 Feb 1859)

RILEY, JAMES, died 2 Aug 1868 at Upper Crossroads, Harford Co., aged 44; the subsequent executrix's notice stated that creditors must exhibit their legal vouchers by 14 Sep 1869 to Margaret Riley, extx. (AI 28 Aug 1868 and 4 Sep 1868); he was later removed from the voter registration list of the 4th District in 1868 (AI 9 Oct 1868)

RILEY, MARGARET, see "James Riley," q.v.

RILEY, MARY E. (Miss) and J. H. Sutton, both of Harford Co., m. 15 Aug 1870 by Rev. Franck (AI 2 Dec 1870; HD 2 Dec 1870 gave her name as "Nanny E.")

RILEY, SUSAN, see "William Riley," q.v.

RILEY, THOMAS, died ---- (date not given) and the executrix's notice stated that creditors must exhibit their legal vouchers by 7 Jan 1865 to Susan Riley and Mary C. Riley, extxs. (SA 29 Jan 1864)

RILEY, WILLIAM, died 15 Aug 1862 at his residence in Harford Co., aged 68, and the executrix's notice stated that creditors must exhibit their legal vouchers by 19 Aug 1863 to Susan Riley, extx. (SA 23 Aug 1862)

RILEY, WILLIAM J. S. and Miss Fannie Whiteford, both of Harford Co., m. 1 Jul 1869 at Long Green Church by Rev. Father Nysson (HD 16 Jul 1869)

RISER, MRS., died last week in Berkeley Co., VA, aged 113 (HM 22 Jul 1852)

RITCHIE, JOHN, see "Archer H. Jarrett," q.v.

ROBERTS, GEORGE, alias George Russem, was killed in a brawl on Tues. night last week at Back Creek, Cecil Co., MD, by George Harris and Benjamin Bolt; he was shot and stabbed through the heart; the parties surrendered themselves and are now in custody; Harris was subsequently convicted of murder and came close to being hung, but on Dec 16th his sentence will be commuted to life imprisonment (AI 7 Jan 1870 and 25 Nov 1870)

ROBERTS, JOHN, of Philadelphia, and Miss Lizzie J. Sadler, eldest dau. of Capt. Thomas Sadler, of Havre de Grace, m. on the morning of 1 Jan 1857, at the residence of the bride's father, by Rev. T. Myers (HM 15 Jan 1857)

ROBERTS, JOHN B. and Mary M. Ellicott, dau. of William M. Ellicott, m. 20 Jun 1871 at Friends Meeting House on Eutaw Street in Baltimore (HD 30 Jun 1871)

ROBERTS, LEWIS, of Philadelphia, and Miss Mary Ady, of Harford Co., m. 18 Mar 1865, at Towsontown, by Rev. P. O. McConnell (AI 7 Apr 1865)

ROBERTS, T. H., see "Holland Greenland," q.v.

ROBERTS, WILLIAM G. and Mary F. Butler, only dau. of Clement Butler, Esq., all of Harford Co., m. 6 Jan 1859 by Rev. Keech (SA 15 Jan 1859)

ROBERTSON, J. E. (Doctor), of Harford Co., and Miss Vinie Price, of Baltimore Co., m. 28 Mar 1865 at the residence of S. D. Price on East Monument St. in Baltimore, by Rev. Charles Reid (AI 14 Apr 1865)

ROBERTSON, MARGARET W., died 19 Aug 1862, in her 89th year, at the residence of A. J. Lewis, Esq., in Philadelphia; obituary contains a brief memorial and poem (SA 30 Aug 1862)

ROBINSON, ANN, of Bel Air, died Sun. morning 4 Dec 1870 (AI 9 Dec 1870)

ROBINSON, CHARLES, died 29 Dec 1862 at his residence near Shawsville, Harford Co., in his 90th year (SA 16Jan 1863)

ROBINSON, DAVID C., of California, and Miss Ellen M. Hays, of Harford Co., m. Wed. 24 Aug 1870, at Dublin Southern Methodist Church, Harford Co., by Rev. Crawford [Easton, MD papers please copy] (AI 26 Aug 1870)

ROBINSON, ELEANOR (Miss) and William H. Prigg, both of Harford Co., m. 13 Mar 1856 at St. Ignatius Church by Rev. Walter (HD 28 Mar 1856)

ROBINSON, ELIZABETH B. (Miss) and John R. King, both of Harford Co., m. 3 Jun 1858 by Rev. Thomas Stuart C. Smith (SA 19 Jun 1858)

ROBINSON, HANNAH, see "Laura C. Baldwin," q.v.

ROBINSON, HANNAH ANN, second dau. of Jason and Mary Ann Robinson, died 17 Nov 1862 at the residence of her grandfather, Shadrack Streett, in her 10th year; obituary contains a long poem written by "M.S." (SA 13 Dec 1862)

ROBINSON, HARRIET ELIZABETH, youngest dau. of Dr. Samuel S. and Mary C. Robinson, died 14 Nov 1864, after a short illness, in her 3rd year (AI 30 Dec 1864)

ROBINSON, J. G., see "Laura C. Baldwin," q.v.

ROBINSON, JASON, see "Hannah Ann Robinson," q.v.

ROBINSON, JOHN, died Mon. 27 May 1867 at his residence near Hickory, in his 75th year (AI 31 May 1867)

ROBINSON, JOSEPH (Doctor), of Baltimore, and Miss Maggie L. Robinson, of Harford Co., m. 18 May 1869 by Rev. D. A. Shermer (AI 28 May 1869)

ROBINSON, LURENNA SLADE (Miss) and Capt. Joseph Augustus Harkins, both of Harford Co., m. 21 Dec 1865 by Rev. J. K. Nichols (AI 5 Jan 1866)

ROBINSON, MAGGIE L. (Miss), of Harford Co., and Dr. Joseph Robinson, of Baltimore, m. 18 May 1869 by Rev. D. A. Shermer (AI 28 May 1869)

ROBINSON, MARTHA, see "Samuel Robinson," q.v.

ROBINSON, MARY, see "Harriet Elizabeth Robinson," q.v.

ROBINSON, MARY A. (Miss) and J. R. Andrews, both of Harford Co., m. 17 Feb 1869, in Deer Creek Chapel, by Rev. D. A. Shermer (AI 26 Feb 1869)

ROBINSON, MARY ANN, see "Hannah Ann Robinson," q.v.

ROBINSON, SAMUEL, died ---- (date not given) and the executrix's notice stated that creditors must exhibit their legal vouchers by 1 Jan 1859 to Martha Robinson, extx. (SA 13 Feb 1858); see "Harriet Elizabeth Robinson," q.v.

ROBINSON, WILLIAM, see "Miss Smith," q.v.

ROCKHOLD, ELIJAH, see "Amelia Hitchcock," q.v.

ROCKHOLD, ELIJAH SR., died Wed. 28 Apr 1863 at his residence in Harford Co.; the subsequent executor's notice stated that creditors must exhibit their legal vouchers by 21 May 1864 to Lysias Rockhold, exec. (SA 1 May 1863 and 29 May 1863)

ROCKHOLD, LYSIAS, see "Elijah Rockhold," q.v.

ROCKWELL, WILLIAM S., of Georgia, died at Abingdon, Harford Co., in 1870 [exact date not given], having resided in that place for some 6 or 8 months, hoping the salubrious air would prove beneficial to his health, which had become much impaired by an attack of paralysis; he had filled many positions of honor and trust in his native State, including U. S. District Judge, Lieutenant Grand Commander of the Supreme Council (of Masons) for the Southern Jurisdiction of the United States, and Past Grand Master of Georgia [obituary in *Baltimore Sun* on 24 Jan 1870] (AI 28 Jan 1870)

RODHAM, MARY, of Harford Co., and Thomas Liddell, of Wisconsin, m. 28 Jan 1864, at the residence of the bride's father, by Rev. H. Singleton (SA 5 Feb 1864)

RODHAM, WILLIAM JR., died 26 Sep 1865 at Knight's Ferry, Stanislaus Co., California, aged 32 (AI 24 Nov 1865)

RODLEY, MARY (Miss) and John H. Lee, both of Baltimore, m. 16 Mar 1871 by Rev. Richard Norris (HD 31 Mar 1871)

ROEBOCK, WARREN, an individual well known among the sporting circles of this city, committed suicide yesterday morning between 12 and 1 o'clock; he was standing on Light St. near the corner of Baltimore St. in conversation with some friends, holding a gun in his hand; one friend told him to put it away before some accident occurred, to which he replied there was no danger; he then walked off and sat down on a door step; a few minutes afterwards a shot was heard and they turned and found him extended upon the pavement; they raised him up, but he never spoke, and died about 15 minutes later; he had shot himself behind the ear, his brain literally blown out; an inquest by Jacob D. Hair, Esq., initially thought it was an accident, but upon hearing Roebock had written a note during the evening, his pockets were searched and the note was found; it was directed to his brother-in-law with whom he had contracted to do what he could not perform; he had therefore determined to bid them all a final adieu, and asked for their forgiveness for what course he was about to pursue (HM 17 May 1844)

ROGERS, CATHERINE, see "Lucinda A. Hoopman," q.v.

ROGERS, ELIJAH B., died Sat. morning 11 Jun 1864, at his residence, aged 55 (AI 17 Jun 1864)

ROGERS, ISAAC, died Sun. 12 Nov 1865, in his 77th year (AI 17 Nov 1865)

ROGERS, JAMES M. and Miss Martha A. Grafton, both of Harford Co., m. 27 Sep 1866 at the Parsonage in Bel Air by Rev. J. N. Nichols (AI 5 Oct 1866)

ROGERS, JOHN, see "Martin J. Purselle," q.v.

ROGERS, JOHN OWEN, died Thurs. 26 Oct 1865 at his residence in Harford Co. (AI 3 Nov 1865)

ROGERS, MARY, died ---- (date not given) and the executor's notice stated that creditors must exhibit their legal vouchers by 19 Nov 1860 to J. R. Ely, exec.. (SA 17 Dec 1859)

ROGERS, R. J., of Harford Co., and Miss Elizzie Hewitt, of Baltimore, m. 27 Aug 1863 in Baltimore by Rev. T. D. Valiant (SA 4 Sep 1863)

ROGERS, ROWLAND, see "Lucinda A. Hoopman" and "Jane Watters," q.v.

ROSEZETTE, REBECCA (Miss) and David Davidson, both of Harford Co., m. 7 Apr 1869 in Rock Spring Church by Rev. W. E. Snowden (AI 14 May 1869)

ROSHER, OFFICER, see "Miss Smith," q.v.

ROSS, DAVID H., died 13 May 1869 at his father's residence near Stafford, Harford Co., of consumption, aged about 26 (AI 4 Jun 1869)

ROSS, ELMA S. (Miss) and George Wonders, Esq., both of Harford Co., m. 19 Apr 1870 by Rev. D. A. Shermer (HD 29 Apr 1870 and AI 29 Apr 1870)

ROSS, ISADORE (Miss), of Harford Co., and Milton T. Lewis, of Lancaster, PA, m. 29 Dec 1867 by Rev. T. M. Crawford, of York Co., PA (AI 17 Jan 1868)

ROSS, JOSEPH, see "Nannie R. Ross" and "William L. Stuart," q.v.

ROSS, NANNIE R., dau. of Joseph Ross, Esq., and James R. Smith, both of Harford Co., m. 12 Sep 1869, at Holy Trinity Church, by Rev. E. A. Colburn (AI 26 Nov 1869)

ROSS, SILAS and Mary E. Warner, both of Harford Co., m. Tues. 20 Oct 1868 at the residence of the bride's father, by Friends' ceremony [Towsontown papers please copy] (AI 23 Oct 1868)

ROUSE, C. C., died ---- (date not given) and was removed from the voter registration list in the 1st District in 1870 (HR 1 Nov 1870)

ROUSE, JOHN G. and Miss Hattie E. Hanway, both of Harford Co., m. Wed. 25 Apr 1866 by Rev. J. K. Nichols (AI 4 May 1866)

ROUSE, STEPHEN and Phebe Walker, of Havre de Grace, m. Thurs. 30 Apr 1868 by Rev. Dr. H. B. Martin, rector of St. John's Church, Havre de Grace (AI 8 May 1868)

ROWAN, JOHN B. (Captain), was killed by the explosion of a shell at the Battle of Nashville, TN, fought on 16 Dec 1864 between the forces of Generals Thomas and Hood ; he commanded at the time of his death a battery in Johnson's Artillery Battalion, Hood's Confederate Army; the letter conveying the intelligence to his friend says "He was the life of the camp, the star of the battalion, the pride of us all" (*Cecil Democrat* quote) [obituary stated he was "of this town" but did clarify if that meant Elkton where the *Cecil Democrat* was published or Bel Air where *The Aegis & Intelligencer* was published] (AI 3 Mar 1865)

ROYDE, ----, and his wife (first names not given) were instantly killed by lightning at their home near Bayview, Cecil Co., during the storm last Sat. evening (HR 4 Aug 1871)

RUFF, MARTHA ANN, aged 7, and Sarah Augusta Ruff, aged 5, daus. of Henry and Alethea Ruff, died Sat. 4 Aug 1866 of dysentery; obituary contains a short verse (AI 17 Aug 1866)

RUMSEY, BILL (Negro man), was murdered in 1858 (exact date not given) in Harford Co. and John Ecton was tried in 1859 for the crime, but was acquitted (HR 14 May 1859)

RUSHMORE, WILLIAM S., of Queen's Co., NY, and Hannah E. Hauks (Hawks), of Harford Co., m. 3 Oct 1867, at Robert Bound's, by Rev. W. M. Meminger [two marriage notices, one of which gave his name as "Rushwood" and another which gave her name as "Hanks"] (AI 11 Oct 1867 and 18 Oct 1867)

RUSSELL, CHARLES, son of Thomas Russell, and Anne T. Kemp, dau. of Thomas Kemp, all of Harford Co., m. 3 Mar 1869 at the residence of the bride's father and according to the order of the Society of Friends (HD 19 Mar 1869)

RUSSELL, JOHN, died ---- (date not given) and the administrator's notice stated that creditors must exhibit their legal vouchers by 1 Oct 1855 to Robert R. Vandiver, admin. (HM 1 Mar 1855)

RUSSELL, JOHN H. and Miss Laura Reed m. 27 Dec 1871 by Rev. George M. Berry (AI 5 Jan 1872); another marriage notice stated Miss Susan Reed and John H. Russell m. 27 Dec 1871, at the residence of John W. Hawkins, by Rev. George M. Berry (HD 5 Jan 1872)

RUSSELL, THOMAS, see "Charles Russell," q.v.

RUSSELLE, ANNA E. (Miss), of Baltimore, and George Walker, of Harford Co., m. 1 Jun 1870, in the Eutaw Street Church, by Rev. Inskip [marriage notice indicated "No cards"] (AI 17 Jun 1870)

RUSSEM, GEORGE, see "George Roberts," q.v.

RUSSUM, ALEXANDER, of Cecil Co., was allegedly murdered (date not given) by Benjamin Bolt and George Harris, all of Cecil Co., and they were brought to trial at Bel Air in Harford Co.; Harris was convicted of murder in the first degree and Bolt of murder in the second degree [his name was spelled once as Aleck Russom] (HR 20 May 1870); see "Benjamin Thompson," q.v.

RUST, A. T. M. and GEN., see "Coleman Yellott," q.v.

RUTHERFORD, EMMA J., dau. of Alexander and Mary P. Rutherford, died 8 Jan 1858 in Baltimore (SA 23 Jan 1858)

RUTLEDGE, ABRAHAM, died 1 Mar 1868, aged 69, at the residence of Elisha England in Harford Co., after a short but painful illness, of pneumonia fever (AI 27 Mar 1868); the subsequent administrator's notice stated that creditors of "Abraham Rutledge, of Harper" must exhibit their legal vouchers by 12 Mar 1869 to John V. St.Clair, admin. (AI 13 Mar 1868); "A. H. Rutledge" was removed from the voter registration list of the 4th District in 1868 (AI 9 Oct 1868); see "James Amos," q.v.

RUTLEDGE, GERARD, died ---- (date not given) and the administrator's notice stated that creditors must exhibit their legal vouchers by 15 Sep 1858 to Mary Rutledge, admin. (SA 21 Nov 1857)

RUTLEDGE, HARPER, see "Abraham Rutledge," q.v.

RUTLEDGE, J. W., see "Mary E. Pocock," q.v.

RUTLEDGE, JACOB, see "Pinkie Rutledge," q.v.

RUTLEDGE, JARRARD, died 20 Jul 1857 at Shawsville, in his 49th year (SA 1 Aug 1857)

RUTLEDGE, JOANNA (Miss) and E. B. Holland, both of Harford Co., m. Thurs. 3 Aug 1865 at Rock Spring Church by Rev. J. H. D. Wingfield (AI 11 Aug 1865)

RUTLEDGE, JOHN W., see "William W. Barton," q.v.

RUTLEDGE, JOSHUA, see "Penelope K. Bastick" and "Penelope Rutledge," q.v.

RUTLEDGE, MARIAN, of Harford Co., and William Meads, of Baltimore, m. 27 Feb 1867 at the Methodist Parsonage at Broadway in Baltimore by Rev. J. W. Black (AI 15 Mar 1867)

RUTLEDGE, MARY, see "Gerard Rutledge," q.v.

RUTLEDGE, MOLLIE A., of Baltimore, and George H. Taylor, of Cecil Co., m. 15 Sep 1870, at the residence of the bride's father, by Rev. Ramsay (AI 23 Sep 1870)

RUTLEDGE, PATRICK H., see "John Wilson," q.v.

RUTLEDGE, PENELOPE (Miss), dau. of the late Joshua Rutledge, of Harford Co., and William Welsh, of Baltimore, m. 19 Apr 1838 by Rev. Holmead (HM 26 Apr 1838)

RUTLEDGE, PINKIE (Miss) and John H. Streett, both of Harford Co., m. 28 Jun 1868, at the residence of Jacob Rutledge, by Rev. B. F. Myers (AI 7 Aug 1868)

SAALFIELD, CHARLES, died ---- (date not given) and the administrator's notice stated that creditors must exhibit their legal vouchers by 1 Nov 1848 to Augustus Henze, admin. (HM 13 Apr 1848)

SADLER, JAMES E. and Miss Sarah W. Cropper, dau. of Capt. E. Cropper, both of Havre de Grace, m. 15 Sep 1863 in Havre de Grace by Rev. Richard Norris (SA 25 Sep 1863)

SADLER, JOSEPH W., of Baltimore, and Miss Susannah Ayers, of Harford Co., m. 26 Sep 1858 in Baltimore by Rev. Alexander Bosserman (SA 2 Oct 1858)

SADLER, LIZZIE J. (Miss), eldest dau. of Capt. Thomas Sadler, of Havre de Grace, and John Roberts, of Philadelphia, m. on the morning of 1 Jan 1857, at the residence of the bride's father, by Rev. T. Myers (HM 15 Jan 1857)

SADLER, MARY C. (Miss), dau. of Thomas Sadler, and Jesse Hilles, Jr., all of Harford Co., m. Thurs. 19 Jan 1865 in Havre de Grace by Rev. W. C. Langdon (AI 10 Feb 1865)

SADLER, THOMAS, see "Lizzie J. Sadler" and "Mary C. Sadler," q.v.

SAMPLE, SARAH, died ---- (date not given) and the executor's notice stated that creditors must exhibit their legal vouchers by 3 Aug 1870 to John Sappington, Jr., exec. (AI 6 Aug 1869)

SANDERS, EDWARD, died ---- (date not given) and was removed from the voter registration list of the 2nd District in 1870 (AI 4 Nov 1870)

SANDERS, MARY E. (Miss) and Samuel J. Greenfield, both of Harford Co., m. 25 Nov 1856 by Rev. H. C. Cushing (HD 28 Nov 1856)

SANDERS, WILLIAM, see "Samuel J. K. Greenfield," q.v.

SANDERSON, ELIZA JANE, wife of F. W. Sanderson, died 11 Nov 1871 in her 43rd year (HR 17 Nov 1871)

SANDS, RICHARD A. and Miss Sarah Murry, both of Baltimore, m. 27 Feb 1865 by Rev. Dr. Dunning (AI 7 Apr 1865)

SAPPINGTON, A. HELEN (Miss), dau. of Dr. John K. Sappington, of Harford Co., and Isaac G. Matthews, of Howard Co., m. Tues. 14 Jun 1864 by Rev. William Finney, at *Blenheim*, the residence of the bride's father (AI 24 Jun 1864)

SAPPINGTON, JOHN JR., see "Sarah Sample," q.v.

SAPPINGTON, JOHN SR. (Doctor), died Thurs. morning 18 Nov 1869, after a short illness, at his residence near Darlington, in his 68th year; he was one of the oldest practicing physicians of Harford Co. and enjoyed a high reputation for medical skill and success in his profession [three death notices appeared in this one issue of the newspaper]; one obituary contains a brief memorial written by "E." and a letter to the editor, written by "S." of Dublin, MD, 23 Nov 1869, also memorialized the deceased and stated he was a member of the Constitutional Convention of 1851; the subsequent administrator's notice stated that creditors must exhibit their legal vouchers by 27 Nov 1870 to Mary A. Sappington and Richard Sappington, admins.; The Medical Society of Harford County passed a resolution in his honor on 26 Apr 1870 and it was published in the newspaper (AI 19 Nov 1869 and 3 Dec 1869 and 13 May 1870)

SAPPINGTON, JOHN K. (Doctor), died 8 Aug 1868 at 3 a.m. at his residence *Blenheim*, Harford Co., in his 78th year, having been indisposed for some time; both the Mason's and Odd Fellow's fraternities attended his funeral at Grove Church, some 150 carriages in attendance [newspaper contains two death notices]; a memorial by the Medical Society of Harford County was presented at their meeting on 11 Aug 1868 and later published in the newspaper; the executor's notice stated that creditors must exhibit their legal vouchers by 26 Aug 1869 to Charlton W. Billingslea, exec. (AI 14 Aug and 28 Aug 1868 and 4 Sep 1868); see "A. Helen Sappington" and "Nathan Ramsay" and "Aquilla D. Keen," q.v.

SAPPINGTON, JOHN, see "Walter B. Sappington," q.v.

SAPPINGTON, MARY, see "Walter B. Sappington" and "John Sappington, Sr.," q.v.

SAPPINGTON, RICHARD, see "John Sappington, Sr.," q.v.

SAPPINGTON, WALTER B., youngest son of Dr. John and Mary A. Sappington, died Sun. 16 Aug 1868, at the residence of his father, aged 19 years, 1 month and 11 days (AI 28 Aug 1868)

SAPPINGTON, WILLIAM (Doctor), died ---- (date not given) and the administrator's notice stated that testator's property in Havre de Grace will be sold on 9 Oct 1856 by Otho Scott, trustee (HD 3 Oct 1856)

SAUNDERS, ISAAC, died ---- (date not given) and the administrator's notice stated that creditors must exhibit their legal vouchers by 12 Feb 1856 to William Welch, admin. (HM 1 Mar 1855)

SAWYER, JOHN and Miss Lizzie E. Burke, eldest dau. of William G. Burke, Esq., both of Harford Co., m. 6 Jun 1871 by Rev. Dr. Martin (HR 23 Jun 1871)

SAWYER, WILLIAM, died 29 Jan 1857, in his 70th year, at his residence in Harford Co. (HD 13 Feb 1857)

SCARBORO, J. THOMAS R., died 20 Sep 1871 at his father's residence in Baltimore Co., aged 22; obituary contains a brief memorial written by "A.W.S., Dublin, MD, 25 Sep 1871" (HD 29 Sep 1871)

SCARBORO, MARY E. (Miss) and Daniel L. Baily, both of Harford Co., m. Thurs. 7 May 1863 by Rev. William Colburn (SA 8 May 1863)

SCARBORO, WALLACE, died ---- (date not given) and was removed from the voter registration list in the 5th District in 1871 (HR 29 Sep 1871)

SCARBOROUGH, ABIGAIL, see "Edward A. Scarborough," q.v.

SCARBOROUGH, ARCHER, see "Archibald Scarborough," q.v.

SCARBOROUGH, ARCHIBALD, died ---- (date not given) and the executor's notice stated that creditors must exhibit their legal vouchers by 16 Aug 1870 to Archer Scarborough, exec. (AI 20 Aug 1869)

SCARBOROUGH, EDWARD A., died 7 Jan 1870, after a lingering illness, in his 56th year; obituary contains a poem; the subsequent executor's notice stated that creditors must exhibit their legal vouchers by 31 Jan 1871 to Abigail H. Scarborough and Philip J. Scarborough, execs.(AI 21 Jan 1870 and 4 Feb 1870)

SCARBOROUGH, EUCLYDES, died ---- (date not given) and the administrator's notice stated that creditors must exhibit their legal vouchers by 25 Jul 1860 to Daniel Scott, admin. (SA 24 Sep 1859)

SCARBOROUGH, FRANCES A. (Miss) and Elisha England, both of Harford Co., m. 8 Dec 1870, at the residence of the bride, by Rev. George M. Berry (AI 16 Dec 1870)

SCARBOROUGH, HARMAN H. and Miss Sarah E. Groscup, dau. of Rev. Frederick Groscup, all of Harford Co., m. 19 Nov 1868 at Friendship M. E. Church by Rev. William A. McKee [*Baltimore Sun* please copy] (AI 11 Dec 1868)

SCARBOROUGH, ISABELLA (Miss) and Wakeman Rickey, both of Harford Co., m. 14 Feb 1871 at the residence of the bride's father, near Dublin, MD, by Rev. George M. Berry (HD 31 Mar 1871)

SCARBOROUGH, LETITIA J., of Harford Co., and Andrew W. Harris, of Cecil Co., m. Fri. 27 Jul 1866 in Elkton by Rev. M. D. Kurtz (AI 10 Aug 1866)

SCARBOROUGH, PHILIP, see "Edward A. Scarborough," q.v.

SCARF, J. L., of Missouri, and Miss Emeline Smithson, of Baltimore Co., m. 17 May 1859 in Baltimore by Rev. Isaac P. Cook (SA 21 May 1859)

SCARFF, ALVERDA (Miss) and William J. Norris, both of Harford Co., m. Thurs. 20 Oct 1870 at the M. P. Parsonage in Jarrettsville by Rev. J. C. Hagey (HD 28 Oct 1870)

SCARFF, ALVERDA (Miss) and William J. Norris, both of Harford Co., m. Thurs. 20 Oct 1870 at the M. P. Parsonage, Jarrettsville, by Rev. J. C. Hagey (AI 28 Oct 1870)

SCARFF, JAMES, died Mon. 20 Aug 1869 at his residence in Marshall's District, Harford Co., in his 55th year (AI 3 Sep 1869)

SCARFF, JAMES H., died Mon. 30 Aug 1869, aged about 56 (HD 3 Sep 1869)

SCARFF, JAMES K., a middle aged bachelor and owner of large landed estates, died very suddenly of heart disease at his residence near Jarrettsville in Marshall's District on Mon. evening (HR 2 Sep 1869)

SCARFF, JOHN (of John), died ---- (date not given) and the administrator's notice stated that creditors must exhibit their legal vouchers by 4 Mar 1869 to George R. Scarff, admin. [George's name was misspelled "Scabrf"] (AI 6 Mar 1868); John Scarff, of J., was removed from the voter registration list in the 4th District in 1868 (AI 9 Oct 1868)

SCARFF, JOSHUA H., see "John Delcamp," q.v.

SCARFF, SARAH M. (Miss) and Richard Taylor, both of Harford Co., m. 29 Apr 1869 by Rev. T. S. C. Smith (AI 14 May 1869 and HD 7 May 1869)

SCHOLFIELD, JOHN P., of California, and Elizabeth Eyre Allibone, dau. of Thomas Allibone, Esq., of Harford Co., m. 19 Nov 1868 at *Brookdale Farm*, Maryland, by Rev. William A. Newbold (AI 4 Dec 1868)

SCOTT, ANNA, consort of James Scott, died Tues. 3 Jun 1862 (SA 14 Jun 1862)

SCOTT, DANIEL, Esq., and Miss Cornelia Norris, both of Harford Co., m. Wed. 18 Nov 1863 (SA 20 Nov 1863); see "Elizabeth A. Jenkins" and "Euclydes Scarborough" and "Lester St. Clair" and "Otho Scott" and "Robert Miskimmon" and "Washington Carlile," q.v.

SCOTT, ELIZABETH, consort of Otho Scott, died Fri. 28 Mar 1862, in her 47th year (SA 5 Apr 1862)

SCOTT, JAMES, see "Anna Scott," q.v.

SCOTT, JAMES A., of Adams Co., PA, and Miss Mary A. Cole, of Harford Co., m. Wed. 5 Apr 1865, in Baltimore, by Rev. John R. Nichols (AI 14 Apr 1865)

SCOTT, MARTHA (Miss), died Sun. 18 Dec 1864 at the residence of William B. Beall, near Bel Air, at an advanced age (AI 23 Dec 1864)

SCOTT, MARY, died ---- (date not given), late of the State of Kentucky; the administrator's notice stated that creditors must exhibit their legal vouchers by 21 Jun 1871 to Henry W. Archer, Harford Co., admin. (AI 8 Jul 1870)

SCOTT, OTHO, died Wed. 9 Mar 1864 in Baltimore, in his 67th year; the executor's notice stated that creditors must exhibit their legal vouchers by 16 Mar 1865 to Henry D. Farnandis and Daniel Scott, execs. (AI 18 Mar 1864); see "Elizabeth Preston" and "Sue Winchester" and "William Sappington" and "Elizabeth Scott," q.v.

SCOTTEN, MOLLIE E., of Harford Co., and John C. Proctor, of Baltimore Co., m. Thurs. 28 Oct 1869 by Rev. Marsh (AI 19 Nov 1869)

SELBY, ELIAS G., of Carroll Co., and Miss America A. Gilbert, dau. of Amos Gilbert, Esq., of Harford Co., m. 2 May 1867 by Rev. T. S. C. Smith (AI 10 May 1867)

SELF, JAMES, died ---- (date not given) and was removed from voter registration list in 1869 [district not clarified, but either 4th, 5th or 6th] (HD 22 Oct 1869 and AI 1 Oct 1869)

SENECA, KATE (Miss), dau. of Dorus Seneca, of Havre de Grace, and William Greenleaf, of Vermont, m. on the morning of 17 Jan 1867 at Havre de Grace by Rev. Hyde (AI 25 Jan 1867)

SEWELL, CHARLES, see "James M. Sewell," q.v.

SEWELL, FIELDER BOWIE, youngest son of Septimus D. and Maria L. Sewell, died Wed. 29 Jan 1868 at *Rose Hill*, Harford Co., aged 23 months (AI 7 Feb 1868)

SEWELL, JAMES M. and Annie O. Reese, both of Harford Co., m. 12 Oct 1865 at the Parsonage by Rev. Dr. Backus (AI 20 Oct 1865)

SEWELL, JAMES M. and Harry Lee and Septimus Sewell, all of Abingdon, drowned last Fri. when their boat capsized while crabbing on Bush River near the P. W. & B. Railroad bridge; their bodies were recovered for burial (HR 12 Aug 1869); another newspaper account gave the names of those involved as Dr. John C. Pope, James Cochran, James Cage, Washington Dorney and his two sons (not named), William George Diffenderffer, James M. Sewell, Septimus D. Sewell, Harry Lee and Josiah Lee (nephews of the last two named), Charles Sewell (son of Septimus D. Sewell), and a colored boy employed by the Sewells, plus two others (names unknown); Harry Lee, aged about 22, single, was buried in Greenmount Cemetery, and James Sewell and Septimus D. Sewell, both m. with families, were buried in Abingdon (HD 13 Aug 1869);

another newspaper gave the names of the thirteen people as Dr. John C. Polk, James M. Sewell, Septimus D. Sewell, Harry Lee, Josiah Lee, George Diffenderffer, James Cochran, Wash. Dorney, Albert Dorney, Edward Hall, William Hall, James Cage, and a colored man in the employ of S. D. Sewell; it also contains more details about the accident, mentioning a colored man named Charles Gilbert who went to the sunken boat and brought in the body of James M. Sewell; he leaves a widow, but no children; he and S. D. Sewell were buried in the family burying ground near Abingdon; Harry Lee, aged about 22, son of the late Josiah Lee and brother of Josiah Lee, Jr., was found floating a considerable distance away; he and his brother had just returned from a tour through Europe; he was buried in Greenmount Cemetery in Baltimore (AI 13 Aug 1869)

SEWELL, MARIA, see "Septimus D. Sewell" and "Fielder Bowie Sewell," q.v.

SEWELL, SEPTIMUS, see "Fielder Bowie Sewell," q.v.

SEWELL, SEPTIMUS D. and Harry Lee and James M. Sewell, all of Abingdon, drowned last Fri. when their boat capsized while crabbing on Bush River near the P. W. & B. Railroad bridge; their bodies were recovered for burial; the subsequent administratrix's notice for Septimus D. Sewell stated that creditors must exhibit their legal vouchers by 23 Aug 1870 to Maria Louisa Sewell, admx. [see further details under "James M. Sewell," q.v.] (HR 12 Aug 1869 and AI 27 Aug 1869)

SEYMOUR, LIZZIE, dau. of Col. John Seymour, of Baltimore Co., and W. H. W. Reed, of Harford Co., m. 7 Dec 1865 by Rev. L. A. Lefevre (AI 22 Dec 1865)

SHANE, MATILDA (Miss), dau. of the late Rev. Joseph Shane, and Samuel Kramer, all of Baltimore, m. Mon. evening 21 Feb 1870 by Rev. Dr. Ryan, assisted by Rev. G. W. Cooper (AI 25 Feb 1870)

SHANNESSEY, JAMES, son of James, aged 16, of No. 233 W. Fayette St. in Baltimore, was frightened to death by a vicious dog a few days ago; he was passing along Raborg St., between Pine and Arch Sts., when the dog suddenly jumped at him, but did not get a hold of him; the frightened youth fell to the ground, got up, and fell a second time, when he expired (SA 31 Jul 1858)

SHANNON, FRANCES (Miss), of Harford County, and Joshua Proctor, of Baltimore Co., and Miss Frances Shannon, m. 25 Feb 1858 by Rev. H. B. Ridgaway (SA 6 Mar 1858)

SHAW, AMOS B., died 16 Apr 1869 in Buckingham, Bucks Co., PA, in his 63rd year (HD 30 Apr 1869)

SHEARS, BENJAMIN, died Thurs. 22 Apr 1869 while cleaning out a well in Aberdeen for George Harris; the walls caved in and buried him under 20 feet of earth and debris around 2½ o'clock that afternoon; efforts to rescue him began immediately and at 8 o'clock his groaning ceased; he was presumed dead, but the rescue continued and his body was recovered the next morning; he leaves a wife and several children; William Oldfield, who recovered the body, started a subscription and raised upwards of $100 for them (HR 29 Apr 1869 and AI 30 Apr 1869)

SHEKELL, ANNIE W. (Miss) and H. Harrison Bradford, both of Harford Co., m. 23 Jun 1865 by Rev. Nichols (AI 30 Jun 1865)

SHEPARD, CHARLES S., of Baltimore, and Miss Mary T. Archer, of Harford Co., m. 13 Sep 1870 by Rev. J. E. Reed (AI 30 Sep 1870)

SHEPHERD, MARY ADDELL, only dau. of G. P. and Susie H. Shepherd, died 25 Jul 1870, near Woodville, Harford Co., aged 6 months and 25 days (AI 5 Aug 1870)

SHERIDAN, ASBURY, died 23 May 1869 at his residence near Hopewell, of a lingering disease, aged about 53 (AI 4 Jun 1869)

SHERNDAN, JAMES and Miss Kate James, both of Harford Co., m. 31 Dec 1868, at home, by Rev. J. G. Moore (HD 19 Feb 1869 and AI 12 Feb 1869)

SHERWOOD, CLARA (Miss), of Baltimore, and John H. Watters (Waters), of Charles Co., MD, m. 28 Apr 1870 by Rev. Father Jordan (AI 6 May 1870)

SHIELDS, OWEN, see "John Gregory," q.v.

SHRIVER, JOHN, see "Charles Vice," q.v.

SHROFF, GRAFTON WILLIAM, died Sun. 17 Jul 1864, aged 21, at the residence of his father in Fallston (AI 22 Jul 1864)

SHROFF, JOHN WASHINGTON, eldest son of Joseph and Sarah Shroff, died 14 Oct 1865 in the morning, at the residence of his father in Fallston, Harford Co., in his 30th year (AI 20 Oct 1865)

SHROFF, JOSEPH, see "John Washington Shroff," q.v.

SHULTZ, LOUISA (Miss), died last Tues. evening at her father's residence in Franklinville; she had lived with the family of A. H. Greenfield, Esq., of Bel Air, for several years and worked as a saleswoman in Mr. Greenfield's store; she had been visiting her parents for a few days and was not feeling well before she left for the visit; she went to bed on Tues. evening and was found dead the next morning; death was supposedly caused by the rush of blood to the head (AI 14 Jun 1867)

SHURE, CHARLES A. (Doctor) and Miss Georgie Gwinn m. 24 Jun 1869 at Port Deposit, Cecil Co., by the bride's brother Rev. W. R. Gwinn, assisted by Rev. H. Branch and Rev. W. E. England (AI 2 Jul 1869)

SICKLES, DANIEL E., see "Philip Barton Key," q.v.

SILLS, RACHEL A. (Miss) and George McMorris, both of Harford Co., m. 19 Sep 1871 by Rev. John Roberts (HD 22 Sep 1871)

SILLS, WILLIAM and Miss Priscilla Barnaby, both of Havre de Grace, m. Tues. 3 Nov 1868 by Rev. C. F. Thomas (HR 5 Nov 1868 and AI 13 Nov 1868)

SILVER, ALICE H., wife of P. W. Silver, died 28 Jan 1868 at Darlington, after a long and painful illness, in her 62nd year;

obituary contains a poem; the subsequent executrix's notice stated that creditors must exhibit their legal vouchers by 15 Feb 1869 to Mary Silver, extx. (AI 28 Feb 1868)

SILVER, ALLIE, dau. of P. W. Silver, died Fri. evening 13 Jul 1866 at Darlington, in her 25th year; after completing her education in Baltimore she returned home and for four years she suffered with a lingering illness that eventually took her life; obituary contains a memorial and poem written by "S." (AI 27 Jul 1866)

SILVER, AMOS, see "Sarah Jane Silver," q.v.

SILVER, BENJAMIN, died ---- (date not given) and the administrator's notice stated that creditors must exhibit their legal vouchers by 24 Mar 1870 to Hannah Silver and R. L. Morgan, Admin. C.T.A. (AI 26 Mar 1869)

SILVER, BENJAMIN, SR., died ---- (date not given) and the administrator's notice stated that creditors must exhibit their legal vouchers by 1 Aug 1848 to Philip W. Silver, admin. (HM 13 Jan 1848)

SILVER, GEORGE B. and Miss C. Kate Hughes, both of Harford Co., m. Tues. 28 Nov 1865, at the residence of the lady's father, by Rev. Samuel Bayless (AI 8 Dec 1865)

SILVER, HANNAH, see "Benjamin Silver," q.v.

SILVER, HENRY A., see "Thomas Swift," q.v.

SILVER, J. P., see "Richard I. Jackson," q.v.

SILVER, MARGARET (Miss), of Harford Co., and George F. Groome, of Baltimore, m. 19 Aug 1851 by Rev. Finney (HM 28 Aug 1851)

SILVER, MARY, see "Alice H. Silver," q.v.

SILVER, MR., see "Susan Pannell," q.v.

SILVER, P. W., see "Alice H. Silver" and "Allie Silver," q.v.

SILVER. PHILIP W., see "Benjamin Silver, Sr.," q.v.

SILVER, SALLIE A. (Miss), dau. of the late Samuel B. Silver, of Harford Co., and Thomas S. Hughes, of Baltimore, m. 8 Jun 1865 at the bride's residence in Harford Co., by Rev. John K. Cramer (AI 16 Jun 1865)

SILVER, SAMUEL B., see "Sallie A. Silver," q.v.

SILVER, SARAH JANE, eldest dau. of Sarah A. and the late Amos Silver, died Sat. 23 Dec 1871 at 10 minutes to 7 o'clock p.m. (AI 5 Jan 1872)

SILVER, SILAS, of Harford Co., and Susan Solomon, dau. of Isaac Solomon, of Wilmington, DE, m. 22 Nov 1837 at Wilmington by Rev. E. Kennard (HM 7 Dec 1837)

SILVER, WILLIAM P., died during the night of 4 Sep 1856 at *Greenwood Glen*, Harford Co., in his 39th year; obituary contains a poem written by "S." (HM 11 Sep 1856)

SIMMONS, JOSEPH N., of Baltimore, and Miss Caroline Wells, dau. of the late Zenas Wells, of Havre de Grace, m. 18 Apr 1847 by Rev. Happerset (HM 28 May 1847)

SIMMS, WILLIAM and Miss Mary Carr, both of Harford Co., m. 28 Nov 1867 by Rev. Lemmon (AI 13 Dec 1867)

SINGLETON, ----, a son of John Singleton, of Havre de Grace, drowned one day last week [March, 1867] while doing something with his boat, which was near the shore of the river in water not over one foot deep; he was subject to fits and apparently fell over the side of the boat and was found with his head and part of his body in the water (AI 8 Mar 1867)

SINGLETON, ----, a son of the late Herman Singleton, drowned one day last week while bathing in the Susquehanna River; it is not known how the accident happened; he was in the habit of bathing and swimming in the river and perhaps was disabled by a cramp; he was about 11 years old and lived in Havre de Grace; a later notice stated he was aged 11, the son of Mrs. Singleton, and he drowned on Sat. 4 Jul 1868 (AI 10 Jul 1868 and 24 Jul 1868)

SINGLETON, AMOS, see "John Singleton," q.v.

SINGLETON, JOHN, died ---- (date not given) and the notice of the public sale of his personal property on 14 Dec 1837 was published in the paper by his administrator Amos Singleton (HM 7 Dec 1837)

SLADE, ABRAHAM, died ---- (date not given) and the executor's notice stated that creditors must exhibit their legal vouchers by 17 Dec 1861 to Rosanna Slade and William B. Tipton, execs. (SA 19 Jan 1861)

SLADE, DIXON, see "Susan Slade," q.v.

SLADE, MARTHA, see "Washington M. Slade," q.v.

SLADE, MARY, wife of Washington M. Slade, died 13 May 1859 in Harford Co., in her 64th year (SA 21 May 1859)

SLADE, MARY JANE, see "William Slade," q.v.

SLADE, MRS., died Wed. 22 Apr 1863 in her 84th year, at the residence of her son in Baltimore Co.; obituary contains a short verse (SA 1 May 1863)

SLADE, ROSANNA, see "Abraham Slade," q.v.

SLADE, SUSAN (Miss), youngest dau. of Dixon Slade, of Harford Co., and John W. Hall, of Baltimore Co., m. Thurs. 21 Dec 1837 by Rev. Andrew B. Cross (HM 28 Dec 1837)

SLADE, WASHINGTON M., died Thurs. 12 Dec 1867 at this residence in Harford Co., in his 72nd year; the subsequent executrix's notice stated that creditors must exhibit their legal vouchers by 20 Jan 1869 to Martha Slade, extx. (AI 20 Dec 1867 and 31 Jan 1868); he was removed from the voter registration list of the 4th District in 1868 (AI 9 Oct 1868); see "Mary Slade," q.v.

SLADE, WASHINGTON M.. Esq., and Miss Martha Amos, both of Harford Co., m. 29 Jan 1867 by Rev. T. S. C. Smith (AI 8 Feb 1867)

SLADE, WILLIAM, died ---- (date not given) and the administratrix's notice stated that creditors must exhibit their legal vouchers by 23 Nov 1860 to Mary Jane Slade, admx. (SA 10 Dec 1859)

SLAYMAKER, JOHN (Captain), died last week in Lancaster, PA, in his 91st year; he was a veteran of the Revolutionary War and the War of 1812; his father, John Slaymaker, was in Braddock's Campaign as a wagoner, and afterwards, in 1776, he marched at the head of a company to Bergen, NJ (SA 11 Sep 1863)

SLEE, ELIZA, see "Cassandra Brookheart," q.v.

SLEE, FLORENCE and Robert E. Hanna, both of Harford Co., m. 12 Sep 1867 (AI 20 Sep 1867)

SLEE, GEORGE, see "John Slee," q.v.

SLEE, JOHN, youngest son of George W. and Mary Slee, died 13 Dec 1863, in the morning, aged 3 years and 6 months; obituary contains a short poem (SA 25 Dec 1863)

SMITH, ---- (Negro man), accidentally shot in the head and face in a house in southwest part of Havre de Grace on Wed. evening and died almost instantly (HR 26 Nov 1868 and AI 4 Dec 1868)

SMITH, ----, an old soldier of the War of 1812, aged 86, was struck by a locomotive on the Port Deposit branch road near Perryville last Wed. morning [March, 1871]; he had been walking along side the railroad and just before the train reached him he stepped onto the track ahead of the engine; he was killed instantly; it is said he had five sons in the Union Army during the war, four whom were killed, and the other one, who lost a leg in the service, is a resident of Havre de Grace and took charge of his unfortunate parent (HR 31 Mar 1871)

SMITH, ALEXANDER, died ---- (date not given) and the administrator's sale of his personal state will be held on 12 Oct 1871 by R. R. Vandiver, admin., at Havre de Grace (HR 6 Oct 1871)

SMITH, ANN, died ---- (date not given) and the executor's notice stated that creditors must exhibit their legal vouchers by 23 Apr 1871 to Joseph H. Jewett, exec. (AI 29 Apr 1870)

SMITH, AVARILLA (Miss) and Daniel McGonigal, both of Harford Co., m. Thurs. 27 Sep 1838, in Baltimore, by Rev. John Smith (HM 18 Oct 1838)

SMITH, BARNEY, of Havre de Grace, was killed on Thurs. of last week [May, 1867] by the cars at Canton ; he was a brakeman on the Port Deposit and Baltimore train; he either lost his balance and fell or came in contact with a post which stood near where he was found; he was an industrious young man who served in the army during the late war and was in the battle before Petersburg; he leaves a mother, now advanced in years (AI 24 May 1867)

SMITH, CAROLINE H., wife of Charles F. Smith, died Tues. 10 Mar 1869, aged 41 years and 11 months, at Maxwell's Point in Harford Co., leaving a husband and children; one obituary contains a brief memorial (HD 19 Mar 1869 and AI 26 Mar 1869)

SMITH, CAROLINE PRISCILLA, died 13 Sep 1867, in her 19th year (AI 20 Sep 1867)

SMITH, CHARLES, a coal heaver of Havre de Grace, died 21 Nov 1868 when the gun he was loading exploded in his hands and both barrels going off and entering his head, carried the entire face away, killing him instantly; verdict of the jury was that he died by his own hand (AI 4 Dec 1868)

SMITH, CHARLES F., see "Caroline H. Smith," q.v.

SMITH, CHRISTIAN, died ---- (date not given) and was removed from the voter registration list in the 3rd District in 1870 (HR 1 Nov 1870)

SMITH, ELIZA ANN, wife of Richard Smith and eldest dau. of William and Jane Hanna, died Thurs. evening 18 Nov 1869 near Churchville (AI 26 Nov 1869)

SMITH, HENRY A. and Miss Ellen C. Jones, both of Harford Co., m. 27 Feb 1871 at the residence of the bride's father, John P. Jones, Esq., near Dublin, MD, by Rev. George M. Berry (HD 7 Apr 1871)

SMITH, HUGH, died ---- (date not given) and the notice stated that creditors must exhibit their legal vouchers by 28 Aug 1844; petition in chancery of Thomas Smith, and others, dated 28 Jun 1843 (HM 17 Nov 1843)

SMITH, JAMES R. and Nannie R. Ross, dau. of Joseph Ross, Esq., both of Harford Co., m. 12 Sep 1869, at Holy Trinity Church, by Rev. E. A. Colburn (AI 26 Nov 1869)

SMITH, MARY H., see "T. S. C. Smith," q.v.

SMITH, MISS, died last week in Baltimore, in her 64th year, from injuries sustained when she was brutally outraged some weeks by a Negro named Jim Quinn near Jarrettsville, Harford Co., and for which crime he was lynched (AI 5 Nov 1869); Miss Smith was on a visit from Baltimore to the family of William Robinson who resides in the neighborhood between Upper Cross Roads and Jarrettsville, and about noon on Tues. 5 Oct 1869 she left to visit J. Henderson Kirkwood's family who lived about a half mile away; she was approached by a young Negro man, known in the community as Jim Crow, aged about 18, who had been cutting corn for Mr. Robinson that day; he grabbed her and dragged her from the public road into the woods and accomplished his horrible designs upon her; he then abandoned her and she managed to make her way back to Mr. Robinson's house; the Negro man was captured last Sat. by Officer Rosher, of Baltimore County, in Glen Rock, just over the line in PA; he was placed in a car on the Northern Central Railroad to be taken to Towsontown jail, but when arriving at White Hall a party of about 30 men took him from the train and set out to Bel Air jail instead of Towsontown; within 2 miles of Jarrettsville, on what is called King's Road, upon his confessing to the crime and giving all the particulars, they halted under a tree and hung him upon a limb of it; he was left suspended during Sat. night until about 12 o'clock Sun. when his remains were cut down and buried in the neighborhood; the condition of Miss Smith is precarious in the extreme and it is feared that she would not long survive her injuries (AI 8 Oct 1869)

SMITH, NATHAN R., see "Hannah Archer," q.v.

SMITH, PACA, see "Richard Dallam," q.v.

SMITH, R. STUMP and Miss Laura Brannan, both of Harford Co., m. 16 Dec 1862 in Baltimore by Rev. H. C. Cushing (SA 27 Dec 1862)

SMITH, RICHARD, see "Eliza Ann Smith," q.v.

SMITH, SARAH (Miss), dau. of the late Col. Smith, died Wed. 14 Mar 1866 at her residence in Harford Co., in her 70th year (AI 23 Mar 1866)

SMITH, THOMAS, died ---- (date not given) and the administrator's notice stated that creditors must exhibit their legal vouchers by 5 Jan 1866 to Thomas Cord, admin. (AI 27 Jan 1865); see "Hugh Smith," q.v.

SMITH, THOMAS S. (Reverend) and Miss Mary H. Stump, eldest dau. of John Stump, Esq., of Perryville, m. 10 Apr 1856 by Rev. W. Finney (HD 18 Apr 1856)

SMITH, Thomas S. C. (Reverend), died Sat. 17 Jul 1869 at his residence in Harford Co., aged 43; a lengthy memorial was written by "J.P.C." and published in *The Aegis & Intelligencer* on 3 Sep 1869, stating he has suffered from impaired health for some months previous, the result of years of incessant labor, both mental and physical; he was a native of Nova Scotia and came to the U. S. to be educated at Dickinson College in PA, followed by his theological course at Princeton Seminary; his first pastoral charge was at Havre de Grace, where he remained a short time before becoming Principal of the Bel Air Academy, in connection with the pastoral charge of the Franklinville Church, a few miles distant; from the academy he was called to Bethel Church, of Harford Co., and in a short time was called to the united pastoral charge of Bel Air and Franklinville, at which charge he resigned at the recent meeting of the Presbytery of Baltimore; during the first part of his last pastoral charge he presided over Bel Air Academy and during the latter part he held the office of County Superintendent of Public Schools [the memorial contains more details about his exemplary character and teaching abilities] (AI 23 Jul 1869 and 3 Sep 1869); another newspaper stated Rev. T. S. C. Smith died suddenly of typhoid fever at his residence at Jerusalem Mills (date not given); his remains passed through Havre de Grace last Mon. for interment in Elkton, Cecil Co.; an ordained minister of the Presbyterian Church, he was Examiner of the Public Schools at the time of his death, and leaves a wife and 6 children (HR 22 Jul 1869); and, another obituary stated he died Sat. 17 Jul 1869 at his residence near Franklinville, in his 43rd year; the subsequent administratrix's notice stated that creditors must exhibit their legal vouchers by 2 Dec 1870 to Mary H. Smith, admx. (HD 23 Jul 1869 and 17 Dec 1869)

SMITH, WILLIAM H. and Miss Margaret A. Kirk, both of Harford Co.,
m. Wed. 3 Jun 1863 by Rev. Welty (SA 12 Jun 1863)
SMITHSON, EMELINE (Miss), of Baltimore Co., and J. L. Scarf, of
Missouri, m. 17 May 1859 in Baltimore by Rev. Isaac P. Cook (SA
21 May 1859)
SMITHSON, GABRIEL, see "John Smithson," q.v.
SMITHSON, JAMES L., aged 26, died on 20 Mar 1856 of consumption
in Baltimore and within 37 hours his brother Thomas M. Smithson,
aged 23, died of the same disease on 23 Mar 1856 in Harford Co.
(HD 28 Mar 1856)
SMITHSON, JOHN, died ---- (date not given) and the executor's notice
stated that creditors must exhibit their legal vouchers by 3 Jun 1858
to Gabriel Smithson, exec. (SA 25 Jul 1857)
SMITHSON, LAURA P. (Miss), of Cecil Co., and George D. Forwood,
of Harford Co., m. 23 Nov 1867 at Port Deposit by Rev. Henry
Branch (AI 29 Nov 1867)
SMITHSON, THOMAS M., see "James L. Smithson," q.v.
SMITHSON, WILLIAM H. and Mary A. Galloway, both of Harford Co.,
m. 4 Oct 1868 in the evening at the Parsonage of Exeter Street M.
E. Church [in Baltimore] by Rev. J. A. Price (HD 9 Oct 1868)
SNOWDEN, ARTHUR (Doctor), formerly of Prince George's Co., MD,
and a surgeon in the Confederate Army during the war, fell
overboard from the steamer *Wenonah* on the Chesapeake Bay, on
Wed. night of last week, and drowned (AI 6 Aug 1869)
SNOWDEN, RACHAEL, see "Hannah Waters Bageley," q.v.
SOLOMON, SUSAN, dau. of Isaac Solomon, of Wilmington, DE, and
Silas Silver, of Harford Co., m. 22 Nov 1837 at Wilmington by
Rev. E. Kennard (HM 7 Dec 1837)
SOMERS, MARY A. (Miss) and John Taylor m. Tues. 11 Oct 1864,
near Harford Furnace (AI 25 Nov 1864)
SPECK, DR. J. F., see "John Lamb," q.v.
SPEDDEN, REBECCA and John Garrison, both of Harford Co., m.
Mon. 2 May 1864 by Rev. E. Kinsey (AI 6 May 1864)
SPENCER, A. D. R. and Miss Agnes Patterson, dau. of the late Samuel
Patterson, of Havre de Grace, m. 10 Jun 1869 at the residence of the
bride, Havre de Grace, by Rev. W. H. Cook [Philadelphia, PA and
San Francisco, CA papers please copy] (AI 18 Jun 1869 and 2 Jul
1869; the former edition spelled the name "Pattison")
SPENCER, DANIEL D. and Miss Rachel Bounce, both of Harford Co.,
m. Thurs. 28 Aug 1862 by Rev. Shoaff (SA 6 Sep 1862)
SPENCER, J. N. and Miss Maggie R. Kelchner, dau. of Peter Kelchner,
stove dealer, all of Havre de Grace, m. 25 May 1869, at the
residence of the bride, by Rev. M. L. Smiser (AI 18 Jun 1869 and
25 Jun 1869; the former edition spelled the name "Kelsner")
SPENCER, JOHN W., died ---- (date not given) and the administrator's
notice stated that creditors must exhibit their legal vouchers by 6

Feb 1856 to Rebecca Spencer and Silas Spencer, admins. (HM 1
Mar 1855)

SPENCER, REBECCA, see "John W. Spencer," q.v.

SPENCER, SILAS, see "John W. Spencer," q.v.

SPICER, ALBERT E., of Harford Co., and India M. Davis, of Baltimore,
m. 21 Feb 1871 by Rev. Dr. Fuller (HD 31 Mar 1871)

SPICER, JAMES and Miss Sarah P. Timmons, both of Harford Co., m.
12 Nov 1857 by Rev. T. S. C. Smith (SA 21 Nov 1857)

SPICER, JAMES, died ---- (date not given) and the executor's notice
stated that creditors must exhibit their legal vouchers by 28 Mar
1871 to John T. Spicer, exec. (AI 8 Apr 1870); he was subsequently
removed from the voter registration list of the 6th District in 1870
(HD 7 Oct 1870 and 4 Nov 1870)

SPICER, JOHN T., see "James Spicer," q.v.

SPICER, JUDGE, see "William Young," q.v.

SPICER, MARY ANN (Miss), of Baltimore, and William P. Tucker, of
Harford Co., m. Mon. evening 13 Nov 1843, in Baltimore, by Rev.
Larkins (HM 17 Nov 1843)

SPINK, S. LEWIS, Esq., and Miss Lizzie Cooley m. 10 Mar 1857 in
Burlington, Iowa by Rev. S. Reynolds (HD 27 Mar 1857)

SPRINGER, J. HENDERSON, of Harford Co., and Eliza S. H. Carter,
dau. of the late Durden B. Carter, Esq., of Philadelphia, m. Thurs. 3
Jun 1858 at the Church of the Ascension in Philadelphia (SA 12 Jun
1858)

ST. CLAIR, BAILEY, see "Elizabeth St. Clair," q.v.

ST. CLAIR, DAVID, see "Elizabeth St. Clair," q.v.

ST. CLAIR, ELIZABETH, died ---- (date not given) and the executor's
notice stated that creditors must exhibit their legal vouchers by 27
Sep 1866 to Bailey St. Clair and David St. Clair, execs. (AI 27 Oct
1865)

ST. CLAIR, JAMES, died ---- (date not given) and the administrator's
notice stated that creditors must exhibit their legal vouchers by 1
Mar 1870 to John V. St. Clair, admin. (AI 5 Mar 1869)

ST. CLAIR, JOHN V., see "Abraham Rutledge" and "Asa Hart" and
"James St. Clair," q.v.

ST. CLAIR, JOSEPH, of Cecil Co., and Miss Mary J. Coburn, of
Harford Co., m. 15 Sep 1869, at Abingdon, by Rev. J. G. Moore (AI
24 Sep 1869)

ST. CLAIR, LESTER, died ---- (date not given) and the trustee's sale
notice stated that his farm will be offered at public sale on 26 Apr
1856 by Daniel Scott, trustee (HD 21 Mar 1856)

STABLER, HENRY, see "George Briggs," q.v.

STANDIFORD, ELLEN J., wife of Isaac Standiford, died Sat. 16 Mar
1867, aged 33; obituary contains a memorial to "Dear Nellie"
written by a "Friend" (AI 29 Mar 1867)

STANDIFORD, ISAAC, see "Ellen J. Standiford," q.v.

STANDIFORD, LLOYD, died Fri. 6 Feb 1863, in his 31st year; obituary
contains a poem written "by his friend" (SA 20 Feb 1863)

STANDIFORD, MALTEER, see "Winfield Scott Standiford," q.v.

STANDIFORD, MARY, see "Winfield Scott Standiford," q.v.

STANDIFORD, MRS. MARY, died Sun. 28 Nov 1863 at her residence,
at an advanced age (SA 4 Dec 1863)

STANDIFORD, WINFIELD SCOTT, son of Malteer and Mary E.
Standiford, died 12 Jul 1870, in the evening, aged 7 months and 27
days (AI 29 Jul 1870)

STANSBURY, ELIZABETH (Mrs.) and William Nelson, Esq., both of
Harford Co., m. Mon. evening 16 Apr 1838 by Rev. Andrew B.
Cross (HM 26Apr 1838)

STANSBURY, ISAAC (Colonel), died 12 Feb 1865, in his 76th year, at
his residence in Harford Co. (AI 24 Feb 1865)

STAPLES, JOHN M., died ---- (date not given) and was removed from
the voter registration list in the 6th District in 1870 (HR 4 Oct 1870)

STARR, GEORGIANNA (Miss) and James Dowling, both of Harford
Co., m. 24 Jun 1856 at the Parsonage in Bel Air by Rev. H. C.
Cushing (HD 27 Jun 1856)

STARR, JOSEPH, see "James Gallion," q.v.

STARRETT, LUTETIA, widow of the late John Starrett, died 11 Feb
1864 at the residence of her son, near Shawsville, in her 73rd year
(SA 19 Feb 1864)

START, ROBERT, died ---- (date not given) and was removed from the
voter registration list in the 5th District in 1870 (AI 4 Nov 1870)

STEARNS, J. OSCAR, of Harford Co., and Miss Ella Milligan, of
Lancaster Co., PA, m. Tues. 17 Nov 1868 at the Presbyterian
Parsonage in Bart Township, near Georgetown, PA, by Rev. J. M.
Rittenhouse (AI 27 Nov 1868)

STEARNS, JOHN L., died ---- (date not given) and the administrator's
notice stated that creditors must exhibit their legal vouchers by 6
Jun 1868 to John O. Stearns, admin. (AI 7 Jun 1867)

STEBINS, HARVY, formerly of Springfield, Massachusetts, died 4 Jan
1868 at his residence, 2 miles west of Havre de Grace, in his 69th
year; he was a kind husband, affectionate father, and a good
neighbor, clear of sectional prejudices and bigotry (AI 24 Jan 1868)

STEEL, ALLEN, committed suicide last Wed. afternoon [June, 1867] by
jumping into the river at Peach Bottom; he was walking with two
men, directly opposite the place known as the "Deeps," when he
remarked that it would be a good place for a person to drown; he
took off his suspenders, tied a stone to one end, tied the other
around his neck, and plunged into the river; the men in company,
thinking he was in jest, made no effort to restrain him until it was
too late to save him; his body was recovered on Thurs. [article from
the *Lancaster Intelligencer*] (AI 28 Jun 1867)

STEINRIDER, HENRY, died ---- (date not given) and the
administrator's notice stated that creditors must exhibit their legal

vouchers by 17 Oct 1855 to John A. Hopper and Ann Maria Steinrider, admins.[Hopper was acting admin. in 1855] (HM 14 Dec 1854 and 1 Mar 1855)

STEPHENS, CATHARINE SUSANNA and David F. Archer, both of Harford Co., m. 9 Jan 1866, at the house of Joseph Stephens, by Rev. J. K. Nichols (AI 26 Jan 1866)

STEPHENSON, CARRIE VIRGINIA RUTLEDGE, dau. of James and Elizabeth N. Stephenson, died 29 Oct 1870, aged 9 [*Baltimore Sun* and *Baltimore Gazette* please copy] (AI 4 Nov 1870)

STEPHENSON, ELIZABETH, see "Carrie V. R. Stephenson," q.v.

STEPHENSON, JAMES, died ---- (date not given) and the executor's notice stated that creditors must exhibit their legal vouchers by 30 Jun 1839 to William B. Stephenson, exec. (HM 28 Jun 1838)

STEPHENSON, JAMES, see "Carrie V. R. Stephenson," q.v.

STEPHENSON, LLOYD (colored), died ---- (date not given) and the administrator's notice stated that creditors must exhibit their legal vouchers by 15 May 1870 to Albert Davis, admin. (AI 21 May 1869)

STEPHENSON, WILLIAM, died ---- (date not given) and was removed from the voter registration list of the 2nd District in 1870 (AI 4 Nov 1870)

STEPHENSON, WILLIAM B., see "James Stephenson," q.v.

STEPHENSON, WILLIAM P., died ---- (date not given) and the administrator's notice stated that creditors must exhibit their legal vouchers by 5 Nov 1858 to David Lee, admin. (SA 14 Nov 1857)

STERLING, B. F., of Harford Co., and Mary A. Price, of Baltimore Co., m. 27 Dec 1868 in Baltimore by Rev. Munsey (HD 1 Jan 1869)

STEVENS, F. C. and Caroline McAlister, both of Washington, D.C., m. 25 Nov 1869 in Baltimore by Rev. John Poisal (AI 24 Dec 1869)

STEWART, ALFRED, formerly of Harford Co., died suddenly 4 Sep 1868 in New York, in his 47th year (AI 11 Sep 1868)

STEWART, DAVID (Hon.), a prominent lawyer, died 5 Jan 1858 in Baltimore (SA 9 Jan 1858)

STEWART, LOU. E. and Oliver G. Kenly m. 1 Oct 1867 at St. Vincent's Church by Rev. Father Myers (AI 11 Oct 1867)

STEWART, ROBERT, died 4 Nov 1869 near Darlington [age not given]; formerly of Scotland, but for the last 25 years a resident of Harford Co. (AI 10 Dec 1869); the subsequent administrator's notice stated that creditors must exhibit their legal vouchers by 20 Dec 1870 to Joseph H. Jewett, admin. (AI 24 Dec 1869)

STEWART, SYLVANIA (Miss), of Philadelphia, and Thomas Livezy, of Harford Co., m. 19 Aug 1868 by Rev. T. S. C. Smith (AI 4 Sep 1868)

STINCHCOMB, N. S. and Mary Enger, formerly of Georgetown, but late of Harford Co., m. 26 May 1857 at St. Vincent's Parsonage in Baltimore by Rev. Obermeyer (HD 5 Jun 1857)

STOCKHAM, CORNELIA E. (Miss), dau. of Thomas Stockham, Esq.,
and Rev. John H. Baker, all of Harford Co., m. Wed. 21 Oct 1868,
at the residence of the bride's father, by Rev. J. G. Moore (AI 6 Nov
1868; HD 30 Oct 1868 gave her father's name as "James")

STOCKHAM, JAMES, see "Cornelia E. Stockham," q.v.

STOCKHAM, JOHN Q., of Harford Co., and Miss Mary L. Bowyer, of
Baltimore, m. 15 Jun 1864 by Rev. J. McKendry Reiley in
Baltimore (AI 24 Jun 1864 spelled his name "Stokham")

STOCKHAM, THOMAS, see "Cornelia E. Stockham," q.v.

STOKES, MR., a German who lived near Aberdeen, Harford Co., died
last Thurs. evening in an accident near Perrymansville; he was
returning from Bush River Neck in a light two-horse wagon and in
crossing the P. W. & B. Railroad, about a quarter of a mile west of
Perrymansville, was struck by the engine of the evening train from
Baltimore; the wagon was struck about the center of the body and
smashed to atoms, the seat and cushions of which were found, on
stopping the train, under the mangled body of Mr. Stokes, which lay
upon the cow catcher; he was alone at the time of the accident, and
leaves a family (AI 21 Dec 1866)

STRAUSBAUGH, A. HENRY, of Howard Co., MD, and Isabella W.
Pannell, youngest dau. of the late James Pannell, of Harford Co., m.
30 Oct 1862 at *Silverton*, in Harford Co., by Rev. William Finney
(SA 8 Nov 1862)

STREET, CHARLOTTE JANE, died 13 Oct 1861, aged 32, at the
residence of her father (SA 16 Nov 1861)

STREET, JOHN, see "Henry R. Amos," q.v.

STREETT, A. J., died ---- (date not given) and was removed from the
voter registration list of the 4th District in 1868 (AI 9 Oct 1868)

STREETT, ABRAHAM J. (Doctor), died 9 Nov 1867 at Clermont,
Harford Co., in his 69th year; the administrator's notice stated that
creditors must exhibit their legal vouchers by 11 Nov 1868 to
Joseph M. Streett, admin. (AI 22 Nov 1867 and 29 Nov 1867)

STREETT, ABRAHAM R., of Harford Co., and Miss Mattie McCurdy,
of York Co., PA, m. 6 Jan 1859 by Rev. Crawford (SA 15 Jan
1859)

STREETT, CHARLES, see "Thomas Nelson," q.v.

STREETT, DAVID, see "Sarah Streett," q.v.

STREETT, ELIZABETH, see "Emma Streett," q.v.

STREETT, EMMA, dau. of J. R. and Elizabeth Streett, died 13 Dec 1857
of scarlet fever, aged 4 years and 5 months (SA 26 Dec 1857)

STREETT, GEORGE W., died 20 Nov 1862 near Winchester, VA, in his
31st year (SA 27 Dec 1862)

STREETT, J. R., see "Emma Streett," q.v.

STREETT, JACOB RUTLEDGE, only son of John H. and Pinkie E.
Streett, died Sat. 18 Dec 1869, aged 4 months and 3 weeks (AI 24
Dec 1869)

STREETT, JAMES AUGUSTUS, formerly of Harford Co., died 25 Oct 1861 at his residence in Memphis, TN (SA 19 Jul 1862)

STREETT, JOHN, see "Jacob Rutledge Streett" and "Henry H. Johns" and "Richard Dallam," q.v.

STREETT, JOHN H. and Miss Pinkie Rutledge, both of Harford Co., m. 28 Jun 1868, at the residence of Jacob Rutledge, by Rev. B. F. Myers (AI 7 Aug 1868)

STREETT, JOHN J., see "Henry Frederick" and "Kate M. Streett," q.v.

STREETT, JOHN R., see "St. Clair Streett," q.v.

STREETT, JOSEPH, see "Marion Streett" and "Abraham J. Streett" and "Edward Fisher" and "Joshua M. Amoss," q.v.

STREETT, JOSEPHINE VICTORIA (Miss), second dau. of Dr. Abraham J. Streett, of Harford Co., and William H. Waters, of *Water Vale*, Harford Co., m. Tues. 12 May 1863 at Rock Spring Church by Rev. R. J. Keeling (SA 15 May 1863)

STREETT, JULIET, see "Marion Streett," q.v.

STREETT, KATE M., wife of John Joshua Streett, Esq., died Sat. 28 May 1870 at her residence in Harford Co., in her 34th year (HD 3 Jun 1870; AI 3 Jun 1870 contains a brief memorial)

STREETT, Marion, infant dau. of Joseph M. and Juliet E. Streett, died 17 May 1870 [age not given] (AI 20 May 1870)

STREETT, PINKIE, see "Jacob Rutledge Streett," q.v.

STREETT, RUTH A. and William A. Wilson, both of Harford Co., m. 19 Feb 1858 by Rev. William Wilson (SA 6 Mar 1858)

STREETT, SARAH, widow of David Streett, of Harford Co., died suddenly on the morning of 26 Mar 1857 after a protracted attack of pneumonia (HD 3 Apr 1857)

STREETT, SHADRACK, see "Hannah Ann Robinson," q.v.

STREETT, ST. CLAIR, died ---- (date not given) and the executor's notice stated that creditors must exhibit their legal vouchers by 2 Dec 1865 to John R. Streett, exec.. (AI 16 Dec 1864)

STREETT, ST. CLAIR, formerly of Harford Co., died 4 Sep 1865 at Tippecanoe, Harrison Co., Ohio, in his 43rd year; obituary contains a poem written by "M.S." [Weekly *Sun* please copy] (AI 29 Sep 1865)

STREETT, WILLIAM and Rose Butler, both of Harford Co., m. Thurs. 12 Aug 1869 at the pastoral residence of St. Ignatius' Church, Harford Co., by Rev. P. F. O'Connor (AI 20 Aug 1869)

STRICKLAND, LAVINIA and William S. Ely, both of Harford Co., m. at the M. E. Parsonage in Bel Air by Rev. W. M. Meminger (AI 1 Jun 1866)

STRITEHOFF, JOHN W. and Miss Mary A. Tucker, both of Harford Co., m. 9 Nov 1869, at Centre M. E. Church, by Rev. J. C. Hagey (AI 19 Nov 1869)

STUART, WILLIAM L., died Sun. morning 12 Apr 1868 at the residence of Joseph Ross, Harford Co., in his 23rd year (AI 17 Apr 1868)

STUMP, ANNIE J. (Miss), of Cecil Co., and William Webster, of Harford Co., m. Thurs. 5 Oct 1865 at Perry Point, Cecil Co., by Rev. William Finney (AI 13 Oct 1865)

STUMP, CASSANDRA, died ---- (date not given) and the executor's notice stated that creditors must exhibit their legal vouchers by 17 Nov 1847 to Henry Stump, exec. (HM 26 Mar 1847)

STUMP, FREDERICK, of Cecil Co., and Miss Mary A. Stump, of Harford Co., m. Tues. 19 May 1863 by Rev. Thomas S. C. Smith (SA 29 May 1863); see "Mary A. Stump" and "William Henry Stump," q.v.

STUMP, HENRIETTA (Miss) and Alexander Mitchell, of Philadelphia, m. 27 Apr 1865, at *Perry Farm* in Cecil Co., by Rev. T. S. C. Smith (AI 5 May 1865)

STUMP, HENRY, see "Hugh S. Holloway" and "Cassandra Stump," q.v.

STUMP, HERMAN, see "Francis Hill" and "Martha Lester," q.v.

STUMP, JOHN, see "Mary H. Stump," q.v.

STUMP, JOHN KELLY, died ---- (date not given) and the administrator's notice stated that creditors must exhibit their legal vouchers by 11 Mar 1863 to William Henry Stump, admin. (SA 15 Mar 1862)

STUMP, JOHN W. (Colonel), formerly of Harford Co., died suddenly 21 May 1867 of disease of the heart, at Houston, Texas, aged 45; he was the son of John W. Stump, Esq., of Oakington, Harford Co., and went to Texas in 1850; he was one of the engineers who located and built the B. B. B. & C. Railroad and also the Tap Road to Columbia; he leaves many friends and an esteemed family [information from *Houston Journal*] (AI 14 Jun 1867)

STUMP, JOHN W., died Tues. morning 21 Oct 1862, at Stafford, at an advanced age; he was one of the oldest and most respected citizens of Harford Co., and leaves a large circle of relatives and friends (SA 25 Oct 1862); see "Cassandra Norris," q.v.

STUMP, KATE W. (Miss) and Dr. James M. Magraw m. 1 Jun 1869 at *Perry Farm*, Cecil Co., by Rev. T. S. C. Smith (AI 11 Jun 1869)

STUMP, MARY A., of Harford Co., and Frederick Stump, of Cecil Co., m. Tues. 19 May 1863 by Rev. Thomas S. C. Smith (SA 29 May 1863)

STUMP, MARY A., wife of Frederick Stump, of Cecil Co., died Mon. 17 Apr 1865 at *Evergreen* in Harford Co. (AI 21 Apr 1865)

STUMP, MARY H. (Miss), eldest dau. of John Stump, Esq., of Perryville, and Thomas S. Smith, m. 10 Apr 1856 by Rev. W. Finney (HD 18 Apr 1856)

STUMP, T. B. COLEMAN, of Harford Co., and Addie F. Wray, dau. of James Wray, of Philadelphia, m. 11 Oct 1865 at Philadelphia by Rev. Reed (AI 3 Nov 1865)

STUMP, THOMAS C., see "William Henry Stump," q.v.

STUMP, WILLIAM HENRY, died ---- (date not given) and the executor's notice stated that creditors must exhibit their legal vouchers by 25 Feb 1868 to Frederick Stump, exec. (AI 1 Mar 1867); see "John Kelly Stump," q.v.

STUMP, WILLIAM HENRY, son of the late Thomas C. Stump, died 19 Feb 1865 at his residence, *Evergreen*, Harford Co., in his 24th year; obituary contains a long memorial and two short poems written by "W.S.F." (AI 24 Feb 1865)

SULLIVAN, EMMA, dau. of the late James T. Sullivan, of Havre de Grace, and Samuel B. Mann, of Flemington, NJ, m. 3 Jan 1865 by Ref. James K. Cramer (AI 27 Jan 1865)

SUNDERLAND, MARY T. (Miss), of Philadelphia, and Jacob E. Bull, of Harford Co., m. 5 Feb 1863 by Rev. J. H. Kean in Philadelphia (SA 13 Feb 1863)

SUTOR, H. P. and M. C. Leattor m. Wed. morning 13 Aug 1843, at St. John's Church, by Rev. Billopp (HM 18 Aug 1843)

SUTTON, ALMIRA, of Harford Co., and A. H. Churchill, of Louisville, Kentucky, m. 6 Jan 1857 by Rev. Sharpley (HM 15 Jan 1857)

SUTTON, ARABELLA (Miss), of Baltimore Co., and John R. Archer, of Harford Co., m. 5 Nov 1866 at the Parsonage in Bel Air by Rev. J. K. Nichols (AI 9 Nov 1866)

SUTTON, J. H. and Miss Mary E. Riley, both of Harford Co., m. 15 Aug 1870 by Rev. Franck (AI 2 Dec 1870; HD 2 Dec 1870 gave her name as "Nanny E.")

SUTTON, J. P. S., died ---- (date not given) and the executor's notice stated that creditors must exhibit their legal vouchers by 29 Aug 1869 to Thomas Sutton, exec. (AI 4 Sep 1868)

SUTTON, THOMAS, see "James Tobin," q.v.

SWEETING, BELLE S. (Miss) and Alonzo Bowman, both of Harford Co., m. 10 Feb 1870 by Rev. J. A. Price (AI 18 Feb 1870)

SWIFT, J. H., see "Loretto Francis Swift," q.v.

SWIFT, LIZZIE E. (Miss) and George Unkle, both of Harford Co., m. 29 Mar 1870 at the residence of the bride's brother, Baltimore, by Rev. W. G. Hillman (AI 1 Apr 1870)

SWIFT, LORETTO FRANCIS, only child of J. H. and Lowie Swift, died 12 Feb 1870, aged 2 months and 9 days (AI 18 Feb 1870)

SWIFT, LOWIE, see "Loretto Francis Swift," q.v.

SWIFT, THOMAS, died ---- (date not given) and the executor's notice stated that creditors must exhibit their legal vouchers by 15 Mar 1865 to Henry A. Silver, exec. (AI 1 Apr 1864)

SYKES, MARTHA, wife of James Sykes and youngest dau. of the late George G. Presbury, formerly of Harford Co., died Sun. evening 14 Feb 1869 in Baltimore (HD 19 Feb 1869)

SYLVESTER, WILLIAM, of Harford Co., died Thurs. 16 Oct 1870, aged 21, at the residence of Rev. William F. Brand (AI 4 Nov 1870); William H. Sylvester was removed from the voter registration list in the 1st District in 1871 (HR 3 Nov 1871)

TALLEY, ISAAC (colored man), while crossing Winter's Run on a log near Waters' Mill last Mon., fell off and struck a large stone in his fall; he was severely injured and would have drown but for the exertions of some companions; it is thought that he cannot recover (AI 26 Feb 1869)

TAMMANY, WILLIAM H., of Cecil Co., and Miss Jane E. Nash, of Harford Co., m. 14 Oct 1868 (AI 16 Oct 1868)

TANGUY, ALFRED A., died ---- (date not given) and the administratrix's notice stated that creditors must exhibit their legal vouchers by 28 May 1871 to Ruth Ann Tanguy, Admx. C.T.A. (AI 3 Jun 1870)

TARLETON, JAMES R., of Baltimore, and Miss Margaret "Maggie" J. Wright, of Havre de Grace, m. Thurs. 29 Oct 1868, at Havre de Grace" by Rev. William H. Cooke (HR 5 Nov 1868 and AI 13 Nov 1868 and HD 6 Nov 1868)

TARLTON, JAMES R., died ---- (date not given) and was removed from the voter registration list in the 6th District in 1870 (HR 4 Oct 1870)

TATE, ALBERT E. and Miss Phebe Walker, both of Harford Co., m. Thurs. 6 May 1869, at the residence of Thomas Cunningham, by Rev. Smith (AI 14 May 1869 and HD 7 May 1869)

TAYLOR, ANN (ANNA), see "Preston Taylor," q.v.

TAYLOR, ELIZABETH H. (Miss) and Philip T. Quinlin, farmer, both of Harford Co., m. Thurs. 26 Mar 1857 by Rev. Crawford (HD 27 Mar 1857)

TAYLOR, GILDER, see "Willie A. Taylor," q.v.

TAYLOR, HENRY S., see "Isaiah Taylor," q.v.

TAYLOR, ISAIAH, died ---- (date not given) and the administrator's notice stated that creditors must exhibit their legal vouchers by 1 Feb 1847 to Henry S. Taylor and Isaiah C. Taylor, admins. (HM 20 Aug 1846)

TAYLOR, J. J., see "Sallie M. Taylor," q.v.

TAYLOR, JOHN and Miss Mary A. Somers m. Tues. 11 Oct 1864, near Harford Furnace (AI 25 Nov 1864)

TAYLOR, MARY, see "Willie A. Taylor," q.v.

TAYLOR, MRS., wife of W. A. Taylor, Esq., committed suicide by cutting her throat with a razor on Thurs. of last week and died Wed. night last; she had been in delicate health and mentally depressed for some time (HR 22 Apr 1870)

TAYLOR, P. D., see "Preston Taylor," q.v.

TAYLOR, PRESTON, son of P. D. and Ann Taylor, died 28 Feb 1869 at Dublin, Harford Co., in his 19th year (HD 5 Mar 1869; AI 5 Mar 1869 gave her name as "Anna")

TAYLOR, RICHARD and Miss Sarah M. Scarff, both of Harford Co., m. 29 Apr 1869 by Rev. T. S. C. Smith (AI 14 May 1869 and HD 7 May 1869)

TAYLOR, ROBERT B., of Harford Co., and Miss Irene L. Cockrell, of Prince William Co., VA, m. 25 Nov 1869 at the M. E. Church

South in Alexandria, VA, by Rev. Dr. Hough [*Baltimore Sun* please copy] (AI 28 Jan 1870)

TAYLOR, ROBERT G. and Mrs. Mary E. Greenfield, both of Harford Co., m. 31 May 1867 by Rev. T. S. C. Smith (AI 7 Jun 1867)

TAYLOR, SALLIE M., youngest dau. of J. J. Taylor, of Norristown, PA, and John H. Lytle, of Magnolia, MD, m. 16 Jun 1869, at the residence of the bride's father, by Rev. Hardin Wheat (AI 25 Jun 1869)

TAYLOR, W. A., see "Mrs. Taylor," q.v.

TAYLOR, WILLIE A., only child of Gilder G. and Mary A. Taylor, died Fri. morning 25 Aug 1865 at 10½ o'clock, aged 2 years, 4 months and 12 days; obituary contains a brief memorial written by "S.E.A." (AI 1 Sep 1865)

TEMPLE, AMANDA, consort of James Temple, died Mon. 11 Feb 1867 at the residence of her husband [age not given] (AI 15 Feb 1867); see "Mary Lizzie Temple," q.v.

TEMPLE, JAMES, see "Amanda Temple" and "Mary Lizzie Temple," q.v.

TEMPLE, MARY LIZZIE, only child of James and Amanda Temple, died 2 Sep 1865 in the evening, near Bel Air, aged 3 years and 11 months; obituary contains a short poem (AI 15 Sep 1865)

TEMPLE, WILLIAM C., died Thurs. 14 Mar 1867, in his 83rd year (AI 22 Mar 1867)

TENLY, HENRY, see "John Campbell," q.v.

THOMAS, ADELIA (Miss) and Newton McCourtney, both of Harford Co., m. 20 Jan 1870 by Rev. D. A. Shermer (AI 28 Jan 1870)

THOMAS, ALFRED and Miss Nancy J. Enfield, both of Dublin District, Harford Co., m. 21 Apr 1870 by Rev. T. M. Crawford (AI 29 Apr 1870)

THOMAS, DAVID E. JR., of Baltimore, and Virginia Quarles, of Harford Co., m. 2 Sep 1865 at *Oak Hall*, the residence of Hon. A. M. Hancock, by Rev. W. F. Brand (AI 8 Sep 1865)

THOMAS, HARMAN, formerly of Abingdon, Harford Co., died 14 Jun 1858 at the residence of his son-in-law in Baltimore, aged 59 years, 11 months and 7 days (SA 19 Jun 1858)

THOMAS, MARY GOLDSBOROUGH, of Talbot Co., MD, and John Paca Dallam, of Harford Co., m. Thurs. 9 Oct 1862 by Rev. L. F. Morgan (SA 18 Oct 1862)

THOMAS, OLIVER H., of Bel Air, and Miss Nannie H. Archer, dau. of the late Dr. John Archer, of Rock Run, Harford Co., m. Tues. 1 Dec 1868 at the residence of Mrs. Constable, sister of the bride, in Cecil Co., by Rev. Squire (AI 4 Dec 1868)

THOMAS, OLIVER H. (Colonel), died ---- (date not given) in his 47th year; he was born in 1823 in Havre de Grace and took up the practice of law, first in Bel Air and then in Chicago; in 1852 he moved to San Francisco, California; when the Civil War broke out he went to Virginia and served in the Confederate Army; his intimate friend Col. James J. Archer, of Maryland, then commanding the 5th Texas, was promoted to Brig. General at the Battle of Seven Pines and immediately appointed Col. Thomas as his aide (article contains a lengthy discussion of his war activities); after the war, and in feeble health, he moved to Baltimore and a year later he moved to Bel Air where he again began his law practice; in the fall of 1868 he m. a sister of Gen. Archer; the week before last he was in Elkton, Cecil Co., to try a case when he suddenly became ill and died at the home of a friend Mr. Constable; a memorial resolution was made in his honor on 10 Oct 1870 by the Bel Air Bar (HD 7 Oct 1870 and 14 Oct 1870); another newspaper obituary stated Col. Oliver H. Thomas, Esq., of Bel Air, engaged as counsel in the murder case of the State vs. The Negroes Williams, removed to Elkton in Cecil Co. to try said case on Wed. of last week and after his arrival was attached with hemorrhage; he was taken to the residence of Albert Constable, Esq., a relative, and medical aid was summoned and he recovered considerably; on Fri. evening at 7 o'clock he was on the back porch with Mr. Constable when he was again seized with hemorrhages and died before he could be gotten in the house; his wife had arrived about two hours before he died; his remains were conveyed to the depot on Mon. last and then to Spesutia Church near Perrymansville where he was interred; a large majority of the Bar accompanied the procession to the depot, including P. M. G. Cresswell and many Harford friends; he was in his 47th year; during the war he supported the Southern cause and became a colonel on the staff of Gen. James Archer in the Virginia Campaigns; he served under Gen. Ewell at the Battle of Gettysburg and although he escaped, he was attacked with a hemorrhage that prostrated his strength and gave further symptom of his fatal disease; after the war he m. Miss Archer, dau. of the late Dr. John Archer and sister of Gen. James Archer; resolutions were later passed in his honor by the Circuit Court for Cecil County and The Bel Air Bar and published in *The Aegis & Intelligencer* (HR 30 Sep 1870; AI 30 Sep 1870 and 8 Oct 1870 and 14 Oct 1870); O. H. Thomas was removed from the voter registration list in the 3rd District in 1870 (HR 28 Oct 1870)

THOMAS, RALPH H. and Miss Rebecca Finley, both of Harford Co., m. 5 Jan 1858 at the Parsonage in Bel Air by Rev. H. C. Cushing (SA 16 Jan 1858)

THOMPSON, ANDREW, see "Henry C. Fletcher," q.v.

THOMPSON, ANGELINE, see "Mary Thompson," q.v.

THOMPSON, BENJAMIN, alias Benjamin Bolt, on trial for killing Aleck Russom in Cecil Co. last December; article contains a summary of the evidence (HD 13 May 1870)

THOMPSON, CHARLES, see "George Hays Thompson," q.v.

THOMPSON, ELIJAH, died Thurs. 17 Sep 1863 at his residence near Havre de Grace, in his 53rd year; obituary contains a poem (SA 25 Sep 1863)

THOMPSON, G. W., died ---- (date not given) and was removed from the voter registration list in the 4th District in 1868 (AI 9 Oct 1868)

THOMPSON, GEORGE HAYS, son of Matilda J. and Charles H. Thompson, died 14 Mar 1859 near Havre de Grace, aged 13 months and 24 days; obituary contains a poem (SA 9 Apr 1859)

THOMPSON, JOHN (colored man), in the employ of Capt. R. E. Duvall, was bathing in the dam at Mitchell's Mill near Bel Air last Sun., with another colored man, when he ventured beyond his depth and, being unable to swim, was drowned in spite of the efforts of the other man to rescue him (AI 3 Jul 1868)

THOMPSON, LEVI, died ---- (date not given) and was removed from the voter registration list in the 5th District in 1870 (AI 4 Nov 1870)

THOMPSON, MAHLON, see "Mary Thompson," q.v.

THOMPSON, MARY, only dau. of Angeline and Mahlon Thompson, died 12 May 1858, aged 5 years, 3 months and 12 days; obituary contains a short poem (SA 12 Jun 1858)

THOMPSON, MATILDA, see "George Hays Thompson," q.v.

THOMPSON, SARAH KEZIAH, died 5 Mar 1869, aged 11 years and 2 months, third dau. of Sarah A. and William Thompson (AI 26 Mar 1869)

THOMPSON, WILLIAM, see "Mary Susannah Michael" and "Sarah Keziah Thompson," q.v.

THOMSON, WILLIAM H. (Captain), of Havre de Grace, died last Tues. morning after a long and painful illness; funeral took place yesterday from the residence of Capt. William Myers (HR 6 Jan 1871)

THOMPSON, WILLIAM J. and Miss Sarah R. Huff, both of Harford Co., m. 11 Jan 1870, at the residence of the bride, by Rev. George M. Berry (HD 11 Feb 1870 and AI 21 Jan 1870)

THORPE, MARY M. (Miss) and George W. Carver, Jr., both of Bel Air, m. 6 May 1867 by Rev. T. S. C. Smith (AI 10 May 1867)

TIMMONS, SARAH P. (Miss) and James Spicer, both of Harford Co., m. 12 Nov 1857 by Rev. T. S. C. Smith (SA 21 Nov 1857)

TIPTON, CATHERINE, see "Frances Tipton" and "Mary L. Tipton" and "Rebecca Tipton," q.v.

TIPTON, FRANCES, fourth dau. of William B. and Catherine Tipton, died 25 Sep 1863, aged 3 weeks; obituary contains a short poem (SA 9 Oct 1863 misspelled her name as "Francis")

TIPTON, MARY L., third dau. of William B. and Catherine Tipton, died 6 Oct 1863, aged 2 years, 4 months and 15 days (SA 30 Oct 1863)

TIPTON, REBECCA, second dau. of William B. and Catherine Tipton, died Thurs. 19 Feb 1863, in her 3rd year (SA 27 Feb 1863)

TIPTON, WILLIAM, see "Frances Tipton" and "Mary L. Tipton" and "Rebecca Tipton" and "Abraham Slade," q.v.

TOBIN, JAMES, died Mon. 3 Sep 1866 at his residence in Harford Co., in his 66th year; another notice indicated the public sale of his personal property will be held on 24 Sep 1866; the subsequent executor's notice stated that creditors must exhibit their legal vouchers by 8 Sep 1867 to Thomas Sutton, exec. (AI 17 Aug 1866 and 14 Sep 1866)

TOBIN, JEREMIAH, residing at No. 161 Forrest St. in Baltimore, but formerly of near Bel Air, Harford Co., died very suddenly on the morning of 14 Apr 1870, in his 37th year; he had been suffering for the past 3 years with a complication of diseases of the heart and lungs; he leaves a wife and 3 children; Coroner Carr determined that death was from natural causes and declined holding an inquest [death notice appeared in *"Baltimore Sun of Monday"*] (AI 15 Apr 1870 and HD 15 Apr 1870)

TODD, ELLA R. (Miss) and Dr. A. J. Foard, both of Baltimore, m. 2 Nov 1871 in the evening, at the Universalist Church in Baltimore, by Rev. Alexander Kent (SA 10 Nov 1871)

TOLLEY (TOLLY), JAMES AND MARY, see "Walter Tolley" and "Thomas Howard Tolly," q.v.

TOLLEY, WALTER, son of James W. and Mary Tolley, died Sat. 30 Sep 1864, in his 18th year (AI 26 Aug 1864)

TOLLY, THOMAS HOWARD, eldest son of James W. and Mary Tolly, died Tues. 12 May 1857, aged 18 years and 6 months (HD 15 May 1857)

TOUCHTON, BELLE, wife of Alfred M. Touchton, died 6 Mar 1870 at Bayview, in her 21st year (HR 18 Mar 1870)

TOY, JOHN, see "John H. Toy" and "Lizzie K. Toy," q.v.

TOY, JOHN H., died ---- (date not given) and the administrator's notice stated that creditors must exhibit their legal vouchers by 19 Jan 1870 to John Toy and William J. Toy, admins. (AI 29 Jan 1869)

TOY, LIZZIE K. (Miss), dau. of John Toy, Esq.., of Baltimore Co., and John A. Harkins m. 3 Mar 1859 by Rev. Hart (SA 12 Mar 1859)

TOY, SALLIE E. (Miss) and John H. Harkins, both of Harford Co., m. 11 Nov 1868 by Rev. R. A. Norris (AI 18 Dec 1868)

TOY, WILLIAM J., see "John H. Toy," q.v.

TRACEY, RACHEL, died Thurs. 17 Feb 1870 at the residence of her brother-in-law Joseph Miller, in the 4th District of Harford Co., at an advanced age (AI 25 Feb 1870)

TRACY, ELIZABETH, an old lady who lived near Wiley's Mill in Marshall's District, was so badly burned by her clothes taking fire last Sun. that she died the next day; she was alone in the house at the time (SA 15 Jan 1859)

TRAILL, MARY V., dau. of Edward Traill, Esq., and John I. Yellott, of Baltimore Co., m. ---- (date not given) at the residence of the bride's father in Frederick, MD, by Rev. Osborn Ingle (AI 12 Jun 1868)

TREADWAY, ELLEN C. (Miss) and Edward T. Monks, both of Harford Co., m. 13 Aug 1866 at the Parsonage in Bel Air by Rev. J. K. Nichols (AI 17 Aug 1866)

TREADWAY, JOHN E., died ---- (date not given) and the executor's notice stated that creditors must exhibit their legal vouchers by 21 Nov 1866 to Edward T. Monks, exec. (AI 12 Jan 1866)

TREADWAY, MARTHA (Mrs.) and Leonard Ady, both of Harford Co., m. 10 Oct 1871 by Rev. J. Roberts (SA 13 Oct 1871)

TREADWELL, ELIZABETH, wife of the late James Treadwell, died at her residence in Baltimore on Wed. 8 Jul 1859, in her 41st year [*Baltimore Sun* please copy] (SA 16 Jul 1859)

TREADWELL, HARRIET S., consort of James H. Treadwell, died Mon. 20 Apr 1868, aged 36; one obituary contains a poem (AI 1 May 1868 and 22 May 1868)

TREADWELL, JAMES, died 15 Feb 1858 at his residence in Harford Co., aged 66, leaving an aged and afflicted partner and their children (SA 20 Feb 1858)

TREADWELL, JAMES H., see "Harriet S. Treadwell," q.v.

TREADWELL, WILLIAM H., of Harford Co., and Miss Julia A. Clayton, of Baltimore Co., m. 25 Jan 1866, at the Parsonage in Bel Air, by Rev. J. K. Nichols (AI 2 Feb 1866)

TREGER, SQUIRE, see "Albert D. Hartman," q.v.

TREUSCH, ADAM, who died at the age of 65 and was buried in Baltimore Cemetery on 28 Nov 1861, was disinterred last Sat. for the purpose of removal to Greenmount Cemetery; the body was found to be almost as perfect in appearance as at the time of burial, except that it was completely petrified; the deceased was a very large man and weighed about 300 lbs. at the time of death; still, 8 years later, it took the strength of four men to lift the remains from the grave; there were several other bodies in the same lot, members of his family, but they showed the usual signs of decay; Mr. Harryman, the superintendent of the cemetery, stated this was the first case of petrifaction that he has seen in 20 years [article also appeared in the *Baltimore Sun*] (AI 25 Jun 1869)

TREUSCH, CHARLES, see "William Buckingham," q.v.

TRIMBLE, ANN, wife of Joseph Trimble, died the 31st day of the 2nd month, 1870 [*sic*], at the residence of Darlington Hoopes, in her 68th year [another obituary states she died at her residence in Harford Co.]; one obituary contains a memorial (AI 11 Feb 1870 and 25 Mar 1870)

TRIMBLE, JOSEPH, died the 17th day of the 3rd month, 1870, at the residence of Darlington Hoopes, in his 98th year (AI 25 Mar 1870)

TROTT, GEORGE L., see "Mary Louisa Trott," q.v.

TROTT, JAMES, of Baltimore, and Miss Sallie E. Cowen, of Harford Co., m. 22 Apr 1862 by Rev. Neville Rolfe (SA 3 May 1862)

TROTT, MARY LOUISA (Miss), eldest dau. of the late Dr. George L. Trott, formerly of Louisiana, and Eugene E. Marriott, of Baltimore

Co., m. 9 Jul 1870, in the Second Presbyterian Church, by Rev. Dr. Edwards (AI 15 Jul 1870)

TROUT, ----, see "Henry C. Fletcher," q.v.

TRUMAN, GEORGE (Negro), convicted of the murder of an unknown stranger near Catoctin Mountain in Frederick Co., suffered the extreme penalty of the law at the jail yard in Frederick City last Fri.; he made full confession of his guilt for robbery and murder previous to his execution (AI 4 Jun 1869)

TRUMP, MICHAEL, died ---- (date not given) and the notice of the public sale of his real estate between Port Deposit and Rowlandsville in Cecil Co., plus five lots in the lower part of Port Deposit, on 6 Dec 1837 was published in the paper by his executrix Eliza Trump (HM 1 Dec 1837)

TUCKER, FANNIE, see "Lillie Helen Tucker," q.v.

TUCKER, LEMUEL, see "Lillie Helen Tucker," q.v.

TUCKER, LILLIE HELEN, dau. of Lemuel J. and Fannie Tucker, died 20 Jul 1871 at the residence of her parents at Mill Creek in Calvert Co., age 1 year (HD 28 Jul 1871)

TUCKER, MARGARET C., of Harford Co., and David Deever, of Lancaster, PA, m. Tues. 1 May 1866 at the residence of the bride's father, by Rev. John W. Smith (AI 4 May 1866)

TUCKER, MARY A. (Miss) and John W. Stritehoff, both of Harford Co., m. 9 Nov 1869, at Centre M. E. Church, by Rev. J. C. Hagey (AI 19 Nov 1869)

TUCKER, MARY LIZZIE (Miss), dau. of William Tucker, Esq., and John W. Preston, all of Harford Co., m. Thurs. 4 Feb 1869 by Rev. William A. McKee (AI 12 Feb 1869)

TUCKER, WILLIAM, see "Mary Lizzie Tucker," q.v.

TUCKER, WILLIAM P., of Harford Co., and Miss Mary Ann Spicer, of Baltimore, m. Mon. evening 13 Nov 1843, in Baltimore, by Rev. Larkins (HM 17 Nov 1843)

TUDER, JOSEPH H., of Baltimore, and Miss Annie E. Denbow, of Harford Co., m. 29 Aug 1870 by Rev. J. E. Moss (AI 2 Sep 1870)

TURNER, ANDREW, see "Olivia Turner," q.v.

TURNER, ANDREW and Miss Julia Ann Whiteford, both of Harford Co., m. 19 Jan 1858 by Rev. T. S. C. Smith (SA 6 Feb 1858)

TURNER, ANDREW, died ---- (date not given) and the administratrix's notice stated that creditors must exhibit their legal vouchers by 14 Jan 1868 to Juliann Turner, admx. (AI 18 Jan 1867)

TURNER, ELI SR., died 28 Sep 1863, Harford Co., in his 69th year; obituary contains a brief memorial; the subsequent executor's notice stated that creditors must exhibit their legal vouchers by 20 Oct 1864 to Eli Turner, Jr., exec. (SA 23 Oct 1863 and 30 Oct 1863); see "Thomas Turner," q.v.

TURNER, ELLEN, see "Thomas Turner," q.v.

TURNER, JULIANN, see "Andrew Turner," q.v.

TURNER, MARY ANN, see "Olivia Turner," q.v.

TURNER, MARY JANE and James S. Cage, both of Harford Co., m. 14 Jun 1858 in Baltimore by Rev. E. J. Drinkhouse (SA 19 Jun 1858)

TURNER, MAYBERRY, see "Thomas Woolen," q.v.

TURNER, OLIVIA, only dau. of Andrew and Mary Ann Turner, of Harford Co., died 1 Jan 1863 in Baltimore, in her 18th year; obituary contains a poem (SA 30 Jan 1863)

TURNER, THOMAS, youngest son of Eli and Ellen Turner, died 14 Dec 1862 at his father's residence in Marshall's District, in his 25th year; obituary contains a poem (SA 16 Jan 1863)

TURNER, WILLIAM, died ---- (date not given) and was removed from the voter registration list of the 4th District in 1868 (AI 9 Oct 1868)

TWO BOYS KILLED, one a nephew of Mr. Lambdin of near Churchville and the other a black boy, while driving some cows, and riding on the same horse, were thrown from the horse against a tree, killing the black boy instantly and the white boy died about 4 hours later; one of the boys broke a switch while passing through a strip of woods and it is supposed the high-spirited horse was struck, causing it to run away (AI 26 Jul 1867)

UNKLE, GEORGE and Miss Lizzie E. Swift, both of Harford Co., m. 29 Mar 1870 at the residence of the bride's brother, Baltimore, by Rev. W. G. Hillman (AI 1 Apr 1870)

UNKNOWN BOYS, see "Two Boys Killed," q.v.

UNKNOWN CHILD (Negro), about one week old, and bearing marks of violence, was found last Fri. morning in a field adjoining the new burial ground in Havre de Grace, where it had been dug out of the ground by some dogs; it was taken in charge of the constable and properly interred (HM 6 Jul 1854)

UNKNOWN COLORED CITIZENS, of Havre de Grace, died during the past week or two from a very malignant type of fever; the mortality has been considerable in comparison with the small population on which the fever had to operate (HD 2 Jun 1871)

UNKNOWN COLORED MAN, found dead last Sun. in Mr. Hopper's stables in Havre de Grace; his body was wedged in between two bales of hay; he was a stranger here and had been about town but a few days; it is said he was subject to fits (HR 6 May 1870)

UNKNOWN DEATHS, names not given; article reported that no less than eight deaths occurred in Havre de Grace last week, an unusually large number for our usually healthy town (HR 13 Jan 1871)

UNKNOWN MAN, one of the workmen at Oakington, loaded his gun to go out shooting last Tues., but by some accident the gun discharged and killed him instantly (HD 30 Oct 1868)

UNKNOWN MAN, who came down from Philadelphia on the morning train last Sat. for the purpose of a gunning excursion on Spesutia Island, was taken ill and expired almost immediately; his remains were taken back to Philadelphia that evening (AI 19 Oct 1866)

UNKNOWN NEGRO BOY, aged about 10, belonging to Alexander Norris, Esq., drowned last Mon. while attempting to cross the ford at Whitaker's Mill during the heavy rains; he fell in and was carried downstream and his body has not been recovered (HD 5 Jun 1857)

UNKNOWN WOMAN, was shot and killed at Chase's Station [in Baltimore Co.] on the P. W. & B. Railroad last Fri. evening; from the description she was no doubt the same young woman who arrived in Havre de Grace from Port Deposit on Thurs. of last week and attracted considerable attention by her singular conduct during her wanderings about town; she called at DeCourcey's barber shop and offered $10 to have her hair curled as she was going to a picnic; some who had knowledge of this woman, but had forgotten her name, said her father resides above Port Deposit in Cecil Co. (HR 30 Jun 1871)

UPDERGRAPH, W. H. HARRISON, of York, Jefferson Co., Ohio, and Miss Eliza M. Wallis, for the past two years a resident of the same place, formerly of Harford Co., m. Tues. 8 May 1838 by Rev. John Lawrence (HM 31 May 1838)

VANDERFORD, WILLIAM H., Esq., editor of the *Democratic Advocate*, Westminster, MD, and Miss Addie R. Neil, dau. of Francis Neil, Esq., of Baltimore, m. Thurs. 25 Nov 1869 at Loyola College, Baltimore, by Rev. Father Boone [her surname was given as both Neil and Neal]; the editor of *The Aegis & Intelligencer* offered his congratulations to his brother editor (AI 10 Dec 1869)

VANDEVER, VINCENT A. Q., of Rising Sun, Cecil Co., MD, committed suicide last week by shooting himself through the heart with a pistol; he was lately a conductor on a street car in Philadelphia and had been arrested for larceny in that city; he gave bond for his appearance and returned home to his father's in Cecil Co.; his sureties became alarmed and sent an officer to arrest him, which he prevented by the above act (AI 24 Dec 1869)

VANDIVER, R. R., see "Alexander Smith," q.v.

VANDIVER, ROBERT R., see "John Russell," q.v.

VANDIVER, SALLIE J. (Miss), of Harford Co., and George K. Bird, of Philadelphia, m. 14 Feb 1871 at Havre de Grace by Rev. William H. Cooke (HD 17 Feb 1871)

VANSANT, JENNIE E. (Miss), of Harford Co., and H. Everett Mechem, of Chicago, IL, m. 19 Oct 1870 at the Washington House, Bel Air, by Rev. D. A. Shermer (AI 21 Oct 1870)

VICE, CHARLES, died 22 May 1867 as the result of a scuffle with John Shriver on 18 May 1867; both men were employees of Messrs. Coale & Bailey who were engaged in fishing on Watson's Island, within the limits of Cecil Co., opposite Havre de Grace; they had a few words and Shriver then pushed Vice down and one of the blood vessels in his neck was cut or broke, thereby causing his death [information from the *Cecil Whig*] (AI 31 May 1867)

WAKELAND, JOHN, died ---- (date not given) and was removed from the voter registration list in the 3rd District in 1870 (HR 1 Nov 1870)

WAKELAND, JOHN E., died Sun. 8 Jun 1862 at his residence, in his 44th year (SA 14 Jun 1862)

WAKELAND, m. C. and F. B. Hanson, both of Harford Co., m. 10 Jan 1867 by Rev. J. S. Stuchell (AI 18 Jan 1867)

WALES, IDA, youngest dau. of Wesley and Susan E. Wales, died 19 Sep 1870, aged 14 years and 7 months (AI 16 Sep 1870)

WALKER, ELIZABETH (Miss), of Harford Co., and William Freeman, of Baltimore Co., m. 11 Nov 1847 by Rev. McJilton (HM 2 Dec 1847)

WALKER, GEORGE, of Harford Co., and Miss Anna E. Russelle, of Baltimore, m. 1 Jun 1870, in the Eutaw Street Church, by Rev. Inskip [marriage notice indicated "No cards"] (AI 17 Jun 1870)

WALKER, GEORGE F. and Laura H. Elliott, dau. of William M. Elliott, m. Thurs. evening 27 Nov 1862, at the residence of the bride's father, by Rev. Dr. F. Swentzell (SA 13 Dec 1862)

WALKER, GEORGE W. and Miss Sarah A. Hopkins, dau. of George Hopkins, Esq., all of Harford Co., m. 26 Nov 1868 at Rock Run M. E. Church by Rev. J. G. Moore, assisted by Rev. Groschell (AI 4 Dec 1868)

WALKER, JAMES, died 28 Oct 1871, in his 65th year (SA 10 Nov 1871)

WALKER, JOHN, died ---- (date not given) and was removed from the voter registration list in the 6th District in 1870 (HR 21 Oct 1870)

WALKER, LIZZIE (Miss) and James W. McKendless, both of Harford Co., m. Tues. 6 Dec 1864 by Rev. Hoblitzell (AI 9 Dec 1864)

WALKER, PHEBE (Miss) and Albert E. Tate, both of Harford Co., m. 6 May 1869, at the residence of Thomas Cunningham, by Rev. Smith (HD 7 May 1869 and 14 May 1869)

WALKER, PHEBE, of Havre de Grace, and Stephen Rouse m. Thurs. 30 Apr 1868 by Rev. Dr. H. B. Martin, rector of St. John's Church, Havre de Grace (AI 8 May 1868)

WALLACE, ARCHIBALD and Miss Eliza L. Howlett, both of Harford Co., m. 9 Jan 1868 by Rev. T. M. Crawford [of York Co., PA] (AI 17 Jan 1868)

WALLICK, CONSTABLE, see "Albert D. Hartman," q.v.

WALLIS, ELIZA M. (Miss), for the past two years a resident of York, Jefferson Co., Ohio, formerly of Harford Co., and W. H. Harrison Updergraph, of the same place, m. Tues. 8 May 1838 by Rev. John Lawrence (HM 31 May 1838)

WALLIS, MARGARET, wife of Samuel R. Wallis, died 11 Aug 1859, in her 52nd year; obituary contains a memorial (SA 20 Aug 1859)

WALLIS, NANNIE W. (Miss) and Aquilla B. Whitaker, both of Harford Co., m. Wed. 6 Apr 1870 at Jarrettsville by Rev. J. C. Hagey (HD 15 Apr 1870 and AI 8 Apr 1870)

WALLIS, WILLIAM H. and Mary A. Cannon, both of Harford Co., m. 13 Aug 1862 by Rev. R. H. B. Mitchell (SA 30 Aug 1862)

WALLIS, WILLIAM H., died Thurs. 5 Feb 1863 at his residence in Harford Co., aged 46 (SA 13 Feb 1863)

WALLIS, WILLIAM R. and Miss Sarah Kellogg, both of Harford Co., m. 7 Feb 1867, at the residence of the bride's father, by Rev. W. M. Meminger (AI 15 Feb 1867)

WALTER, LAURA J. (Miss), formerly of Baltimore Co., and John Judd, of Harford Co., m. Tues. 24 Nov 1868 at St. Ignatius Church, near the Hickory, by Rev. P. F. O'Connor (AI 18 Dec 1868)

WALTHAM, HESTHER, died ---- (date not given) and the executor's notice stated that creditors must exhibit their legal vouchers by 4 Aug 1858 to William Billingslea, exec. (SA 5 Dec 1857)

WANN, BENJAMIN F. and Miss Mary E. Dallam, both of Harford Co., m. 29 Dec 1869 by Rev. A. D. Shermer (HD 7 Jan 1870); another marriage notice spelled his name "Waun" and stated they m. 28 Dec 1869 (AI 7 Jan 1870)

WANN, J., see "John S. Kennedy," q.v.

WANN, JAMES H., of Harford Co., and Miss Nellie E. Hammond, dau. of Dominick Hammond, of Baltimore Co., m. 3 Dec 1868 at the Green Street M. P. Church by Rev. T. D. Valiant (HD 1 Jan 1869 and AI 1 Jan 1869)

WANN, JOHN SR., died ---- (date not given) and was removed from the voter registration list of the 3rd District in 1870 (HR 28 Oct 1870)

WANN, JOHN, Esq., died at his residence, near Hickory, last Mon. morning, in his 84th year; throughout his long life he had won and preserved the esteem and respect of his fellow citizens to an extent rarely paralleled; he was a Justice of the Peace for many years and was trusted by his fellow men as a man of strict integrity and scrupulous honesty of purpose; he was probably the oldest member of Mt. Ararat Lodge, A.F.& A.M., in Harford Co., and was always much devoted to the principles of masonry; his portrait, painted in oil, adorns the lodge room at Bel Air, and is regarded by the surviving members of the Lodge as a valuable memento of their venerated brother who has passed away (AI 6 May 1870)

WANN, MARY JANE (Miss) and Josiah M. Herrman, both of Harford Co., m. 12 May 1868 at the Methodist Protestant Church, Bel Air, by Rev. D. A. Shermer (AI 22 May 1868)

WARD, CHARLES, died ---- (date not given) and the administratrix's notice stated that creditors must exhibit their legal vouchers by 9 Oct 1866 to Elizabeth Ward, admx. (AI 13 Oct 1865)

WARD, ELIZA J. (Miss) and Andrew A. W. Banister, both of Harford Co., m. 31 Jan 1856 by Rev. Cushing (HD 1 Feb 1856)

WARD, ELIZABETH, see "Charles Ward," q.v.

WARD, JOHN, see "M. Virginia Ward," q.v.

WARD, JOHN S., died ---- (date not given) and was removed from the voter registration list in the 5th District in 1870 (AI 4 Nov 1870)

WARD, JOHN T. and Miss Hester J. Harkins, both of Harford Co., m. 20 May 1868 by Rev. D. A. Shermer at the Methodist Protestant Church in Bel Air (AI 22 May 1868)

WARD, M. VIRGINIA, fourth dau. of John Ward, Esq., of Bel Air, and Jerry Young m. 26 Nov 1857, in Baltimore, by Rev. Hedges (SA 5 Dec 1857) .

WARDEN, MARY E., died ---- (date not given) and the administrator's notice stated that creditors must exhibit their legal vouchers by 17 Oct 1867 to Cyrus Minnick, admin. (AI 30 Nov 1866)

WAREHAM, GEORGE T. and Miss Susan E. Keen, both of Harford Co., m. Wed. 6 Jul 1853 by Rev. T. S. C. Smith, of Havre de Grace (HM 7 Jul 1853)

WAREHAM, GEORGE, of Havre de Grace, died Tues. night 27 Jul 1852, aged about 62, after a protracted illness; he leaves a large family and a train of friends; the subsequent administrator's notice stated that creditors must exhibit their legal vouchers by 1 Jun 1853 to John Wareham, admin.[George's name was spelled "Wareman" in the first notice] (HM 29 Jul 1852 and 28 Oct 1852)

WAREHAM, JOHN, Esq., died ---- (date not given) from a recent prostration of paralysis; one of the oldest and most respected citizens of Havre de Grace; John L. Williams was exec. of his estate (HR 10 Jun 1870 and HD 22 Jul 1870); he was removed from the voter registration list of the 6th District in 1870 (HR 21 Oct 1870); see "George Wareham," q.v.

WARNER, EDWARD, died 15 Dec 1846 near Darlington, Harford Co., after a lingering illness, in his 31st year; obituary contains a memorial and poem (HM 1 Jan 1847)

WARNER, LUCINDA (Miss) and Jacob Iley, both of Harford Co., m. 6 Dec 1859 by Rev. Zulauf (SA 31 Dec 1859)

WARNER, MARY E. and Silas Ross, both of Harford Co., m. Tues. 20 Oct 1868 at the residence of the bride's father, by Friends' ceremony [Towsontown papers please copy] (AI 23 Oct 1868)

WASHINGTON, ----, son of Isaac Washington (colored), of near Hopewell Crossroads, died 1 Jan 1870, aged about 14; while driving a yoke of oxen attached to a cart; the cart turned into another road one of the wheels mounted the roots of a large hickory tree and turned over and crushed the boy's head; James Foley was standing about 150 yards away and witnessed the accident; when he arrived at the spot the boy was dead (HD 7 Jan 1870)

WATERMAN, CHARLES S. and Miss Alice E. Gilbert, both of Harford Co., m. Tues. 19 Feb 1867 by Rev. T. S. C. Smith (AI 22 Feb 1867)

WATERS, AMOS, died Mon. 1 Nov 1869 at his residence, *Watervale*, Harford Co., in his 82nd year; the subsequent executor's notice stated that creditors must exhibit their legal vouchers by 8 Nov 1870 to William H. Waters, exec. (AI 12 Nov 1869); he was removed from the voter registration list of the 3rd District in 1870 (HR 28 Oct 1870)

WATERS, CAROLINE, see "Sarah Rebecca Waters," q.v.

WATERS, ISAAC, see "Sarah Rebecca Waters," q.v.

WATERS, SARAH REBECCA, youngest dau. of Caroline and Isaac Waters, of Harford Co., died Thurs. morning 12 May 1859, of consumption, aged 16 years and 7 months (SA 28 May 1859)

WATERS, T. C. SYDENHAM, died 5 Mar 1857, in his 21st year, in Baltimore (HD 13 Mar 1857)

WATERS, WALTER, died 30 Oct 1871 at Cooptown, in his 90th year (HD 3 Nov 1871)

WATERS, WILLIAM H., of Water Vale, Harford Co., and Miss Josephine Victoria Streett, second dau. of Dr. Abraham J. Streett, of Harford Co., m. Tues. 12 May 1863 at Rock Spring Church by Rev. R. J. Keeling (SA 15 May 1863); see "Amos Waters," q.v.

WATKINS, JOHN, see "Rachel Watkins," q.v.

WATKINS, JOHN B., of Long Green, Baltimore Co., and Clara A. Bagley, dau. of J. Orrick Bagley, of Harford Co., m. Thurs. 25 Mar 1869, at Monument Street M. E. Church, by Rev. Richard Norris (AI 2 Apr 1869 and 9 Apr 1869)

WATKINS, RACHEL, died ---- (date not given) and the executor's notice stated that creditors must exhibit their legal vouchers by 20 Nov 1864 to John Watkins, exec. (SA 27 Nov 1863)

WATSON, JAMES T., see "Mary Ann Norris," q.v.

WATT, JAMES, died ---- (date not given) and the administrator's notice stated that creditors must exhibit their legal vouchers by 6 Sep 1867 to James Watt, admin. (AI 14 Sep 1866)

WATT, JAMES (Doctor) and Miss Ellie Merryman, both of Harford Co., m. 19 Dec 1865 by Rev. Crever (AI 22 Dec 1865)

WATT, JAMES, see "Robert S. Watt," q.v.

WATT, MARY, see "Robert S. Watt," q.v.

WATT, ROBERT S., died 13 Sep 1859, aged 28, and his twin brother William M. Watt died 22 Sep 1859, sons of James and Mary Watt, at the residence of their father on Deer Creek [Baltimore papers please copy] (SA 8 Oct 1859)

WATT, WILLIAM M., see "Robert S. Watt," q.v.

WATTERS, ALEXANDER Y., see "Laura J. Watters," q.v.

WATTERS, DANIEL R., Esq., an old and well respected citizen, died suddenly last Mon. morning at his residence a few miles from Bel Air (SA 15 Aug 1857)

WATTERS, ELLEN S., wife of Dr. John H. Watters, formerly of Harford Co., died 26 Apr 1857 in St. Louis, MO (HD 8 May 1857)

WATTERS, JAMES D. and Fanny H. Munnikhuysen, dau. of John A. Munnikhuysen, Esq., all of Harford Co., m. Tues. evening 20 Oct 1868 at the M. P. Church, Bel Air, by Rev. T. D. Valiant (AI 23 Oct 1868)

WATTERS, JANE, relict of the late William Watters, died Wed. 25 Jan 1865 in Bel Air, in her 65th year (AI 27 Jan 1865); the subsequent executor's notice stated that creditors must exhibit their legal vouchers by 24 Mar 1866 to Rowland J. Rogers, exec. (AI 31 Mar 1865)

WATTERS, JOHN H. (Doctor), died ---- (date not given) and was removed from the voter registration list of the 3rd District in 1870 (HR 1 Nov 1870); see "Ellen S. Watters," q.v.

WATTERS (WATERS), JOHN H., of Charles Co., MD, and Miss Clara Sherwood, of Baltimore, m. 28 Apr 1870 by Rev. Father Jordan (AI 6 May 1870 gave his name as both Waters and Watters in the same marriage notice)

WATTERS, LAURA J., dau. of Alexander Y. Watters, Esq., and Dr. R. Dickey, of West Chester, PA, m. 23 Dec 1863 in the afternoon, at the residence of the bride at *Oakland*, Harford Co., by Rev. William G. Ferguson (SA 3 Jan 1863)

WATTERS, MARY ANN, see "Stephen Watters," q.v.

WATTERS, RUTH A. (Mrs.), died Tues. 2 Feb 1864, in her 72nd year (SA 12 Feb 1864); see "Mary Ann Woods," q.v.

WATTERS, STEPHEN, died ---- (date not given) and the notice of the sale of his personal and real estate located at the mouth of Winter's Run on 8 Dec 1837 was published by his executrix Mary Ann Watters (HM 1 Dec 1837)

WATTERS, WILLIAM, see "Jane Watters," q.v.

WAUN, BENJAMIN F., see "Benjamin F. Wann," q.v.

WAXWOOD, BENEDICT (colored), died 8 Nov 1868 near Hopewell Crossroads, in his 71st year; he was familiarly called "Ben" and was a well behaved man who left behind him a good name; it would be well for those of his race to imitate his example (AI 4 Dec 1868)

WEAVER, EMMA L. W., of Pottsville, Schuylkill Co., PA, and Columbus K. Gilmore, of Port Deposit, Cecil Co., MD, m. 20 Jul 1869 by Rev. H. Branch (AI 30 Jul 1869)

WEBSTER, ANNA, see "Martha Hanson Webster," q.v.

WEBSTER, HENRY, died ---- (date not given) and was removed from the voter registration list in the 3rd District in 1870 (HR 1 Nov 1870); see "Sallie F. Webster," q.v.

WEBSTER, ISAAC, see "Joseph Webster," q.v.

WEBSTER, ISAAC P., youngest son of Capt. John A. Webster, of Harford Co., died 1 Jul 1862 of camp fever, in the camp before Richmond, aged 22 (SA 2 Aug 1862)

WEBSTER, JOHN A., see "Isaac P. Webster" and "Mary Alice Dorsey" and "Rachel Webster," q.v.

WEBSTER, JOHN L., died ---- (date not given) and the administrator's notice stated that creditors must exhibit their legal vouchers by 29 Nov 1866 to James R. Chesney, admin. (AI 12 Jan 1866)

WEBSTER, JOHN LESTER, died 11 Sep 1869 in his 71st year (HD 17 Sep 1869)

WEBSTER, JOSEPH, aged 76, son of the late Isaac and Sarah Webster of Harford Co., died "on the seventh day morning" (AI 4 Jun 1869)

WEBSTER, LOU. L., dau. of Rev. Dr. Webster, the officiating clergyman, and George J. Finney, of Harford Co., m. 26 Apr 1865 in Baltimore by Rev. Dr. Webster (AI 5 May 1865)

WEBSTER, MARTHA HANSON, only child of William and Anna J. Webster, died Fri. 13 Mar 1868 of scarlet fever, at *Webster's Forest*, aged 19 months (AI 20 Mar 1868)

WEBSTER, MOSES, died ---- (date not given) and the administrator's notice stated that creditors must exhibit their legal vouchers by 29 Jan 1868 to Stephen S. Johns, admin. (AI 15 Feb 1867)

WEBSTER, RACHEL, wife of Capt. John A. Webster, U.S.R.M., died 3 Oct 1869 at *Mount Adams*, Harford Co., in her 73rd year (AI 8 Oct 1869)

WEBSTER, REV. DR., see " Lou. L. Webster," q.v.

WEBSTER, RICHARD E. and Sophia C. Norris, dau. of William B. Norris, Esq., all of Harford Co., m. 6 Jun 1867 at St. Luke's Church, Baltimore, by Rev. William F. Brand (AI 14 Jun 1867)

WEBSTER, SALLIE F., dau. of Henry Webster, Esq., of Harford Co., and Thomas J. Keating, of Queen Anne's Co., m. 12 Jun 1862 in Harford Co. by Rev. Dr. A. Webster (SA 21 Jun 1862)

WEBSTER, SARAH, see "Joseph Webster," q.v.

WEBSTER, WILLIAM , see "Martha Hanson Webster," q.v.

WEBSTER, WILLIAM, of Harford Co., and Miss Annie J. Stump, of Cecil Co., m. Thurs. 5 Oct 1865 at Perry Point, Cecil Co., by Rev. William Finney (AI 13 Oct 1865)

WEEKS, WILLIAM (Reverend), died Mon. 7 Apr 1862 at the residence of Mrs. Maulsby near Bel Air, in his 68th year; he was for many years a minister of the Methodist Episcopal Church and for some years since had charge of the circuit, but for some time previous to his death had been greatly afflicted and was compelled to retire from the pulpit (SA 12 Apr 1862)

WEEMS, ANNIE S. (Miss) and Oliver C. Bramble, both of Harford Co., m. 4 Apr 1869 at the M. E. Parsonage, Abingdon, by Rev. J. G. Moore (AI 9 Apr 1869)

WEITZEL, JOHN C., of Baltimore, and Miss Ida A. Wilson, of Harford Co., m. ---- (date not given) at the Parsonage of Caroline Station [in Baltimore] by Rev. R. A. Riley (HD 26 Mar 1869)

WELBOURNE, VIRGINIA M. and Alexander Hogg, both of Baltimore, m. 5 Jan 1865 in that city by Rev. John W. Williams (AI 13 Jan 1865)

WELCH, MARTIN, died ---- (date not given) and was removed from the voter registration list of the 4th District in 1868 (AI 9 Oct 1868)

WELCH, NANCY, consort of William Welch, died Fri. 1 Feb 1867, near Churchville, in her 69th year (AI 8 Feb 1867)

WELCH, WILLIAM and Miss Susan McCullough, both of Baltimore Co., m. 16 Feb 1869 by Rev. Creaver (HD 5 Mar 1869)

WELCH, WILLIAM, see "Isaac Saunders" and "Nancy Welch," q.v.

WELLS, BENJAMIN and Miss Bertie Richardson, both of Harford Co., m. 15 Jun 1870, in Aberdeen M. E. Church, by Rev. J. G. Moore (AI 24 Jun 1870)

WELLS, BENJAMIN, see "Olivia Baker," q.v.

WELLS, CAROLINE (Miss), dau. of the late Zenas Wells, of Havre de Grace, and Joseph N. Simmons, of Baltimore, m. 18 Apr 1847 by Rev. Happerset (HM 28 May 1847)

WELLS, JOSEPH, see "Sallie R. Wells," q.v.

WELLS, SALLIE R. (Miss), dau. of Joseph Wells, Esq., and Luther Osborn, all of Harford Co., m. 10 Dec 1868, at home, by Rev. J. G. Moore (AI 25 Dec 1868)

WELLS, ZENAS, see "Caroline Wells," q.v.

WELSH, MRS. ----, wife of Theodore Welsh, and her child (name not given), drowned last Mon. as Samuel Grier was driving with his sister and her child over a run near Broad Creek; after the heavy rains of that day, the force of the water was so strong as to upset the buggy; they were carried downstream; Mr. Grier and his horse survived (SA 15 Aug 1857)

WELSH, THEODORE, see "Mrs. Welsh," q.v.

WELSH, WILLIAM, of Baltimore, and Miss Penelope Rutledge, dau. of the late Joshua Rutledge, of Harford Co., m. 19 Apr 1838 by Rev. Holmead (HM 26 Apr 1838)

WESLEY, J. M., died ---- (date not given) and was removed from the voter registration list of the 2nd District in 1870 (AI 4 Nov 1870)

WEST, REBECCA, died 9 Aug 1851 in Harford Co., in her 78th year (HM 28 Aug 1851)

WEST, WILSON D. and Miss Ann M. Ewing, both of Harford Co., m. 8 Aug 1867 in the M. E. Church, Dublin, by Rev. W. M. Meminger (AI 16 Aug 1867)

WETHERALL, WILLIAM G., see "Edward Griffith," q.v.

WETHERILL, JENNIE (Miss) and J. Thomas Gross, both of Harford Co., m. 21 Dec 1871 by Rev. J. C. Hagey (AI 12 Jan 1872)

WHALAND, HARRIET H., wife of Robert W. Whaland, died Tues. 25 Jan 1870; obituary contains a short verse [*Baltimore Sun* and Kent County papers copy] (AI 4 Feb 1870); see "John T. Whaland," q.v.

WHALAND, JOHN T., only child of R. W. and Harriet H. Whaland, died 25 Feb 1857, in his 21st year, after a lingering and painful illness, conscious to the last (HD 6 Mar 1857)

WHALAND, R. W., see "John T. Whaland," q.v.

WHANN, SAMUEL and Mrs. Sarah E. Flaharty (Flaherty), both of Harford Co., m. 25 Nov 1869 by Rev. George M. Berry (AI 17 Dec 1869 and HD 17 Dec 1869)

WHARTON, GEORGE, died ---- (date not given) and was removed from voter registration list in 1869 [district not clarified, but either 4th, 5th or 6th] (HD 22 Oct 1869 and AI 1 Oct 1869)

WHEELER, L. (Mrs.), died Thurs. 14 Jan 1864, at an advanced age (SA 22 Jan 1864)

WHEELER, SYLVESTER, of Harford Co., and Miss Martha A. Glacken, of Lancaster Co., PA, m. 4 Feb 1869 at St. Ignatius Church by Rev. Father O'Connor [*Lancaster Intelligencer* please copy] (HD 19 Feb 1869 and AI 12 Feb 1869)

WHISTLER, LOTTIE, of Harford Co., and R. C. Herbert, of Perrymansville, m. 11 Jan 1866, at the house of Mr. Whistler, by Rev. J. K. Nichols (AI 26 Jan 1866)

WHITAKER, AQUILLA B. and Miss Nannie W. Wallis, both of Harford Co., m. Wed. 6 Apr 1870 at Jarrettsville by Rev. J. C. Hagey (HD 15 Apr 1870 and AI 8 Apr 1870)

WHITAKER, AVARILLA B. (Mrs.), of Harford Co., and Absalom Galloway, of Marshall Co., Illinois, m. 20 Sep 1866 by Rev. J. K. Nichols (AI 5 Oct 1866)

WHITAKER, FRANKLIN, see "Charles H. Raitt" and "Samuel Whitaker, Jr.," q.v.

WHITAKER, SAMUEL JR., son of Franklin Whitaker, Esq., of Dunkale Mills, on Winter's Run, Harford Co., died Thurs. night after a brief illness of typhoid fever, in his 23rd year; at the time of his death he was Captain, Co. B, 8th Cavalry Bttn., M. N. G., of Bel Air, having been elected last August; he was also a member of Mt. Ararat Lodge, A.F.& A.M.; his interment was in St. Mary's Church Cemetery at 10½ o'clock this morning; his company passed a resolution in his honor and it was subsequently published (AI 23 Dec 1870 and 30 Dec 1870)

WHITAKER, TABITHA E. (Miss) and John C. Monks, both of Harford Co., m. 5 Mar 1857 in Baltimore by Rev. G. F. Adams (HD 13 Mar 1857)

WHITE, ANN, see "William Thomas White," q.v.

WHITE, JOSHUA, see "William Thomas White," q.v.

WHITE, WILLIAM THOMAS, son of Joshua W. and Anna M. White, died 11 Nov 1867 near Aberdeen, Harford Co., aged 3 months and 11 days (AI 29 Nov 1867)

WHITEFORD, C. J., died ---- (date not given) and was removed from the voter registration list of the 1st District in 1870 (HR 1 Nov 1870)

WHITEFORD, CHARLES H. A. and Miss Cassandra Finley, of Lancaster Co., PA, m. Tues. 4 Dec 1866 at the residence of Philip H. Love, near Bel Air, by Rev. T. M. Crawford of York Co., PA (AI 7 Dec 1866); see "Capt. Clough," q.v.

WHITEFORD, CUNNINGHAM, see "Mary Ann Whiteford," q.v.

WHITEFORD, FANNIE (Miss) and William J. S. Riley, both of Harford Co., m. 1 Jul 1869 at Long Green Church by Rev. Father Nysson (HD 16 Jul 1869)

WHITEFORD, HUGH C., see "Robert R. Jones," q.v.

WHITEFORD, JULIA ANN (Miss) and Andrew Turner, both of Harford Co., m. 19 Jan 1858 by Rev. T. S. C. Smith (SA 6 Feb 1858)

WHITEFORD, LIZZIE (Miss) and John L. Glenn, both of Harford Co., m. Tues. 6 Sep 1870 at the residence of F. B. Glenn, Bel Air, by Rev. W. B. Brown (AI 9 Sep 1870)

WHITEFORD, M. CROOK, of Harford Co., and Lizzie B. Lucy, only dau. of Prof. Thomas Lucy, of Baltimore, m. 27 Jul 1869 by Rev. Dr. Dalrymple [marriage notice indicated "No cards"] (AI 13 Aug 1869)

WHITEFORD, MARTHA LOUISA (Miss) and Abraham Durham, both of Harford Co., m. 22 Dec 1870, at the residence of the bride's mother, by Rev. James Smith (AI 23 Dec 1870)

WHITEFORD, MARY ANN, dau. of Cunningham Whiteford, of Harford Co., died last Fri. (HM 31 May 1838)

WHITEFORD, SAMUEL M. and Miss Sarah J. Heaps, both of Harford Co., m. 14 Dec 1865 by Rev. Smith (AI 22 Dec 1865)

WHITEFORD, SUSAN E. (Miss) and James Kilgore, both of Harford Co., m. 9 Jan 1868 by Rev. T. M. Crawford, of York Co., PA, assisted by Rev. J. D. Smith and Rev. J. Y. Cowhick (AI 17 Jan 1868)

WHITSON, SARAH R. (Miss) and George H. Garrettson, both of Harford Co., m. Thurs. 6 Jan 1870, at Friendship Meeting House, by Rev. Daniel Reese (AI 14 Jan 1870)

WICKS, WILLIAM A., died ---- (date not given) and was removed from voter registration list in 1869 [district not clarified, but either 4th, 5th or 6th] (AI 1 Oct 1869 and HD 22 Oct 1869)

WILEMAN, ANNA (Miss) and James H. Marshall, both of Harford Co., m. 19 Jul 1871, at Havre de Grace, by Rev. William H. Cooke (HD 28 Jul 1871 and HD 28 Jul 1871)

WILES, AQUILA, see "William Wiles," q.v.

WILES, WILLIAM, died ---- (date not given) and the administrator's notice stated that creditors must exhibit their legal vouchers by 1 Jan 1839 to Aquila Wiles, admin. (HM 25 Oct 1838)

WILEY, CAROLINE, see "William Wiley," q.v.

WILEY, JOSEPH, died ---- (date not given) and the administrator's notice stated that creditors must exhibit their legal vouchers by 19 May 1864 to David Wiley, admin. (SA 22 May 1863)

WILEY, MATTHEW, died ---- (date not given) and the executor's notice stated that creditors must exhibit their legal vouchers by 31 Feb [sic] 1841 to William Wiley, exec. (HM 10 Oct 1840)

WILEY, WILLIAM, died ---- (date not given) and the administratrix's notice stated that creditors must exhibit their legal vouchers by 4 Mar 1847 to Caroline Wiley, admx. (HM 25 Jun 1846); see "Matthew Wiley," q.v.

WILGIS, ELIZABETH, see "Richard Hall Wilgis," q.v.

WILGIS, GEORGE, see "Richard Hall Wilgis," q.v.

WILGIS, RICHARD HALL, son of George and Elizabeth Wilgis, died 24 Sep 1865, aged 11 years and 9 months (AI 29 Sep 1865)

WILGUS, ANN MARIA and Andrew T. Miller m. 6 Aug 1867 by Rev.
W. M. Meminger (AI 16 Aug 1867)

WILGUS, JAMES and Hannah A. Flowers, both of Harford Co., m. 2
Jan 1866 by Rev. E. Kinsey at the M. E. Parsonage in Bel Air
[Baltimore papers please copy] (AI 5 Jan 1866)

WILGUS, SUE J. (Miss) and James P. Beal, both of Harford Co., m. 15
Jan 1867 at Mt. Zion M. P. Church, near Bel Air, by Rev. J. K.
Nichols (AI 8 Feb 1867)

WILLIAMS. B. H., died ---- (date not given) and was removed from the
voter registration list of the 1st District in 1870 (HR 1 Nov 1870)

WILLIAMS, BILL, see "James Williams," q.v.

WILLIAMS, CHARLES, see "James Williams," q.v.

WILLIAMS, CORNELIA (Miss) and Oliver T. Bailey, both of Havre de
Grace, m. Tues. morning 27 Oct 1868, at Havre de Grace, by Rev.
C. F. Thomas (HD 6 Nov 1868; AI 13 Nov 1868 gave the date as 7
Oct 1868)

WILLIAMS, JAMES (Negro man), was apparently poisoned to death by
his nephew Bill Williams, who was put in jail on Wed.; he lived in
the neighborhood of Deer Creek Iron Works; he was sick at the time
and his nephew allegedly put arsenic in his medicine; a post mortem
examination showed the presence of arsenic in the stomach of the
deceased, and the accused had purchased the poison a short time
prior to the occurrence; however, when the case went to trial at the
end of February, 1870, it stated that Charles Williams, Negro [not
Bill Williams] was indicted for the murder of James Williams,
Negro, by poisoning; newspaper article contains details about the
trial; another article indicated Charles and Sarah Ann Williams
(Negroes), whose trial had been removed to Cecil Co., were found
not guilty of the murder of James Williams (AI 17 Sep 1869 and 4
Mar 1870 and 7 Oct 1870); see "Oliver H. Thomas," q.v.

WILLIAMS, JOHN L. and Miss Mary A. Mitchell, both of Harford Co.,
m. Thurs. 28 Jan 1864 at St. John's Church, Havre de Grace, by
Rev. W. C. Langdon (SA 5 Feb 1864)

WILLIAMS, JOHN L. and Miss Amanda S. Mitchell, dau. of Bernard
Mitchell, Esq., m. Tues. 21 Jan 1868 at St. John's Church, Havre de
Grace, by Rev. Henry B. Martin, M.D.. (AI 24 Jan 1868)

WILLIAMS, KATE , see "Philip Williams," q.v.

WILLIAMS, PHILIP, died Sun. 15 Jan 1865, aged 4 years and 5 months,
his sister Kate Williams died Mon. 16 Jan 1865, aged 5 years and
11 months, and their sister Rose Whitridge Williams died Tues. 17
Jan 1865, aged 3 years and 1 month; all died of diphtheria; they
were the only children of Dr. Philip C. and Mary Williams, of
Baltimore; their obituary contains a brief verse (AI 27 Jan 1865)

WILLIAMS, PHILIP, of Winchester, VA, died Thurs. 2 Apr 1868, in his
76th year (AI 10 Apr 1868)

WILLIAMS, ROSE W., see "Philip Williams," q.v.

WILLIAMS, SARAH ANN, see "James Williams," q.v.

WILLIAMSON, LIZZIE C., wife of John G. Williamson, died 7 Apr 1868, aged 27 (AI 15 May 1868)

WILLLIAMSON, JAMES P., a druggist on Gay St. near High, in Baltimore, committed suicide last Tues. by taking prussic acid; a short time before he died he told his wife what he had done; he leaves a widow and 3 children (SA 8 Jan 1859)

WILLIAMSON, JOHN G., see "Lizzie C. Williamson," q.v.

WILSON, ASBURY, see "Elizabeth Wilson," q.v.

WILSON, DR. J., see "Harriet A. Dickson," q.v.

WILSON, ELIZABETH, wife of William H. Wilson, of Havre de Grace, went from religious services in the Methodist Church at North East, Tues. night of last week, to the residence of her brother-in-law, Asbury Wilson, and died while sitting in a chair, in less than half an hour after she entered the house; supposed cause of death was heart disease (AI 18 Feb 1870)

WILSON, FANNIE R., eldest dau. of Isaac Wilson, and William E. Griffith, both of Baltimore, m. 8 May 1862 by Rev. William N. Elliott of Elkton, MD (SA 17 May 1862)

WILSON, G. W., died ---- (date not given) and was removed from the voter registration list in the 4th District in 1868 (AI 9 Oct 1868)

WILSON, H. A., see "Samuel Middleton Dickson," q.v.

WILSON, IDA A. (Miss), of Harford Co., and John C. Weitzel, of Baltimore, m. ---- (date not given) at the Parsonage of Caroline Station [in Baltimore] by Rev. R. A. Riley (HD 26 Mar 1869)

WILSON, ISAAC, see "Fannie R. Wilson" and "Margaret M. Wilson," q.v.

WILSON, J. L., died ---- (date not given) and was removed from the voter registration list in the 4th District in 1868 (AI 9 Oct 1868)

WILSON, JAMES F., died ---- (date not given) and was removed from voter registration list in 1869 [district not clarified, but either 4th, 5th or 6th] (HD 22 Oct 1869 and AI 1 Oct 1869)

WILSON, JAMES T., of Havre de Grace, died last Mon. after a brief illness; he leaves a wife and 3 children (HR 19 Nov 1868)

WILSON, JOHN, died ---- (date not given) and the administrator's notice stated that creditors must exhibit their legal vouchers by 10 Apr 1857 to Patrick H. Rutledge, admin. (HD 18 Apr 1856)

WILSON, JOSEPH ADDISON, youngest child of Rev. William and Margaret Wilson, died 25 Nov 1866 in Harford Co., aged 13 years and 10 months (AI 7 Dec 1866)

WILSON, LEE, died ---- (date not given) and the administrator's notice stated that creditors must exhibit their legal vouchers by 14 Mar 1868 to John H. Kirkwood, admin. (AI 22 Mar 1867)

WILSON, MARGARET, see "Joseph Addison Wilson," q.v.

WILSON, MARGARET M., consort of Isaac C. Wilson, died Sun. 18 Mar 1866 near Darlington, Harford Co. (AI 23 Mar 1866)

WILSON, MRS., wife of Capt. William Wilson, of Havre de Grace, died very suddenly last Mon. evening; she had gone over to North East a few days since to attend the funeral of a relative and remained there a few days; upon returning she later complained of feeling unwell, and sitting down, said "I am going to die" and in a few moments expired; she leaves a large and interesting family (HR 11 Feb 1870)

WILSON, PAMELA (Miss) and Dr. W. S. Forwood, both of Harford Co., m. 16 Jun 1857 at the 2nd Presbyterian Church in Baltimore by Rev. Smith (HD 19 Jun 1857)

WILSON, SAMUEL, died ---- (date not given) and was removed from the voter registration list in the 4th District in 1868 (AI 9 Oct 1868)

WILSON, WILLIAM, see "Robert C. Amos" and "Mrs. Wilson" and "Joseph Addison Wilson" and "Elizabeth Wilson," q.v.

WILSON, WILLIAM, a young man, drowned last Fri. night off Spesutia Island while engaged in gilling; it became dark and stormy and he was somehow knocked off his boat; his body was recovered by means of a seine on Sat. morning; the Mount Vernon Lodge of Odd Fellows from Abingdon took the body in charge (SA 28 May 1859)

WILSON, WILLIAM A. and Ruth A. Streett, both of Harford Co., m. 19 Feb 1858 by Rev. William Wilson (SA 6 Mar 1858)

WILSON, WILLIAM G. (Doctor) and Frances A. Lee, both of Harford Co., m. 15 Apr 1867, at the residence of the bride's mother, by Rev. W. M. Meminger (AI 26 Apr 1867)

WILSON, WILLIAM H., Esq., of Harford Co., and Malinda J. Colison, of Baltimore, m. 6 Jan 1857 by Rev. W. Stevenson (HM 15 Jan 1857)

WINCHESTER, A. PARKS, see "Sue Winchester," q.v.

WINCHESTER, SUE, wife of A. Parks Winchester and dau. of the late Otho Scott, died 25 Dec 1868 at Hunting Ridge in Baltimore Co. (HD 1 Jan 1869)

WINDSOR, WALTER EDMUND, of Baltimore, died 20 Nov 1862 in Bel Air, aged 23 (SA 29 Nov 1862)

WINFIELD, SUSAN (Miss) and Francis A. Knott, both of Bel Air, m. 28 Nov 1837 by Rev. Kirtz (HM 14 Dec 1837)

WINGFIELD, BETTY, see "Paul Wingfield" and "Richard H. L. Wingfield," q.v.

WINGFIELD, J. H. D., see "Paul Wingfield" and "Richard H. L. Wingfield" and "Mary Imogen Wingfield," q.v.

WINGFIELD, MARY IMOGEN, wife of Rev. J. H. D. Wingfield, died Sat. 15 Sep 1864 in Bel Air, aged 25; obituary contains a short poem [*Baltimore Gazette* and Norfolk and Portsmouth (VA) papers please copy] (AI 23 Sep 1864)

WINGFIELD, PAUL, son of Rev. J. H. D. and Bettie D. Wingfield, died Sun. 19 Jul 1868 at Petersburg, VA, aged 8 months (AI 24 Jul 1868)

WINGFIELD, RICHARD HENRY LEE, son of Rev. J. H. D. and Betty D. Wingfield, died Mon. 26 Aug 1867, aged 9 months (AI 6 Sep 1867)

WINSTANLEY, WILLIAM and Miss Mary E. Phelps m. 26 Mar 1868, at the residence of the bride's father, by Rev. Thomas M. Cathcart (AI 17 Apr 1868)

WONDERS, GEORGE, Esq., and Miss Elma S. Ross, both of Harford Co., m. 19 Apr 1870 by Rev. D. A. Shermer (HD 29 Apr 1870 and AI 29 Apr 1870)

WOOD, G. W., died ---- (date not given) and was removed from the voter registration list in the 4th District in 1868 (AI 9 Oct 1868)

WOOD, JAMES, see "Dorcas Durham," q.v.

WOOD, MARY E., of Baltimore, and James A. Wiles, of Harford Co., m. 13 Sep 1870 by Rev. Blake (AI 23 Sep 1870)

WOOD, WILLIAM D., died Sun. 18 Apr 1869 at his residence near Jarrettsville, of consumption, aged 28 (AI 23 Apr 1869)

WOODHOUSE, INDIANA CLARK (Miss), of Havre de Grace, and Elbridge Warren Hosmer, of Massachusetts, m. Sun. evening 27 Jan 1867 at the Episcopal Church in Havre de Grace by Rev. Dr. Henry B. Martin (AI 1 Feb 1867)

WOODS, MARY ANN, wife of John Woods and dau. of John and Ruth Watters, died 20 Jul 1859, in her 31st year (SA 30 Jul 1859)

WOOLEN, THOMAS, and Col. Mayberry Turner (believed to be his father-in-law), were seriously, if not fatally, stabbed by an Italian organ grinder at their residence near Loudenslager's Hill in Baltimore last Sat. night; when they discovered their ice house door had been broken in, they apprehended the man involved and while considering whether to let him go, the man drew a long knife, stabbing Turner in the arm and side and Woolen in the breast, entering some five inches into a lung; the man fled but was caught by a man named Pantz, who was then cut across the arm, but managed to capture the attacker; a crowd assembled and wanted to hang the organ grinder, but Col. Turner's brother and the police convinced them otherwise; Turner, formerly a Democratic Party candidate for Mayor of Baltimore, and Woolen are now both working members of the American Party; Turner is expected to recover, but Woolen's condition almost precludes the possibility of any hope (HM 25 Sep 1856)

WOOLSEY, HENRY, died Tues. 11 Oct 1864 at his residence in Harford Co., aged about 52 (AI 14 Oct 1864)

WOOLSEY, JASON, died ---- (date not given) at his residence in Harford Co., aged about 60 (AI 4 Jan 1867)

WORTHINGTON, CHARLES, son of J. E. and E. O. Worthington, died Mon. 11 May 1868, aged 11 weeks, at the residence of his father near Trappe Church, Harford Co. (AI 22 May 1868); see "Drucie Worthington," q.v.

WORTHINGTON, DRUCIE, dau. of Charles Worthington, Esq., and Thomas H. C. Reed, both of Harford Co., m. Thurs. 20 Dec 1866 at St. Peter's Church, Baltimore, by Rev. Julius E. Grammer (AI 28 Dec 1866)

WORTHINGTON, E. O., see "Charles Worthington," q.v.

WORTHINGTON, EMILY, dau. of Mary W. and the late William Worthington, died 28 Jun 1868 near Darlington, in her 17th year (AI 10 Jul 1868)

WORTHINGTON, J. E., see "Charles Worthington," q.v.

WORTHINGTON, JAMES, see "Joseph Worthington" and "Thomas Worthington," q.v.

WORTHINGTON, JOHN S., of Harford Co., and Miss Mollie E. Reed, of Baltimore, m. 24 May 1870, in Baltimore, by Rev. Edward Kinsey (AI 17 Jun 1870)

WORTHINGTON, JOSEPH, aged about 15 or 16, son of James Worthington, Esq., of Abingdon District, died last Tues. on the road to Baltimore; he and his father were driving a team which was run over by another team which followed behind, the horses of which had ran off; his injuries were so great that he died immediately upon reaching Baltimore; a subsequent article stated he died 24 Feb 1857 in his 16th year; in the death of this youth a parent has lost a dutiful child, and brothers and sisters a kind and affectionate companion (HD 27 Feb 1857 and 6 Mar 1857)

WORTHINGTON, MARY, see "Emily Worthington," q.v.

WORTHINGTON, THOMAS, died ---- (date not given) and the executor's notice stated that creditors must exhibit their legal vouchers by 2 Aug 1856 to James C. Worthington, exec. (HM 11 Oct 1855)

WORTHINGTON, WILLIAM, see "Emily Worthington," q.v.

WRAY, ADDIE F., dau. of James Wray, of Philadelphia, and T. B. Coleman Stump, of Harford Co., m. 11 Oct 1865 at Philadelphia by Rev. Reed (AI 3 Nov 1865)

WRIGHT, AMELIA (Miss), niece of Joshua Wright, Esq., who lived on the Baltimore and Harford Turnpike about 8 miles from Bel Air, was thrown from her horse and was dangerously if not fatally injured; while riding near Mr. Dampman's Hotel her horse took fright at some passing carriages and ran away; she either fell or jumped and was picked up in a speechless condition and remained so to Wed. morning; no hopes were entertained for her recovery; she died on 2 Oct 1866 at the residence of her uncle in Baltimore Co., aged 13 years and 7 months, dau. of the late William Wright; obituary contains a poem written by "W." (AI 5 Oct 1866 and 12 Oct 1866)

WRIGHT, EDWARD CURRY and Miss Elizabeth A. Foster m. 1 Jul 1856 at the Exeter Street Parsonage in Baltimore by Rev. J. S. Martin (HD 4 Jul 1856)

WRIGHT, ELIZA G. (Miss) and J. Frank Devoe, both of Harford Co., m. Thurs. 13 Feb 1868 at the residence of the bride's father (AI 27 Mar 1868)

WRIGHT, ELIZABETH and Isaac H. Cairnes, both of Harford Co., m. Tues. 30 Jun 1868 by Rev. Thomas M. Cathcart (AI 10 Jul 1868)

WRIGHT, ELONOR E. (Miss), died ---- (date not given); no obituary is given, but rather a poem written by an unnamed friend (SA 22 Mar 1862)

WRIGHT, J. THOMAS, of Jerusalem Mills, Harford Co., and Miss Sallie A. Bond, of Baltimore, m. Thurs. 2 Feb 1865 by Rev. Andrew B. Cross (AI 10 Feb 1865)

WRIGHT, JOSHUA, see "Amelia Wright," q.v.

WRIGHT, MARGARET "MAGGIE" J. (Miss), of Havre de Grace, and James R. Tarleton, of Baltimore, m. Thurs. 29 Oct 1868 by Rev. William H. Cooke [one obituary spelled her name as "Maggy" and the minister's name as "Cook"] (HR 5 Nov 1868 and AI 13 Nov 1868 and HD 6 Nov 1868)

WRIGHT, WILLIAM, see "Amelia Wright," q.v.

WYATT, DELIA (Mrs.), died Wed. 1 Aug 1866 at her residence in Winchester, VA, in her 68th year (AI 3 Aug 1866)

WYATT, LOUISE, of Winchester, VA, and William Munnikhuysen, of Harford Co., m. 10 Nov 1869 at Christ Church, Winchester, by Rev. J. B. Avirett (AI 26 Nov 1869)

WYATT, WILLIAM E. (Reverend), aged 75, rector of St. Paul's Protestant Episcopal Church, died last Fri. at his residence in Baltimore; he was a native of Halifax, N. S. and settled in Baltimore about 1814; the *Baltimore Sun* states he was the oldest presbyter in the Diocese of Maryland; two of his sons are in the Episcopal ministry (AI 1 Jul 1864)

YARNALL, JOHN L., died last Sun. night, an enterprising and respectable citizen of Port Deposit, Cecil Co. (HM 25 Jan 1855)

YATES, JOHN, died ---- (date not given) and the administrator's notice stated that creditors must exhibit their legal vouchers by 31 Dec 1856 to John Daugherty, admin. (HD 25 Jan 1856)

YELLOTT, COLEMAN, Esq., died 28 Jul 1870, aged 49, at Leesburg, Loudoun Co., VA; he was a native of Harford Co., a member of the Maryland Bar, and first practiced law in Calvert Co. before removing to Baltimore; he was elected State Senator on the American Party in 1859 and at the outbreak of the war in 1861 was a supporter of the rights of the South; he was elected one of the peace commissioners to visit the President of the Southern Confederacy to urge a suspension of hostilities, etc., and went to Montgomery, Alabama for this purpose, but did not return until after the war ended; he served as a major in the Army of Northern Virginia for 3 years under Gen. Lee; in 1865 he moved his family from Leesburg to Lexington, VA, and returned to Baltimore in December 1869, forming a new law partnership with R. Emmett Jones; overtaken with illness, he returned with his family to the home of his late father-in-law Gen. Rust, in Leesburg, and died of congestion of the liver; his brother, Judge Yellott, of Baltimore Co., was with him at the time of his death [article from *Baltimore Sun*] (AI 5 Aug 1870); another obituary states Coleman Yellott, Esq., of

the law firm of Yellott & Jones in Baltimore, died on 28 Jul 1870 at
Leesburg in Loudon Co., VA, of a disease of the liver; he was born
in Harford Co. in 1821 and was admitted to the Baltimore Bar when
quite a young man; in 1860 he was elected to the State Senate and
the following year he went to Virginia and joined the Confederate
Army, rising to the rank of major; in 1866 he began practicing law
in Lexington, VA until 1869 when he was solicited to return to
Baltimore; he brought his family to the city in December and took
up his law practice with R. Emmett Jones; a few months later he
was attacked with disease of the liver and went to Virginia for the
purpose of recuperating his health; after a second attack he died at
the residence of his brother-in-law Col. A. T. M. Rust in Loudon
Co. (HD 5 Aug 1870)
YELLOTT, JOHN I., of Baltimore Co., and Mary V. Traill, dau. of
Edward Traill, Esq., m. ---- (date not given) at the residence of the
bride's father in Frederick, MD, by Rev. Osborn Ingle (AI 12 Jun
1868)
YOUNG, BLANCH BAKER, youngest child of William and Mary E.
Young, died Wed. 5 Oct 1870, aged 7 months; one obituary
contains a short verse (HD 7 Oct 1870; AI 7 Oct 1870 gave her
name only as "Blanche")
YOUNG, JERRY and Miss M. Virginia Ward, fourth dau. of John Ward,
Esq., of Bel Air, m. 26 Nov 1857, in Baltimore, by Rev. Hedges
(SA 5 Dec 1857)
YOUNG, MARY, see "Blanch Baker Young," q.v.
YOUNG, OFFICER, see "---- Bennett (Negro)," q.v.
YOUNG, WILLIAM, an aged man, of Irish birth, was found dead last
Sat. by the side of the Bel Air and Baltimore Turnpike near the farm
of Lee Amoss; he could not have been dead but a few hours as he
had been seen passing by the Amoss farm about the middle of the
day; he had been living at the Alms House for some time, and was
quite feeble, but able to take light exercise; an inquest by Judge
Spicer determined he had died from exposure to the heat of the sun;
his body was returned to the Alms House and buried at the expense
of the county (AI 13 Jul 1866)
YOUNG, WILLIAM, see "Blanch Baker Young," q.v.
ZELL, GUILLERMO A., of New York, and Kate H. Richardson, eldest
dau. of Henry Richardson, Esq., of Bel Air, and Guillermo A. Zell,
of New York, m. Tues. 17 May 1870, at St. Ignatius Church, by
Rev. Father O'Connor (AI 20 May 1870)
ZIMMERMAN, E. DORA (Miss), youngest dau. of John and Elizabeth
Zimmerman, and William C. Harward, of Philadelphia, formerly of
Harford Co., m. 9 Apr 1870 at the residence of the bride's father in
Baltimore Co. (HD 15 Apr 1870)
ZIMMERMAN, ELIZABETH, see "E. Dora Zimmerman," q.v.
ZIMMERMAN, HENRY S., see "Isaac Zimmerman," q.v.

ZIMMERMAN, ISAAC, died ---- (date not given) and the executor's notice stated that creditors must exhibit their legal vouchers by 5 Jan 1866 to Henry S. Zimmerman, exec. (AI 13 Jan 1865); see "Lizzie Zimmerman," q.v.

ZIMMERMAN, JOHN, see "E. Dora Zimmerman," q.v.

ZIMMERMAN, LIZZIE, only dau. of Isaac Zimmerman, Esq., of Harford Co., and John E. Bennett m. 19 Feb 1863 by Rev. Shoaff (SA 27 Feb 1863)

ZIMMERMAN, W. H. H., of Baltimore Co., and Miss Jennie N. Reed, of Baltimore, m. Thurs. 4 Jun 1863 in Harford Co. by Rev. H. Dunning (SA 12 Jun 1863)

ZOLLINGER, ELIZABETH, wife of Capt. Henry A. Zollinger and dau. of the late Capt. Thomas Courtney, of Harford Co., died Sat. 8 Dec 1866 at Lewistown, PA, in her 42nd year (AI 28 Dec 1866)

Heritage Books by Henry C. Peden, Jr.:

*A Closer Look at St. John's Parish Registers
[Baltimore County, Maryland], 1701–1801*

A Collection of Maryland Church Records

*A Guide to Genealogical Research in Maryland:
5th Edition, Revised and Enlarged*

*Abstracts of Marriages and Deaths in Harford County,
Maryland, Newspapers, 1837–1871*

*Abstracts of the Ledgers and Accounts of the Bush Store
and Rock Run Store, 1759–1771*

Abstracts of the Orphans Court Proceedings of Harford County, 1778–1800

Abstracts of Wills, Harford County, Maryland, 1800–1805

Anne Arundel County, Maryland, Marriage References 1658–1800
Henry C. Peden, Jr. and Veronica Clarke Peden

Baltimore City [Maryland] Deaths and Burials, 1834–1840

Baltimore County, Maryland, Overseers of Roads, 1693–1793

Bastardy Cases in Baltimore County, Maryland, 1673–1783

Bastardy Cases in Harford County, Maryland, 1774–1844

Bible and Family Records of Harford County, Maryland, Families: Volume V

Cecil County, Maryland Marriage References, 1674–1824
Henry C. Peden, Jr. and Veronica Clarke Peden

Children of Harford County: Indentures and Guardianships, 1801–1830

Colonial Delaware Soldiers and Sailors, 1638–1776

*Colonial Families of the Eastern Shore of Maryland
Volumes 5, 6, 7, 8, 9, 11, 12, 13, 14, 16, and 19*
Henry C. Peden, Jr. and F. Edward Wright

*Colonial Families of the Eastern Shore of Maryland
Volume 21 and Volume 23*

Colonial Maryland Soldiers and Sailors, 1634–1734

Colonial Tavern Keepers of Maryland and Delaware, 1634–1776

Dorchester County, Maryland, Marriage References, 1669–1800
Henry C. Peden, Jr. and Veronica Clarke Peden

Dr. John Archer's First Medical Ledger, 1767–1769, Annotated Abstracts

Early Anglican Records of Cecil County

*Early Harford Countians, Individuals Living in
Harford County, Maryland in Its Formative Years
Volume 1: A to K, Volume 2: L to Z, and Volume 3: Supplement*

Family Cemeteries and Grave Sites in Harford County, Maryland

First Presbyterian Church Records, Baltimore, Maryland, 1840–1879

*Frederick County, Maryland, Marriage References
and Family Relationships, 1748–1800*
Henry C. Peden, Jr. and Veronica Clarke Peden

Genealogical Gleanings from Harford County,
Maryland, Medical Records, 1772–1852
Winner of the Norris Harris Prize from MHS for
the best genealogical reference book in 2016!

Harford (Maryland) Homicides

Harford County Taxpayers in 1870, 1872 and 1883

Harford County, Maryland Death Records, 1849–1899

Harford County, Maryland Deponents, 1775–1835

Harford County, Maryland Divorces and Separations, 1823–1923

Harford County, Maryland, Death Certificates, 1898–1918: An Annotated Index

Harford County, Maryland, Divorce Cases, 1827–1912: An Annotated Index

Harford County, Maryland, Inventories, 1774–1804

Harford County, Maryland, Marriage References
and Family Relationships, 1774–1824
Henry C. Peden, Jr. and Veronica Clarke Peden

Harford County, Maryland, Marriage References
and Family Relationships, 1825–1850

Harford County, Maryland, Marriage References
and Family Relationships, 1851–1860
Henry C. Peden, Jr. and Veronica Clarke Peden

Harford County, Maryland, Marriage References
and Family Relationships, 1861–1870
Henry C. Peden, Jr. and Veronica Clarke Peden

Harford County, Maryland, Marriage References
and Family Relationships, 1871–1875

Harford (Old Brick Baptist) Church, Harford County, Maryland,
Records and Members (1742–1974), Tombstones, Burials (1775–2009)
and Family Relationships

Heirs and Legatees of Harford County, Maryland, 1774–1802

Heirs and Legatees of Harford County, Maryland, 1802–1846

Inhabitants of Baltimore County, Maryland, 1763–1774

Inhabitants of Cecil County, Maryland 1774–1800

Inhabitants of Cecil County, Maryland, 1649–1774

Inhabitants of Harford County, Maryland, 1791–1800

Inhabitants of Kent County, Maryland, 1637–1787

Joseph A. Pennington & Co., Havre De Grace, Maryland, Funeral Home Records:
Volume II, 1877–1882, 1893–1900

Kent County, Maryland Marriage References, 1642–1800
Henry C. Peden, Jr. and Veronica Clarke Peden

Marriages and Deaths from Baltimore Newspapers, 1817–1824

Maryland Bible Records, Volume 1: Baltimore and Harford Counties

Maryland Bible Records, Volume 2: Baltimore and Harford Counties

Maryland Bible Records, Volume 3: Carroll County

Maryland Bible Records, Volume 4: Eastern Shore

Maryland Bible Records, Volume 5: Harford, Baltimore and Carroll Counties

Maryland Bible Records, Volume 7: Baltimore, Harford and Frederick Counties

Maryland Deponents, 1634–1799

Maryland Deponents: Volume 3, 1634–1776

Maryland Prisoners Languishing in Goal, Volume 1: 1635–1765

Maryland Prisoners Languishing in Goal, Volume 2: 1766–1800

Maryland Public Service Records, 1775–1783:
A Compendium of Men and Women of Maryland
Who Rendered Aid in Support of the American Cause
against Great Britain during the Revolutionary War

Marylanders and Delawareans in the French and Indian War, 1756–1763

Marylanders to Carolina: Migration of Marylanders to
North Carolina and South Carolina prior to 1800

Marylanders to Kentucky, 1775–1825

Marylanders to Ohio and Indiana, Migration Prior to 1835

Marylanders to Tennessee

Methodist Records of Baltimore City, Maryland: Volume 1, 1799–1829

Methodist Records of Baltimore City, Maryland: Volume 2, 1830–1839

Methodist Records of Baltimore City, Maryland: Volume 3, 1840–1850
(East City Station)

More Maryland Deponents, 1716–1799

More Marylanders to Carolina: Migration of Marylanders to
North Carolina and South Carolina prior to 1800

More Marylanders to Kentucky, 1778–1828

More Marylanders to Ohio and Indiana: Migrations Prior to 1835

Orphans and Indentured Children of Baltimore County, Maryland, 1777–1797

Outpensioners of Harford County, Maryland, 1856–1896

Presbyterian Records of Baltimore City, Maryland, 1765–1840

Quaker Records of Baltimore and Harford Counties, Maryland, 1801–1825

Quaker Records of Northern Maryland, 1716–1800

Quaker Records of Southern Maryland, 1658–1800

Revolutionary Patriots of Anne Arundel County, Maryland, 1775–1783

Revolutionary Patriots of Baltimore Town and Baltimore County, 1775–1783

Revolutionary Patriots of Calvert
and St. Mary's Counties, Maryland, 1775–1783

Revolutionary Patriots of Caroline County, Maryland, 1775–1783

Revolutionary Patriots of Cecil County, Maryland, 1775–1783

Revolutionary Patriots of Charles County, Maryland, 1775–1783

Revolutionary Patriots of Delaware, 1775–1783

Revolutionary Patriots of Dorchester County, Maryland, 1775–1783

www.ingramcontent.com/pod-product-compliance
Lightning Source LLC
Chambersburg PA
CBHW070304290326
41930CB00040B/2075